Fairies

FAIRIES
A HISTORY

FRANCIS YOUNG

polity

Copyright © Francis Young 2026

The right of Francis Young to be identified as Author of this Work has been asserted in accordance with the UK Copyright, Designs and Patents Act 1988.

First published in 2026 by Polity Press Ltd

Polity Press Ltd
65 Bridge Street
Cambridge CB2 1UR, UK

Polity Press Ltd
111 River Street
Hoboken, NJ 07030, USA

All rights reserved. Except for the quotation of short passages for the purpose of criticism and review, no part of this publication may be reproduced, stored in a retrieval system, or transmitted, in any form or by any means, electronic, mechanical, photocopying, recording, or otherwise, without the prior permission of the publisher.

ISBN-13: 978-1-5095-6677-8

A catalogue record for this book is available from the British Library.

Library of Congress Control Number: 2025940286

Typeset in 11.5 on 14pt Adobe Garamond
by Cheshire Typesetting Ltd, Cuddington, Cheshire
Printed and bound in Great Britain by CPI Group (UK) Ltd, Croydon

The publisher has used its best endeavours to ensure that the URLs for external websites referred to in this book are correct and active at the time of going to press. However, the publisher has no responsibility for the websites and can make no guarantee that a site will remain live or that the content is or will remain appropriate.

Every effort has been made to trace all copyright holders, but if any have been overlooked the publisher will be pleased to include any necessary credits in any subsequent reprint or edition.

For further information on Polity, visit our website:
politybooks.com

For Abi and Tali

Contents

Preface		*page* ix
Introduction: the fairy-haunted world		1
1	The hills are alive: sacred nature in ancient Europe	28
2	Between heaven and hell: monotheism and ambiguous spirits	52
3	Here be monsters: otherworld beings in the Middle Ages	78
4	Founding fairyland: the late Middle Ages	106
5	The reformation of fairyland: early modern fairies	131
6	Trying the spirits: fairies and the enchanted Enlightenment	159
7	Fairies go global	184
8	The coming (back) of the fairies: the nineteenth and twentieth centuries	205
9	Rewilding fairyland: fairies today	238
Conclusion		268
Notes		272
Bibliography		296
Index		325

Preface

> If, however, the scrupulous inquirer should ask me what I feel about the truth of this tale, I reply with Augustine that the wondrous things of God are to be marvelled at, not debated with disputation; and I do not, by denying it, place limits on divine power; but nor do I, by affirming it, insolently stretch what cannot be stretched.
>
> Gerald of Wales, *Journey through Wales* 1.8

In March 1188, in the town of Loughor near Swansea in South Wales, Bishop Dewi of St Davids told Gerald of Wales what a priest named Elidyr had once told the bishop had happened to him as a boy. At the age of twelve, Elidyr had run away from his harsh teachers, and hidden under an overhanging riverbank. There the young Elidyr was approached by beautiful, diminutive beings and visited their land; but after he stole a golden ball from the fairies, they shunned him and he was never able to find his way back to their realm. Just as it would to us, the story of Elidyr seemed fantastical to Gerald; but Bishop Dewi had been struck by Elidyr's sincerity. Elidyr could not tell the story without weeping for the lost joys of fairyland, and Gerald decided he could not deny the possibility the story was true. As a medieval churchman, Gerald had to submit his judgement and his reason to God, and he could not be entirely sure that God would *not* permit such wonders to exist.

Fairies have always existed in this realm of uncertainty. Unlike angels, demons, ghosts, or witches, there were no sound biblical or theological grounds for believing in them. But people like Elidyr kept meeting them. Some people even claim to meet fairies today. Of all supernatural beings, fairies have always fascinated me the most. Perhaps that is because they are the weirdest beings of folklore, and the hardest to classify; or perhaps it is because fairies (and the fairyland they inhabit) embody magic in their very being. Fairies are said to be like us, yet unlike us; they are simultaneously physical beings, yet eternally elusive, their nature governed by mysterious laws we can never fully understand. Fairies speak to our desire for enchantment, for escape from the mundane; yet they are also creatures of glamour and illusion. As a child I collected books about fairies obsessively, until adolescence rendered such an interest embarrassing; but, like so many childhood passions, my interest in fairy lore returned in adulthood. I was not, like the hapless Elidyr, searching fruitlessly for re-entry to their realm. Rather, I was searching as a historian and as a folklorist for answers about the origins of this most intriguing of cultural phenomena: humanity's belief in a mirror-community of non-human social supernatural beings.

This is my third book about fairies. The first, *Suffolk Fairylore* (2018), examined in depth the fairy traditions of one English county. This was followed by *Twilight of the Godlings* (2023), in which I endeavoured to trace the origins of Britain's fairies. The present book is more ambitious still, and is about the origins of all European fairies – as well as the global fairies who fanned out across the world from the sixteenth century onwards, whose ancestry can be traced back to European folklore. Folklorists have shown a great deal of interest in fairies, yet fairyland has received only sporadic attention from historians and historically minded folklorists. Indeed, no one has ever attempted a complete history of European fairy belief. This book aims to fill the need for such a history, but it has its limits; rather than being a comprehensive cultural history of the fairy theme, it is a study of the origins of past and present fairy beliefs, and a history of the human search for fairies. Its primary focus is on the history of the human experience of encountering fairies, and on the effort to make sense of them – rather than on fairies in art, literature, drama, and film (although cultural portrayals of fairies have, of course, influenced the way people claim to experience them).

Two themes that run through this book are the interaction of fairy lore with Christianity (as a semi-acknowledged element of Christian popular cosmologies) and the fundamental importance of fairy encounters as a way of experiencing the world for pre-modern (and some modern) people. It is a history of fairies, but it is also a plea for fairies to be taken seriously as a feature of human culture, and perhaps even as a characteristic of human consciousness.

I am grateful to Dr George Owers of Polity for his interest in commissioning the book, to the librarians of Cambridge University Library and the Bodleian Library in Oxford for facilitating my research, and to Dr Nicholas Wilkinson for reading some of this book before publication and sharing his insights. Thanks are also due to my daughters Abigail and Talitha for always asking me the most challenging questions about fairies. All translations in the text are my own, unless otherwise stated; quotations from the Bible are taken from the Authorized Version. All images were sourced from Wikimedia Commons unless otherwise stated. The following abbreviations are used in the text:

PG *Patrologia Graeca*, ed. J.-P. Migne (Paris, 1857–66), 161 vols.
PL *Patrologia Latina*, ed. J.-P. Migne (Paris, 1844–64), 221 vols.

Francis Young
Peterborough
February 2025

Introduction: the fairy-haunted world

In around 1880, an Orthodox priest was summoned to a farm in the parish of Karksi in the Mulgimaa region of southern Estonia. Estonia was then part of the vast Russian Empire, but the majority of its rural inhabitants were neither Russian-speakers nor Orthodox Christians, but rather Finno-Ugric-speaking Estonians whose ancestral paganism remained a powerful force.[1] But the peasants of Karksi evidently believed that an Orthodox priest might be able to help them with an exorcism – because a domestic spirit, Pell, was causing havoc in a local granary. Almost eighty years later, speaking to a folklorist in Soviet-occupied Estonia in 1958, an old woman described what she had witnessed as a young girl. The priest arrived and challenged Pell, who eventually emerged from the granary. Pell sat 'like a completely naked person' on the granary's high wooden steps, nursing an infant. She argued with the priest, but at last she agreed to depart.[2]

The Estonian granary spirit Pell is about as far as most of us can imagine from the stereotyped fairy of contemporary popular culture – the sort of being the average British or American child might draw when prompted to depict a fairy: tiny, probably female, winged, and perhaps holding a magic wand. But fairies – or at least beings who seemingly occupy the same space in culture and folk belief as fairies – are a diverse, global phenomenon. And whereas people are most likely to encounter fairies as imagined or fictional entities in the contemporary Western world, for most of history (and indeed until very recently) they have been encountered as real beings. In some cases, as we shall see, they still are. The old woman who saw Pell exorcised from a granary was still sure, even after years of Soviet marginalization of Estonian folk culture, that she had seen a granary spirit in physical form.

While the unsettling figure of Pell is hardly Disney's Tinker Bell, we can discern in Pell some of the key characteristics that distinguish fairies from other categories of supernatural being. Crucially, fairies are physical beings, not apparitions (even if they can sometimes defy the laws of physics). They have bodies, of a kind. Fairies have a humanoid appearance (usually) but they are decidedly non-human. Fairies are neither wholly good nor wholly evil, but – like us – are capable of both; note that the priest argued with Pell, rather than simply banishing her like a demon. And fairies are social beings: like us, they have children, live in families, and form societies and hierarchies. People have actually claimed to see and encounter fairies; they are not beings whose existence is confined to traditional stories, and it is not enough to write them off as mere cultural archetypes. Furthermore, my decision to open this book with a fairy encounter taken from Estonia is a very deliberate choice: to make the point that fairies are not beings exclusive to, or emanating from, the folklore of Britain and Ireland – as they are so often perceived to be.

'Fairy', for the purposes of this book at least, is a generic term that covers any supernatural, human-like non-human beings – from the fays of medieval French romance literature and the aos sí of Ireland to elves, dwarfs, trolls, gnomes, nereids, vilas, leprechauns, pixies, brownies, and so on. This is a book about the human experience of encounter with such beings, in all their diversity. It is possible, of course, to explain away what the Estonian girl saw that day at the granary: perhaps the 'spirit' who looked like a naked human being really was just a human woman, a desperate vagrant who had taken refuge in the granary and was trying to keep her child alive. That may or may not be true; we have no way of knowing now. What matters for the folklorist is the lens of 'belief' through which the witness interpreted what she saw; she was quite certain that she witnessed the spirit Pell, because the entity fulfilled her expectations. This book is a history of fairies, and therefore it is a history of how people have experienced the world around them. I am not interested in 'explaining away' the experiences of people who claim to have seen or encountered fairies, or in finding ways to account for those experiences in some other way. Fairies are part of the rich history of human experience, and I do not see why belief in them or claims of encounters with them are any less worthy of respect than, say, religious beliefs or reports of religious experiences.

At the same time, however, fairies have a history. They are not simply a baffling, inexplicable phenomenon in human culture – weird as they are. We can try to trace their genesis in human belief from the earliest times to the present day. Fairies mirror human societies and are as diverse as the different human cultures that encounter them. Real or imagined, the history of fairies is also our history, and I will argue in this book that the human relationship with fairies may be entangled with the emergence of consciousness, and therefore perhaps a foundational aspect of what it is to be human. But we are about to enter a very murky world indeed: a land where nothing means quite what we think it means, where nothing remains the same as we thought it would, and where the unwary are easily led astray and trapped forever in illusions and misconceptions. For we are about to enter that unstable fairyland that is the history of fairies.

Naming the good people

The very word 'fairy' can be a stumbling block for some people. It immediately evokes (both in the English-speaking world and now well beyond it) a tiny winged humanoid, probably female, associated with enchantment, with childhood, and even with childish*ness* – a byword for the sort of nonsense we should have grown out of as adults. It is perhaps for this reason that some who want to take fairies more seriously choose to spell the word differently, reverting to the archaic 'faery' or 'faerie', or speaking of 'the fae'. This is understandable; it introduces an element of otherness that makes us pause, rather than assuming that the 'faeries' being talked about are the cultural pap of children's cartoons and colouring books. As Diane Purkiss put it, 'we can forget our preconceptions of fairies, and encounter their truly alien quality for the first time'.[3] But the fact remains that 'fairy' is the standard English spelling of a word that refers both to benign childhood fantasies and to deeply unsettling entities of folklore. This paradox is, in my view, an interesting feature of the history of fairies in its own right – and the question of how fairies stopped being 'scary' is one of the questions this book will explore.

But 'fairy' is also a deeply unsatisfactory word for this kind of being, because it has a very particular cultural history rooted in the collapse of the Western Roman Empire, the development of the Romance languages, and the influence of one of those languages (French) on medieval England.[4] Even in England, 'fairy' was a latecomer, replacing Middle English *pouke* (puck) in the south of the country only in the fifteenth century, while the medieval English word favoured in the north, 'elf', survived and still thrives.⁵ 'Fairy' is a word that usage has pulled from a particular cultural context – in this case, early modern Britain and Ireland – and applied globally to a category of being for which we have no name we can all agree on.

The problem, however, is that fairies are beings of folklore and popular culture; they are not, like angels and demons, the subjects of dogmas and theological definitions. Nor are they, like witches, the subject of a historical legacy of endless judicial debate. There are few learned discussions from the Middle Ages or the early modern period about what fairies actually *are*, and certainly no agreement was reached then or now. So we are left using a word from Britain (even if it has cognates in most of the Romance languages) to name a vast swathe of folkloric beings who, in many cases, have no known historical relationship with the British and Irish 'fairy'. It is a bit like English speakers using the word 'pear' to describe any vaguely pear-shaped fruit, from avocado pears to prickly pears. And it should also be remembered that, even if 'fairy' is a word with a fairly fixed meaning today, that does not mean it had a fixed meaning in the past.⁶

It is ironic that naming these beings presents a problem for modern scholars, given that naming the fairies is an ancient taboo. Again and again in fairy traditions, euphemisms like 'the good people', 'the good neighbours', or 'the gentry' have been preferred to a direct statement of who or what these beings are. Yet the issue facing the contemporary historian of fairyland is not so much one of averting misfortune as one of securing meaning. Some scholars may be tempted to wave a hand and breezily declare that specific names hardly matter, and what we are dealing with here is a broad category of supernatural being that we can expect to find across most human cultures. These beings might have local names, but they reflect a human desire to imagine a 'hidden' population of non-human beings coexisting alongside us. 'Fairies', on this view, are best examined from the perspective of anthropology. The question we should be asking is what it is about being human, and the human experience of the world, that causes cultures to perceive and tell stories about these 'mirror people' who reflect ourselves.

To a certain extent, the generalization holds. It is possible to define fairies, at least provisionally, as a frequently invisible population of uncanny non-human (yet human-like) living beings, reported by folklore, who share our world. The extent of the supernatural powers fairies are said to possess, the nature of their social and political organization, their moral character, their size, their location, their dwelling in an otherworld (and so on) can be set aside as mere contingent window-dressing to the basic idea of non-human people. But the difficulty with a generalized approach is that it makes it difficult to study the *history* of fairies. For history requires specifics, including the origins of specific names, and how they came to be applied. Folkloric accounts of fairies, by contrast, often seem to exist outside historical time. Such accounts are good at noting similarities and differences, but lack any plan or method for establishing *how* and *why* some fairies came to be more closely related to one another than others, and they do not offer any coherent account of how fairy belief in any particular place took the form it does. These interpreters of fairy lore are those that Michael Ostling and Richard Forest call the 'lumpers': interpreters who, both now and in the past, tended to lump all miscellaneous supernatural beings together.[7] In the past, this 'lumping' might have taken the form of identifying all supernatural beings (other than angels) as demons, while now it usually takes the form of cryptic pronouncements on the universality of anthropological categories.

The opposite approach to that of the 'lumpers' is that of the 'splitters', who 'prefer a hierarchical typology of named beings, each with its own specified habits, habitation, and abilities'.[8] It is an approach to fairy lore best embodied, perhaps, in the English folklorist Katharine Briggs's *A Dictionary of Fairies* (1976),[9] which has spawned an entire genre of fairy encyclopaedias that minutely divide the fairy world into a multiplicity of local spirits. This too was a well-established trend in scholarship long before the twentieth century – early modern demonologists were eager to subdivide, name, and categorize spirits in order to demonstrate their prowess in understanding the complexities of the devil's delusions.

The difficulty with this 'splitting' approach, however, is that the way a demonologist or folklorist might subdivide supernatural beings may not reflect the way such beings actually function in folklore and vernacular culture, which is much more fluid and chaotic. Once we start dividing up the fairy realm into neat categories, people are apt to take such divisions too seriously, with lasting effects for our conceptualization of the supernatural world of folk belief. But, as Jakobsson points out, such taxonomization is itself a product of the European Enlightenment and derives from botany and zoology; it is not part of the fairy tradition, and when we examine that tradition closely, 'What emerges is not a neat classification . . . but rather a vast and confusing array of words'.[10]

One possible response to both the 'lumpers' and the 'splitters' is to reject the meaningfulness of fairy terminology altogether. On this reading, 'fairy' is a term applied to an imaginary being, and since everyone imagines a fairy differently (and every culture has its own supernatural beings and its own names for them), 'fairies' as a category of being are ultimately meaningless, especially when we try to apply any kind of analysis across cultures. If this is true, then all I am doing in describing vilas as 'the fairies of the Slavic world' or nereids as 'the Greek equivalent of fairies' is superimposing the blinkered worldview of a British folklorist on another culture – and thus any attempt to write a history of fairies is just another sorry exercise in cultural imperialism. Michael Ostling and Richard Forest adopt an approach similar to this, arguing that the study of fairies is 'the study of rhetorical patterns', and that any kind of reification of fairies is misguided and impossible.[11]

I am less pessimistic. While we should be alive to the dangers of eliding important cultural differences and historical genealogies, it is nevertheless hard to avoid the conclusion that fairy-like beings do play similar roles in widely different cultures. Looked at another way, claims that fairies belong only to Britain and Ireland, and that fairies are too diffuse to be meaningful, can themselves be viewed as a chauvinistic. They risk excluding beings from discussion who are outside the cultural ambit of familiarity. The refusal to reify fairies imposes an arbitrary distinction between vernacular, marginalized, and uncodified beliefs such as fairies, on the one hand, and mainstream religious belief on the other. After all, whether they believe in him or not, historians of religion accept the reification of the deity of Christianity as a being to be treated *as if* real in the lives and experiences of believers. Ultimately, the fact that historians are not willing to approach fairies in the same way as deities comes down to a lack of respect for folk belief.

It is no accident that no single agreed way of talking about fairies exists; and it is no accident that fairy terminology is diffuse and struggles to achieve the sort of unity of meaning that would make fairies a respectable subject of academic discussion. Fairies are beings who have been pushed to the fringes of folk culture; the shared conceptual frameworks available for beings such as angels and demons, who were the focus of extensive learned discussion, are unavailable for fairies. They are poor relations in intellectual history. It is easy (and sometimes tempting) to engage in a puritanical repudiation of the meaningfulness of tricky concepts; after all, with enough determination, any concept can be deconstructed and exposed as 'meaningless', from money to love. But such deconstructions disregard the fact that people carry on using the concepts that clever theorists have long since pronounced meaningless, and people continue to find them useful in their lives. One famous example is the distinction between religion and magic, two terms which are notoriously difficult to define. And yet, on a practical level, everyone seems to have a sense of what sort of human behaviours are being referred to by the words 'magic' and 'religion', and that they differ from one another.[12]

Cleverly deconstructing commonly understood words and concepts removes the historian so far from everyday life and discussion that, quite justifiably, most people will stop listening. Furthermore, such an approach privileges elite discourses where the conceptual identities of beings were clearly formed, and makes it impossible to discuss folk culture, where such identities were often more diffuse. Saying that a concept is simply meaningless fails to answer any historical questions. The reality is that many concepts that matter a great deal to us have no clear or agreed-upon definitions, and the absence of an adequate definition or a universal name does not, in and of itself, invalidate the reality of a concept or deny it a history. So I do not think it is helpful, or fair to people in the past, to say that 'fairy' is conceptually meaningless.

Yet fairies are notoriously hard to define – to the point that we might even be tempted to say that the elusiveness of a definition for them is one of their defining characteristics.[13] However, as scholars become increasingly interested in fairies (the result of a flourishing literature on the history of supernatural belief), broad attempts to define them have begun to emerge. For Peter Narváez, fairies were 'challenging, "significant other" societies of *liminal personae*, creatures "betwixt and between", possessing supernatural powers that can be used for evil or good'.[14] Narváez's approach to fairies as a *society* anticipated Simon Young and Davide Ermacora's classification of the fairies as the 'social supernatural'.[15] Whereas other supernatural beings are either part of the human community (such as witches and sorcerers) or solitary non-human phenomena (such as ghosts or bogeys), social supernatural beings are non-human, humanlike beings who form and live in societies and include the elves of Iceland, the trolls of Scandinavia, the nereids of Greece, the vilas of the Slavic world, and so on. So far, Young and Ermacora's formulation seems to have stood up to scrutiny; while there are a few isolated examples of other types of supernatural beings living socially, it does indeed seem that social life is largely confined in folklore to the fairies and their ilk.

But it is not just their identity as social beings that defines this sort of supernatural creature. While it is important to avoid unqualified universalizing claims, it remains true that social supernatural beings are associated, in most European cultures, with some of the same beliefs, fears, and phenomena. These include the abduction of children, their replacement with 'changelings' from an otherworld realm (apparently an explanation for developmentally disabled or neurodivergent children, and perhaps a justification for infanticide), unusual fossils, prehistoric artefacts and fungi (especially the mycological phenomenon of the 'fairy ring'), dancing (especially in circles), buried treasure, hills and mounds, bodies of water, and certain kinds of illness and debility. On the other hand, there are also major differences between social supernatural beings in different parts of Europe. The trolls of Scandinavia are, in general, uglier and more malevolent than the fairies of Britain and Ireland. The elves of Iceland, in contrast to British fairies, seemingly follow the Christian faith (although this is occasionally found in Ireland). The godlings of Western Europe tend to live in an otherworld realm under the ground, whereas in the central and eastern regions of the continent they tend to dwell in the forest or in lakes. And, perhaps most strikingly, in Eastern and Southeastern Europe, the societies of such beings are entirely female.

My approach to fairies in this book is inclusive, because I believe there is more to be gained by including potential denizens of the fairy realm than by excluding them. However, it is necessary to draw some borders. Those borders are both geographical and cultural; fairies, as considered here, are beings of European folklore. In saying this, I do not make any claim that fairy-like beings are exclusive to European cultures, which is clearly false. As we shall see in chapter 2 below, fairies ultimately share a common ancestry with the jinn of Islam and can trace some of their origins to the ancient Near East. But the jinn are a vast subject in their own right and, like the 'small gods' of African traditional religions (for example), they deserve separate treatment. It is possible that a global survey of 'small gods' in all human cultures could be written, but few have a broad enough knowledge of global religion and anthropology to attempt it; as a specialist in the folklore of Britain and the Baltic states, I am already aware of my limitations when it comes to surveying the fairy lore of the whole of Europe. Nevertheless, this book does range beyond Europe's geographical limits (even if it remains within its cultural borders) by considering the development of fairy lore in colonial societies (especially in North and South America and Australasia) where European culture had a dominant and lasting influence, and in that sense it is a global history of the European fairy.

Interpreting fairy lore: diffusion, ancestry, and environment

The question posed by the existence of similarities in traditions of social supernatural beings across diverse cultures is *how* (and indeed *whether*) fairies in different cultures are related. There are broadly three approaches to this problem. The first is diffusionism – the idea that at some point in the past, different cultures have come into contact with one another and transmitted folkloric ideas. For instance, the Lithuanian folklorist Jonas Balys, noting the similarity between the Baltic laumės (supernatural forest-dwelling women) and 'Celtic' fairies, assumed that at some unknown point in history there had been British or Irish influence on the ancient Lithuanians – as difficult as this is to imagine.[16] Similarly, Éva Pócs has noted 'the remarkable typological similarities between the Celtic and the Slavic fairy world'.[17] And it is true that there are some remarkable and seemingly detailed similarities; for instance, the Scottish fairy seer Isobel Gowdie reported encountering fairies who had no backs, but appeared hollow from behind, and the same feature is characteristic of the Nordic skogsrå and the bohyni of the Slavic world, as well as cropping up in at least one account from medieval England.[18] But when, and how, did Slavic, Nordic, and Celtic folklore come into contact with one another in order to cross-fertilize this idea?

A second approach to the similarities in widely dispersed traditions of fairy lore is to seek a common ancestor for fairy belief across cultures. Perhaps fairies were brought by the Indo-Europeans, who brought Indo-European languages into Europe from the steppes of Eastern Europe.

Perhaps they preceded the Indo-Europeans, and represent a survival of 'Old European' religion that came before the sky-gods of the steppe people. Perhaps they are a relic of Mesolithic animism that has resiliently survived beneath the imposition of numerous different religions, belief systems, and worldviews over the past 5,000 years. The idea that fairies have prehistoric origins is one that deserves to be taken seriously, and this book will do so. But it is also impossible to demonstrate, to the standards usually required by historians, that such remote origins exist – especially for *specific* features of fairy lore rather than just for the general idea of fairies themselves as an otherworld population.

The third approach to explaining similarities in fairy traditions is to appeal to the importance of the environments people live in for the development of their folklore, as well as simple coincidence. People living similar lifestyles, in similar landscapes, and under similar climatic conditions of the temperate northern hemisphere will produce similar ideas about supernatural otherworlds. If we apply Ockham's razor to similarities in folklore across cultures by prioritizing the simplest explanation, the 'environmentalists' say, this is a less outlandish hypothesis than insisting on historically unverifiable scenarios of cultural contact or common cultural ancestry. Just as the building of ziggurats in both Mesoamerica and Mesopotamia is to do with the physics of constructing stable monumental structures rather than imagined civilizational contact (or, worse still, 'ancient aliens'), so fundamental environmental factors shaped patterns of supernatural belief in agrarian subsistence societies. Folklore, on this reading, is subject to a kind of 'convergent evolution' that is determined by human nature, human interaction with the natural world, and the creation of complex human cultures. Each society is as capable as any other of inventing from whole cloth a group of beings to account for the same set of otherwise inexplicable phenomena – from disappearing children to sleep paralysis and rings of especially green grass – whom we now lump together as a single category of 'fairies'.

It is possible, of course, that all three approaches to explaining similarities in fairy traditions have an element of truth to them. We know that fairy beliefs can be historically linked between cultures, because we have some well-documented cases of such links. But this does not mean *all* fairy belief is linked in this way. What we are probably looking at, when surveying the totality of European fairy belief, is a mixture of spontaneous creativity by different cultures and folkloric interaction between cultures, now overlaid one upon the other in such a complex way that it is now difficult, if not impossible, to disentangle their precise origins.

The relationship of the fairies of the two islands of Great Britain and Ireland is a case in point. Ireland's fairies bear the same name (in English) as their British counterparts, but because early medieval Ireland's vernacular literature survives from a very early period, we know that the fairies of Ireland have nothing to do with Britain, or with England: they are the aos sí, with a historical pedigree beyond anything the English fairy whose name they have adopted could possibly imagine. At the same time, however, it is still possible – perhaps even likely – that British and Irish fairies *do* share a common ancestor, and that a long-forgotten equivalent of the aos sí existed in Iron Age Britain, whose culture and language were seemingly very similar to Ireland's. But we can never know this for sure.

As this example of the neighbouring islands of Britain and Ireland shows, questions of similarity and difference become very complicated as soon as we examine them closely. In 1957, Katharine Briggs observed that the question of the origin of fairies is 'a detective story in which the crime turns out to have been committed not by one main criminal but by a number of fortuitous minor criminals, who has each unwittingly contributed to the main crime, and who have scattered clues about with bewildering profusion'.[19] In other words, it is impossible to produce a reductive explanation for where fairies come from, because folklore has somehow constituted a single category of being from multiple sources and origins, just as the diverse perpetrators on the Orient Express produce a single victim and a single murder. As the Hungarian folklorist Éva Pócs puts it, the fairies of Eastern Europe 'show an amalgamation of the most varied mythical and ritual legacies and fragments: from ancient goddesses, fate women, Greek nymphs, Slavic and Albanian nature spirits to storm demons and the souls of those who have died prematurely and are now to be found in storm clouds'.[20]

Again, different interpretations of this diversity are possible. Perhaps fairies are a sort of dustbin of supernatural belief, used to explain anything that does not fit comfortably into any other category. This might, *inter alia*, explain why fairies are sometimes good and sometimes bad. There may be an element of truth to this. But perhaps fairies should be seen instead as an especially flexible and accommodating folkloric vernacular, capable of absorbing elements of other beliefs in much the same way as the English language is especially good at absorbing vocabulary from other languages.

Because fairies are beings of folk belief, they have been studied all too often only at the local and national level. It is easy enough to find books about the fairies of Ireland, the fairies of Britain, the fairies of Wales, the fairies of Newfoundland, and so on – and indeed studies of fairy traditions in individual regions and counties; I myself wrote one about the English county of Suffolk.[21] This is because it is easier to study beings with very specific local characteristics and traditions at a local level. But if the historical study of fairy belief never moves beyond the local, the broader significance of intermediate beings in European and European settler-colonial societies will never be realized.

At present, the broader study of fairy-like beings in an international context is still in its infancy, and we would benefit from more studies that lean into the unfamiliarity of fairy traditions, such as Daniela Simina's comparison of Irish and Romanian fairy beliefs.[22] At the same time, however, comparative study should never become a simplistic process of looking for imagined common origins; we need to think deeply about the diversity of reasons why belief systems that are spread across different cultures and large geographical distances look the same – and they are not always the reasons we might at first assume.

All too often, fairies have been seen as 'survivals' of an earlier, ancient stratum of belief that underlies present-day belief systems, but this conception of fairies as lingering relics of the past rests on a particular vision of folklore as an inflexible inheritance, and rural people as passive recipients of that inheritance. People believed in fairies, in other words, because other aspects of their belief system had failed to displace them. But this seems an excessively passive view of folk belief. In reality, the continuity of fairy belief is (in Margaret Alexiou's words), 'less a process of survival than of constant assimilation and integration with other influences'.[23] In other words, communities creatively and continually fashion new roles for fairies and new supernatural beings according to need. Exact taxonomies of the fairy world, mimicking the work of biologists, thus miss the point; they imply that each supernatural being in the fairy world is clearly distinct, and that differences of name correspond to differences of nature (and, indeed, that *similarities* of name point to convergence of nature). Fairies exist on the unstable terrain of folklore, and it makes more sense to study their characteristics in more general terms than it does to get drawn into fine distinctions between brownies and goblins, pucks and pixies.

Patently ridiculous?

If you are reading this book, you probably think fairies are interesting. But there may be some readers who wonder why a subject as silly as fairies deserves serious historical attention. Belief in fairies holds a special status in modern Western culture as a paradigmatic example – indeed, a sort of cultural type-specimen – of a belief held to be absurd, childish, and obviously ridiculous. Only the belief that the earth is flat seriously rivals believing in fairies as a proverbial instance of absurd belief. While few would feel the need to *condemn* actual belief in fairies – it is supposed to be self-evidently absurd, after all – fairy belief is invoked pejoratively and metaphorically, almost as an unthinking reflex, in the denigration of unacceptable beliefs. Beliefs deemed absurd are dismissed as 'fairy tales', with atheists mocking the Abrahamic religions as 'Bronze Age fairy tales' or calling God a 'sky fairy', while speakers of British English might reply to an implausible claim with a sarcastic 'and there are fairies at the bottom of my garden'. Neither religion, belief in paranormal phenomena such as ghosts and poltergeists, nor belief in divination provoke scorn quite like belief in fairies – even if some thoroughgoing atheists and sceptics are insistent that all such beliefs are as absurd as each other. Indeed, belief in fairies stands out from other socially unsanctioned beliefs insofar as it is deemed so absurd that it is more likely to provoke *laughter* than hostility.

Just as in J. M. Barrie's *Peter Pan* a fairy dies every time a child says 'I don't believe in fairies', so it seems that a reputation dies every time a modern, Western, 'educated' adult says that fairies are real. The cultural image of the weak-minded and credulous believer in fairies was fixed (at least in Britain) by the publication of Sir Arthur Conan Doyle's *The Coming of the Fairies* (1922), in which the celebrated creator of Sherlock Holmes avowed faith in the reality of the infamous Cottingley fairy photographs. The Cottingley fairies and their cultural consequences will be examined in more detail in chapter 8 below, but it is noteworthy that the reputation of Conan Doyle's contemporary W. B. Yeats

(1865–1939) never seems to have suffered in the same way from his open avowal of belief in the reality of fairies. The difference was, perhaps, that Yeats had an established reputation as a fanciful poet and explorer of mysticism – not to mention the fact that, as an Irishman, he might have been expected to believe in fairies. Conan Doyle's fairy belief, on the other hand, seemed shocking (his own Irish descent notwithstanding) because it did not fit with his public persona; and even today, some readers of J. R. R. Tolkien and C. S. Lewis are horrified to discover that these 'serious' authors contemplated the possibility that fairies might be real.

Because fairy belief stands outside the mainstream of culture and religion, it is unprotected by the degree of traditional deference accorded to the dogmas of mainstream religions – which, even if we do not accept them, a multifaith society encourages us to respect (or at least leave alone) for the sake of harmonious coexistence with our fellow citizens. Belief in fairies is marginal in modern Britain, and not associated with any particular ethnicity or culture (except perhaps the Irish), and thus vulnerable to mockery. Fairies are one belief it is safe to make fun of. Yet it is difficult to imagine anyone other than an Islamophobic bigot choosing to mock Muslim belief in the jinn, whose existence is sanctioned by the Qur'an itself.

Up to now, I have used the term 'belief' to describe the response of people who think and act as if fairies are part of reality. But the notion of 'belief' is a particularly Christian (and indeed particularly Protestant) one, implying an act of confession – an active assent of the mind and will to the reality of fairies, like a Christian reciting the Creed.[24] 'Belief in fairies' is not, of course, an article of any faith, and like the person who says 'I don't believe in ghosts, but I'm afraid of them', or 'I don't believe in ghosts, but I've seen one', fairies have been experienced as part of reality by many people who would have preferred they were not. As Lizanne Henderson and Edward Cowan note, the question 'Do you believe in fairies?' would have baffled people in pre-industrial Scotland – 'The only dispute concerned . . . whether the guid neighbours were manifestations of divine providence or the legions of hell'.[25] The question worth discussing, in other words, was not whether fairies (or fairy phenomena) existed, but how fairies fitted into a Christian cosmology.

It is difficult for most of us to understand, in a (Western) world where faith in unseen beings seems like a deliberate, countercultural choice, that people in the past did not engage with the fairies (as so many contemporary fairy believers do) because they *chose* to believe in them. Rather, people in the past found themselves confronted with phenomena they could account for in no other way within their cultural worldviews than by the activity of the fairies. And therefore people feared the fairies – for fear does seem, historically, to have been the most common response to them; and fear, as anyone overwhelmed by irrational terror alone in a house at night can testify, does not require *belief*. I can still be frightened out of my wits by unexplained noises or shadows while being *rationally* certain there is no one in my house.

Furthermore, up to the end of the seventeenth century even learned people dwelt within an intellectual framework where the authority of the ancients largely went without question. Doubt might be cast on the moral worth and correct interpretation of ancient pagan authors, but their basic truthfulness in reporting the existence of beings such as nymphs, fauns, and satyrs was usually beyond question. Again, what mattered was whether these beings were purely corporeal monsters, evil demons trying to deceive human beings, or something else entirely. Furthermore, to pre-modern people it did not so much matter whether they encountered strange beings in dream, trance, waking consciousness, or even story; what mattered was establishing what sort of spirits they were.[26]

I am not suggesting that no one should be permitted to make fun of those who treat fairies as part of reality. Everyone is free to respond to fairies as they choose. But I do propose in this book that there is historically nothing especially funny about fairies, or about the business of believing in them (or, more accurately, about experiencing reality in such a way that fairies are part of it). Certainly, the idea that fairy belief is childish, and suited only to children, is one that the evidence of history challenges. Indeed, even if children are the one group in modern Western societies who continue to believe in fairies until their education in adult ways of perceiving the world drives the fairies away, the disturbing possibility remains that children remain closer to perceiving reality as it truly is. The otherness of children in their modes of perception and behaviour is a source of fear in grown-ups.[27] And yet we convince ourselves that fairy belief belongs to an inferior, childish stage of psychological development in order to avoid grappling with the thought that other modes of perceiving reality are possible. On this interpretation, adult laughter at the mention of fairies is as much nervous laughter as it is contemptuous mockery: the performance of derision against a possibility so threatening to our established worldview that only laughter can exorcise it and banish it once again to the nursery.

J. R. R. Tolkien took the view that fairy tales (by which he did not necessarily mean tales featuring fairies) were no more intrinsically suitable for children than they were for adults, and that if someone possessed an intrinsic taste for such tales, it would only grow with age.[28] The children's author Rosemary Sutcliff turned the idea of fairies as childish on its head, suggesting that it is only because the honesty of children renders them better able to confront fundamental matters of life and death, good and evil, that they appreciate fairy tales: 'The young have a strong feeling for the primitive and fundamental things of life. That is why myths and legends certainly not meant for children in the first place have been largely taken over by them.'[29] In other words, it is an unflattering reflection on the unseriousness of our adult society that we consign the most protean narratives to children's literature, even if they were once the guiding myths of peoples and cultures. Whether or not you, the reader, consider belief in fairies to be absurd, I remain convinced that fairy belief is as deserving of a history as any other culturally important aspect of human belief. Indeed, I would make the case that marginalized beliefs such as that in fairies are especially deserving of the historian's attention, not least because it is easy for people to hold on to long-since-discredited historiographies when a subject is not front and centre in popular awareness.

Indeed, the loss of fairy belief may be more serious than we think. The palaeoanthropologist Ludovic Slimak holds up the disappearance of fairy belief ('with the last wild dreams of wild children') as a paradigmatic example of the kind of cultural extinction – the collapse of a mythical world – that may presage the extinction of our species itself. In the same way that Indigenous peoples are left disoriented and their lives without meaning when modernity strips them of their worldviews, so Slimak theorizes that other humanities (such as the Neanderthals) may have fallen victim to a fatal mythological collapse in the aftermath of first contact with *Homo sapiens*.[30] The collapse of fairy belief alienates us from a fundamental aspect of our ancestors' perception of reality, and impoverishes the richness of our relationship with surrounding nature.

But such a view may be unnecessarily alarmist; it assumes, after all, that fairy belief *has* gone away or is at risk of doing so. And this, as we shall see, is far from the whole story.

Fairy belief has come under sustained attack since the seventeenth century on what are essentially grounds of plausibility: the unlikelihood that beings such as the fairies exist, and the absence of any good reason for them to exist. Ockham's razor shaved the fairies away as a category of beings whose existence is unnecessary to account for any aspect of the world we live in; after all, we now have alternative explanations for rings of lush grass, fossils, prehistoric artefacts, horses found in a sweat despite spending all night in the stable, and so on. The difficulty with such an approach to fairies, however, is that it assumes that fairies primarily served an explanatory function in the first place, filling in gaps in the understanding of rural people who knew no better. A merely 'functional' account of the fairies, where they fulfil certain prescribed roles determined by ignorance of the 'true' nature of physical reality, simply will not do – because the stories told about fairies, and the power with which they were invested, vastly exceed any explanatory function the fairies could be said to perform. This is not to say that fairies do *not* fulfil various social functions in societies where their existence is accepted,[31] but the fulfilment of those functions is not a sufficient explanation for why fairies are part of human experience. We might *think* we know what medieval or early modern people imagined fairies to be, but in reality there is no 'single master narrative';[32] the fairy encounters people reported were always somehow weirder than we can imagine.

The fundamental weakness of Enlightenment-derived dismissals of fairy belief as 'superstition' or ignorance is that neither superstition nor ignorance accounted for the richness and complexity of fairy lore. Why would ignorance, even coupled with extreme credulity, give rise to belief in such extraordinary and complex beings, and such rich narrative traditions about them? Scepticism, however potent, leaves behind the troubling question of *why* people held such elaborate beliefs in beings that (we are assured by right-thinking people) are not real. The difficulty, I would suggest, is that the Enlightenment was preoccupied with questions of ontology. What beings are there? Which beings are real, and which imaginary? We too, as inheritors of the Enlightenment, find it hard to escape this way of thinking.

But we might get closer to the mystery of why people believe in fairies (even today) by approaching fairies not as a hypothesized category of entities which stands or falls by the standards of scientific observation, but as a mode of perception inherited (or chosen) by some cultures and individuals. This is the question of the relationship between fairy belief and animism that will be explored in chapter 1 below. The shift from belief in (and fear of) fairies to public ridicule of fairy belief, which in Britain took place in the second half of the seventeenth century, was not so much determined by the influx of new kinds of *knowledge* as by the abandonment of older ways of perceiving the world. And if this is true, it raises questions about the future of fairies, since our ways of perceiving the world may yet change – a theme explored in the book's final chapter.

Fairies and Christianity

Fairies are, as we have seen, difficult to define; and they are as diverse across cultures as they are similar. But there is one characteristic that all European fairies share, and that is their coexistence alongside, and interaction with, the Christian faith for the last few centuries – in some cases, for a millennium and a half or more. The dogged coexistence of fairies alongside Christianity is perhaps the most remarkable fact about them, insofar as Christian doctrine ostensibly makes no room for the existence of such beings. Other supernatural and folkloric beings – angels, demons, ghosts, witches, even giants and dragons – either could be found in the Bible or could be accounted for, with a few slight adjustments of interpretation, within a Christian cosmology. But there are, on the face of it, no fairies in the Bible – no morally and ontologically ambivalent beings with natures somewhere between the human and the demonic. The Ukrainian folklorist Natalie Kononenko goes so far as to define fairies as 'spirit beings who are not part of the Christian religious pantheon'.[33] Fairies are, in other words, beings of folklore that stand outside the 'official' Christian cosmology of the Bible and the church.

The relentless moral ambiguity of fairies – their failure to conform to Christian ideas of either good or evil spirits, and the church's failure to turn them into one or the other, or stamp them out entirely – is a historical puzzle whose solution Jacqueline Simpson sought in human nature: 'Clear-cut moral divisions do not reflect the way we experience life, where good luck and misfortune bear no relation to virtue and vice.'[34] They are outsiders in a Christian cosmology because they are outsiders in relation to Christian cosmology. It seems obvious, to some, that the only explanation for this uncomfortable coexistence that makes sense is that fairies are 'pagan survivals', half-remembered gods and goddesses who somehow made it through the nuclear winter of Christianization and lingered on as degraded versions of themselves. But this does not follow. As Ronald Hutton has shown, Christian societies were more than capable of fashioning folkloric figures from whole cloth who had no obvious connection with the Christian faith, such as Mother Earth.[35] A supernatural being's poor fit with Christianity need not be seen as evidence of its origins in a pre-Christian cosmology, and it is a key argument of this book that folk Christianity *did* make strenuous efforts to incorporate fairies into unofficial Christian cosmologies.

The fraught relationship between fairies and Christianity has sometimes been considered as something that primarily troubled the learned, and not the 'folk' themselves, who happily coexisted with fairies in their semi-pagan ignorance. But this runs against the evidence for fairy belief, which suggests that attempts to make sense of fairies within a Christian cosmology often came from ordinary people themselves, or was at least a shared endeavour between the 'folk' and the learned elite. This should not surprise us; learned culture has an impact, sooner or later, on folk belief, and learned speculations feed into folklore. Furthermore, 'ordinary' people (by whom I mean non-elite individuals who were not engaged in the production of written sources) were often no less devout Christians than the learned, and equally concerned with remaining faithful to a Christian outlook while also experiencing fairies as part of their day-to-day reality.

Fairies are, thus, beings of popular Christianity who were formed (at least in part) by the imposition of layers of Christian interpretation over them – provided the distinction between official and popular Christianity is properly understood. It is important to set aside simplistic ideas of an oppressive medieval church imposing rigid dogmas on a quasi-pagan populace, who simply hid their real beliefs beneath a Christian veneer. From the church's point of view, the reality was even worse: people did not reject Christianity or pretend to be Christians, but instead developed their own forms of unorthodox Christianity. The inevitable price paid by the church for the process of Christianization in any culture is that people will make Christianity their own, inflected by their cultural distinctiveness, and a popular Christianity will develop that does not always have much to do with official theology. 'Folk demonology' was often at variance with official views of angels and demons, and proved resistant to categories of absolute good and absolute evil, preserving a messier and more ambivalent picture of the spiritual world.[36] But although 'folk demonology' may have arisen from and among ordinary people, it was picked up soon enough by preachers, for whom warning people against contact with the fairies was a pastoral imperative.

Fairies are therefore best understood as 'parareligious' beings within Christian cosmology: they are not properly intruders or pagan holdovers, but formed an integral part of the Christian worldviews of many ordinary people in spite of their failure to gain official recognition from the church. In this respect, as we shall see, Christianity differs from Islam, where the appearance of the jinn in the Qur'an ensured that belief in intermediate non-human beings was officially sanctioned by Muslim doctrine.

The absence of official doctrinal recognition did not, however, stop Christian clergy acknowledging fairies as a presence (and a threat) at the local level. Joyce Salisbury, in a study of folk beliefs in Galicia, argued that people clung on to fairy beliefs for as long as the church failed to provide a functional alternative to such spirits.[37] In some cases, this was never; Christianity was always a bit too unworldly to cater to all of the spiritual needs people felt they had, and so there was always a space left for the fairies.[38] As Heiki Valk puts it, in relation to Estonia, 'the higher cult was expelled much earlier by the Church and Christianity than that practised at the lowest, personal level'.[39]

Fairies may or may not have ultimately pagan origins. But in one sense it does not really matter. Fairies can and did coexist with Christianity regardless, and until the late Middle Ages little or no effort was made to stamp out belief in them – that is why there is so little evidence of fairy belief from the records of church courts, which tried to regulate acceptable and unacceptable belief. The key point is that the history of fairies and Christianity is predominantly one of coexistence and accommodation – and sheer indifference – rather than opposition and hostility; although, as we shall see, Christian clerics did eventually become interested in fairy belief and made attempts both to suppress it and to borrow from it for the development of their own demonologies.

Fairylands, fairy tales, fairy fictions

The very word 'fairy' contains within itself not just the name of a kind of being, but the name of a place: *féerie* or *faerie*, the land or realm of the *fées*, which later became muddled with the singular 'fay' in the English language. Not all fairies inhabit an otherworld; the domestic fairies, who are often solitary, do not seem to have any particular connection with an otherworld realm, and in some cultures fairies inhabit 'earthly otherworlds' such as the forest or bodies of water. In Iceland, the elves coexist, usually invisibly, in the same physical space as human communities. But in Irish, British, and French tradition, and in the countries that came under their influence, fairies inhabit an otherworld realm that is usually accessed via (but is not identical with) mounds, hills, and prehistoric monuments of various kinds. The fairy otherworld is characterized by 'glamour' – a kind of enchantment that lies upon everything, lending it a grander and more beautiful appearance than it has in reality – and time moves differently in fairyland from in the human world, with the result that people who spend a short time in fairyland will often find that many years have passed for their family and friends. Furthermore, eating the food of the fairy otherworld has the effect of trapping a human being within it.

Fairyland is often ruled by a king, a queen, or both, and is a hierarchically structured society mirroring our own. Another theme in many tales is the fairies' need of mortals – as midwives, as playmates, and (more sinisterly) as surrogate children, with fairy changelings sent to replace the abducted mortal infants who then swell the ranks of fairyland. In Scottish tradition, the dead are sometimes taken to fairyland too, and are seen at Hallowe'en among the 'fairy rade', when the fairies processed through the countryside. The study of fairies is, then, not just an enquiry into a particular kind of folkloric being, but into a whole supernatural society. The question is not just 'what is a fairy?' but how fairies organize their society and interact and coexist with one another as social supernatural beings.

There is no shortage of narratives of human encounters with fairies and human visits to fairyland, but such narratives can be divided into three broad – and very different – categories. In one category, we might place 'veridical' fairy narratives (what folklorists sometimes call 'memorates'), which claim to be factual accounts of someone's encounter with the fairies – such as the tale of Elidyr, or the narrative of the 'Green Children of Woolpit' (see chapter 3 below), or the reports published by Edmund Jones in eighteenth-century Wales (see chapter 6). In another category, we can place 'fairy tales', traditional tales which are sometimes presented as factual narratives of an actual encounter, but more usually were told for entertainment or for moral instruction. Indeed, it is not always clear that fairy tales are about the fairies at all; they have their own logic and their own history.[40] As the Lithuanian folklorist Norbertas Vėlius put it, whereas fairy tales are 'strictly stereotypical' and lack a 'supernatural shield' (because the supernatural is taken as given in fairy tale), legends of encounters with supernatural beings remain 'realistic' and take place in the everyday world.[41] Furthermore, the fairies of fairy tale differ from the fairies of folk belief – for instance, trolls often live under bridges in fairy tales, but have no association with bridges in Scandinavian folk belief.[42] In the third category are fairy fictions: self-consciously crafted uses of fairies in literary or dramatic narratives, from the medieval Romances to Shakespeare's *Midsummer Night's Dream* and Victorian pantomime, from the fairies of J. M. Barrie to the elves of J. R. R. Tolkien. Because a great deal of academic writing on fairies emerges from literary studies, there is much excellent scholarship on literary fairies.[43]

The relationship between fairies and literature has proved a very fruitful one, but it also raises a 'chicken and egg' question: to what extent did literature derive from fairy folklore, and to what extent did literature inspire popular perceptions of fairies at any given time? Were the medieval Romance tradition's stately mistresses of enchantment, the likes of Morgan Le Fay, inspired by what ordinary people believed about fairies? James Wade and Richard Firth Green have argued that it is far from clear that they were, and that it is just as likely that the authors of Romances simply seized upon fairies as convenient narrative devices that could function as a sort of *deus ex machina* to introduce elements of the fantastical and magical into a story.[44]

But if the fairies of literature did not depend on folklore, did literary portrayals of fairies inform folkloric conceptions of fairies?[45] In one sense, this seems obviously true: most people who claim to encounter fairies in the twentieth and twenty-first centuries seem to meet winged 'flower fairies' whose roots lie in literature. But this is a late phenomenon. The prominence of fairies in literary studies can risk giving the impression that fairies are first and foremost a literary construction which somehow irrupted into folklore – and, indeed, Ronald Hutton has advanced an argument for the formation of medieval British fairies in which literature did play a key role.[46] But Richard Firth Green cautions that 'we have been conditioned by post-medieval attitudes to fairies to construe any story containing them as a literary fantasy, and we tend unreflectively to project such conditioning back upon our medieval ancestors'.[47]

In other words, fairies have not always been just story, and fiction and folklore are not the same thing. Folklore is constructed by communities, not devised by individual artists. This does not stop communities adopting the visions of artists and writers, of course – this is the process folklorists call 'ostension', whereby something originating in story begins to manifest as part of people's experience or enactment of reality. Ostension, as I shall argue in subsequent chapters of this book, has played an important role in the development of fairy beliefs – the invocation of fairies in magic was apparently inspired by literature and art, as, later, were 'SWFs' ('Small, Winged Fairies').[48] But this is not the same thing as saying that *all* fairy belief is ostension rooted in literature.

Literary fairies, while culturally important, are not the principal focus of this book, which is about fairies *as encountered* rather than fairies *as imagined*. In other words, this is a book about fairy *narratives* rather than fairy tales or fairy fictions. This is not to deny that fairies have a long history as beings serving useful narrative functions, as well as beings people claimed to encounter as part of their experience of reality. However, as a historian, I am interested in the origins of beliefs rather than in the origins of legendary or literary tropes, which do not necessarily have anything to do with the way people perceive the world. For too long, scholars have often thought it sufficient to study the cultural impact of folklore and belief without engaging directly with folkloric beings as part of people's experience of the world. People met (and meet) fairies; fairies were (and are) part of their experience of reality. The question the historian should be asking is how this came to be.

A history of fairies

Fairies are peculiarly resistant to historical analysis, which is probably why so few attempts have been made to trace their history. This is not only because fairies are difficult to define and classify, but also because discussions of them in learned sources are quite rare – and, of course, before the age of print (and for quite some time after), most of the historical sources we possess were produced by a literate elite who only sporadically discussed folk culture. Folk culture is always hard to historicize, and few would now have the confidence of the Victorians in 'reverse engineering' folk narratives to become 'evidence' for ancient patterns of story reaching back into prehistory. A history requires historical evidence. There is also the question of how that evidence should be interpreted. If we take fairies themselves as historical actors, then, as Jeremy Harte notes, we face the problem that fairies do not act like human beings, according to human rules, or in ways we understand. There is therefore no causation (as we understand it) in fairy encounters, and thus there can be no history – all that is possible is 'an inquiry about what events meant at the time',[49] without the usual questions historians ask, such as 'Did it really happen?'

While Harte may be correct that the motivations of fairies are unfathomable, that is often true of human beings as well. The historian can never be sure why anyone acted the way they did. If fairyland is a foreign country whose rules often make little sense to us, so is the past. I am not convinced that the challenges of studying fairy lore mean we should shy away from a historical investigation of fairies as encountered by human beings, and that is what this book aims to provide. It is neither a miscellany of folklore nor a comprehensive catalogue of fairy beings, nor is it an attempt to offer some watertight and complete definition of what fairies are or how they behave. It is, rather, a history of what humans have written about fairies, and how they have encountered them, and it is particularly focussed on what people thought fairies were and where they thought they came from – as well as how we ended up with the fairies we are familiar with today. These are questions that can be profitably explored regardless of whether fairies themselves are real as historical actors.

The structure of this book is broadly chronological, which reflects the importance of rescuing fairies from the timeless limbo in which folklore sometimes leaves them. At the same time, however, fairies are composite beings whose elements derive from multiple traditions, and the first two chapters of this book address the two main root systems that converge to form the tree of European fairy lore. The first of those roots is belief in 'godlings' or spirits of nature in the religious traditions of pre-Christian Europe – about which we know frustratingly little, with the exception of Graeco-Roman culture. Chapter 1 explores the possibility that the roots of fairy belief lie in 'animistic' or 'shamanistic' outlooks on the human relationship with the natural and divine worlds, arguing for the primacy of 'godlings' as a religious category. Fairies are not, in other words, decayed remnants of pagan gods – rather, 'godlings' are an irreducible category of being in their own right, who have existed in both pre-Christian and Christianized European societies.

Chapter 2 turns to the second fundamental root of European fairy belief, which is Jewish and Christian belief in intermediate spirit-beings between the angelic and the demonic. This is a belief that has never gained any kind of official acceptance in Christianity (in contrast to Islam), but has nevertheless emerged repeatedly in unofficial 'folk theologies', especially in early medieval Ireland. Generally speaking, the extent to which fairy belief has been influenced by the Bible and by the speculations of the Church Fathers has been insufficiently acknowledged in most explorations of the history of fairy belief. The Christianization of Europe resulted in the interaction and integration of existing beliefs in godlings with learned speculations about the Bible and Classical mythology to result in fairies who were partly demonic, partly angelic, partly Graeco-Roman, and partly vernacular.

It was these ambiguous beings, still in the process of formation, who became the fairies of the Middle Ages – and they are the subject of chapter 3, which explores the place of ambiguous otherworld beings in the still-forming imaginative world of the early Middle Ages. Medieval authors were uncertain about the extent of God's creation, and entertained the possibility of the existence of 'monstrous' races, combining human and animal characteristics as well as supernatural powers, both in distant lands and closer to home. Heterodox (or at least theologically creative) understandings of intermediate beings developed, especially in Ireland and Scandinavia, drawing upon a mixture of euhemerism and theological speculation. But it is clear that no definitive understanding of who or what such otherworlders were existed before the fourteenth century (at the earliest), and fairies swirled in a linguistic and conceptual soup for much of the Middle Ages.

The subject of chapter 4, 'Founding fairyland', is the formation of more familiar conceptions of fairies and their realm in the later Middle Ages. This happened in part owing to the rise of fairies to prominence in the French and British Romance traditions of vernacular literature, but it was also tied to greater ecclesiastical interest in (and censure of) fairy belief. At the end of the Middle Ages, fairy belief began a transformation that was to continue into the early modern period, and which I refer to in chapter 5 as the 'reformation of fairyland'. This 'reformation' was, in part, a demonization and 'witchification' of folklore by the reformers of the Protestant Reformation, who were determined to collapse fairyland entirely into the demonic realm. But it was also a more complex transformation that began before the Protestant Reformation and involved Catholics as well as Protestants, leading to a more structured fairyland, a Renaissance classicizing influence on ideas of what fairies looked like, and the rise of fairy magic – the idea that it was actually possible to communicate with and draw supernatural power from the fairies.

The social marginalization and decline of belief in fairies – at least in some parts of Europe – is the subject of chapter 6. Yet, as the chapter's title suggests, the Enlightenment involved enchantment as well as disenchantment. While authors of the late seventeenth century such as Balthasar Bekker led a relentless attack on the richness of the inherited supernatural world of late medieval Christianity, the speculative intellectual climate of the period led others, such as the Scottish clergyman Robert Kirk and the Welsh minister Edmund Jones, to investigate the fairies as a subject in their own right, while antiquaries like John Aubrey allowed their unchecked curiosity to range as far as the fairy realm. In an unstable atmosphere of speculation about occult forces and unknown powers, fairies were not as marginal to the Enlightenment as some might assume, even if they were undergoing a parallel transformation to stereotyped forms onstage, in art, and in literature. It was also in this period that European fairy belief began to move outwards into the lands settled and colonized by Europeans in the so-called 'age of discovery', and this is the subject of chapter 7. From Newfoundland and New England to New France and Latin America, Old World fairy beliefs continued in settler communities as well as interacting with Indigenous belief systems.

The nineteenth and twentieth centuries, which are the subject of chapter 8, saw the return of fairies to the cultural mainstream. This was the era of systematic folklore collection throughout Europe, when vast numbers of fairy traditions were collected across the continent, and fairy fictions became immensely popular. But it was also an era when, as rural fairy traditions slipped away in many places, a few Spiritualists and Theosophists sought to revive belief in fairies among a new class of believer – educated people who consciously chose to believe in fairies, such as Sir Arthur Conan Doyle and others convinced by the photographs of the Cottingley fairies. The affair of the Cottingley fairies redefined the popular image of fairies forever. In Ireland and elsewhere, the cultural value placed on fairy lore by nationalist folklorists became a political weapon wielded in aid of national independence movements, and authors such as Lewis and Tolkien treated fairies with deep seriousness. At the same time, the eccentric members of the Fairy Investigation Society dedicated themselves to finding and contacting otherworld peoples.

Chapter 9 considers the phenomenon of fairy belief today – which is sometimes sincere, and sometimes less so (especially when tourism is involved). It considers the role played by fairies in contemporary religious, spiritual, and ecological movements, from alternative spiritualities to contemporary Paganism. It considers efforts to collate reports of fairy sightings in modern media from online surveys to podcasts; the relationship between fairies and UFOs; the role of fairies in psychedelia, in modern Christianity, and in efforts to re-enchant the world – and, finally, it looks ahead to what the future may hold for humanity's long and complex relationship with fairies.

ONE

The hills are alive: sacred nature in ancient Europe

In February 1692, a Sámi man from the far north of Sweden, Anders Povelsen, was put on trial in Vadsø in Norway, accused of possessing and using a banned ritual drum. The Sámi tradition of creating 'rune drums' for divination, painted with different figures to signify sources of sacred power, is in all likelihood a very ancient one indeed, stretching back into prehistory. Povelsen was questioned in detail by the Norwegian court about the meaning of the figures on his drum, who included the thunder god Dierpmis and the goddesses Maddarakka and Sáráhkká, as well as reindeer – as might have been expected in a reindeer-herding culture. This testimony met the court's expectations that the Sámi, as an unconverted and still pagan people, threatened the unity and godliness of Denmark-Norway as a Lutheran kingdom.

But the overtly 'pagan' imagery on Povelsen's drum (which was finally returned to the Sámi by the queen of Denmark in 2022) was accompanied by something stranger: Christian images, such as 'God the Father', 'God's Son', the Virgin Mary, a church, and St Anne the 'sister' (actually the mother) of the Virgin Mary. Strangest of all, perhaps, were the 'Christmas men' (*Juovlagázzi*), personifications of the twelve days of Christmas who performed helpful tasks for Sámi families in the midwinter period.[1]

The Sámi 'Christmas men' were humanoid personifications of the twelve days of Christmas, a little like Charles Dickens's ghosts of Christmas past, present, and yet to come. Outside literature, however, the idea of experiencing units of time as personified beings is so alien to a conventional Western way of thinking that it is, perhaps, scarcely comprehensible unless we come to terms with the Sámi approach to reality. The word we might use for that experience of reality is 'animism', which Graham Harvey has defined as 'a concern with knowing how to behave appropriately towards persons, only some of whom are human'.[2] Animism is sometimes confused with anthropomorphism – the tendency to ascribe human or human-like qualities to non-human beings or things – but the very concept of anthropomorphism assumes that a culture identifies personhood with humanness, since the only way a non-human can be perceived as a person is when 'human' qualities are imposed upon them/it. But animists do not need to anthropomorphize, because for them personhood itself extends beyond the human. Animals, inanimate objects, and even (as with the Sámi) divisions of time can be persons. One Inuit shaman reported that the first spirit who ever helped him was a personified manifestation of his name.[3] Animists have experiences of this kind because they 'put less emphasis on classification and more on observation'. Thus the Ojibwa of North America's Great Lakes considered some stones to be living, because they observed some stones behaving like living things by shifting position, changing shape, or becoming larger or smaller.[4]

This chapter will consider the idea that the beings we call fairies have their ultimate origin in an animist approach to reality. The idea that fairy belief is animistic is not a new one; as long ago as 1911, Walter Evans-Wentz (1878–1965) proposed that fairy lore represented a 'considerable degeneration from what must have been in pagan times a widespread and highly developed animistic creed'.[5] As we shall see, there are reasons to take seriously the idea that fairy belief is a manifestation of animism, although it is also far from clear that this really explains where fairies come from. But if it is true that fairies emerge from animism, the implications are profound – for it would mean that fairies may be, at least among Europeans and people of European heritage, the oldest surviving of all popular beliefs. So old, in fact, that the human experience of a community of unseen others may have something to tell us about the emergence of consciousness itself. Coexistence with fairies might, then, be seen as a fundamental feature of what it is to be human – a sort of epiphenomenon of personal consciousness. But this is not an easy question to explore. The question of the ultimate origin of fairies tests history to its limits, and requires the invocation of other disciplines such as anthropology and developmental psychology – a sure sign that we have wandered into an unreliable realm where nothing is certain, but where deep questions nonetheless arise about humanity's relationship with nature and with the cosmos.

Animist fairies

The idea that personhood extends beyond human beings – the sense that we are not alone – is at the very foundation of fairy belief. In this respect it is tempting to classify fairy belief as a kind of animism. Animism is 'an animal- and spirit-related mode of vernacular sensitivity, a complex way of perception, thought, and action that encompasses human and other-than-human persons';[6] the animist's experience of reality is, in other words, a complex and delicate negotiation with persons. Fairy belief seems to hark back to a time when humans experienced reality in terms of persons; when personification, in fact, was a *mode* of perception. This is not 'religion' as we might understand it, and it is probably a category error to bracket animism with religion; indeed, anthropologists and historians long denigrated animism because it was viewed as a 'primitive' evolutionary stage of religious belief.[7] But, as the Ojibwa show, animism is not a matter of belief but of observation; it is about the forging of relationships with non-human beings, rather than abstract faith commitments.[8] And there is no single 'animism', as if it is a coherent ideology (or an ideology at all); rather, all cultures will express the making of relationships with non-human beings in different ways. Put another way, there is no *content* to animism; it is a behaviour and an activity, not a set of beliefs.

What Ronald Hutton calls 'a capacity to conceive of worlds beyond the material and the immediate' seems to have been a defining feature of anatomically modern *Homo sapiens sapiens* for as long as we have existed, expressed first of all in rituals surrounding the disposal of the dead and in the creation of painted or carved representations of people and animals.[9] It is possible that what we call animism is as old as the Upper Palaeolithic – up to 50,000 years ago – but we have to confront the fact that everything we think we know about our ancestors in deep prehistory comes from a combination of very ephemeral archaeological remains and analogies drawn from contemporary populations who have seemingly retained 'prehistoric' ways of life. Drawing these analogies requires us to make many assumptions: to assume, for instance, that human perceptions of reality essentially stood still for 50,000 years until 'modern' religion came along, and that contemporary animists are largely untouched by modern concerns. Stereotyping prehistoric worldviews as 'totemism', 'animism', or 'shamanism' is usually uninformative and unhelpful.[10] Many contemporary animists inhabit complex and overlapping cosmologies, worldviews, and worlds of belief, just as Anders Povelsen did in seventeenth-century Norway. But within those complex and overlapping cosmologies, an animist element will often ensure that personification remains a mode of perception.

'Animism' is a term of anthropology rather than history; when using it, therefore, it is important to avoid the pitfalls of early anthropology, which had a tendency to 'flatten' the complexities of human culture by assuming that all human beings in the same 'stage of development' would have similar approaches to reality and religion. The days of generalizing claims about all human cultures are largely gone – as is the idea that all humans exist in a hierarchy of stages of religious development – and this book is focussed on the otherworld supernatural beings of Europe and of the global European diaspora rather than the otherworld social supernatural beings of humanity in general. A book about all otherworld beings across all cultures probably *could* be written, but it could scarcely claim to be a work of history, since it is impossible to demonstrate historical connections between the invisible worlds of every culture. When dealing with the deep past, acknowledgement of our shared humanity (important as that is) needs to be balanced against recognizing the uniqueness of cultures – and the ways in which that uniqueness lends meaningfulness to cultural concepts.

While exercising appropriate caution in refraining from anthropological generalizations, therefore, it does seem that human interest in forming relationships with non-human beings often fixes on the same sorts of places. Thus, Ken Dowden has argued that an awareness of the specialness of trees, stones, water sources, and groves (natural enclosures formed by trees) constitutes a nucleus for the subsequent development of what we call 'religion' out of 'raw ecology'.[11] It is striking, for example, that the making of offerings on unusual stones in the Baltic (where ritual use of stones continued into the twentieth century[12]) seemingly paralleled Neolithic practices in Britain – with cup-marked stones existing in both regions. Similarly, heavily forested areas of Europe that are widely dispersed over vast distances seem to have developed similar traditions regarding groves, sacred trees, and offerings to forest spirits for successful hunting.[13] While there may be 'contact theories' for such similarities, a hypothesis of contact may be surplus to requirements. If the forest is essential to a people's survival, is it really surprising that people will independently find ways to make the forest sacred? But here again, the general must be balanced against the particular. To me, as a lifelong inhabitant of temperate northern Europe, the typical features in a European landscape that seem 'special' or unusual are more obvious than they would be to a visitor from another region. But a different set of features, beyond my capacity to imagine, might be significant in a different climate zone and ecological context, such as the Australian Outback.

If ecology and anthropology have something to tell us about the human tendency to animism, it is possible that developmental psychology also reveals clues about the origins of our yearning to form connections with non-human persons. Developmental psychologists and educationalists have long been aware of children's apparent tendency to 'animist', anthropomorphic, personifying, and teleological language in forming an early understanding of science – and there is a corresponding debate about whether or not teachers should use such language.[14] Is it acceptable to say that steam is trying to escape from a pressure cooker? That lightning is looking for the tallest structure to strike, in order to earth itself? That a river is finding the quickest way to the sea? It is impossible to know whether such ways of thinking and speaking are 'natural' to children – but most children nevertheless seem to move from such language towards more 'scientific' and depersonalized ways of speaking about natural phenomena as they grow up.

It is surely no accident that children are also more open to fairies as part of their experience of reality; the notion that non-human persons exist is not self-evidently absurd to them. For young children, personhood might be a highly dispersed category, with no clear distinction between animate and inanimate objects, living and non-living things – indeed, the idea of a relationship with a non-living thing fashioned to look like a human or animal is arguably the basis for the appeal of young children's toys. Again, however, it is difficult to be sure if children's openness to fairies derives from some sort of 'innate animism' or from the fact that adults think fairies will appeal to children, and therefore they talk about them to children as if part of reality – leading in turn to childhood fairy belief. The pioneering developmental psychologist Jean Piaget famously identified children's tendency to 'magical thinking', 'animism', or 'superstition' (understood as an erroneous understanding of causality) as an inability to distinguish between mental and non-mental realities.[15]

It should be noted, however, that such a diagnosis presumes a degree of confidence in our understanding of what causation really is, as well as certainty that mental and non-mental realities *do not* permeate one another (a question to which we will return in chapter 9). The human capacity to project life and sentience onto the non-living and the non-sentient seems to be an epiphenomenon or by-product of our own sentience – although it is perhaps only in a technologized, manufactured world that such projection is stigmatized as a perceptual error. In a hunter-gatherer society, after all, almost everything non-human that a human interacts with *is* alive, and it is only in the last few millennia of our existence that humans have been able to live in surroundings largely manufactured by human artifice. The perception of universal, interpenetrating life that aided the hunter-gatherer has thus become a glitch in modern, industrialized human life. But is it a glitch that somehow gives rise to fairies?

The idea that fairies are in some sense an expression of lingering animism has been advocated in recent years (among others) by Emma Wilby and Michael Ostling, who have argued that animism might be viewed as a kind of 'bedrock' of popular belief that continues to exist beneath layers of religion, resilient to religious changes.[16] Like a linguistic 'substrate' that lingers beneath living languages, although long since extinct in and of itself in most Christianized societies, lingering animism can still be detected in the shape of popular belief. For Wilby, fairy belief is 'an amalgamation of many of the animistic beliefs and rituals surrounding nature spirits, deities, ghosts and so on which had not been completely homogenized into Catholic hagiolatry and the cult of the dead'.[17] The idea that fairies are a more comfortable fit with animism than with polytheism is not a new one;[18] there is a long tradition in Classical studies of identifying the Roman notion of *numen* (divine power) as a kind of *mana* or impersonal animistic spirit.[19] This was enthusiastically advanced by comparativist scholars keen to view the ancient world through the lens of anthropology, although it is out of fashion now.[20]

If fairies seem animistic because they point towards a more dispersed understanding of personhood than most modern Westerners are used to, others have noted that fairy belief suggests a permeability of the human and animal worlds. As Tolkien observed, 'absence of the sense of separation of ourselves from beasts' is a characteristic feature of fairy tales that seems to speak to some deep longing as old as time (which Tolkien himself connected with the Christian doctrine of the Fall).[21] Therianthropy, the mingling of animal and human characteristics (as well as animal transformation), is a recurring theme in portrayals of the fairy world, and some scholars have linked this in turn to an ancient human practice of transgressing the boundaries of the human and animal worlds: shamanism. It is to the idea of fairies as manifestations of a therianthropic and shamanic worldview that we now turn.

Therianthropic and shamanic fairies

Ronald Hutton has observed that the earliest human art was characterized by therianthropic figures – hybrid human–animal depictions, of whom the most famous are the Hohlenstein-Stadel 'lion man' figure (figure 1.1) and the 'Sorcerer' of the Cave of the Trois-Frères (an apparent depiction

Figure 1.1 The Hohlenstein-Stadel 'lion man'

of a man metamorphosing into a stag, or vice versa).[22] It is striking that almost all contemporary portrayals of fairies and elves, from Tinker Bell to Elrond and Santa Claus's elf helpers, are notionally therianthropic in one detail: the pointed ears that have become a universally recognized shorthand for fairies and elves, and derive ultimately from the goat-like or asinine ears of the Greek god Pan. As we shall see in chapter 5, Pan and the satyrs and fauns that broadly shared his therianthropic appearance became the basis for early modern depictions of elves and fairies (probably because the Latin word *faunus* so often glossed vernacular words for this kind of being).

In and of itself, an iconographic development in early modern Europe has little relevance to the ultimate origins of fairies in the deep history of humanity. However, traditions of fairies shifting to and from animal forms go back a great deal further than the sixteenth century. In Estonia, where animist traditions lingered longer than in most other European nations, the spirits of the forest could appear to people in animal, human, or mingled therianthropic forms.[23] Furthermore, the spirits were not conceived of as distinct from the singular spirit of the forest itself, leading Ivar Paulson to coin a distinct term, 'animatism', to describe the Estonian experience of the forest.[24] Like the Estonian forest spirits, the fairies of other European cultures still seem entangled with and embedded in the land in a manner unlike any other kind of supernatural being – and one way to account for this is via the emergence of fairy belief from some sort of 'animatism', where the landscape was simultaneously imbued with spirit yet could also manifest itself in personified forms.

Therianthropy has historically been linked with the idea of 'shamanism', a problematic term drawn originally from ethnographic study of Siberian trance practices but subsequently applied to many circumpolar and North American peoples, including the Sámi and Native Americans, when it is not clear that any relationship exists between their cultures. Like 'animism', 'shamanism' is an anthropological term of convenience rather than a real conceptual category (and certainly not a coherent religious tradition).[25] Shamanism has also been projected back into the past onto prehistoric cultures – on the basis of archaeological evidence such as the Mesolithic antler headdresses found at Star Carr in Yorkshire – accompanied by the assumption that shamanism represents an early form of human religiosity that we might expect to find in hunter-gatherer societies.[26] Most accounts of shamanism are dominated by the idea that shamans make contact with the spirit world in an altered state of consciousness, sometimes assuming the behaviours and identities of animals. The shaman thus becomes a therianthropic being, located somewhere between the human and animal worlds – and thus, like fairies, a being who falls into the uncanny category of the 'almost human'.[27]

The Arcadian pastoralist god Pan, whose physical appearance influenced the portrayal of both male godlings in the ancient world and fairies in medieval and early modern Europe, is perhaps the best-known of Europe's therianthropic deities. Speculation about Pan's possible origins as an animistic, therianthropic, or shamanistic spirit of wild places who was shoehorned into the polytheistic Greek pantheon at a later date has long formed part of scholarly discussion of Pan's origins.[28] Certainly, Pan's therianthropic character sets him apart from the other Olympians, and it is noteworthy that Pan was seldom worshipped in temples (caves sacred to Pan were more common), suggesting a cult with archaic origins pre-dating Greece's urban (and urbane) polytheism. Furthermore, there was always a degree of ambiguity as to whether Pan was a singular deity or a representative of a class of beings – the *panes* – who were all therianthropic goat-men.[29] This kind of singular–plural ambiguity is detectable in British godlings from the Romano-British period onwards,[30] and could be taken as an indication that these figures represent an earlier (or at least different) iteration of collective divinity that contrasts with straightforwardly anthropomorphic polytheistic gods.[31] As we shall see in chapter 2, the idea of 'god-peoples' even survived Christianization in early medieval Ireland.

The best-known of all the therianthropes of folklore is the werewolf, who in the Baltic region was viewed not as an object of fear but as a positive (or at least ambivalent) figure – and, rather like the fairies, as a corrector of injustice.[32] One seventeenth-century Latvian man even identified himself as 'God's werewolf'.[33] The Lithuanian and Latvian words *vilkólakis/vilkolakas* (cognate with Polish *wilkołak*) literally mean 'wolf-skin',[34] and in some traditions people did indeed 'become' a wolf by putting on its skin, suggestive of a tradition with possible shamanic origins. In Estonia, people believed they could transform themselves into both wolves and bears by putting on their skins,[35] and the Norse tradition of the 'berserker' who mentally became a bear in battle is well known.

Fairy-like beings throughout Europe are ascribed miscellaneous animal features, which in folk tales often provide a way of distinguishing them from normal human beings – such as the cow's tail of the beautiful Norse huldra, who lures men into her embraces in remote places,[36] and the hooves and bird-legs of the Slavic vilas and bohyni.[37] As we shall see in chapter 2, the Irish aos sí transform themselves into animals in many tales, and there is a long tradition of fairy animals in British folklore.[38] Furthermore, Emma Wilby has argued that the frequent appearance of animal familiar spirits in British witch trials ought to be understood in 'shamanic' terms, as the manifestation of spirit animals.[39]

However, against the idea that fairies are, at root, shamanic therianthropes stands the fact that fairies do not *always* have any animal features. Folkloric narratives are full of ways in which fairies appear at first glance to be human, but are in fact not quite human – from the Slavic tradition of vilas without backs (the back of a vila just looks like a hollow tree trunk) to the Icelandic idea that elves lack a septum. Wilby's familiars appear to her shaman-witches 'in clearly defined, three-dimensional human or animal forms'[40] – which is not how shamans experience contact with animal spirits in trance states.[41]

Perhaps, therefore, we should not read too much into the phenomenon of therianthropy, which (like the recurring theme of diminutive stature) might just be another way of signalling the monstrosity or 'otherness' of fairies. Nevertheless, it makes sense that the fairies should have an affinity with animals, as the living things who bridge the divide between human beings and nature. Animality, on this reading, is a conceptual shorthand for the almost human. But both 'shamanism' and 'animism' are uncomfortably hazy concepts; they are rather too easy to apply across widely different eras and societies, raising troubling questions about how meaningful such terms are.[42]

While it seems clear that the 'social supernatural' of fairyland in some way mirrors human society, some scholars have taken this idea of mirroring even further by arguing that fairies are in some sense doppelgängers. The French historian Claude Lecouteux advocated the idea that the fairy should be seen as a sort of psychic double,[43] while Éva Pócs sees in Hungarian fairies an analogue for the 'possession' of magical practitioners in trance states.[44] The fairy is, in other words, a projection of the trance-worker's self – what the Sámi called a person's *gand* and the Norse their *gandr*.⁴⁵ The boundary between Hungarian fairies (*szépasszony*) and humans can be transgressed by humans who 'walk with' the *szépasszony* and in some sense become them, but only because the humans who do this already have a 'double soul'.⁴⁶ Similarly, ideas of witches as people with a 'double soul', simultaneously human and non-human, can be found in Russian tradition,⁴⁷ and in the Scottish idea of fairies as 'co-walkers' or 'reflex-men' who mirrored the experiencer.⁴⁸ As we shall see, there was a tradition of confusion between human witches and supernatural magical beings, as if witches could become these beings or vice versa. Against the idea that fairies are projected magical doubles, however, stands the idea that fairies are so often encountered as a *community* rather than simply as individuals. As ever, no explanation seems fully to account for the richness and variety of fairy belief.

Dawn of the godlings

The major challenge when it comes to tracing the ultimate origins of fairy-like beings in most cultures is that records of folk belief rarely begin earlier than the sixteenth century, when church and state concerned themselves as never before with the details of what people believed. The earliest folklore collection, however – in the sense of sustained efforts to record the stories people told about supernatural beings – took place in the seventeenth century, and the majority of folklore collections were made in the nineteenth. A further difficulty is that belief in godlings is almost impervious to archaeology, since minor deities of nature tend not to be associated with buildings. But there are exceptions to this evidential darkness: Greece and Rome, most obviously, where we have detailed written records from the ancient world; and Ireland, where we have detailed literary explorations of otherworld beings from the early medieval period.

It is perilous to infer too much from the few examples we have of belief in godlings reaching back into the ancient world, but what we do see among the Greeks and Romans (and, later, the Irish) is a fairly clear distinction between the beings we might call godlings and the 'higher' gods. Indeed, the lower reaches of divinity for the Romans were a permeable and fluid category, and semi- or quasi-divine beings included heroes (often the hybrid offspring of a divine being and a human mother or father), genii (tutelary spirits of a place or person), lares and penates (domestic spirits, peculiar to each household), and the di manes (quasi-divine spirits of the ancestors) – not to mention the collections of non-human and theriomorphic beings in the retinue of gods such as Bacchus, Pan, and Dionysus: nymphs, satyrs, fauns, centaurs, sylvans, pans, naiads, dryads, and so on.

Commenting on religious developments in 1970s Bali, Clifford Geertz observed a movement from a diffuse conception of divinity in the natural world towards 'a nucleate . . . concept of the divine',[49] where divinity was concentrated in specific polytheistic personalities – a development similar to the evolution of polytheism from nature cults in the ancient world, as advocated by Ken Dowden.[50] On this interpretation, godlings of nature like the nymphs and satyrs are beings left behind from an earlier stage of 'religious development' – although they are in some cases sublimated into divine personalities who can be placed, in theory, alongside the Classical polytheistic gods of Olympus, such as Pan and Faunus. But there was always a lingering sense that these 'old' or 'rustic' gods were more limited, less universal, and more tied to the land than their Olympian counterparts: 'spirits like us have our limits', declares the god Faunus to King Numa in Ovid's *Fasti*, 'we are rustic gods who have dominion in the high mountains'.[51]

This Roman religious interpretation of the 'animistic', aniconic gods of nature as 'old' and the polytheistic, cosmopolitan, temple-centred Olympians as 'new' has proved influential down the centuries. In its modern form, it is the archaeologist Marija Gimbutas's theory that the patriarchal, hierarchical Indo-Europeans brought their polytheistic gods into Central and Western Europe, replacing a pre-existing 'Old European' matriarchal cult of goddesses.[52] On this interpretation, Europe's godlings might be seen as a 'relic population' of pre-Indo-European divinities.

But there is no good evidence that this is the case, and it is just as likely that godlings have always coexisted alongside more exalted divine beings. Indeed, the existence of groups of deities in Vedic tradition might mean that the 'fluctuation between plural and singular' that we find with deities such as Faunus and Silvanus is actually a characteristic feature of the Indo-European religious heritage, rather than a relic of something older.[53] Furthermore, Hutton has questioned the characterization of fairies as 'nature spirits', since their role as guardians of nature emerged from literature and reflected human preoccupations with a world being reshaped by industrialization.[54] It might be more accurate, perhaps, to view fairies as 'land spirits' (as indeed they are called in the Scandinavian languages, *landvættir*) since they often live literally *inside* the land.

In a study of popular religion in Galicia over a long period of time (from prehistory to the early Middle Ages), Joyce Salisbury argued for 'deep religious needs integral to rural culture' that did not essentially change, whether pagan Celtiberians and Romans or Christian Visigoths were in charge, and which perpetuated the veneration of rural godlings. Put simply, godlings exist because people need them to exist – and not necessarily because they have inherited half-understood belief systems from deep prehistory. From Roman antiquarians onwards, the temptation to view rural popular beliefs as somehow antiquated or marginal has proved a strong one. But, as Salisbury argues, there is no justification for characterizing popular religion as 'persisting superstitions' or as 'peripheral, archaic or deviant religiosity'.[55] Nor is there any justification for regarding it as unsophisticated or, still worse, 'primitive'. People living a hand-to-mouth existence from the land feel the need to secure the direct assistance of spirits intimately associated with the land, and thus the placation of godlings was an integral part of rural life in the Classical world.

The nymphs of ancient Greece are one group of godlings whose development we can trace from the Homeric era (perhaps as long ago as the ninth century BCE) to present-day Greek folklore; and indeed many countries in Central and Eastern Europe, well beyond Greece, share similar traditions of all-female societies of social supernatural beings. The ancient Greek nymphs were *kourotrophic*, which meant they were particularly concerned with the well-being of children, both as infants and in puberty, as children approached adulthood. At the same time, the nymphs personified and were closely connected with bodies of water.[56] This entanglement of nature spirits with human destiny and human cycles of birth, infancy, and adolescence is something we encounter again and again in fairy lore. The nymphs are human enough to form part of human genealogies – again, the theme of the 'fairy bride' is a recurring one throughout European folklore – but they are also immortal personifications of rivers, streams, and springs who seemingly flit in and out of humanness, and even in and out of anthropomorphism.[57]

Figure 1.2 Three nymphs from a Greek marble relief, c.320–300 BCE

The Greek nymphs often appeared in triads (see figure 1.2),[58] an association between supernatural women and the number three that seems to be a deep feature of European culture.[59] Furthermore, just as later fairies were associated with underground dwellings and underground otherworlds, so the nymphs were associated with caves;[60] and the nymphs were said to 'seize' or 'possess' people in the phenomenon of 'nympholepsy' (literally 'caught by the nymphs' in Greek),[61] which those more inclined to see relics of shamanism in fairy belief might see as a link with trance states. Nympholepsy was certainly linked with prophecy and divination[62] – an early manifestation, perhaps, of the long-standing connection between fairies and magic.

It is tempting to view the nymphs and other godlings like them as what animistic spirits become when a polytheistic culture is not quite sure what to make of them. Polytheists are not, generally speaking, in the business of abolishing and supplanting local gods, and polytheistic outlooks tend to absorb and accommodate rather than exclude deities;

but what to do, then, with deities that are so different from exalted temple-deities such as Zeus or Athena? These are deities who do not constitute distinct divine personalities but rather groups of beings, glimmering between the human and the non-human, who walk the hills and meadows, and are inseparable from the natural features they enchant, imbue, represent, and personify. Did beings like the nymphs emerge from a sort of syncretism of animism with polytheism, where animistic spirits are given an appearance and identity that makes some sort of sense within a polytheistic outlook? It is difficult to do anything more than speculate.

But godlings of nature such as Pan and the nymphs, whose origins we might suspect lie in rural animism, were not the only kind of godling in the ancient world. Rather different, and more appealing to the learned and the philosophically minded, was the *daimōn* (Latin *daemon*), which was not tied to specific places or features of nature as the nymphs were. The Greek words *daimōn* and *theos* may have had similar meanings at one time; in Homer's *Iliad* the two terms seem to be interchangeable, but signs of differentiation emerge in Hesiod's *Works and Days*. The differentiation of higher and lesser deities seems to have been a more general trend in the second and first millennia BCE across the interlocking cultures of the ancient Near East and Mediterranean. We see it, for example, in the exorcistic texts of Mesopotamia (where it came to be recognized that malign spirits could be cast out by the invocation of more powerful deities). Similarly, the Persian young Avesta begin to distinguish a hierarchy of evil beings, known as *daevas*, from a corresponding hierarchy of benign beings called *ahuras* in the first half of the first millennium BCE.[63] As the *ahuras* were subordinate to the benign deity Ahura Mazda, so the *daevas* served his destructive adversary Ahriman.

The Greeks had begun to distinguish higher and lower divinities by the separate terms *theos* and *daimōn* by the fourth century BCE, but in contrast to the Mesopotamians and Persians they did not draw a moral distinction between the two. Greek daemons could do good or bad. Plato mentioned *daimōnia* in his dialogue *Timaeus*, but it was Philip of Opus in the *Epinomis* (a work long misattributed to Plato himself) who claimed the daemons inhabited the elements of earth, air, fire, and water.[64] The *daimōn* as a subordinate divine being came into its own in the Hellenistic period, elaborated from hints found in the philosophy of Plato and the speculations of Neoplatonists. A kind of demonological *koine* (cultural vernacular) regarding daemons passed from the Greek to the Roman world, as the works of Plutarch and Apuleius testify. Here, 'daemons are spiritual beings who think so intensely that they produce vibrations in the air that enable other spiritual beings . . . as well as highly sensitive men and women, to "receive" their thoughts'. In this way, daemons can become the source of phenomena such as clairvoyance, prophecy, artistic inspiration, and genius.[65]

In the third century, Plotinus thought a personal daemon simultaneously was within a person like an intellectual principle and could manifest as a transcendent being.[66] And for the fourth-century CE Roman philosopher Calcidius, the existence of daemons was a logical necessity, given the existence of the immortal celestial bodies and the mortal, perishable world:

> it is necessary that there is another, middle genus, that participates in the celestial nature as well as in the earthly one, which is both immortal and bound by passion. Such is the nature of daemons, I think, sharing with the divine because of its immortality, and sharing with the perishing since it is passible and is not immune to passions, whose goodness takes care of the good.[67]

There is one crucial respect, however, in which Greek and Roman daemons differed from later fairies, and the daemons should not be conflated with the nature godlings of the ancient world. Daemons were invisible, aerial beings whose bodies, according to Calcidius, contain no earth.[68] In contrast to fairies, therefore, daemons are not chthonic beings who come out of the earth, but rather inhabitants of the space between the earth and the sphere of the Moon. As we shall see, the daemons of Hellenistic pagan belief assumed great significance in early Christianity, where they acquired an almost exclusively negative identity and were elided with the 'unclean spirits' of first-century Judaism.

Diane Purkiss sees neither godlings or nature nor Hellenistic daemons at the root of fairy belief, emphasizing instead the possible influence of 'nursery bogies' such as Mormo and Lamia.[69] Lamia is a figure of Graeco-Roman mythology who does not quite correspond to anything in modern folk belief – a kind of non-human female vampire, 'associated with death, with the devouring of her victims, and with sexuality or obscenity'.[70] Like the nymphs, however, Lamia was not a singular being but also the embodiment of a class of lamias. Wilby has attempted to link lamias and other cannibalistic spirits of antiquity with the lingering survival of shamanism;[71] in prehistoric societies, the entering of trance states may have been associated with deliberately transgressive practices such as the eating of human flesh. Whatever the truth, Purkiss's case is that figures of terror in the ancient world – especially figures of terror to children – underwent a gradual process of domestication via euphemism. It is a process best summed up, perhaps, by the novelist Terry Pratchett in his 1992 novel *Lords and Ladies*: 'You said: The Shining Ones. You said: The Fair Folk. And you spat, and touched iron. But generations later, you forgot about the spitting and the iron, and you forgot why you used those names for them, and you remembered only that they were beautiful.'[72]

In other words, people use euphemistic and ingratiating terms for frightening otherworld beings as a way of placating them, but over time this use of euphemisms like 'the good neighbours' or 'the fair folk' leads to a process of collective forgetting whereby the euphemism itself (now taken literally) seems to affect the way people imagine and experience otherworlders. Paradoxically, the fairies come to be imagined as benevolent and beautiful beings for the very reason that people were *so* afraid of them they dared only say positive things about them.

Indeed, there is some archaeological evidence for such seemingly perverse behaviour; in 1751, a Roman altar was discovered at Benwell on Hadrian's Wall, dedicated to 'the three lamias' – a unique instance of worship of lamias in the Classical world, and presumably motivated by fear rather than love.[73] However, the idea that *all* fairy belief derives in some way from various kinds of half-forgotten 'scarelore' seems unlikely, for fairies are neither completely evil nor completely benevolent; their moral ambiguity and unpredictable relations with human beings suggest that they are something far more complex, and far stranger, than either bogeys invented to scare or fantasies woven to reassure.

What is certain is that lamias survived from the ancient into the medieval world, becoming female demons who kidnapped and devoured newborns during the night,[74] an identity that was conferred on them by the authority of Isidore of Seville and Augustine.[75] This should not surprise us – given that Christianity usually demonized the godlings of the Classical world, it made sense for Christian authors to adopt wholesale those beings whom the ancients *already* demonized.[76] The identification of Lamia with the biblical and Talmudic demoness Lilith is a further factor, which will be considered in chapter 2 below.

Deified ancestors and dancing goddesses

Any consideration of the deep origins of fairy belief must consider not only the possibility that fairies originate from animism or therianthropic shamanism, but also the long-standing theory that fairies are in some way linked to prehistoric ancestor worship. The idea that the fairies are in some sense the ancient dead is associated with Katharine Briggs. Briggs's observation that fairies were called 'ghosts' in many English tales can perhaps be set aside, given that in early modern English 'ghost' was a synonym for 'spirit' (and fairies are often called simply 'spirits'). However, the fact that the dead were often seen in the company of the fairies is indeed suggestive of some connection,[77] and by 1967 Briggs had concluded that 'the half-deified spirits of the dead' formed an important part of the origins of fairies.[78]

The appearance of the dead among the fairies need not mean that the fairies *are* the dead, however; in ancient Greece, children who died prematurely (and especially those who drowned) were said to have been taken and 'made sacred' by the nymphs,[79] and the notion that the souls of the unbaptized and suicides were taken by fairy-like beings (and subsequently seen among them) was widespread throughout Christian Europe. In Ukraine, young women who committed suicide, usually by drowning after becoming pregnant outside of wedlock, were said to become Rusalkas.[80] But the once-human Rusalkas remained distinct from the decidedly non-human bohyni, so it is impossible to make any simplistic equivalence between the unholy dead and the fairies. Eastern European fairies are connected with the dead, but not in any uncomplicated way; 'in periods dedicated to the dead', they enforce taboos linked to humans transgressing areas associated with the dead.[81] But this does not necessarily mean that the fairies are themselves the dead. It was also possible, of course, for human beings to be lured into or to willingly join the fairy realm; human children stolen by the fairies joined their number, thus creating a peculiar ambiguity about the humanness or non-humanness of the fairies.

One variation of the argument that fairies originated as ancestors (or rather, the dead of a community) is advanced by Elizabeth Wayland Barber, although she considers the Eastern and Southern European vilas and 'willies' that are the focus of her argument somewhat different from the fairies.[82] In Barber's view, these supernatural women were

> young women born into the clan who had died before having any children . . . had not used their store of fertility. So, people reasoned, if we're especially nice to them, they might bestow that unused fertility on us. Because unmarried girls in the living community spent much of their time singing and dancing together, people inferred by analogy that the spirits of dead girls might band together and spend their time singing, dancing, swimming, laughing, and so on. These Dancing Goddesses inhabited the wilds, controlling the rain and other waters, creating the fertility and healing powers people needed.[83]

For Barber, the origins of Eastern and Southern European belief in communities of dancing supernatural women can be traced to the Neolithic, when the priorities of the first farmers were establishing land boundaries and achieving social cohesion within agricultural communities. The digging of ditches and building of fences only enhanced Neolithic people's awareness of a dangerous 'other' (both natural and supernatural) that lay beyond the physical boundaries that now fixed domestic and civic space. Dancing, argues Barber, arose as a cultural response to the need for social cohesion in new farming communities as it bonded the community together in a shared activity that became associated with fertility and, in particular, with young women. It was these young women who, when they died young (and thereby remained forever young), became a focus for supernatural hopes of fertility in the community, although the spirits of such women were also banished to the otherworld that lay beyond the boundaries of the community.[84]

All of this is very speculative, and it is all too easy to use the archaeological evidence of prehistory to build castles in the air that may or may not have any relevance to prehistoric reality. The connection between fairies and dancing, however, is seemingly both ancient and widespread across Europe. We might think of the Bacchic *thiasos*, the retinue of godlings that accompanies the god Dionysus in his revels, and dances across the great dish of the Mildenhall Treasure in the British Museum,[85] or the portrayal of (and invocation of) the Roman lares (household spirits) in dance.[86] This is the 'choral action' typical of the social supernatural, which often occurs in the form of dance.[87]

But there are many different ways to interpret the association of social supernatural beings with dance, and with circular dances in particular. One highly reductive approach would be to see it as an explanation for 'fairy rings' on the grass (although traditions of dancing godlings long pre-date any mention of 'fairy rings', so such reductivism is probably misguided). Another would be to point to the simultaneous playfulness and solemnity that is possible in dance, and the way in which participation in a dance places a person at one remove from reality (rather like acting). The circle dance further removes its participants from time: it is without a clear end or beginning, and thus dancing in a circle could serve as a kind of instantiated symbol for otherworldliness and timelessness, as well as a ritual action to generate magical power (another typical characteristic of the fairies). But this, too, is speculation rather than fact.

It is perhaps difficult for us, who view the dead primarily as human lives and relationships lost to us, to comprehend the extent to which prehistoric people believed the ancestors became a different sort of being. Recent archaeological discoveries at Cladh Hallan on the Hebridean island of South Uist have revealed that Bronze Age islanders not only carefully mummified their dead and continued to live alongside their mortal remains, but also created composite mummies that mingled the body parts of ancestors. The Cladh Hallan mummies were 'neither alive nor dead, both at once', and may have been treated as divine beings;[88] certainly, their mortal remains seem to have transcended personal identities they had in life. As sites of public worship in the landscape declined in Bronze Age Britain (the henges and stone circles of the Neolithic), it seems to have relocated to domestic spaces, where it may well have been focussed on deified ancestors.[89] But such a transmutation of human beings to the status of gods may also have been possible in life; in 2020, an archaeogenetic study of individuals buried in Neolithic passage graves in Ireland revealed they practised first-degree incestuous unions, a transgression of matrimonial norms that in some ancient societies signified a quasi-divine status[90] – although whether a distant memory of these 'god-people' fed into stories of the mound-dwelling *síde* must remain speculation.

The sacrality of domestic spaces, perhaps established by the burial of ancestors (or stillborn children) within that space, may be reflected in the tradition of household spirits. In the Germanic world at least, these began as 'room-gods' or kobolds (from Old High German *kofewalt*, 'room spirit', *cofgodas* in Old English), which eventually became the French *gobelin* and re-entered English as 'goblin'.[91] In the Iberian world, they were the *dueños de casa*, whose name (like their stature) became shortened over time to *duendes* (dwarfs).[92] Similarly, the possibility that the fairies are, in some sense, a memory of the deified, transformed, and transmuted prehistoric dead is hinted at by the medieval association between fairies and barrows and tumuli in the British landscape, as well as the ongoing significance accorded to barrows as places of supernatural encounter and sites of burial.[93] But it is important not to push these connections between folklore and prehistory too far, and to remain mindful of the vast expanses of time involved, which render implausible most proposals of direct or unproblematic connections.

Fairies and witches

While the witch is considered today to be a human supernatural figure, in the Middle Ages the boundary between the human witch and the non-human 'hag' was far from clear-cut.[94] Perhaps the most famous instance of such ambiguity is the 'Weird Sisters' of Shakespeare's *Macbeth*, referred to in a stage direction as 'witches' but nowhere called witches in the play itself, since they are in fact the Norns – the three sisters of destiny in Norse mythology. An early viewer of the play, the magician Simon Forman (who did not, of course, read the stage direction), immediately recognized the Weird Sisters as fairies.[95]

The Old English word *hæg* (the ancestor of 'hag') referred not to human witches but to night-riding supernatural warrior women.[96] These supernatural women can be found in British sources too, like the mysterious trident-wielding *theomacha* encountered in a forest by the seventh-century Breton St Samson of Dol.[97] However, a process of cultural elision between non-human supernatural beings and humans (usually women) suspected of evil supernatural intent seems to have occurred, perhaps as early as the Roman period in Britain. At Kimmeridge in Dorset, a group of women received 'deviant' burials in the third century (their skulls were placed between their feet, and their jaws removed) and each was buried with a spindle whorl. One possible interpretation of the spindle whorls is that they were a kind of mockery of women who were accused of trying to influence human fortunes by divination or magic, like the Parcae whom the Romans believed span the fates of human beings.[98]

It is possible, then, that the identification of human beings with supernatural beings such as the Parcae (and, later, hags) began as a kind of dark joke, but gradually gained momentum. The line between witches and fairies was porous in Britain before the early modern period, and both fairies and witches were put forward as rival explanations for misfortune.[99] In some regions, such as Gaelic Ireland and the Baltic, belief in witchcraft remained restricted to certain times of danger during the year, or to particular activities such as the stealing of milk or butter, while fear of non-human social supernatural beings was much more widespread.[100] Linguistic and conceptual slippage between non-human supernatural beings and humans accused of malefice was a feature of several cultures, and it is difficult to ascribe this entirely to confusion about the nature of supernatural beings. For example, by the twelfth century the Latin word *fadus* (derived from *fata*, the root of the word 'fairy') had the meaning of a male witch or warlock,[101] and the word *fatata* (bewitched, or enchanted) could refer to someone under the influence of a fairy or a human witch.[102] Julian Goodare has shown that, in early sixteenth-century Scotland, the women who venerated the 'seely wights' (fairy-like beings) in the hope of deriving power from them came to be called the 'seely wights' themselves.[103]

The relationship between fairies and witches confronts us with a 'chicken and egg' question: did belief in harm by supernatural beings come first, and later come to be transferred to human agents? Or were the original witches human beings, fear of whom transmuted them into imagined wholly supernatural beings?[104] On balance, the former seems more likely than the latter; the oldest evidence usually points to witches originating as non-human beings. In Lithuania, for example, where Christianization came especially late, the all-female group of nature godlings known as the laumės came to assume monstrous and therianthropic characteristics (such as chicken legs) only as a result of Christian demonization. Furthermore, the practice of hanging dead magpies in stables to deter the laumės came to be aimed against human witches, who were thought to transform themselves into magpies to reach the witches' sabbath – an elision of older ideas and imported demonologies of human witchcraft.[105] Similarly, it was in Russia – largely untouched until the seventeenth century by learned demonologies – that the non-human 'folk tale' witch or *baba-iaga* survived alongside the human *ved'ma*.[106] Monstrous and cannibalistic (especially of children), the *baba-iaga* lived in the forest and seems to be linked, ultimately, with the Lamia of the ancient world. Similar ideas of night-flying, blood-sucking 'witches' who were probably not thought of as human at all could be found from Poland to the Canary Islands.[107] By the sixteenth century, the distinction between witches (as human authors of malefice) and fairies as non-human supernatural beings (who might be responsible for certain kinds of malefice) seems to have been more clear-cut, at least in Britain; but even here some ambiguities remained.[108]

'Everything is fairies'?

As I noted in the Introduction, it is possible to view fairies as a sort of 'dustbin' of supernatural belief, a way for folklore to account for all sorts of odd things that do not obviously lend themselves to other straightforward explanations – from fairy rings in the grass to elfshot (prehistoric flint arrowheads). But it is also possible to turn this perspective on its head, and to see fairies as the most versatile of all supernatural beings because they are also the most *fundamental*. On this view, fairy belief came first, emerging from the ancestral animism of most human cultures – indeed, perhaps emerging alongside human consciousness itself – and later diversified into belief in ghosts, witches, possession, and so on. The beings we call fairies were those left behind, who did not evolve into other manifestations of the supernatural. But there is a danger to this 'everything is fairies' approach; if fairies are seen as fundamental to all folklore, it becomes nearly impossible to confer on them any kind of distinctive identity.

Perhaps a better approach than trying to see fairies at the root of every folk belief – which will lead ultimately to reductivism – is to recognize fairies as a diffuse mythology.[109] The transformations undergone over time by fairies – or by those strands of folk belief that eventually became the fairies we recognize – were so fundamental and so complex that it is fruitless to search for an 'original'. Which strand should we follow back into the past, when there are so many? Nevertheless, as we shall see throughout this book, the idea that fairies represent 'a basic experience of the spiritual world from before that world became subject to the classifications of demonologists'[110] does seem to be supported by the historical evidence. Refinements to people's understanding of the spiritual world often came in response to a pre-existing background of fairy lore that was no longer considered adequate, or doctrinally sound. But the fairies always survived, and represented a kind of unmoored supernatural, with its own internal life – an intellectually untethered strangeness that defied neat classification. This is what makes the fairies such a fascinating historical subject, yet also an endlessly frustrating one.

But even if we did know everything we would like to about the animism of prehistoric Europe or the godlings of the ancient world, that knowledge would only give us a partial understanding of the origins of fairies. For Europe's fairies are not just land spirits of the pre-Christian world, they are also constructions of a Christian (or sub-Christian) mythology with origins reaching back to the roots of monotheism itself in the ancient Near East. It is to the Near East, therefore, that we now turn – in order to explore the origins of those ambiguous spirit-beings between heaven and hell who would one day inspire or become the fairies.

TWO

Between heaven and hell: monotheism and ambiguous spirits

Some time in ninth-century Ireland, the abbot of Louth, Caenchomrac (d. 898), was chanting the Psalms on an island in Lough Ree, when he saw the form of a tall man emerge from the waters of the lough. The man informed Caenchomrac that he belonged to an otherworld community that lived at the bottom of the lough, and that the community had a monastery. However, the young monks had rebelled and been expelled from the monastery in the form of swine (the aos sí frequently transform into animals in Irish tales), and were now being hunted by local people in the hills; one pig-monk had already been given to Caenchomrac's human monks and was now roasting over a fire, and the tall man from the lough was the pig-monk's father and was clutching his son's psalter to prove it. Caenchomrac followed the man to the bottom of the lake and visited the underwater monastery of the aos sí, and the 'Psalter of the Pig' which had belonged to the unfortunate monk of the aos sí was preserved for centuries thereafter as a wonder at the monastery of Clonmacnoise.[1]

While this story was recorded much later in the Middle Ages – and probably originated as a way of explaining the peculiar name of the 'Psalter of the Pig' preserved at Clonmacnoise – it nevertheless shows that medieval Irish people could contemplate the idea of the aos sí, Ireland's fairies, having their own monasteries. Similarly, in Iceland the elves were said to have their own churches, which far outnumbered human places of worship.[2] The idea that fairies are Christians and worship God is not by any means a universal tradition; they are more often portrayed as alienated from God in some way. But the story of Caenchomrac's visit to an underwater fairy monastery illustrates the ambiguity of the fairies' relationship with Christian monotheism, in which they have never enjoyed an official status.

Nevertheless, each of the monotheistic Abrahamic religions (Judaism, Christianity, and Islam) has developed traditions in dealing with non-divine spirit-beings. With the exception of a few sects such as the ancient Sadducees and modern Karaites, Abrahamic monotheists do not believe that the absolute sovereignty of God requires the believer to deny the existence of 'transmundane' spirit-beings; indeed, the coexistence of spirit-beings alongside a supreme, transcendent creator God is a characteristic feature of these religions, even if they vary in their classification of these beings and their account of their origins.

The subject of this chapter is the relationship between intermediate, morally ambiguous spirits and monotheism, and the development of belief in such beings in a monotheistic context. For a crucial factor in fairies remaining part of the popular cosmologies of Christian Europeans was the fact that it was possible for Christianity to account for them, wholly or partially. The monotheistic heritage of 'transmundane' beings is, along with the prehistoric inheritance of godlings and land spirits, the second pillar that supports fairy belief. But in order to find out how, we need to understand how the ancient Jewish heritage of spirit-belief in monotheism affected early Christianity. We shall then consider how the Church Fathers (the theologians of the first few centuries of the Christian church) interpreted spirits that were neither the angels of heaven nor the demons of hell, before considering the specific case of early Christian Ireland as a culture where unusual and distinctive ideas about intermediate beings developed in the centuries following Christianization.

The Abrahamic monotheisms emerged in the ancient Near East, where a belief in divine attendants, messengers, and demons was widespread, and the monotheistic faiths carry this deep cultural legacy. References to such beings became embedded in the scriptures of the monotheistic faiths, making it difficult to deny their existence – although, as we shall see in chapter 6 below, this is exactly what some Christians managed to do from the late seventeenth century onwards.

However, for many ancient believers the existence of a divine court and divine messengers enhanced rather than detracted from the transcendence of an omnipotent God (who was served not just by human beings, but also by much more exalted entities), and allowed him to act in the world through his agents and messengers without compromising his transcendence. Furthermore, the existence of malign spirit-beings (demons) provided a theodicy: an account of why evil occurs in the world that exculpates the supreme deity.

The idea of intermediate spirit-beings who dwell on earth and may be either helpful or harmful to humans became especially significant in Islam (as the jinn) but always occupied a more ambiguous and unestablished position within Judaism and Christianity – belonging to the realm of pseudepigraphic and apocryphal writings, and later the speculations of the Church Fathers, rather than to official doctrine. However, intermediate spirits were part of the cosmology of Hellenistic Jews and early Christians; and, as we shall see, such speculations provided an important precedent for later fairy belief in Christianized cultures.

The ancient Jewish heritage: ambiguous spirits in the Old Testament

Scholars of the Hebrew Bible have long recognized that the development of monotheism (or perhaps more accurately, *monolatry* – the worship of one God) in ancient Israel was a gradual process.[3] The proliferation of names for Israel's God, and most famously the use of a plural name for him – *Elohim* – in the Book of Genesis, has long alerted scholars to the possibility that much older traditions were incorporated into the biblical portrayal of the deity who eventually came to be worshipped by the Israelites as the one God, YHWH or Yahweh, whose cult may have subsumed within it older local traditions of supreme deities. By the same token, the biblical narrative of the history of Israel and Judah repeatedly references ongoing forms of unauthorized worship at local shrines (most notably, the cult of the goddess Asherah[4]), suggesting that Israelite polytheism died hard in the pre-Exilic period (the era before the deportation of the population of Jerusalem to Babylon in the sixth century BCE).

So, while we might be inclined to think of monotheism as a clearly defined faith claim – that there exists only one supreme, transcendent, and omnipotent God – the reality of biblical monotheism was rather different from the rationalist monotheism of the modern world. While the Hebrew Bible is unambiguously insistent that only one deity should be worshipped, there is no clarity on the question of whether other gods actually exist or not. There are frequent assertions that other gods are nothing more than idols, but this seems to be a rhetorical attack on other gods as powerless rather than a coherent ontological claim about their non-existence, since in other places the gods are referred to as real beings.

Biblical monotheism was, then, as much rhetoric as it was theology. It was about the subordination of other divine beings to God, much like the submission of conquered princes who become the satraps and councillors of their new overlord. Monotheism was, in other words, a reclassification of divine beings and a readjustment of the dynamics of power between them; paradoxically (in a monotheistic cosmology), divine multiplicity elevated YHWH as 'a great king above all gods' (Psalm 95:3).[5] Biblical scholars continue to debate how the ancient Israelites came to believe in a dualistic universe of spirit-beings who serve YHWH (the angels) and spirit-beings who oppose him (the demons). This angels/demons dualism had significant consequences for subsequent Christian ideas about the spiritual world, pushing belief in ambiguous spirit-beings such as fairies to the margins of orthodoxy, so it is important to understand how this binary developed.

In the first place, it is important to recognize that the angels/demons binary in contemporary Christian belief does not correspond to ancient Jewish ideas – most notably the Christian idea that angels are benign and heaven-dwelling and demons are evil and hell-dwelling. In the Hebrew Bible, angels are far from benign, such as the 'destroyer' or 'angel of death' of Exodus 12:23 who kills the firstborn children of Egypt. Indeed, the word 'angel' is merely a designation of the task given by God to a spirit-being (that of God's messenger), rather than an indication of that being's origin or moral character. It is far from clear from the biblical narrative that all angels dwell in heaven with God; and the ancient Israelites did not have a Dante-esque conception of demons as fallen angels ejected from heaven and cast down into a subterranean hell.

Annette Yoshiko Reed has argued that Jewish interest in 'intermediate spirits' between human beings and God, including angels and demons, emerged in the third century BCE from a combination of interest in Hellenistic culture and 'Mesopotamian scholasticism', which was often intensely concerned with the categorization of demons and the best ways to exorcise them.[6] Pseudepigraphic Jewish writings (non-canonical texts written in the style of scriptures) of this era did not present a straightforward dualistic theodicy in which a benevolent God and his angels are confronted with an evil devil and his demons. Rather, the pseudepigrapha ascribe no single cause for earthly evils and present a much messier picture than later Christian outlooks on good and evil, where angels were often responsible for evil and demons sometimes played a more benign role.[7]

The Hebrew Bible shows little interest in angels, and even less in demons – there is little discussion of what angels are, perhaps in conscious reaction against the prominence of angels and demons in the religious traditions of neighbouring Near Eastern peoples, and a preoccupation with genealogy seems to have taken the place of angelological and demonological speculations in ancient Judaism.[8] Nevertheless, the heavenly realm of the Hebrew Bible seems to be teeming with different kinds of life, and God is said at various times to preside over a council of the gods (Psalm 82:1) and to have sons (Genesis 6, Job), which may reflect the lingering survival of earlier forms of monotheism where the gods of other nations were incorporated into Jewish cosmology as councillors or sons of YHWH. On another interpretation, the *mal'akim* of the Hebrew Bible are shadowy manifestations of YHWH himself in a mode of multiplicity; certainly, the nature or ontology of such beings is of no interest to the biblical authors, who adopt a 'counter-classificatory' approach that depicts an anonymous host who serve God.[9]

Similarly, on the rare occasions when we encounter references to an 'evil spirit' (Judges 9:23–4, 1 Samuel 16:19), there is no reason to think this refers to a distinct category of spirit-beings (still less 'fallen angels', a much later idea) who are defined by an evil character.[10] Rather, it seems that YHWH might send out angels to cause harm as well as good, like the 'destroyer' of Exodus 12:23 or the 'evil angels' of Psalm 78:49. The emergence of a more coherent conception of a distinct class of spirit-beings who serve God in heaven (for want of a better word, the angels) and a distinct class of spirit-beings who cause human misfortunes on earth (for want of a better word, the demons) came later. Jewish culture came under greater external influence from Hellenistic, Mesopotamian, and Persian culture, where parallel developments in the classification of higher and lower and good and evil spirit-beings were also under way.[11]

Our interest, however, is not in the formation of the ideas of angels and demons inherited by Christianity, but in the idea of intermediate spirit-beings who stood between purely good angels in divine service and purely evil demons in opposition to God: the sort of beings who could become fairies, or at least provide a precedent for them. There is, in fact, one particularly mysterious passage of Genesis (6:1–4) that inspired Jewish speculation about beings intermediate in nature between the divine and human:

> And it came to pass, when men began to multiply on the face of the earth, and daughters were born unto them, that the sons of God saw the daughters of men that they were fair; and they took them wives of all which they chose. And the Lord said, My spirit shall not always strive with man, for that he also is flesh: yet his days shall be an hundred and twenty years. There were giants in the earth in those days; and also after that, when the sons of God came in unto the daughters of men, and they bare children to them, the same became mighty men which were of old, men of renown.

The original meaning of Genesis 6 is obscure; it could be interpreted as reflecting earlier Hebrew conceptions of God as a collective and physical being that somehow survived into Yahwistic narratives. But whatever the truth, the story seemed to suggest that in the antediluvian world, angels (if this was who the 'sons of God' were) took physical form and had sexual relationships with human women, who gave birth to hybrid human/non-human beings ('giants') who exceeded normal human strength and became heroes, 'the mighty men . . . of old'.

In the third century BCE, one group of Jewish scribes produced a very detailed narrative inspired by Genesis 6, *The Book of the Watchers*, in which it is one particular group of angels (the 'Watchers') who decide to come down to earth in order to father children with human women. Inspired by Genesis 6:5 ('And God saw that the wickedness of man was great in the earth, and that every imagination of the thoughts of his heart was only evil continually'), the authors of *The Book of the Watchers* concluded that the Watchers must also have had an intellectual influence on humans. The Watchers are thus exiled to earth by their own choice (and not, it should be noted, thrust down to hell by divine power), and teach human beings arts of divination and magic, as well as other arts such as the manufacture of weaponry and cosmetics.

It is humans' possession of these arts that angers God and causes him to flood the world to rid it of the Watchers, the giants, and humans who have learnt evil arts from the Watchers. However, the giants are not entirely killed by the Flood and become discarnate demonic forces instead.[12] The idea that the demons issue from the bodies of the giants after their deaths is found also in the pseudepigraphical 1 Enoch.[13] *The Book of the Watchers* is significant to the subsequent development of speculation about ambiguous spiritual beings, including fairies, because it diverges from a purely punitive portrayal of the fall of the angels – the Watchers make their own decision to leave heaven, swearing an oath to do so on Mount Hermon, and they are exiled to earth rather than banished to some infernal realm.[14] By fathering hybrid children, the Watchers mingle flesh and spirit, reminding us of the corporeal yet invisible nature of the fairies in many traditions. And the arts the Watchers teach human beings (including metalworking, dyeing, and the making of weapons, jewellery, and cosmetics) are undeniably useful. The fallen Watchers are negative figures in *The Book of the Watchers*, but they are not so much portrayed as malign as *corrupting*; although well-intentioned (they are motivated by a natural attraction to the beauty of human women, rather than by hatred of humanity), the Watchers end up leading humans astray by teaching them arts unsuitable for humans to know.

The Book of the Watchers and the pseudepigraphical tradition it represented seem to have seeded the idea (denied by *The Book of the Watchers* itself) that some representatives of a non-Adamic race could have survived the Flood. Again and again, the fairies are represented in folklore as what the seventeenth-century author John Webster called 'non-Adamick Creatures'[15] – creations of God who did not take their descent (as all humans did) from Adam and Eve.

One creative piece of speculative theology to explain how hybrid non-human spirit-beings could exist, which originated in Judaism, was the legend of Lilith. Lilith is mentioned once in the Bible (Isaiah 34:14), as a denizen of the wilderness left behind by the prophesied desolation of Israel's enemies, although her name is translated as 'the screech owl' in the Authorized Version. Jerome's choice of *lamia* in the Latin Vulgate is perhaps more appropriate, since in Jewish demonology Lilith became a Lamia-like figure. The Lilith legend seems to have originated from the attempts of Talmudic scholars to harmonize the two separate accounts of the creation of man and woman in the Book of Genesis, by speculating that Adam had received a bride before Eve, who was Lilith.

In its first fully developed form, in the medieval *Alphabet of Ben Sira*, Adam and Lilith argue over sexual positions and Lilith asserts her equality with Adam because they were both made from earth, before speaking

Figure 2.1 The Queen of the Night relief (Burney Relief), *c*.1800–1750 BC

the name of God and flying off into the air. Adam complains to God, who sends three angels to persuade Lilith to return. The angels catch up with Lilith in the waters of the Red Sea and try to drown her; she declares she will weaken newborn children unless they wear a talisman bearing the images of one of the angels, and she accepts God's sentence that a hundred of her children will die every day. These are the demons, her children by Adam, although she will continue to visit men by night in order to have more children by them (figure 2.1).[16] Demons, in Jewish tradition, are not predominantly fallen angels (as they are in Christianity), but the invisible children of Lilith and human males, and for this reason rituals developed for driving away the invisible hybrid human–demon offspring of Jewish men from their bodies after death.[17]

The Lilith legend passed rapidly into Christian tradition; Gershom Scholem even thought the Byzantine version of the story might have preceded the Jewish one. Here Adam's demonic consort is usually known by another name, and the three angels are replaced by three saints, but the story is essentially the same. Lilith's ultimate origins, however, lie in Babylonian demonology.[18] Yet in Jewish and Christian tradition, Lilith is a human being who *becomes* demonic owing to her disobedience towards Adam and God; in this respect, she anticipates traditions of monstrosity that will be explored in the next chapter. But her original human identity renders her demon children ambiguous beings who are neither fully flesh nor fully spirit, opening up the possibility of human-like races descended from Adam and Lilith rather than Adam and Eve. The legend of Lilith shares with *The Book of the Watchers* the idea (common within Judaism) that demons are not fallen angels but hybrid (and therefore unclean) beings born of the union of human and non-human beings.[19] The uncleanness of demons derives not so much from their evil natures, therefore, but from their hybrid nature – a characteristic that would later be shared by fairies in many traditions.

The history of the Old Testament and its related pseudepigrapha does not end with their composition, and choices of translation played a key role in the way the Bible's picture of supernatural beings was received in late antiquity and the Middle Ages. For example, Jerome's rendering of Isaiah 26:13–14 in the Vulgate implied that the giants of Genesis 6 might return: 'O Lord our God, lords besides you have possessed us ... Let not the dead live, let not the giants rise again (*gigantes non resurgant*); on account of which you have visited and struck them, and obliterated all memory of them.'[20] This ambiguous passage simultaneously asserts that the giants have gone, and that they might yet return. Similarly, it was Jerome who chose to translate the Hebrew word *se'īrīm* (goat demons) differently in different places; sometimes the *se'īrīm* are *daemonia* (demons) but in Isaiah 13:21 and 34:14 they are *pilosi* (a variant term for satyrs) – a precedent which allowed *se'īrīm* to be translated as 'satyrs' in the Authorized Version.[21] What the original *se'īrīm* were supposed to be remains unclear; Reed alludes to 'Mesopotamian traditions about malicious spirits shaped like animals',[22] and the *se'īrīm* were probably theriomorphic nature spirits of some kind. But Jerome's translation choice had the unintended consequence of validating the reality of some of the godlings of the ancient world for medieval Christians, and thus played a key role in the eventual development of fairy lore.

Demons and unclean spirits: spirit-beings in the New Testament

The New Testament uses two main terms, seemingly interchangeably, for unwanted spirit-beings, who are usually the object of exorcisms by Jesus or his disciples: *daimōn* (demon) and *pneuma akatharton* (unclean spirit). However, the underlying cosmology and demonology behind these designations are not altogether clear. The focus of the Gospels and Acts is, rather, on the effect these beings have on individuals and the liberation that exorcism can bring. However, the unclean spirits / demons seem to be primarily *tormentors* of humanity rather than tempters, a role that is confined to Satan.[23] The relationship between the unclean spirits and Satan himself is thus less than clear in the text of the New Testament itself, even if later Christian interpretations posited a straightforward hierarchical relationship between Satan as ruler of demons and the lesser unclean spirits as his minions.

In response to this ambiguity, some scholars have argued that the fluid religious environment of the late Roman Mediterranean renders it historically inappropriate to adopt fixed assumptions about the unambiguously evil character of possessing spirits in the early church.[24] But whether or not the unclean spirits of the Gospels and Acts were demons, early Christianity continued a tendency already established in Hellenistic Judaism of using the Greek philosophical term *daimōn* with exclusively negative connotations to identify an evil spirit opposed to God's benevolence. Early Christianity, which was notable for its simultaneous denunciations of and creative new use of terms from Greek philosophy, seemingly took a Greek metaphysical term that was neutral in and of itself – *daimōn* – and made it refer to a class of exclusively evil beings.

However, it seems that even the idea of evil demons was itself a Christian borrowing from Graeco-Roman religion, rather than a religious innovation. According to the Neoplatonist philosopher Calcidius, *daimōnia* of the lowest order – those located closest to earth, and infected by human emotions – are capable of doing harm to humans, and in fact function as 'avengers of crimes and impiety according to the sanction of divine justice', just as they did later in Christianity.[25] The pagan Calcidius' *daimōnia* are 'deserter angels', and it seems that this conception of malign avenger demons was simply taken over by Christians, lock, stock, and barrel, from the Neoplatonists. The Christian borrowing of *daimōnia* from Greek thought was not unprecedented; the Jews had a long history of borrowing transmundane beings from the cosmologies of neighbouring peoples, and Philo admitted that his view of angels was informed by Greek thought on *daimōnia*.[26] What the Christians did that was new was to adopt a conception of malign demons as their *sole* view of demons, and thus the intense moral dualism of Christian demonology and angelology was born. Demons are entirely evil, and angels are entirely good – with only humans as morally ambivalent beings of both flesh and spirit. It was this entrenched demonological dualism in Christianity that created a challenging environment for beliefs in morally ambivalent spirits who were neither angels nor demons – in other words, fairies.

The demons / unclean spirits are not, however, the only spirit-beings spoken of in negative terms in the New Testament. In his Letter to the Romans (8:38), Paul refers to 'angels', 'principalities' (*archai*), and 'powers' (*dynameis*), and in Galatians (4:3) to 'bondage under the elements of the world' (*stoicheia tou kosmou*), while the pseudo-Pauline Letter to the Ephesians (6:12) appears to elaborate this cosmology: 'For we wrestle not against flesh and blood, but against principalities (*archai*), against powers (*exousiai*), against the rulers (*kosmokratoroi*) of the darkness of this world, against spiritual wickedness in high places.'

Clearly, these beings are not the 'unclean spirits' encountered by Jesus and his disciples, but something more cosmic and threatening. Paul was writing against the background of a Middle Platonist 'tendency to create ... personified abstractions for and around God',[27] although Paul's approach was distinctive insofar as he perceived these personifications as a threat rather than an explanatory tool for preserving the omnibenevolence of a monotheistic God. But Christianity was theologically iconoclastic in this respect, emphasizing the absence of barriers and intermediate entities between God and the believer.

For Paul's near contemporary, the Hellenistic Jewish philosopher Philo of Alexandria, the personification of *dynameis* guarded God's transcendence,[28] but such beings were not to be understood as good or bad in and of themselves. Philo declared in his commentary *On the Giants* (on Genesis 6) that 'you will not go wrong if you reckon as angels, not only those who are worthy of the name ... but also those who are unholy and unworthy of the title'.[29] Chris Forbes has argued that Paul's 'elements (*stoicheia*) of the world' are physical elements that Greek and Roman philosophers misidentified (in Paul's view) with gods, when they are 'merely aspects of God's providential management of the world'. They are pitted against the believers because they include the law, sin, and death; but they are personifications rather than truly personal beings and will soon be rendered powerless by a new dispensation of grace under Jesus Christ.

The meaning of Paul's *archai* and *exousiai* (first principles and authorities) is less clear, but in Forbes's view Paul tended away from personifying them. It was only in later Christian tradition, from the writings of Clement of Alexandria onwards, that the *archai* and *exousiai* came to be seen as distinct demonic beings.[30] In Paul's thought they may have been closer to the angels of the Book of Jubilees, emissaries and vice-regents of God who sometimes exceed their authority and cause suffering to the people of God.[31]

Paul made no attempt to systematize his thought by (for instance) identifying these cosmic forces with demons. He was, rather, 'working creatively between the angelology and demonology of his Jewish heritage, and the world-view of the thoughtful Graeco-Roman philosophical amateur'.[32] However, here was another distinctive Christian contribution to demonological thought within Abrahamic monotheism: the characterization as evil of any power between human beings and God, even if those powers were originally created by God, and charged with the governance of part of his creation. Paul's emphasis is on the disruptive, absolute, and exclusive lordship of Jesus Christ, which cuts through and renders malign any previous dispensation of cosmic powers governing the world.

The impact of this rejection of subordinate powers within Christian cosmology was to make impossible any kind of rapprochement between Christianity and Graeco-Roman religion; there was no possibility, for instance, that the pagan gods could be refigured as angels and added to an inclusive 'Christian pantheon' under Christ's overall tutelage. In order to understand the subsequent development of fairy lore within Christianized societies, it is important to recognize that Christianity introduce not only new religious concepts (such as Christ as the Son of God, or God as Trinity) but also a new set of relationships between human beings and the divine, in which acceptance of the lordship and sovereignty of Jesus Christ supplanted or took precedence over any pre-existing relationships. Against the context of this absolute sovereignty, demons, who had been a misfortune and annoyance in Hellenistic Judaism, were refigured as absolutely evil adversaries of God. Exactly where fairies fitted in would be a problem for both theologians and ordinary people to wrestle with.

Making fairies:
demonization, angelization, and euhemerism in early Christianity

As Christianity transformed the Roman world in its first few centuries, the Christian thinkers of the era (who are generally known collectively as the Church Fathers) were forced to contend with the problem of pagan learning and culture: how much of it should Christians accept, assimilate, transform, and reject? When it came to intermediate spiritual beings, there was a strong prejudice against admitting any possibility of beings that were neither evil demons nor benign angels. But there were chinks in the conceptual armour of the church that allowed more nuanced approaches to the spiritual world to develop.

For instance, the story of the 'sons of God' in Genesis 6 seemed to allow the possibility that some 'demons' might be physical (or partially physical) beings rather than entities of pure spirit. The story apparently coincided with folkloric beliefs in sexual relations between godlings and humans, with the result that it seemingly confirmed the existence of beings such as fauns and satyrs. Thus, Augustine of Hippo, in his *City of God*, was willing to concede

> that Silvani and Pans, commonly called incubi, have often appeared to women as wicked men, trying to sleep with them and succeeding. These same demons, whom the Gauls name Dusii, are relentlessly committed to this defilement, attempting and achieving so many things of such a kind that to deny it would seem brazen. Based on this, I dare not risk a definitive statement as to whether there might be some spirits, aerial in substance (for this substance, when it is set in motion by a fan, is perceived as sensation within the body and as touch), who take bodily form and even experience this sexual desire, so that, by any means they can, they mingle with women sensually. But that the holy angels of God in no way fell in like manner during that era – that I would believe.[33]

Augustine had created the demonological concept of the incubus – an original idea, although it derived from the name *Incubo* (a title of the Roman god Faunus, which did not originally have sexual connotations), and dependent for its scriptural authority on a particular interpretation of Genesis 6.[34] However, by granting that there existed a class of 'demons' who had physical bodies, Augustine opened up the possibility that they were not entirely evil – after all, the irredeemable evil of the fallen angels lay in their spiritual natures and the irreversible decision of a wholly spiritual will. But if some 'demons', such as fauns and satyrs, were corporeal like human beings, then it was not impossible to imagine their redemption – as we shall see in chapter 3 below.

The intense moral dualism of Christianity made it difficult for *daimōnia* to be treated as anything other than unambiguously evil enemies of God. But alternative views were not impossible, and one dispute concerned the *daimōnion* that Socrates claimed guided him. Socrates was a figure of intense interest to many early Christian thinkers, steeped in Neoplatonism, for whom the Athenian philosopher provided a sort of pagan analogue to Christ himself. Committed to truth, accused of impiety towards Athenian polytheism for introducing knowledge of a single deity, and put to death for the sake of truth, the death of Socrates as portrayed by Plato seemed to echo that of Christ. One of the Church Fathers, Justin Martyr, even made the comparison explicit in his *Second Apology* for the Christian faith.[35]

But if Socrates had genuinely been inspired by God, although a gentile lacking knowledge of Christ, this seemed to suggest that the *daimōn* of Socrates could not have been an evil demon. Clement of Alexandria, realizing this, suggested that Socrates' *daimōn* might have been something more like a guardian angel.[36] This idea was by no means universally accepted – indeed, it was fiercely opposed by Cyril of Alexandria, Gregory Nazianzen, and Tertullian, who saw Greek philosophy (and Socrates in particular) as the gateway to the Christian heresy of Gnosticism. But for others, such as Justin Martyr and Minucius Felix, the parallels between Socrates inspired by a *daimōn* and Christ inspired by the Holy Spirit proved irresistible.[37]

Clement of Alexandria was not the only Church Father to allow a more positive role for *daimōnia*. In one passage in his polemic against Celsus, Origen appears to make room for benign 'aerial beings' (*aóratoi*) who purify the air, denying that they are *daimōnia*. In context, however, it seems Origen is referring to angels, since he is challenging Celsus to show that it is *daimōnia*, and not angels, who purify the air.[38] Nevertheless,

Origen's belief that angels perform a function as mundane as purifying the air suggests that the Alexandrian theologian simply replaced daemons with angels in his cosmology (leaving only evil to the daemons), rather than denying that spiritual beings were required at all for these roles. A similar emphasis on the lower angels as powers of nature can be found in the pseudepigraphical Book of Jubilees.[39] Origen thus expands the functions of the angels beyond their typical roles as worshippers and messengers of God, and makes them stewards of the minutiae of nature (not unlike the nature fairies of twentieth-century Theosophists). Eusebius, meanwhile, listed good daemons as part of the order of creation in his response to the pagan philosopher Porphyry – and argued that the pagans worshipped evil daemons, but never explicitly denied the existence of the good ones.[40]

But there was another possible approach to the godlings of the ancient world, other than demonization or 'angelization'. This was euhemerism, the idea that the ancients had mistakenly and ignorantly taken mortal beings and treated them as divinities. Isidore of Seville (d. 636) was perhaps the most influential euhemerist of the early Middle Ages, insisting that pagan worship had arisen out of a misguided desire to honour the memory of the mighty dead.[41] This interpretation allowed for a more sympathetic appraisal of paganism, which was not the worship of demons and a conspiracy against God but rather an honest mistake of fallen human beings. And it allowed for a more 'naturalistic' view of godlings. Thus, Isidore concluded that satyrs were essentially an unusual kind of human: 'The Satyrs are little people with hooked noses; they have horns on their foreheads, and feet like goats' – the kind of creature that Saint Anthony saw in the wilderness . . . There are also said to be a kind of wild men (*silvestres homines*), whom some call Fauns of the fig.'[42]

As we shall see in the next chapter, an entire medieval tradition of *naturalia* developed from Isidore, in which the godlings of the Classical world – and otherworld beings encountered by medieval people – were interpreted in terms of the diversity, monstrosity, and mystery of God's physical creation, rather than in terms of demonology.

If Christian theologians were sometimes ambivalent about the roles and natures of demons (or alleged demons), the popular Christianity of the church's early centuries was even less reliably dualistic. 'Folk devils' often differ from their theological counterparts, lacking the latter's absolute evil.[43] As ordinary Christians became (or remained) involved in practices of magic, it blunted the force of their faith's demonological dualism; ritual magic, after all, is about negotiation with and coercion of transmundane powers and is less concerned with their moral character. It was perhaps as a result of demons' importance in magic that early Coptic Christians adopted 'a scalar understanding' of them, from helpful to evil.[44] David Frankfurter has argued that magicians call upon demons and/or the devil not as representatives of cosmic evil or of opposition to Christ, but rather as chaotic and disorderly powers that might nevertheless be of use to humanity.[45]

Indeed, such an approach was arguably consistent with the role taken by fallen angels in *The Book of the Watchers* who, regardless of their malevolence or lack of it, taught humans undeniably useful arts. Wesley Carr observed 'a mixing of Greek and Jewish or Judaeo-Christian ideas' in the demonology of the early Christian era, producing such mysterious beings as the *angeloi katachthonioi* (angels of the underworld) who occur in some curses.[46] Neither a blurring of the boundaries between angels and demons, therefore, nor a refiguring of demons as useful beings was impossible in early Christianity – and this tradition of transgressing the usual strict demonological dualism of Christianity prepared the way for ambivalent beings such as fairies.

As late as the eleventh century, the Byzantine thinker Michael Psellus avidly retained as much as possible of the ancient Greek doctrine of *daimōnia* as inhabitants of air, earth, and sea, as well as 'the lowest subterranean depths'. Although Psellus insisted that all demons were 'haters of God, and enemies of man', he claimed the aerial and earthly demons were less bad than those who lived underground, or in the sea.[47] And the very idea that demons could be divided into levels of malignancy, and that some remained in the air or on the earth rather than in hell, opened up the possibility of later speculation about a category of morally ambivalent spiritual beings dwelling on earth. Indeed, Psellus's own motives in advancing a Christianized Greek cosmology are not altogether clear. Although he was avowedly a Christian, his writings speak to an intense intellectual interest in paganism and a fascination with magic that perhaps extended into practising it, rendering him a not unambiguously Christian figure.[48]

Psellus was also one of the few Byzantine thinkers to engage with the folklore of his own time. He was aware of the belief of ordinary Greeks in 'the Fair One of the Mountains', a beautiful woman (or women) appearing in lonely and wild places, but he rejected the idea that she should be considered a demon. The Fair One of the Mountains was, rather, 'an affection of the head, produced from harsh vapours, or food digested with difficulty'[49] – just as Jacob Marley was, according to Scrooge, an undigested piece of cheese. The Fair One of the Mountains was a matter for the physician rather than the metaphysician. But Psellus did not deny the existence of daemons, although he suggested that some daemons might be made by magicians, and that they were either inanimate or perhaps drew on the life of some human being, like an animated statue.[50] On this reading, a daemon seems to be some sort of projection of the will of the magician as an apparent (but not really) separate being. At the time, Psellus's speculations were challenging to a prevailing consensus among churchmen that anything non-angelic was from the devil (as were even some angelic apparitions); while Psellus seems to us like a sceptic, the really shocking implication of his eccentric theories about daemons at the time was that not all apparitions were evil.

While it is possible to find positive or neutral evaluations of intermediate spiritual beings among Patristic and Byzantine writers, such speculations remained marginal in Christianity when compared to the official place held by the jinn (morally ambivalent semi-physical beings) in Islam. According to the Qur'an, God created the jinn as beings of free will to serve and worship him, but in contrast to humans (who were fashioned from clay), the jinn were made from 'smokeless fire', and both good and evil jinn exist. In Islamic tradition, some jinn are Muslims and some are unbelievers, and stories about them repeatedly echo European fairy traditions.

For example, the jinn sometimes intermarry with humans, and they constitute a supernatural society and are organized hierarchically under a king or kings.[51] Furthermore, like the fairies in many traditions, the jinn are said to be a 'pre-Adamic' race.[52] Whether or not the jinn represent the incorporation of pre-Islamic spirits of the Arab tribes into Islam, the Qur'an's approach to such spirits is in stark contrast to Christianity's dualism when it came to the spiritual world. While Iblis (the Satan of Islam) is a jinni who disobeys God's command, rather than a fallen angel, not all of the jinn follow Iblis in disobeying God, and Iblis does not envy God or lead a rebellion against him. Indeed, in Islamic theology it would be unthinkable for Iblis to envy God since God is too far above any creature for the thought of usurping God to arise.[53]

As we shall see in chapter 3, however, ideas of 'neutral angels' and morally ambivalent demons – similar to Islamic belief in the jinn – did arise in medieval Christianity. It is possible that this belief arose first in a heretical context among Gnostics; Clement of Alexandria alluded to a Gnostic belief that 'some of the angels, through carelessness, were hurled to the earth, not having yet quite reached that state of oneness, by extricating themselves from the propensity to that duality'.[54] This implied that not all fallen angels were evil or rebels against God, but such a position never attained doctrinal recognition. Demonological dualism was always the default understanding of the relationship between humans, angels, and demons; but popular Christianity, especially when suffused with folklore, slowly but steadily ate away at the integrity of Christianity's 'official' demonology and introduced rationalizations for the existence of the ambiguous beings whose reality was attested by the experiences of ordinary people.

Furthermore, from Ireland to Eastern Europe, the fairies are often portrayed as longing for salvation (in vain, for they lack the humanity that Christ redeemed).[55] None of this would have been possible unless there had been, already embedded in the monotheistic tradition, the possibility of creative interpretation of angelic and demonic natures. And some of the earliest detailed evidence for such creative interaction between native and Christian beliefs comes from the very edge of the Christian world, where the waves of the vast Atlantic battered the last island of Europe and of Christendom.

'Terrestrial gods' in early Christian Ireland

At some point in the fifth century, a British bishop, Patrick, travelled to the island of Ireland in order to convert to Christianity the people who had enslaved him in his youth. It was a remarkable act of faith; the Irish were known as pirates and raiders, and their island was largely unknown and feared as a home of terrifying barbarians. Patrick may not have been the first Christian missionary to the Irish, who had never been conquered by the Romans, but his mission to the Irish was among the first Christian missions to a people outside the Empire. It was also exceptionally successful; by 600 CE (within a century and a half of Patrick's arrival), Ireland had been 'converted on the level of hierarchy and institution', and by 700 even 'increasingly marginalized manifestations of non-Christian religion' were gone from the island.[56] Ireland's rapid assimilation of Christianity as an un-Romanized Iron Age society had important cultural consequences, such as the development of a rich vernacular literature in Old Irish and a flourishing culture of learning that took in native traditions as well as Latin and Greek, producing some of the greatest scholars in Western Europe after the collapse of the Western Roman Empire. It also produced a unique approach to Ireland's religious past that deviated from the standard Christian approach to paganism in the late and former Empire.

That standard approach, exemplified by missionaries such as Martin of Braga (in the Iberian peninsula) and Maximus of Turin (in northern Italy), was to denounce all pre-Christian beliefs about supernatural beings as forbidden idolatry and deceits of demons. While Martin of Braga argued that the gods of the Galician mountaintops were demons who appeared to people to deceive them into offering false worship, Maximus of Turin was especially focussed on stamping out the last remnants of pre-Christian belief from the countryside, targeting clandestine altars to nature spirits erected in fields and granaries.[57] The foundation for this Christian missionary critique of paganism was the Old Testament, where the threat of idolatry constantly loomed against the Israelite kingdoms, and their kings periodically targeted Canaanite holy sites such as Asherah poles and rival temples where YHWH was improperly worshipped as an anthropomorphic deity with a divine consort. Late antique missionary Christianity in Northern Europe inherited the 'paranoid monotheism' of post-Exilic Yahwism, where it was always the expectation that recrudescent idolatry would somehow assert itself unless consciously and repeatedly stamped out.

What is remarkable about Christianity in Ireland, compared to the former provinces of the Roman Empire, is that it did not follow this path in relating to its pagan past or the pagan deities who formed part of the cultural background to early Irish literature. It is possible that Irish Christianity's eccentric approach to pre-Christian deities was informed by its Romano-British roots; Romano-British Christianity, it seems, was unusually at ease with pagan imagery, and there is evidence for a degree of syncretism among Christians in fourth-century Britain.[58] On the other hand, it was precisely this kind of relaxed late Roman 'cultural Christianity' that Patrick seems to have rejected in his *Confessio*, and the Irish church became renowned for the intensity of its faith and commitment. Irish Christians' unusual openness to pre-Christian supernatural beings should be interpreted not as a kind of syncretism, nor even as tolerance, but as a consequence of the 'indigestibility' of parts of the Irish supernatural world encountered by Christian missionaries. It is possible that Ireland was not exceptional in this regard; but the fact remains that only Ireland developed a vernacular literature so soon after conversion in which non-human, semi-divine beings played a significant role. Ireland is thus one of the few European cultures for which we have early evidence for the determined and conscious integration of pre-Christian supernatural beings into a thoroughly Christianized worldview (although the position of the elves in Iceland offers some parallels).

All the evidence suggests that, just as elsewhere in the Christian world, Ireland's missionaries stamped out the worship of pagan deities and destroyed places where sacrifices were offered, early on in the conversion process.[59] This is exactly what we should expect – deriving their knowledge of paganism from the Old and New Testaments, missionaries to pagan lands expected to encounter people worshipping idols of wood and stone, offering animal and food sacrifices to specific deities, and ascribing phenomena such as storms and droughts to the gods. But what if a people's outlook on the supernatural world included not *just* deities of the kind missionaries expected to find, but also beings intermediate between the human and the divine who were not objects of worship? The nature of pre-Christian Irish religion is difficult to determine, for the very reason that Ireland was converted so early and so thoroughly.[60] Given Ireland's geographical, linguistic, and cultural proximity to the island of Britain, however, it seems likely there were some parallels between the religious traditions of Iron Age Ireland and Iron Age Britain.

Yet Ireland also had its peculiarities: most notably belief in the *áes síde* (aos sí in modern Irish), a race of beings who dwell in natural or artificial burial mounds and look like humans, but who are more beautiful, longer-lived (or immortal), and possess supernatural powers (figure 2.2).[61] By

Figure 2.2 'Riders of the sídhe', 1911

the tenth century, these otherworlders had come to be referred to also as 'the people of the goddess Danu' (Tuatha Dé Danaan) and euhemerized in genealogical terms as one of the peoples who had settled Ireland in the distant past.[62] But were the aos sí or the Tuatha Dé Danaan ever worshipped? This is an important question, because if they were once gods, then the fairies of Ireland are decayed deities (as one long-standing tradition of scholarship maintains[63]); but if they were never worshipped, the aos sí are *sui generis* – a class of subordinate godlings (if that is a suitable term for them) distinctive to the Irish context, but also comparable with intermediate godlings elsewhere in Europe who survived as fairy-like beings into subsequent eras.

According to the eighth-century *Hymn of Fiacc*, before the coming of St Patrick, 'On the folk of Ireland there was darkness: the peoples used to worship *sidi*.' Taken literally, this would mean the aos sí were the old gods of pagan Ireland, but Peter Alderson Smith preferred to interpret the *Hymn of Fiacc*'s claim as rhetorical hyperbole rather than an accurate statement about pre-Christian Ireland. There is no mention anywhere in Irish literature of the sí or the Tuatha Dé being offered sacrifices, and while they are often portrayed as pagans, they are also said to have their own priests – suggesting they worship the gods, and so are not gods themselves.[64] Furthermore, no one in the early literature ever swears by the sí or the Tuatha Dé, which one would expect of deities.[65] In fact, as Jacqueline Borsje notes, manuscripts of the *Hymn of Fiacc* vary between *sidi* and *ídla* (idols) in this passage, so it is not altogether clear whether the hymn originally referred to the aos sí at all.[66]

One strand in the Irish tradition demonized the aos sí. For instance, in the story *The Wasting Sickness of Cú Chulainn* we learn that

> the demonic power was great before the faith, and it was so great that the demons used to fight bodily with the human beings and they used to show pleasures and secret places to them, as if they were permanent. It is thus that they used to be believed in. So that it is those apparitions that the ignorant call *síde* and *áes síde*.[67]

But demonization of the sí was not typical. Early Irish literature was intensely focussed on the aos sí, with entire genres devoted to the exploration of the Otherworld. These included *echtrai* (adventures in the Otherworld), *físi* and *baili* (prophecies from the Otherworld), *immrama* (sea voyages to the Otherworld), and *aislingi* (dreams of the Otherworld).[68] And the boundary between the world of Christianity and the world of the sí was decidedly porous. Even St Patrick and his companions were sometimes portrayed with characteristics similar to the sí. In Muirchú moccu Machtheni's late seventh-century hagiography of Patrick, when the pagan King Lóegaire tries to kill Patrick and his followers for lighting an Easter fire, the Christians transform themselves into eight deer with a fawn who run into the wilderness – a therianthropic transformation typical of the sí.[69] Patrick was said to have turned druids into birds and made them fly – a power, ironically, that the druids themselves claimed to have.[70]

On another occasion, according to another early hagiography by Tírechán, two pagan princesses who spotted Patrick and a companion at a well mistook them for 'men of the *síde* or gods of the earth' because they were at the well so early.[71] There is a biblical parallel for the aos sí as *dii terreni* (gods of the earth), since in 1 Samuel 28:13 the woman of Endor whom King Saul has asked to raise the spirit of Samuel declares, 'I saw gods ascending out of the earth.' What this seems to mean is that the spirits of the dead can be conceptualized as divinities who dwell in the earth and have the capacity for prophecy – which is how early medieval Irish literature views the sí.[72] Even claims for the divinity of the sí, therefore, involve interplay between pre-Christian Irish tradition and the Bible; this is a conceptual universe in which there is not always a clear way to separate pre-Christian from Christian thought.

In accounts of his life from the seventh century onwards, Patrick is not a mere mortal, but rather a magical being of a different order whose power is greater than that of the old gods or the aos sí. In such narratives, the sí are typically an annoyance and a distraction from Ireland's new Christian destiny rather than evil opponents of the missionaries, and there are frequent ambiguities. In one account, for example, Patrick banishes the Tuatha Dé Danaan to 'the foreheads of hills and rocks', but even then he foretells that 'thou [wilt] see some poor one of them as transiently he revisits the earth'. Furthermore, Patrick makes a specific exception for one *ollam* (master poet) of the Tuatha Dé, Cascorach, whom he excludes from the sentence of banishment.[73] Lisa Bitel has argued that Irish Christian authors, rather than demonizing the aos sí, 'de-idolized the ancient supernatural' by writing stories in which the aos sí are portrayed as human-like characters with familiar human problems of love, conflict, and destiny.[74]

While it might be going too far to speak of a 'baptism of the gods' in early medieval Ireland, where the old gods were fully incorporated into a Christian worldview,[75] Borsje has argued that medieval Irish Christianity might be viewed as a kind of 'inclusive monotheism'.[76] In *The Courtship of Étaín*, the aos sí are said to be 'without blemish, conceived without sin or crime', and thus not subject to original sin; furthermore, humans are prevented from seeing the aos sí by 'the darkness of Adam's sin' – suggesting that the sí are somehow without sin.[77] Indeed, in one particularly remarkable passage of the seventh- or eighth-century *Voyage of Bran*, Bran encounters the sea god Manannán mac Lir, who declares of himself and his kind,

We are from the beginning of creation
Without old age, without consummation of earth,
Hence we expect not that there should be frailty,
The sin has not come to us.[78]

Scholars have offered various views on how this appearance of Manannán should be interpreted.[79] If Manannán is intended to be an allegory of Christ, taking a pagan deity as an allegory of Christ represents a significant departure from patristic tradition; the old gods were conventionally demonized by the Church Fathers, not divinized. In texts such as *The Courtship of Étaín* and *The Voyage of Bran* the old gods function almost as terrestrial angels, 'images of human perfection'. But the Tuatha Dé Danaan are not mentioned in these texts, and rather than a survival of pre-Christian beliefs into Christian Ireland – which would suggest a heterodox Christianity – they are 'a residue of pre-Christian material transfused with ecclesiastical modes of thought'.[80]

In one old Irish tale, *The Voyage of the Boat of the Uí Chorra*, we encounter what is apparently the earliest iteration of what would become the standard theological rationalization of fairies in Irish culture – that the fairies are fallen angels, but those who took no side in the war of heaven rather than those who sided with Satan. Here the Uí Chorra arrive at an island of birds, where the birds turn out to be neutral angels.[81] The link with the sí, who were turned into birds by St Patrick – and often turn themselves into birds – is at least implied. In the better-known *Voyage of St Brendan*, the birds are also encountered, although they are neutral angels in some manuscripts and simply 'soulbirds' (human souls turned into birds) in others – a sign of anxiety, it seems, about the heterodox notion of neutral angels.[82]

The theme of neutral angels will be explored in more detail in the next chapter, but in such stories early medieval Irish writing on the aos sí emerges as a forest of playful and learned allusion and literary elaboration. On the one hand, it is difficult to be sure how far it reflected beliefs held by ordinary people outside the monastery;[83] but on the other, it seems rather unlikely that Irish monastics adopted the aos sí and the old gods of Ireland as a purely literary exercise, given that doing so put them at odds with patristic tradition. Their immersion in an Irish cultural context where such beings were taken for granted seems the most straightforward explanation for why they adopted such eccentric ideas.

Lord of the Worlds: God among the spirits

In nineteenth-century Croatia, folklorists reported that people would cross themselves when they saw glittering lights in the fields, which they interpreted as the dancing of the vilas, 'for the vilas are divine creatures'.[84] As we have seen, the idea that intermediate spirit-beings are divine – associated with God, and possessed of a quasi-divine nature themselves – is one strand in Abrahamic monotheism that reaches back a long way. In Islam, it reached its fullest expression in the doctrine of the jinn, while Rabbinic Judaism generally declined to elevate demons to the level of fallen angels and treated them as spiritual pests, the offspring of Lilith or of the giants of Genesis 6. In Christianity, however, a demonological dualism dominated – at least officially. What Jacqueline Borsje calls 'inclusive monotheism' did remain as one possible approach to Christianity, even among the Church Fathers themselves.

But it would be wrong to see belief in intermediate spirit-beings as a qualification of the absoluteness of monotheism. The title of 'Lord of the Worlds' given to God in Islam expresses the monotheistic instinct to multiply rather than limit the diversity of creatures and the diversity of natures over which God rules. This multiplication of spirit-life functioned in ancient Judaism, and functions in Islam to this day, as an exaltation of monotheism, not a limitation on it – God is big enough to create and rule over other mysterious forms of life as well as being served by benign angels and even evil demons who do his bidding as tempters and punishers of humanity.

This approach to monotheism never became the norm in Christianity. But it did exist, and its existence made possible the creative incorporation of fairy lore into unofficial Christian cosmologies, which we shall examine in subsequent chapters. For while it may be true that the *matter* of fairy lore often derives from pre-Christian traditions – such as the names of Ireland's quasi-divine beings – fairies slide fairly comfortably into an already existing conceptual structure that was integral to Christian thought. The conceptual *form* of fairies, or at least their conceptual place in the world, is largely an artefact of Christianity in most European cultures, since it was possible to contemplate that fallen-yet-neutral spirit-beings existed. It was also possible to contemplate that non-human beings who were partly spiritual and partly physical existed. In other words, Judaeo-Christian mythologies such as the giants of Genesis 6, the fall of the Watchers, and the children of Lilith made it possible to construct post hoc rationalizations for fairies, rendering fairies as much an outgrowth of Christianity as 'pagan survivals' who thumbed their noses at the new faith.

THREE

Here be monsters: otherworld beings in the Middle Ages

At some point in the first half of the fourth century CE, a Christian hermit living in the Egyptian desert, Anthony, set out to find Paul of Thebes, a man he had heard was even holier than he was. Anthony was already ninety years old, and he had no idea where Paul might be found; but he struggled on in the scorching heat of the noonday sun until he encountered – of all things – a centaur. Anthony, recognizing this creature of pagan myth, immediately made the sign of the cross; but he was also desperate to find his fellow hermit, and so he asked the centaur if he knew where Paul lived. The 'monster' simply pointed, and galloped away. But Anthony followed the centaur's directions, and came upon a dry valley where he spotted a faun with the horns and feet of a goat. Anthony, who was no stranger to temptations from hideous devils, prepared to do spiritual battle with the faun, but to his surprise the creature offered him a palm fruit and declared:

> I am a mortal being, and one of those inhabitants of the desert whom the Gentiles, deluded by various forms of error, worship under the name of fauns, satyrs, and incubi. I am sent to represent my tribe. We pray you in our behalf to entreat the favour of your Lord and ours, who, we have learned, came once to save the world, and 'whose sound is gone forth into all the earth'.

Anthony was moved to tears by the faun's declaration of faith – and Jerome, who recorded this story, added a coda to the effect that a faun had once been captured in the desert and paraded through the streets of Alexandria, if anyone should doubt that such creatures existed.[1] Centuries later, a twelfth-century sculptor depicted Anthony's encounter with the faun on a tympanum of the church of Saint-Paul-de-Varax in Burgundy, under the inscription 'The abbot [i.e. Anthony] was seeking Paul, and the faun taught.'[2]

Figure 3.1 'St Anthony encounters a satyr', 1643–1655, by Herman van Swanevelt

Jerome's decision to include this story is, on the face of it, surprising. After all, Christians usually considered creatures of Graeco-Roman myth such as centaurs and fauns to be nothing more than misshapen demons, less subtle and refined in their deceptions than the Olympian gods who were also fallen angels who lured pagans into worshipping them. Indeed, Jerome implies that Anthony thought this too. But Anthony turns out to be mistaken; the centaurs and fauns are not demons, but mortal monstrous races; creatures of God, who have heard that Christ redeemed the entire creation and want to be part of the story of salvation. At another church in Burgundy, Vézelay, another Romanesque tympanum depicts the Gospel being preached to these monstrous races – such as the *cynocephali* (dogheaded men), the *panotti* (with huge ears that cover their whole bodies), and the pygmies.[3] In this cosmic vision of redemption, the entire creation, and not just the human race, receives the benefits of Christ's death and resurrection.

Jerome's story of Anthony's encounter with the centaur and satyr belonged to a new way of viewing the godlings of the ancient world in late antiquity, as *naturalia* (natural phenomena) rather than as supernatural creatures – even if they remained uncanny, and perhaps also retained some magical powers. It is difficult for us to appreciate, in a world formed by nineteenth-century anxieties about definitively distinguishing the human from the non-human that emerged from Darwin's theory of evolution, that in patristic and early medieval Christianity humanity remained a somewhat porous category. This chapter will examine the initial development of fairies (although they were then seldom so called) in the early Middle Ages. As we shall see, the interpretation of fairies as a natural (albeit unusual) monstrous race was one possible approach to the problem of their existence. But in tracing the origins of the component traditions that would eventually constitute the figure of the fairy, we will also need to examine medieval ideas of neutral angels, helpful demons, water spirits, and poltergeists.

Monstrous and pygmy races

Monsters in the Middle Ages were human-like beings who existed in 'forms seemingly beyond the borders of the humanly possible', in the words of Jeffrey Cohen.[4] A monster was, in other words, not a non-human animal but a being sufficiently human for its departure from the norms of humanity to be alarming. There is an immediate affinity, therefore, between the monster and the almost-human fairy; and, as we have seen, the godlings of the ancient world could be refigured as monsters of the physical world rather than hybrid divine–corporeal beings. This tradition, in fact, pre-dates the hegemony of Christianity, and can be found in the second-century *Physiologus* (whose text formed the basis of most medieval bestiaries), according to which satyrs were a monstrous race living in Ethiopia.[5] The fifth-century Roman author Martianus Capella reported that

> The dance of the long-lived ones (*longaevi*) fills the earth itself, which is inaccessible to humans, who inhabit the woods, groves, lakes, springs and rivers, and are called pans, fauns, *fones*, satyrs, sylvans, nymphs, male and female fate-speakers (*fatui, fatuaeque*), or *Fantaue* or even *Fanae* (from which sanctuaries (*fana*) are so called), who are accustomed to divine the future. These,

after a long age, die like humans; but, however, they have a very present power of foreknowing, attacking and harming.[6]

This account, written at the cusp of Christianity's triumph over Graeco-Roman religion, preserved some of the supernatural characteristics of the godlings of the ancient world – but it rendered these godlings ultimately mortal: monsters, in other words, rather than deities. The basic foundation of the idea of monstrous races was the Hippocratic treatise *On Airs, Waters and Places*, written in the fifth century BCE, which introduced the idea that different kinds of land will produce different kinds of people.[7] But the existence of monstrous races was also supported by the Bible, under some interpretations at least. The hybrid giants of Genesis 6 had been (in theory) destroyed in the Flood, but it was always possible they lingered somewhere in remote regions of the world. Similarly, the mysterious 'mark' set by God on Cain, so that anyone who found him should kill him (Genesis 4:15), could also be interpreted as a source of monstrosity in Cain's descendants, while for others it was the curse placed by Noah on his son Ham and his descendants (Genesis 9:25) that lay at the root of the development of monstrosity, as the outward appearance of certain races came to express their accursed nature.

Augustine's discussion of the monstrous races in his *City of God* proved especially influential. Augustine was by no means certain that the monstrous races really existed, and approached them with caution; but if they did exist, Augustine considered that they were human in spite of their peculiarities – as long as they were rational, mortal animals. The monstrous races, therefore, were descended from Adam – and Augustine wondered if God might permit their existence in order to show that the monstrous births that sometimes occurred in his own society were not failures of the creator, but rather expressions of the diversity God allowed:

> What if God has seen fit to create some races in this way, that we might not suppose that the monstrous births which appear among ourselves are the failures of that wisdom by which he fashions the human nature, as we speak of the failure of a less perfect workman? Accordingly, it ought not to seem absurd to us, that as in individual races there are monstrous births, so in the whole race there are monstrous races.[8]

But while Augustine was concerned with the monstrous races said to live at the edge of the world by ancient writers such as Herodotus, medieval writers also explained the existence of monsters encountered in their own societies by reference to biblical stories. In Anglo-Saxon England, for instance, the author of *Beowulf* took the story of Cain as an explanation for ogres, elves, giants, and the monster Grendel:

> For a long while the unblest creature [Grendel] had inhabited the territory of a species of water-monsters (*fifelcynnes*) since the Creator had proscribed him along with the stock of Cain. The everlasting Lord avenged that murderous act by which he slew Abel. He enjoyed no benefit from that violent assault, for God the Ordainer exiled him for that crime far away from human-kind. From him all misbegotten things were born – ogres (*eotenas*) and elves (*ylfe*) and hellishly deformed beings (*orcneas*) such as the giants who fought for a long time against God; for that he paid them their due.⁹

Similar narratives circulated in Ireland, where Cain was said to have fathered a siren named Ambia who had intercourse with a trout, giving birth to Fomoir (ancestor of the Fomorians) and Becnait (ancestor of the leprechauns).¹⁰ According to the *Book of the Dun Cow* (*c*.1100), 'from the accursed Ham are descended *Luchorpain* (leprechauns), *Fomoraig* (Fomorians), *Goborchinn* (horse-heads) and every human being of unshapely appearance'.¹¹ While monsters were often expressions of an ultimate Other, and therefore threatening beings, they did not always carry negative connotations, especially in the twelfth century. Like Jerome's faun, monstrous beings were capable of delivering moral lessons to the human race – for, after all, they too were creatures of God.¹²

On one interpretation, medieval fairy traditions can be taken as a variant of the medieval belief in monstrous races in which the monsters live not only at the edges of maps, beyond the civilized world, but also hidden in our midst – or in areas of our familiar world, such as underground or in the sea, that are usually inaccessible to us. Indeed, some stories appear to portray monstrous peoples stumbling into our world, like the tale of the shaggy, sea-dwelling wild man of Orford who was caught in fishermen's nets off the Suffolk coast,¹³ or the green boy and girl who stumbled out of underground tunnels near the English village of Woolpit in the twelfth century, perhaps from the imagined 'antipodes' on the other side of the globe.[14] The trolls of Scandinavia were often portrayed as aboriginal giants who inhabited the land before its current inhabitants, implying a link with the giants of Genesis 6,[15] although the medieval terminology of trolls was unstable and at different times they were taken as an equivalent to Latin *daemonia*, *idola*, and even *serpentes et dracones*. Indeed, in medieval Scandinavia, the term 'troll' could seemingly refer to any 'non-human non-dead Other'.[16] The trolls were 'a rather vaguely defined group of supernatural beings in Old Norse mythology . . . sometimes acting as individual characters but mostly spoken of as a harmful collective', but the term 'troll' could also designate humans with uncanny abilities, giving rise to the Norse word for witchcraft, *trolldómr*.[17]

But while trolls are an obvious example of the monstrous fairy, the difficulty with using monstrosity as a key to understanding medieval fairy lore is that only *some* fairies were monstrous. Some beings, like the green children of Woolpit (with their green skin) and the fairies encountered by Elidyr (with their tiny stature), were normal and even pleasing in appearance apart from one strange characteristic. Other fairies, such as elves, were wholly beautiful – and, indeed, defined by their beauty.

In some stories, beauty and monstrosity combine in depictions of the otherworld realm; according to Thomas of Walsingham, Lord Greystoke's horse was detained by an ugly, diminutive 'red man' who led Greystoke to a realm of beautiful women, one of whom cut off Greystoke's head and thereby robbed him of his wits.[18] An interesting feature of this story is that the red man was unstable in size, growing as he grabbed hold of the horse's reins, and this variation as to size is perhaps the oldest and most lasting feature of fairy monstrosity – although it is by no means universal. Ireland's aos sí are not diminutive beings in the medieval literary tradition, and even in the modern Irish fairy lore collected by Dermot Mac Manus and Eddie Lenihan the sí are either stately beings or simply 'the lads from the other side', human-seeming beings who only occasionally become visible (see chapter 8 below). The only exceptions are beings specifically thought of as diminutive in the Irish tradition, such as the leprechaun and clurichaun. Similarly, in the Slavic and Baltic traditions, the vilas and laumės are of human size, as are the elves of Scandinavia (who are distinct from the dwarfs) in all but the most recent traditions; and there is no reason to suppose that the elves of Anglo-Saxon England were imagined as being diminutive, either.

So where did the idea that fairies are smaller than humans come from? Belief in a race of diminutive people, the pygmies, reaches as far back as Homer, who first mentioned the pygmies' legendary battle with the cranes in the *Iliad*. In Greek mythology, the pygmies were a non-human or quasi-human race similar to but essentially different from humans, owing to their inferior intelligence.[19] The question of pygmy humanity, debated by natural philosophers such as Albert the Great, was an 'edge case' for medieval philosophers that helped to clarify the boundaries of the human, but ancient pygmies had no association with magic or enchantment. But some conceptual slippage seems to have occurred between pygmies and ancient godlings; Isidore of Seville discussed the pygmies immediately after his discussion of 'fauns of the fig', and in Walter Map's *De nugis curialium* (On the Trifles of Courtiers), written in the late twelfth century, the pygmy king encountered by King Herla has distinctly faun-like therianthropic characteristics:

> [He was] a pygmy in respect of his low stature, not above that of a monkey ... and [he] might be described in the same terms as Pan; his visage was fiery red, his head huge; he had a long red beard reaching to his chest, which was gaily attired in a spotted fawn's skin: his belly was hairy and his legs declined into goats' hoofs.[20]

Unlike the pygmies of Greek mythology, Walter Map's pygmy king rules over an enchanted otherworld where time moves differently from in our world, with ultimately disastrous consequences for King Herla (who is condemned to wander an unfamiliar Britain on a fairy horse, never dismounting lest he crumble to dust). The pygmies who invade Britain in the Welsh tale *Lludd and Llefelys*, the *coraniaid*, are apparently malignant and monstrous in one respect (their unusually acute hearing), although their appearance is never described.[21]

However, tiny fairies are sometimes beautiful, like the fair-haired Tuath Luchra in one thirteenth- or fourteenth-century story about the Irish hero Fergus. Their tiny king Iubdan is much admired: 'His is a voice clear and sweet as copper's resonance, like the blood-coloured rowan-berry is his cheek; his eye is bland as it were a stream of mead; his colour like that of the swan or of the river's foam.'[22] Likewise, the diminutive people encountered on a riverbank by the twelve-year-old

Elidyr in Gerald of Wales's *Journey through Wales* are beautiful rather than monstrous, and inhabit an enchanted underground world. In fact, Gerald's story is the first in which British fairies assume the characteristics which had become familiar by the end of the Middle Ages (as we shall see in chapter 4 below):

> When [Elidyr] was a young innocent only twelve years old and busy learning to read, he ran away one day and hid under the hollow bank of some river or other, for he had had more than enough of the harsh discipline and frequent blows meted out by his teacher . . . Two days passed and he still lay hidden, with nothing at all to eat. Then two tiny men appeared, no bigger than pygmies. 'If you will come away with us', they said, 'we will take you to a land where all is playtime and pleasure.' The boy agreed to go. He rose to his feet and followed them. They led him first through a dark underground tunnel and then into a most attractive country, where there were lovely rivers and meadows, and delightful woodlands and plains. It was rather dark, because the sun did not shine there. The days were all overcast, as if by clouds, and the nights were pitch-black, for there was no moon nor stars. The boy was taken to see their king and presented to him, with all his court standing round. They were amazed to see him, and the king stared at him for a long time. Then he handed him over to his own son, who was still a child.

According to Elidyr, 'All these men were very tiny, but beautifully made and well-proportioned.' They were vegetarians, living on dairy products, and had fair complexions and long flowing hair like women. They rode horses the size of greyhounds and refused to swear oaths, owing to a hatred of falsehood. These otherworlders 'had no wish for public worship, and what they revered and admired, or so it seemed, was the plain unvarnished truth' – a reverence for the truth that was shared, as it happens, by the leprechaun-king Iubdan. Elidyr carried on living in this underground world, but often returned to his own and visited his mother, who was the only human he told about the otherworld. His mother, hearing that gold was common in the otherworld, asked him to bring back a present; so he brought back a golden ball that he and the Fairy King's son used to play with; but when he reached his mother's threshold and tripped on it, he realized that the little people were in pursuit. Elidyr dropped the ball and two of the fairies snatched it up;

they vanished back into the otherworld, whose entrance Elidyr was never able to find again.[23]

A curious feature of Elidyr's story (about which he was interrogated, in old age, by the bishop of St Davids) was that he claimed to remember fragments of the otherworlders' language, which Gerald noticed had a distinct resemblance to Greek. Gerald believed, in common with most learned men of the period, that the Britons descended from Brutus the Trojan, and therefore the British language (the ancestor of Welsh) had evolved from Greek. By noting that the fairies' language was closer to Greek, Gerald implied that they were somehow Britons and descendants of Brutus – but they had perhaps become separated from the rest of the Britons at an early date and so retained their ancient speech. Just as the eleventh-century *Lebor Gabála Érenn* (Book of the Invasions of Ireland) had portrayed the Tuatha Dé Danaan as a surviving 'relic population' of earlier inhabitants of Ireland, so Gerald seems to have been reaching for a similar notion. As we shall see, the idea that fairies were human relic populations would continue to evolve, reaching the height of its popularity and becoming inflected by racism in the nineteenth century.

While the Greek idea of the pygmies as a monstrous people, mediated via Isidore of Seville, was one potential source for the idea of diminutive otherworlders, there may also have been more prosaic explanations. If otherworlders are thought to live underground, then it makes sense that they should be of small stature, and I have argued elsewhere that the nature of surviving Roman ruins in Britain may have inspired the idea that these structures were once lived in by tiny people.[24] There is a long tradition of tiny artefacts inspiring and confirming belief in the existence of tiny supernatural beings – most famously the phenomenon of 'elfshot' (prehistoric flint arrowheads), but perhaps also the tiny votive offerings found at some Romano-British shrines. In Ireland, the tiny clay pipes dating from a period when tobacco was too expensive for people to smoke it in large quantities were known as 'leprechauns' pipes' and taken as confirmation of the tiny shoemakers' existence.[25]

I have proposed that the British tradition of diminutive, subterranean fairies may have come into contact with English elf lore in the period after the Norman Conquest (when Breton nobles and people of Anglo-Norman descent from the Welsh Marches became culturally influential), and led gradually to a synthesis of the pygmy otherworlders of the

Britons with the elves of the English.[26] But it was not exclusively fairies who were perceived as tiny beings – in 1287, John de Tregoz was healed by a tiny figure of St Thomas Cantilupe, only a foot high, who emerged from the saint's shrine in Hereford Cathedral.[27] Perhaps we should be asking whether human visionary experiences *in general* somehow lend themselves to manifestations of diminutive beings.

Germanic tradition also had its own pygmies – the dwarfs. Although dwarfs are best known from Norse literature, they were not part of medieval Scandinavian folk belief,[28] and although they occur in early England it is not always clear what exactly a *dweorh* was supposed to be (the word also meant 'spider'). All that seems certain is that people feared dwarfs and believed they caused illness.[29] In Norse literature, however, the dwarfs (the alternative plural 'dwarves' was invented by J. R. R. Tolkien) are 'associated with the dead, with battle, with wisdom, with craftsmanship, with the supernatural, and even to some extent with the elves'.[30] In the *Prose Edda*, the dwarfs are created by the gods as divine goldsmiths, and create 'the mead of poetry'; they are intermediate between the gods and the giants,[31] but the dwarfs are only ever vaguely defined in Old Norse tradition, with their absence more prominent than their presence.[32] Dwarfs are apparently unable to bear the light of the sun, which turns them to stone, and it is never quite clear whether they are for or against the gods. The dwarfs become 'otherworld predators' because they are below the status of the gods but possess uncanny powers.[33]

While the dwarfs are not beautiful, the elves or fairies often are. Yet the beauty of fairies in some medieval tales is not necessarily inconsistent with their construction as monstrous peoples; for the marginal peoples of medieval geography (who include the monstrous races) are also beyond the reach of the Gospel, and thus simultaneously unenlightened and innocent. The emphasis on the honesty of the fairies in both the story of King Iubdan of the Tuath Luchra and the tale of Elidyr – and indeed the implication that their reverence for truth somehow takes the place of religion among humans – echoes the reports of medieval travellers (or self-styled travellers) like John Mandeville, who admired pagan peoples for their nobility and honesty rather than disparaging them for their ignorance of Christ.[34] Fairies, even when they were not geographically distant or physically ugly, retained an 'extended monstrosity' insofar as they remained a moral and spiritual other – with all the ambiguities that carried. The monstrous races were an appealing template for fairies because such an interpretation made it possible to square the existence of fairies with the Bible, but it also allowed the fairies to be construed as people dwelling (like pagans) beyond the cultural and spiritual boundaries of the baptized world.

Out of the water

It is a curious feature of several of the earliest names given to fairy-like beings in early medieval Europe that they are associated with water spirits, in spite of the fact that such beings are encountered primarily on land in most of the narratives we have. As we saw at the start of chapter 2 above, Ireland's otherworlders sometimes dwelt at the bottom of loughs. The nereids of Greece, the leprechauns of Ireland, the *lutins* of the francophone world, the *Nixen* of the germanophone world, and the mysterious Portunes of early medieval England all began life (etymologically speaking, anyway) as water sprites, yet only the *Nixen* (and their derivatives such as the Estonian *Näkk*) retained their indelible association with bodies of water into later folklore.[35]

Water spirits who live *in* the water as their otherworld domain should perhaps be distinguished here from fairies who somehow embody and patronize springs. Pierre Gallais argued that the association between the fairy and the spring (which is found, as we have seen, as far back as the link between nymphs and springs in Homeric Greece) was an Indo-European archetype,[36] and I have elsewhere explored the association between fairies and springs in Britain.[37] By the sixteenth century, the proverb 'naked like a fairy coming out of the water' ('nue comme une fée sortant de l'eau') had passed into popular usage in France.[38] But whatever the link between fairies and springs really means – and whether or not it represents a vestige of animistic veneration of water sources – it is not quite the same thing as fairies living *in* a body of water as their otherworld realm.

Indeed, it is possible that the underwater realm, normally accessible to humans, was the original otherworld in much the same way as the sídhe mounds of Ireland were the gateways to an underground otherworld, or the way the forest serves as an otherworld in Baltic and Slavic traditions. The ancient British preoccupation with depositing offerings in bodies of water is suggestive of a belief like this,[39] which may have had less to do with the aquatic nature of the spirits who inhabited waters – or even their patronage of a particular lake, pond, or river – than with the idea of water itself as a veil sundering humans from an otherworld of divinities. In Welsh tradition, the fairies often inhabit 'the hollow banks that overhang the deeper parts of lakes or rivers', and the twelfth-century *Black Book of Carmarthen* alludes to 'every dwarf... beneath the sea'. Indeed, the name of the Welsh water monster *afanc* seems to be cognate with Irish *abacc* (dwarf), and thus may have referred originally to a dwarf-like being.[40]

If deep water itself was an otherworld, it is not altogether surprising that supernatural beings originally associated with the sea migrated to the land as ideas of otherworlds evolved. Thus, in medieval Greece the nymphs were replaced entirely by the nereids, originally the marine female attendants of Poseidon. The nereids retained the nymphs' beauty at times, as well as their dancing and their association with springs and lonely places, but also took on the demonic characteristics of Lamia as potential child-stealers, bringers of sickness, and seducers of the unwary traveller.[41] Similarly, in one early medieval Breton story, a female godling (called a *theomacha*) encountered by St Samson in a forest wields a trident, hinting at a marine origin.[42] In Ireland, the *lupracán* was originally a water spirit, glossed in due course as *luchorpán* (small body), which gave rise to the idea of the leprechauns as dwarfs and, in due course, their reputation as the diminutive shoemakers of the fairies.[43] In the eighth-century *Senchas Már*, the sleeping hero Fergus is carried to the sea by *lupracáin* whom he spares on waking up, on condition that they grant his wish to be able to walk under water. They then lead him on an underwater journey. As late as the twelfth century, the *Acallam na Senórach* (Colloquy of the Ancients) referred to a *loch luchra* (Loch of the Leprechauns), suggesting an underwater association.[44]

The original word *lupracán*, in Jacopo Bisagni's view, derived from the Luperci – young men in ancient Rome who dressed in animal skins for the Lupercalia, who according to Augustine actually turned into wolves by passing through water. In Old Irish texts of *computus* (commentaries on the correct calculation of the church's calendar), the Luperci were transmuted into a monstrous race who dwelt in water, the *lupracáin*.[45] If Bisagni is correct, leprechauns are thus the product of at least five folkloric transformations:

1. Augustine's refiguring of the Luperci as actual lycanthropes
2. early Irish interpretation of the Luperci as a monstrous race
3. the transference of that monstrous race to Irish folklore as the water-dwelling *lupracáin*
4. the misinterpretation of *lupracán* as *luchorpán* and the refiguring of *lupracáin* as dwarfs
5. the transformation of the diminutive *luchorpán* into the fairy shoe-maker of modern Irish folklore

We could even add to this list the commercialization of the leprechaun and its transformation into an internationally recognized (and somewhat degrading) stereotype for the Irish themselves (see chapter 9 below).

The origins and etymology of the *lutin* of modern francophone nations (whose New World incarnation we will meet in chapter 7) are similarly convoluted. Somehow, *neptunus* (from Neptune, the Roman god of the sea) had become a term for spirits of French folk belief by the early thirteenth century, when it is attested by both Gervase of Tilbury and Thomas of Cantimpré.[46] Gervase also described another kind of fairy from England known as the *Portuni*, whose name apparently derived from the Roman god Portunus (god of harbours) – although the Portunes did not survive into subsequent English folklore.[47] Although Gervase and Thomas wrote in Latin, the Old French word they rendered as *neptuni* was presumably *netuns*, which became *nuitons* and then *luitons* – and finally *lutins*.[48] Mia Gerhardt showed that the *netuns* were originally equine water spirits, rather like the Scottish kelpie; twelfth-century romances make several references to horses that were the offspring of a mare and a *netun*.[49] Thereafter *nuiton/luiton* seemingly became a generic term for a monster or demon.

In the thirteenth-century romance *Huon of Bordeaux*, however, a *luiton* (whose natural form is a sea-monster) is able to take the appearance of a handsome young man, Malabron, who acts as the hero's attendant.[50] In another romance of the second half of the thirteenth century, *Gaufrey*, the *luitin* Malabron acts as an invisible noisy spirit in a castle, roaring, blowing out candles, and upending a bier (in modern terms, a poltergeist).[51] Thereafter, Malabron is revealed as a shapeshifter who has been specifically gifted by God with the ability to change his form whenever he chooses, but any particular connection with the sea seems to have disappeared.[52] But a further development then took place in folklore, as the *lutin* somehow evolved into a diminutive being.[53] In time, the *lutins* became a fairy people of northern France, while *follets*, *dracs*, *fadas*, and dolphins predominated in the south of the country.[54]

Like *lutins*, the *dracs* had a name that apparently derived from the sea – the Latin Vulgate translated the sea monster Leviathan as *draco* (dragon) (Psalm 73:13, Ezekiel 32:2) – but Gervase of Tilbury portrayed the *dracs* as dwellers in freshwater rivers and lakes, where they took the form of gold cups floating on the surface of the water. When people reached out to grab the cups, they would fall in and be dragged down to the *dracs'* underwater abode. Strangely, however, the *dracs* are not monsters or serpents but look like humans – although their monstrous character is underlined by their eating of human flesh.[55] In Occitania, *drac* was considered a synonym for *fée*,[56] although the tradition also found its way to Brittany where later folklore featured the theme of an underwater world inhabited by *dracs*.[57] But we should not rule out the possibility that the text of Gervase of Tilbury's *Otia imperialia* itself informed the development of subsequent Breton folklore.

The French tradition of treating dolphins as fairies – which seems to have reached England as well, in the form of the Highclere grampus[58] – is a particularly interesting instance of therianthropy, not least because it involved a real-world animal. Dolphins, like the apes that would later be classed as 'satyrs' and interpreted as monstrous races of almost-human beings,[59] seemed almost human in their behaviour, and it was this almost-humanness that may have given rise to the legend (recorded by Gervase of Tilbury) that the dolphins had once been knights. Gervase also described dolphin–human hybrids and implied that dolphins could assume human form.[60] It was thus appropriate that the dolphin, a magical creature between the human and the supernatural (as well as between the human and the animal), became one of the heraldic symbols of the French monarchy.

The white people

If Ireland was the second culture whose godlings broke upon documented history (after those of the ancient Near East and Mediterranean), the godlings of the Germanic world were the next to emerge from the mists of prehistory: the elves. The proto-Germanic word that gave us English *elf* and Old Norse *alfr* may have been cognate with Latin *albus*, and meant something like 'the white ones' or 'the shining ones',[61] and indeed otherworld beauty was one of the characteristics associated with the elves.[62] However, *albus* and its cognates are not originally Indo-European words and seem to derive from a pre-Indo-European substrate (a lost language preceding the Indo-European languages in Europe). *Albus* may have given rise to words in non-Germanic languages (such as *ellyl* in Welsh and *iele* in Romanian) that also refer to supernatural beings but may not derive from a common Germanic source.[63] However, we should not conclude from this that elves represent survivals of a pre-Indo-European cultural substratum, and Bargan acknowledges that it is just as likely that the *iele* of Romania was inspired in some way by Germanic folklore. Linguistic survival does not equate to religious survival.

In Germanic culture, elves were always ambiguous beings, and the primary response to elves in Anglo-Saxon England seems to have been fear. Elves were beautiful, but they were also intensely threatening and menaced humans with their supernatural shot (which caused sudden, unexplained pains and illness) and were monsters descended from Cain.[64] One prayer book even identified them as devils.[65] In origin, they seem to have been demigods; in the sixth century, Jordanes glossed the Gothic word *anses* (ancestor of Old Norse *æsir*) as *semideos* (demi-gods), and the *æsir* (gods) were said to include the álfar.[66] So perhaps the elves were once worshipped as deities; some Icelandic sagas refer to sacrifices to the álfar (although this could be an instance of inaccurate Christian back-projection, like the *Hymn of Fiacc*'s claim that the pagan Irish worshipped the sí). Yet the álfar and Vanir (Norse gods) were also referred to interchangeably in the Norse sagas, suggesting that the pre-Christian Norse may have regarded them as one and the same.[67]

Furthermore, the sagas seem to suggest that great kings might be venerated as álfar after their deaths – so perhaps the álfar were conceptualized as the mighty ancestral dead, rather like the sí and the Tuatha Dé in Ireland.[68] However, Ármann Jakobsson has argued that the idea of 'the elves' as a supernatural race or parallel society was a later development, on the grounds that 'elf' could be used to refer to dwarfs and trolls as well as the human-like and non-monstrous beings usually associated with the term. So 'elf' was a fairly fluid term, it seems, for supernatural beings in general. Subsequent readers have been misled by the excessive enthusiasm of some medieval authors for classification, such as the Icelandic writer Snorri Sturluson (1179–1241) who seems to have invented the categories of 'light elves' (*ljósálfar*) and 'dark elves' (*døkkálfar*) that so influenced the fantasy fiction of Tolkien and Alan Garner.[69]

The precise nature of what people believed about elves in pre-Christian England (and even in Christian Anglo-Saxon England) remains obscure. In spite of the fact that elves crop up in personal names, place names, and glosses, more questions remain than answers. Yet while the elves of Anglo-Saxon England passed their name to the elves of post-Conquest England, few of the themes of Anglo-Saxon elf-lore can be found in relation to medieval elves – with the exception of the elves' predilection for causing harm and their capacity to seduce men and women (if indeed the Anglo-Saxons believed this). There is no evidence (for example) that the Anglo-Saxons believed elves lived under the ground, inhabited an otherworld, or formed a coherent, hierarchically organized society.[70] Terry Gunnell has drawn attention to the problem that most sources about elves (which come from England and Iceland) are peripheral to the heartland of elf-lore itself, which was Sweden; and he cautions that elves may have been synthesized in the Middle Ages with *landvættir* (land-wights, i.e. nature spirits) as a result of the influence of Norse translations of French romances in the thirteenth and fourteenth centuries.[71] In their earliest attested form, the álfar seem to have been venerated as gods in south-western Sweden, where their cult was associated with offerings made to farm grave mounds; an early Norwegian law book, the eleventh-century *Gulaþingslǫg*, attempted to ban this practice.[72]

Tom Shippey has identified an 'elf problem', which is partly the category problem of where to place elves within a Christian cosmology,[73] and partly the problem of whether the elves should be seen as good or bad (or both), demonic or quasi-divine, given that the medieval sources seem to treat them as both. It is also the problem of who or what counted as an elf, and what different kinds of elves there were, which Tolkien sought to resolve in his fiction.[74] In contrast to the aos sí and later conceptions of the fairies, the earlier medieval evidence suggests that elves were not spirits of nature or of the land, who belonged to a separate category, and a folkloric merging of the álfar with nature spirits seems to have begun in medieval Iceland.[75] This collapsing of earlier conceptual categories might be compared to the evolution of the medieval English elf (rebranded in due course as the English fairy), who was apparently a syncretic being that emerged in the wake of the Norman Conquest,[76] although in Iceland the shift was not to do with cultural mixing but instead, perhaps, linked to the challenges of colonizing an uninhabited and hostile landscape. The Icelanders not only began worshipping and sacrificing to álfar but also began transforming leaders who died into álfar,[77] which may have reflected a novel religious response (reviving the idea of the elves as gods) to the challenge of living in Iceland.

Snorri Sturlusson's distinction between 'light elves' and 'dark elves', which occurs nowhere else, is now widely regarded by scholars as a literary construction rather than a reflection of actual folk beliefs. Sturluson may have been inspired by portrayals of angels in the Old Norse *Elucidarius* to refigure elves as divided into angelic and demonic kinds.[78] If this is what Sturluson was doing, then his treatment of elves echoed the Irish tradition of 'angelizing' the old gods and the concept of fairies as neutral angels that emerged from the *Voyage of St Brendan*, since by inventing the *ljósálfar* Sturluson admitted the possibility that the elves might be perceived as benign and even angelic beings. The sheer diversity of medieval references to elves – where they are sometimes gods, sometimes mirror communities of morally neutral human-like beings, and sometimes fearful beings who caused harm to humans – suggest that these references 'stem from a variety of different belief systems originating in different times and different environments'.[79] In other words, it might be a mistake to seek a single 'ur-elf' whose nature somehow made sense of these disparate characteristics. Rather, it might make more sense to view 'elf' (like 'troll') in its earliest period of use as a generic term for the uncanny or supernatural instead of a label for a distinct and well-defined category of beings.

Neutral angels, benign demons

As we saw in chapter 2 above, the idea that some angels had refused to take sides in the heavenly war between the rebel angel Lucifer and God's heavenly champion Michael (figure 3.2), and that God turned them into birds, emerged in the Middle Ages in Irish *immrama* (tales of otherworld voyages). The eighth-century *Voyage of St Brendan* became a very popular text and it exists in many versions, in several languages. To take just one example, in the fourteenth-century Middle English *Metrical Life of St Brendan*, the birds inform Brendan:

> 'We were', he said, 'once angels shining in heaven;
> As soon as we were created, our master was too proud
> Lucifer, for his fairness, so that he fell soon out,
> And with him also many a one, as their deed was,
> And we fell also down; but for no sin it was,
> And we did not at all assent to his foul injustice,
> But solely to show our Lord's sweet might;
> Lest we be here in sorrow anon; and we are in joy enough,
> And sometimes our sweet Lord's might we see,
> And through the earth we fly, and through the air also.'[80]

Although the association between birds and fairies was a specifically Irish one, in this English version it seems to be implied that the neutral angels have become the fairies, or at least morally neutral sublunary spirits of some kind ('through the earth we fly, and through the air also'). Marcel Dando argued that the idea of the neutral angels – which would become the standard Irish rationalization of fairies within a Christian cosmology – originated in Ireland.[81] Jude Mackley overstates the case, however, in describing belief in neutral angels as a heresy;[82] the basis for this claim seems to be that the Church Father Origen, whose theological views were declared heretical, said that at the end of the world 'angels may become men or demons and again from the latter they may rise to be men or angels'.[83] But to hold that some angels remained neutral was not the same as claiming that angels and demons could ultimately change their moral character; the decision and punishment of the neutral angels might be irrevocable as well. It was an unsupported theological speculation rather than heresy per se, although it was condemned as an error by the University of Paris in 1398.[84]

The fact that belief in neutral angels was controversial may be indicated by its omission from several versions of the *Voyage*.[85] But the idea of neutral angels proved a popular literary device, and it eventually spread out from Ireland to the rest of Europe, featuring in Chrétien de Troyes's *Yvain*, Wolfram von Eschenbach's *Parzifal*, and, most famously of all, in

Figure 3.2 *The Fall of the Rebel Angels*, 1621, by Lucas Emil Vorsterman after Sir Peter Paul Rubens

Dante's *Inferno*, where in the 'vestibule of the futile' the poet meets 'that base band of angels who were neither rebellious nor faithful to God, but stood apart. The heavens drive them out, so as not to be less beautiful; and deep Hell does not receive them, lest the wicked have some glory over them'.[86] We find the idea in Jansen Enikel's popular *Weltchronik* (World Chronicle), written in around 1272,[87] and the idea of neutral angels appealed to magicians. Not only were such angels readily accessible on earth – for God cast them down to dwell alongside humans – but such a rationalization made it possible to perform ritual magic of dubious moral character without invoking demons.[88] In some cases, such as in the fifteenth-century Dutch and German versions of Brendan's *Voyage*, the neutral angels become the therianthropic and monstrous Walserands (hybrid creatures with human bodies and hands but the heads of boars and the necks of cranes and legs of dogs), who tell Brendan that God punished them with a monstrous appearance but banished them to an earthly paradise.[89] In other works, such as the Middle English translation of *Esclarmonde*, the neutral angels are said to govern the fairies but are distinguished from them.[90]

Perhaps the clearest medieval articulation of the idea that the neutral angels became the fairies can be found in the *South English Legendary*, composed in the 1270s or 1280s. The *Legendary* is a collection of verse hagiographies for various feast days – including the feasts of St Michael the Archangel, which required a digression into the events of the war in heaven. It is here that the *Legendary* introduces the neutral angels:

> Others that were somewhat for him [i.e. Lucifer] were in mistaken thought
> And nevertheless they held better with God, and he forbore sending them to hell;
> But they were also cast out of heaven, and are above the others
> And high under the firmament; and they see God's will,
> And so must be somewhat in sorrow, for till the world's end
> They must be here till Doomsday, and go again to heaven.
> And some are also in the earthly paradise,
> And in other places on earth to do their penance
> For their fault in heaven.

The reference here to 'earthly paradise' recalls St Brendan's Isle of Birds, while the idea that the neutral angels are 'high under the firmament' assimilates them to the Hellenistic *daimōnia*. The notion that the neutral angels will eventually return to heaven, but only at the Day of Judgement, links them with purgatory – the idea of a place of temporary punishment for those whose sins are venial rather than mortal (the links between purgatory and fairyland will be explored in the next chapter). The author of the *Legendary* is clear that the entities who cause nightmares and appear in the form of men and women to seduce humans are demons (the incubi); but there are also neutral angels who wander the earth, and these are identified with the elves:

> And often in the form of women, in many a solitary way
> I see of them great company both hop and play
> That are called elves, that often come to town

And by day are much in the wood, and by night upon the high down,
That are of the wretched spirits who were robbed of heaven;
And many of them at Doomsday shall yet come to rest.[91]

The neutral angels' capacity to be syncretized with godlings of pre-Christian origin was 'part of an alternative Christian belief system that was neither fully acknowledged nor condemned by medieval theologians'.[92] However, no Church Council said anything about demons or the fall of Lucifer until 1215, and belief in neutral angels is perhaps better described as an eccentric theological opinion rather than an alternative belief system. Pierre Gallais argued that fairies were not so far from angels in the medieval popular imagination (at least in France); they were less ethereal and closer to the earth and to the people than angels, and therefore the role of helpers and messengers assigned to the angels in the Bible was projected by the medieval French peasant onto fairies – a popular belief which the church had to tolerate.[93] In chapter 4, we will explore the ambiguous relationship between fairies and angels in Joan of Arc's home village of Domrémy.

But if neutral angels could be fairies, so too could demons who abandoned their evil natures and decided to be helpful towards humans. In his *Journey through Wales*, Gerald of Wales told the story of a priest who served a Danish archbishop very efficiently, until one day the priest made a rather strange admission, and told the archbishop:

> Before Jesus Christ was born in the flesh ... devils had great power over human beings; but when He came, this power was greatly diminished. They were dispersed, some here, some there, for they fled headlong from His presence. Some hurled themselves into the sea. Others hid in hollow trees and in the cracks of rocks. I remember that I myself jumped down a well.[94]

The priest, it turned out, was really a demon who had decided to become helpful; and the story seems to furnish an origin story for the fairies, the spirits who dwell 'in hollow trees and in the cracks of rocks', and in wells. They are demons who, having been terrible and fearful before the time of Christ, became diminished in the Christian era – a curious medieval parallel to the later idea that fairies were somehow diminished gods. The German monk Caesarius of Heisterbach (1180–1240) was fascinated by these helpful demons, and gave a series of examples of them in his *Dialogus*. Caesarius explained that when Lucifer rebelled against God, 'it is said that certain ones [i.e. angels] simply consented to join the proud ones with Lucifer against God, these certain ones fell with the rest, but they are less evil, and they do less harm to men'.[95] These, then, are not the neutral angels who might one day be redeemed, but rather demons who, without any hope of heaven, nevertheless choose to help rather than tempt human beings.

In one tale, a knight discovers that the spirit who has been helping him is a demon, and realizes he cannot in conscience continue receiving assistance from an evil spirit; so he gives the demon five silver coins which the spirit returns, asking the knight to buy a bell that will call the faithful to divine service. The implication seems to be that for the demon, who is beyond the possibility of salvation, it still remains possible for him to contribute to the salvation of human beings. Another of Caesarius's exempla concerns a knight called Everhard who received a demon's assistance to obtain a divorce from Rome; the demon then took Everhard on a pilgrimage to Jerusalem and, on his return, helped him save a man from being set upon by robbers in a wood.[96]

If it was not beyond the bounds of possibility to believe that demons could try to be good, and choose to help humans, then attempts to demonize fairies were moot; the speculations of authors such as Gerald and Caesarius undermined the effectiveness of demonization before it had even begun, by suggesting that even if fairies were demons, demons were not always bad. Furthermore, other authors such as Gervase of Tilbury admitted that fairies were demons, but drew a distinction between these minor demons and the demons of hell; they were 'those who sided with the devil but whose pride was less grievous' and accordingly they were 'reserved to provide phantoms of this nature to punish humankind'.[97] If fairies as godlings had confounded demonization by missionaries, then as 'demonlings' they also confounded the demonologists because they seemed consistently less terrifying, less powerful, and less disembodied than demons ought to be.

From Parcae to fairies

While the origin of the fairies as beings of folklore is polyvalent and complex, there seems little doubt that the word 'fairy' itself emerges from one particular tradition rooted in late antique popular religion in the former Western Roman Empire. That tradition is the survival, in an attenuated form, of the Roman Parcae as goddesses of destiny. The Parcae were the Roman equivalent of the Moirai of ancient Greece: three sisters who weave the fates of human beings. The Parcae were sometimes known as the *fata* (literally 'the things said'), which might mean they were originally personifications of the verbal decrees (i.e. *fata*) of the gods, but later became personified as beings in their own right.[98] However, the widespread recurrence of the theme of three supernatural women determining human destiny across multiple cultures (such as the Greek Moirai, the Scandinavian Norns, the Scottish Wyrd Sisters, and the Baltic Laimės) might suggest that the three sisters are a fundamental feature of Indo-European mythology.[99]

It seems that in the wreckage of pre-Christian Gaulish religion, the Parcae became conflated with the Deae Matres (divine mothers) whose cult originated in the Rhineland area and became popular throughout Gaul and Britain.[100] While no myths survive explaining the function of the Deae Matres, their frequent appearance in association with the cornucopia suggests they were goddesses of fertility and abundance. However, the Parcae as *fata* also became conflated with the nymphs as *fatuae* or 'fate-speakers',[101] as multiple different categories of supernatural women who formerly had different functions came to be conflated, perhaps under the pressure of Christian attempts to demonize the pre-Christian supernatural world. The *Decretum* of Burchard of Worms (d. 1025), a penitential (compendium of ecclesiastical offences and corresponding penalties) compiled in the early eleventh century, preserves a valuable record of this hotchpotch of popular beliefs in the early medieval Rhineland. Burchard's *Decretum* takes the form of a series of questions to be posed to penitents by a priest in the confessional:

> Have you believed what some are wont to believe, either that those who are commonly called the Fates exist, or that they can do that which they are believed to do? That is, that while any person is being born, they are able

even then to determine his life to what they wish, so that no matter what the person wants, he can be transformed into a wolf, that which the vulgar call a werewolf, or into any other shape. . . . Have you believed what some are wont to believe, that there are women of the wilds, called 'the sylvan ones' who they say are in bodily form, and when they wish to show themselves to their lovers and, they say, have taken delight with these, and then when they wish to depart and vanish? . . . Have you done as some women are wont to do at certain times of the year? That is, have you prepared the table in your house and set on the table your food and drink, with three knives, that if those three sisters whom past generations and old-time foolishness called the Fates should come they may take refreshment there; and have you taken away the power and name of the Divine Piety and handed it over to the devil, so, I say, as to believe that those whom you call 'the sisters' can do or avail aught for you either now or in the future?[102]

The first point to note about Burchard's *Decretum* is that it is focussed on erroneous belief – in other words, Burchard considered it a sin to *believe* in the Parcae/Fates, not to consort with them. This is the distinction famously made in the well-known *Canon episcopi* first recorded in 906 by Regino of Prüm (and also part of Burchard's text) which made clear the unreality of witchcraft and the night-flights of witches, and imposed penalties for belief in witchcraft rather than for witchcraft itself – in stark contrast to the late medieval church's approach to the subject. In the same way, while later medieval churchmen expressed concerns about fairy belief on the grounds that fairies were probably deceitful demons, Burchard anticipated the scepticism of the late seventeenth century insofar as he does not seem to have believed in these beings at all.

The link drawn by Burchard between the Fates and lycanthropy, which seems to be made nowhere else in this way, is interesting when considered against the background of the association between fairies and therianthropy – and its possible suggestions of animism – discussed in chapter 1 above. But there is insufficient detail in the text for us to be certain that we are dealing here with vestiges of some sort of shamanic practice. Burchard was also the first writer, it seems, to link the Parcae to 'sylvan ones' who seduce men in wild places – the earliest appearance of the erotic female fairy. Some sort of elision of the Parcae with sexually predatory Lamia-like beings, not present in antiquity, seems to have occurred in the early Middle Ages.[103]

By the twelfth century, John of Salisbury was reporting a belief that *lamiae* ate stolen infants at gatherings of those who flew with 'the Queen of the Night', before the goddess took pity on them, making them whole again and returning them to their cradles.[104] Laurence Harf-Lancner argued that fairies of destiny (descended from the Roman Parcae) should be distinguished from the 'Melusinian' fairy, or fairy lover.[105] The erotic fairy seducer or incubus, who could be either male or female, has a complex origin in its own right, and its elision with fairies of destiny in the *Decretum* was central to the formation of the figure of the medieval fairy.[106] The incubus combined elements of belief in seductive and predatory nature spirits, the Watchers of Genesis 6, the speculations of Augustine and other Church Fathers, and the 'night hag' experienced by people suffering from sleep paralysis.[107]

Again, it seems we are here glimpsing a new synthesis of formerly distinct beliefs in the wreckage of the pagan world. Burchard's third question suggests that people did not simply believe in the Fates but also expected to meet them, or to receive a visitation of some kind, since they laid a table for them. It is conceivable that the ritual meal prepared for the Parcae that Burchard records here was some sort of substitute for sacrificial rites, since these had long since been outlawed by the church and their practice forgotten. On this reading, a special meal took the place of sacrifice, with the domestic table standing in for the altars of former days. Yet the Parcae also underwent transformations in this period, and did not simply remain the deities of fate they had been in the Roman era; they came to be associated with the underworld and therefore became chthonic beings – perhaps facilitating the use of 'fairy' as a term for earth-dwelling spirits.[108]

It is possible that something like the beliefs described by Burchard, in which women believed they participated in ecstatic journeys with supernatural beings, survived in Sicily and the Balkans.[109] Evidence from the eighteenth century shows that 'fairy societies' who claimed to combat witches under the patronage of 'St Ilona' (really the Fairy Queen Tündér Ilona) existed in the Balkans, Hungary, and Romania, and they may have been much older.[110] Indeed, according to one interpretation, the nereid and vila traditions of Greece and Slavic Europe, in which fairies appear as exclusively female societies of supernatural women led by a queen (sometimes said to be an immortal sister of Alexander the Great[111]) are a relic of late antique / early medieval Diana cults.[112] However, while this might make sense for Greece, it is unclear how the Slavic world as a whole (which was largely outside the Roman Empire) came to adopt lingering relics of pre-Christian Graeco-Roman cults. While the Byzantine historian Procopius wrote of the Slavs' reverence for nymphs as early as the sixth century,[113] the earliest specific references to vilas can be found in Russia in confessional books of the eleventh and twelfth centuries, as well as in an Old Bulgarian manuscript of the thirteenth century; but there is little detailed information on the fairies of the Slavic world until the systematic folklore collection of the nineteenth century.[114]

Noel Williams argued that in the midst of all this post-pagan confusion, a central and abiding concept became associated with the supernatural women called *fata* or *fatae* (and later *fées* and fairies): that of 'fatedness', 'a quality in the world which can control and direct the actions of humanity, and hence is more powerful than humanity'.[115] However, the medieval Latin word *fatatus* (fated) expressed rather more than notions of fatalism and inevitability – it could also mean 'haunted' or 'enchanted',[116] a richness of meaning still preserved in the Scots word 'fey' (from Old English *faege*), which can describe someone destined or accursed and – often – possessed of some sort of strange enchantment or power.[117] There is a semantic analogy to be drawn, perhaps, with the Old English word *wyrd*, which referred to both destiny and strange supernatural power – hence the modern English 'weird'. A similar analogy could be drawn with the Spanish word *duende*, which has the double meaning of a fairy-like supernatural being and an indefinable quality of earthy authenticity and emotional ecstasy.[118] The Latin word *fatalitas* (fatedness, enchantment) seems to have become *faierie* in Old French, which referred not just to a state of enchantment but also to fairyland, a realm of enchantment. It was this word, for whatever reason, that the English language eventually adopted (rather than the singular 'fay') as a replacement for 'elf' in the late Middle Ages – a development that will be examined in chapter 4 below.[119]

An irony of penitentials such as Burchard's *Decretum* is that, by trying to make sense of popular superstitions through the lens of ancient deities like the Parcae, they may have contributed to the perpetuation of such beliefs. Penitentials were copied and recopied, and confessors continued to ask detailed questions in the confessional about illicit beliefs; yet the terms in which those questions were asked must surely have conditioned people's responses to some degree. If penitents interpreted their own experiences in such a way that they answered in the affirmative to the confessors' enquiries, this created a feedback loop of confirmation for confessors, reassuring them that people continued to venerate the Parcae.[120]

If processes of early medieval synthesis somehow merged godlings of destiny with supernatural lovers, they also set up an association between fairies and children that endures to the present day, albeit in a very different form. In one sense, it is logical that goddesses of destiny such as the Parcae should be particularly concerned with infants because they determined and decided a person's destiny at birth; and the prevalence of infant mortality in the early medieval world rendered it probable that the Parcae would choose to cut the thread of life sooner rather than later. It makes sense, therefore, that goddesses of destiny might have lingered as menacing rather than comforting presences around the cradle.

But the involvement of fairies with children was far more extensive than simply pronouncing destinies, like the fairy godmother of fairy tale. Fairies became, at an early date, stealers of infants, as Lamia had been before them. Yet the identity of supernatural child-stealers was not fixed; in medieval Greece, it was the nereids who stole infants, while in Scandinavia it could be trolls or elves,[121] and in medieval Brittany it was the fauns. Indeed, child-stealing and the changeling myth seem to be a generic fear that happens to have been imposed on the fairies, rather than a core characteristic of who the fairies were,[122] and in some cultures (such as Lithuania), the changeling (*laumiukas*) is indistinguishable from a normal human child but will eventually run off into the woods and join the laumės.[123]

The focus of this chapter has been on one strand of medieval fairy traditions: the idea of fairies as a race of monstrous humans or human-like beings (perhaps of angelic or demonic origin). While it is perilous to attempt to impose exact chronologies on fairy belief, it was this perception of fairies – as a hidden community of otherworlders whose existence was ordained by God as part of some mysterious divine purpose – that largely predominated in the early Middle Ages and into the thirteenth century. Accounts of 'fairies' from this period lacked 'any sense of a coherent belief system to contain and explain the stories being repeated by the authors'.[124]

This is true at one level; but at another level, there *was* a belief that could account for such encounters, and that was belief in the inscrutable wisdom of God and the variety and unlimited wonder of his creation. Carl Watkins has argued that the late twelfth and early thirteenth centuries were a period when 'wonder stories' were allowed to challenge accepted cosmologies, leading to a more open-ended conception of God's creation.[125] As Jeremy Harte says of Walter Map, 'there is no moral, it is all table talk rounded off with "and aren't the works of the Lord marvellous"'.[126] From the mid thirteenth century onwards, however, perceptions of fairies began to shift. As Watkins puts it, 'genre boundaries hardened once more', and 'the wondrous diminished'.[127] Fairies became more heavily demonized as churchmen spent more time rationalizing them theologically, rather than just telling occasional anecdotes about them, and fairies become more intensely associated with magic. Furthermore, the idea of a fairy realm, with rulers and hierarchies, began to come into focus, and fairies became a major theme of medieval literature. It is to these late medieval developments that we now turn.

FOUR

Founding fairyland: the late Middle Ages

In 1536, on the eve of the Reformation in Wales, a Welsh scribe wrote a life of the seventh-century saint Collen. St Collen was in his hermit's cell one day when he heard two men talking about the king of Annwn (the Welsh underworld) and of the fairies, Gwyn ap Nudd. When Collen advised the men that the fairies were nothing more than demons, they warned the hermit he would soon see Gwyn himself; and accordingly, a messenger of the otherworld was soon hammering on Collen's door, commanding him to come and meet Gwyn ap Nudd on the nearby hill (Glastonbury Tor, in some versions of the story) by midday. Collen refused, but the persistent messenger kept coming back and eventually, taking some holy water, the saint set out for the hill:

> On reaching the place, Collen beheld there the most beautiful castle that he had ever seen, with the best-appointed troops; a great number of musicians with all manner of instruments; horses with young men riding them; handsome, sprightly maidens, and everything that became the court of a sumptuous king. When Collen entered, he found the king sitting in a chair of gold. Collen was welcomed by him, and asked to seat himself at the table to eat, adding that beside what he saw thereon, he should have the rarest of all dainties, and plenty of every kind of drink. Collen said, 'I will not eat the tree-leaves.' 'Hast thou ever', asked the king, 'seen men better dressed than these in red and blue?' Collen said, 'Their dress is good enough, for such kind as it is.' 'What kind is that?' asked the king. Collen said that the red on the one side meant burning, and the other, cold. Then he sprinkled holy water over them, and they all vanished, leaving behind them nothing but green tumps.[1]

This story, written at the close of the British Middle Ages, contains most of the characteristic elements of late medieval fairy belief. It makes a concerted attempt to demonize the fairies, portraying them as adversaries of a saint, as demons, and as suffering the pains of hell. It portrays the fairies as hierarchical, having a king (in this case, Gwyn ap Nudd), and implies the existence of a fairy realm (here identified with Annwn). It associates fairies with hills and mounds, and with glamour – the ability to enchant and transfigure the appearance of ordinary things. It portrays the fairies as beautiful and handsome, and references the oft-repeated folkloric theme of the danger to mortals of partaking in fairy food and drink.

The theme of this chapter is the development of fairy lore from the mid thirteenth century onwards. It is a period when we have rich evidence from Britain, Ireland, France, and Scandinavia, where there were established traditions of writing about fairies. The later medieval period, between around 1250 and the advent of the Reformation in the 1530s, was characterized by the production of literature about fairies, by greater anxiety about fairy belief among churchmen, and by the development of more detailed ideas about fairy societies.

Furthermore, it was in this period that the association between fairies and magic became more clearly articulated – both the idea that fairies were in possession of magical powers, and the notion that they might (given the right conditions) share these magical powers with human beings. However, it was also in the late medieval period that the idea that the fairies were departing (or already gone) first emerges – a theme that remains part of fairy lore to the present day. And it was in the late medieval period that the various confused ideas about godlings, otherworlders, and monstrous peoples that existed in the early Middle Ages began to coalesce into the recognizable figure of the modern fairy, through a complex synthesis of literary, religious, and folkloric ideas in several different countries.

Demonization, undemonization, and degradation

As we have seen in the foregoing chapters, the binary division of spirit-beings into benign angels and evil demons was the standard Christian approach to the cosmos from the Church Fathers onwards, even if there were notable exceptions to this trend such as the survival of the 'god-peoples' in early medieval Ireland and belief in neutral angels and benign demons. Yet these were marginal phenomena; on the whole, medieval Christianity – or, at least, the medieval institutional church – was liable to treat any unsanctified being of folk belief as demonic. This does not mean, of course, that such beings were treated as demonic or evil at the level of popular Christianity; nor does it mean that theologians did not draw distinctions between different kinds of demons. Furthermore, merely turning a being of folk belief into a demon, and convincing people that it was a demon, did not necessarily result in people fearing that demon; as Jeremy Harte has shown, the devil of English folklore was usually a very different being from the devil of theology,[2] and the same goes for the portrayal of Velnias (the pre-Christian god identified with the devil) in Baltic folklore, who was often a helper of the poor and oppressed.[3]

The process of 'demonization' (the refiguring of characters of folk belief as demons) is one of the most important for understanding the formation of fairy lore. Yet it was by no means a straightforward one-way process in which Christianity took beings of pre-Christian belief and discredited them. In its simplest form, demonization accompanied a conversion event and involved convincing people that the gods they had hitherto been worshipping were actually demons who had tricked their ancestors into offering sacrifice, thereby establishing their hold over an entire society as false gods.

Demonization became fraught with difficulty, however, when it ran up against beings who did not obviously fit the pattern of the biblical gods of the Canaanites denounced by the Old Testament prophets or the Graeco-Roman deities denounced by St Paul and the Church Fathers. If godlings, minor spirits of nature or of the home, were identified as demons, this raised more questions than it answered. Why were these demons so lacking in power in comparison to those who had persuaded people to worship them as false gods? If demons were disembodied beings, why did people so often encounter these minor godlings as physical beings who consumed food, had sex, and had children and families? And, most disturbingly of all, was there a possibility that demonizing such minor beings (who showed no sign of being banished from folk belief) actually risked *elevating* their status to equality with the banished gods?

It is noteworthy, in this regard, that the earliest ecclesiastical approaches to fairy belief (from Burchard of Worms onwards) tended to deny the fairies' existence altogether;[4] not because an eleventh-century churchman such as Burchard was *certain* that fairies did not exist (in the same way as an Enlightenment clerical *philosophe* might have been certain), but because Burchard seems to have understood that denouncing fairies as demons was counterproductive. The idea that demonization is a counterproductive missionary strategy, and actually helps *preserve* pre-Christian beliefs, has been explored by the sociologist of religion Joel Robbins,[5] as well as by David Frankfurter in the context of contemporary Sri Lanka and by Pasi Enges in the context of nineteenth-century Sápmi, among others.[6] Demons are objects of religious awe, as well as fear; demonization reinforces the reality of the existence of such beings, placing them in a different relation to the believer, but still an important one. Since demons in Christianity are fallen angels and beings of terrifying power, the assertion that animistic spirits are demons might have the effect of elevating them from their former status; and if missionaries are unable to provide satisfying narratives for the newly demonized gods and spirits, it is likely that people will supply their own in which demonized folk spirits are perhaps not as evil as the missionaries intended them to be.

It is here that we encounter a frustrating 'chicken and egg' question: does the portrayal of demons and the devil as sympathetic or ambivalent beings in folklore reflect ordinary people's assessment of demons as less threatening than the clergy considered them? Or does it reflect the imposition of a 'demonic' identity on folkloric beings who had not previously been demons? In Harte's view, this question is essentially unanswerable; all we can do is say that people told an ever-shifting repertoire of stories about folk spirits, in some of which the spirits were good, in some of which they were bad, and in some of which they were morally ambivalent.[7]

However, it is worth noting that the complexity of the church's own tradition with regard to engagement with godlings undermined efforts at demonization. As we have seen, the Church Fathers were not unanimous in the view that godlings were demons (in the sense of fallen angels banished to hell), and even Augustine considered godlings such as fauns to belong to a different, more earthly variety of demons, while the story of the giants in Genesis 6 continued to lend credibility to the idea that spirit-beings could have sex with humans.

In the Scholastic philosophy of the thirteenth century, however, such ambiguities were increasingly unacceptable. Under the influence of the

Aristotelian impulse to introduce clear distinctions between different kinds of creature, the Scholastics sought unambiguous definitions of what counted as human, angelic, and demonic. Although the philosophical impetus for this strict taxonomic approach to creation was Aristotelian, the impetus for a renewed focus on demonology was theological. The Catholic church's confrontation with unorthodox beliefs about the devil during the Albigensian Crusades led to a dogmatic definition of the devil's status as a fallen angel at the Fourth Lateran Council (1215) – the first time the church had ever pronounced officially on who or what the devil was (although there were, of course, long-established traditions of scriptural interpretation on this). If the devil was a fallen angel, that implied that the rest of the demons were too – and if demons had been angels, then they were subject to the metaphysical speculations of the Scholastic angelologists.

Accordingly, older ideas about neutral angels and benign demons were squeezed out of the ambit of acceptable orthodox Christian belief,[8] and speculations about monstrous races as an explanation for the godlings of the ancient world similarly began to break down. The Scholastic philosopher William of Auvergne (d. 1249) was puzzled, therefore, by an account of a faun killed by arrows during a battle, since he considered all beings of that kind to be immortal.[9] Elaborate naturalistic explanations about the condensation of air had to be concocted to explain the apparent physicality of beings who, according to the philosophers, were by nature bodiless and discarnate. Yet, paradoxically, concern about the threat of incubi (demons who had sex with human beings) only grew in the later Middle Ages.[10] The church was caught in a difficult position between doctrine and folklore, teaching a philosophically sophisticated doctrine of demonology that de-emphasized demonic physicality, yet simultaneously obliged to deal with penitents who confessed to having sex with incubi – and obliged to take such confessions seriously, on account of Genesis 6. Furthermore, until Thomas Aquinas elaborated a theory of how disembodied demons could inseminate women, it was generally assumed that the demons who did this belonged to a specific, more earthly category of fallen angel – in other words, fairies.[11] The exchange between folklore and theology was a two-way one, and demonology was all too easily 'infiltrated by vernacular conceptions of fairyland'.[12]

As Richard Firth Green has demonstrated, once we accept that most accounts of encounters with incubi from the later Middle Ages were fairy encounters, and that *incubus* was usually a synonym for fairy,[13] we are able to unlock a rich seam of medieval fairy lore. But while demonization may have produced a folklore of its own, I have also argued for the existence of a parallel or subsequent process of 'undemonization', whereby folklore undermined ecclesiastical efforts to demonize pre-Christian beings by giving them a morally ambivalent character. In folk tale, the devil and demons can become figures of fun and even adventure; familiarity breeds contempt, and the more preachers spoke about demons and the more artists portrayed them on the walls of churches, the less afraid of them some people became. Indeed, on the principle that there is no such thing as bad publicity, the preachers may simply have been advertising the seductive powers of demons to an adventurous minority who might receive such warnings as an invitation to explore the demonic world, via ritual magic.[14] As John Bromyard noted in the mid fourteenth century, people sometimes actively resisted attempts to prohibit fairy magic, such as the parishioners who denied they had received their rituals for finding stolen property from the devil, but had them from 'the fair folk' (*pulchrum populum*).[15]

Folk culture's 'undemonization' of beings the church sought to discredit might also be accompanied by a process of 're-personification', whereby communities fashioned new supernatural entities according to need even in the Christian era.[16] Hutton has shown that the figure of 'Mother Earth' developed in this way in the Middle Ages,[17] rendering unnecessary the often fruitless search for pagan antecedents for such beings. The philosophical speculations of Scholastics were simply too ethereal to matter much to ordinary Christians in the Middle Ages, for whom it made much more sense that demons would be physical beings – and if demonization succeeded at all, it was usually by transforming formerly benign or ambivalent beings into monstrous bogeys. Thus, in the Baltic region, which was Christianized especially late, the 'Mother of Rye' (*Rugių Boba*) who had been invoked as a goddess in the sixteenth century was, by the nineteenth century, a hideous hag who lurked in the rye fields and stole children,[18] and the beautiful laumės (the female fairies of the Baltic) had come to be portrayed as shapeshifting hags with hens' feet.[19]

Yet bogeys were corporeal monsters who evoked fear (and often provided useful 'scarelore' that discouraged children from risky behaviour), not the demons of theology. This was degradation rather than demonization, and such degradation was not necessarily accompanied by ideas of absolute evil. The old gods were, rather, banished to the margins, like the degraded Baltic deities who live in forest shacks in some nineteenth-century folklore,[20] or the version of Manannán mac Lir who becomes a wandering conjurer in sixteenth-century Irish tales.[21] And when it came to the fairies, degradation was hardly a threat for beings who already existed at the bottom of the ontological pecking order of divinities. Fairies proved to be the scum at the bottom of the cultural barrel that the disinfectant of demonization could never quite succeed in clearing out – because the fairies were too different from the pagan gods who were the primary targets of Christianization. Christianity itself was conflicted in the relative importance it assigned to doctrine and folklore – and, after all, the fairies may have emerged anew in a Christian context anyway.

Perhaps the best-known attempt to demonize fairies in late medieval Europe, and certainly the most politically charged, took place at the trial of Joan of Arc before the inquisitor Pierre Cauchon at Rouen in 1431. The English and Burgundians were intent on tracing Joan's apparent supernatural powers to a demonic rather than a divine source, and accordingly Joan was questioned intensely about a beech tree next to a healing well on the lands of the Château de Bourlément, known as the Tree of the Fairies (*arbre des fées*), Tree of the Ladies, or 'Le Beau Mai' (the beautiful May). On the fourth Sunday of Lent, Laetare Sunday, it was traditional for the young unmarried women of Domrémy to hang garlands of flowers on the tree (figure 4.1). Cauchon sent investigators to Domrémy in an effort to establish whether the ceremonies associated with the tree were superstitious or, indeed, diabolical. Joan was questioned about whether she heard the voices she claimed to be those of angels and saints under the tree, which she denied, testifying instead that she heard them in the fields when the church bells rang. She denied ever having seen fairies under the tree, 'as far as she knew', although her godmother claimed to have seen them. She knew nothing of the claimed healing properties of the well, she said, and although she had hung garlands on the tree as a child she had done so in honour of the Virgin Mary, Notre Dame de Domrémy. The cult of the tree of Domrémy was entangled, therefore, with Marian devo-

Figure 4.1 'In Domrémy, the Tree of the Ladies', 1860
Source: Yolanda Perera Sánchez / Alamy Stock Photo. Used with permission

tion in a way that some sites in England, such as Evesham and Woolpit, may also have mingled fairy lore with popular Marian piety.[22]

Nevertheless, Joan confessed that she had sometimes heard her voices under the tree – but that they had never come *from* the tree. She was questioned about whether her godmother claimed to be a wisewoman, recalling the usual claims of deriving some sort of power from the fairies, made by people who had seen them. Ironically, the cult of the tree and well of Domrémy suffered suppression not when Joan of Arc was executed, but when she was rehabilitated by the church twenty-five years after her death – for it was then even more important to avoid any suspicion of superstition associated with the site, and accordingly Gospel readings by the local priest replaced the old devotions, while local people were encouraged to deny their visits to the holy well.[23]

However, while the case of the tree of Domrémy illustrates how thoroughly the late medieval church *could* demonize fairies and the places associated with them, it is important to bear in mind that such thoroughgoing demonization rarely took place. The tiny number of instances of fairy belief that came to the attention of English church courts leave one wondering how many people must have carried on commerce with the fairies without ever drawing the notice of the authorities. Yet it is striking that the inquisitors in Joan's trial proceeded on the assumption that the fairies who lived under the tree of Domrémy were real; there was no hint of the ecclesiastical scepticism of the earlier Middle Ages.

Fairies and literature

Characters identified as *fées* first emerged in French vernacular romance literature of the twelfth century. Indeed, 'fairy' first emerged as a literary word.[24] The fairies of medieval romance are usually beautiful women in possession of magical powers, but the romances give no coherent account of who these fairies are, or even whether they are non-human supernatural beings or human sorceresses who have learnt to master *féerie* or enchantment, and are therefore *fées* by association.[25] Katharine Briggs thought that the fairies of the medieval romances began life as human enchantresses and only later turned into non-human fairies;[26] but it is difficult to be sure of this, and there is a danger that the 'fairies from literature' debate becomes another never-ending and unproductive chicken-and-egg debate in which there is insufficient evidence either way – that the enchantresses of romance are adaptations of non-human fairies or that the fairies of romance are adaptations of human enchantresses.[27] In the end, we are dealing here with creative fiction, where the narrative functions played by fairy characters were more significant than their ontological status or origins in folk tradition.

One of those narrative functions of literary fairies was to act as a *deus ex machina*; fairy magic helped to advance or resolve a story, and added an element of the wondrous without introducing theologically problematic beings such as pagan gods, angels, or demons. In the romance tradition, 'the fantastic took the place of the pagan marvellous', and fairies took the place of gods since magic required the intervention of supernatural beings who were preferably neither angels nor demons (the wizard Merlin, for example, has a special status as the hybrid offspring of a demon and a human mother).[28] Fairies also functioned as placeholders for other entities who might otherwise have rendered a story problematic. In the Middle English romance *Sir Orfeo* (*c.*1300), the role of Pluto is taken by the Fairy King. Likewise, Chaucer's Fairy King and Queen in *The Merchant's Tale* are named Pluto and Proserpina, while Morgan le Fay bears many characteristics of Circe and Medea.[29]

This 'fairyization' of the pre-Christian world could also be found in the landscape, as with the prehistoric offering stones in late medieval Sweden that became *älvkvarnar* (elf-mills).[30] Fairies were figures with the capacity to act somewhat like the deities of the ancient world, but they remained at arm's length from the contested realm of theology, as well as providing an outlet for classicizing impulses.[31] Ultimately, however, the literary fairy of medieval romance was an artefact of Christianization, reflecting a cultural forgetting of the pagan past. Yes, fairies avoided the controversial religious associations of pagan deities; but for most people they were also more familiar figures, and to declare that Proserpina was a fairy was more readily comprehensible than calling her a goddess.

Hutton has argued that by the middle of the thirteenth century there were three strands to British fairy belief: a tradition of elves (derived ultimately from the Anglo-Saxons) as harmful, yet also healing and seductive, entities; a literary tradition of beautiful, magical fairy women; and belief in human-like otherworlders that did not fit neatly into either of these traditions. By the end of the thirteenth century, efforts were under way to make sense of these beings, and thus the *South English Legendary* distinguished between evil, earthbound spirits who seduced men and women and brought nightmares, and the neutral angels who became the elves, seen dancing at night.[32] Robert of Gloucester (d. 1300) sought to make sense of the elves in his *Metrical Chronicle* partly by reference to folk belief and partly by reference to Hellenistic philosophy, identifying them simultaneously as the aerial daemons of the Greeks and as the elves who are seen in lonely places and seduce men and women by night:

> The clerks said that it is in philosophy found
> That there are in the air on high, far from the ground,
> A manner of spirits (*gostes*), 'wights' as it were,
> And men may often see them on earth in wild places;
> And often in men's form they come to women,

And often in women's form they come to men also
These that men call elves . . .³³

What remains unclear is the extent to which literary portrayals of fairies affected the shape of actual popular belief in them. Hutton believes it did, arguing that fairies crossed over from literature in a fairly short period between the thirteenth and fifteenth centuries in a kind of ostension – the manifestation and performance of literary themes in the form of actual belief.³⁴ Hutton's argument is based on the difference in character between the structured fairy belief of the late Middle Ages (at least in Britain) and the rather diffuse and confused ideas about otherworld beings found before around 1250.³⁵ That structured belief consisted, according to Hutton, of seven main elements:

1. Belief in a parallel world with human-like inhabitants with their own ruler and society, often in some ways superior to human society
2. Belief in the ability of otherworld beings to enter our world (and steal children from it), while humans can sometimes enter the otherworld realm
3. The belief that lakes, woods, hills, and artificial tumuli could be portals to the otherworld
4. Belief in supernatural women who dance in lonely places at night and can be abducted by mortal men, but will ultimately return to their own realm
5. An association between otherworld beings and the colour green
6. The belief that otherworld beings might bless humans who helped them, but might also torment humans by, for example, leading them astray at night
7. Belief in human-like creatures who come into people's homes and are either helpful or play tricks on the inhabitants³⁶

As we have already seen, some of these beliefs have ancient antecedents. There is certainly some truth to the contention that late medieval fairy belief was literary ostension; as we shall see, the idea of involving fairies in ritual magic was indeed ostension, and emerged from literature. Furthermore, the idea of a 'Fairy Queen' does seem to have crossed from literature into folk belief only in the fifteenth century.³⁷ But literary influence is not the only explanation for the greater systematization of fairy belief in the late medieval period, and Richard Firth Green emphasizes the influence of preaching and preachers' manuals that sought to demonize the fairies and, in doing so, more thoroughly systematized them. Fairyland, for example, bore a certain resemblance to late medieval ideas of purgatory.[38] Popular fairy belief was indeed under the constant influence of elite culture,[39] which affected and was in turn affected by folklore like the reflections in a hall of mirrors, but that influence cannot be characterized as mainly or exclusively *literary* in nature.

Just as vernacular literature transformed perceptions of fairies in France and Britain, so in late medieval Ireland the ongoing vernacular tradition of fantastical tales continued to develop ideas about the Tuatha Dé Danaan. For example, in the fifteenth century, Franciscan friars at Multyfarnham in Co. Westmeath first wrote down the story *The Children of Lir*, in which Aoife, the stepmother of Lir's children, transforms them into swans; the children remain swans for 900 years, at which time the monk Mochaomhóg breaks Aoife's spell and returns the children to a decrepit human form; he then baptizes them and they die.

The story is notable for the idea that the Tuatha Dé Danaan are (eventually) mortal; indeed, the children's own mother dies in childbirth. Furthermore, the story tells us that the Tuatha Dé can become Christians, but the story departs from simple euhemerism (refiguring the Tuatha Dé as humans) since the evil stepmother Aoife becomes 'a demon of the air'.[40] *The Children of Lir* thus continues the Irish tradition of holding in tension the question of whether the Tuatha Dé are human or non-human, mortals or gods.

An even later tale, *The Tale of the Kern in the Narrow Stripes*, simultaneously transforms the figure of Manannán mac Lir into a mysterious travelling conjurer and plants him squarely in the present day (or recent past). In the story, Hugh 'the Black' O'Donnell (d. 1537), son of Hugh 'the Red' O'Donnell, king of Tyrconnell, is feasting with his kerns[41] at Ballyshannon when a mysterious kern arrives wearing narrow stripes, a worn, ragged mantle, waterlogged shoes, and carrying his sword without a scabbard. Hugh initially tries to eject the kern but he charms the company with his angelic skill on the harp. However, he also causes havoc among the other kerns and later displays his otherworld powers, and at the end of the story we are told that he was 'Manannan mac Lir of the *tuatha dé danaan*, who was wont thus to ramble in the character of a prestidigitator, of a professor in divers arts, of one that on all and sundry played off tricks of wizardry.'[42] The capacity of the sí and Tuatha Dé to break into current events was characteristic of medieval Irish literature; in 1317, according to *The Triumphs of Turlough*, Donchad O'Brien was riding to battle when he ran into Bronach of Burren of the Tuatha Dé Danaan, who forewarned him of his death.[43] However, the appearance of such elements might be accounted for by the fact that Irish bards enjoyed playing with their own contemporaries as literary characters (as Dante did) rather than, like the authors of romance, setting their tales in fantasy otherworlds. The elements of the fantastical thus seem to break in upon the 'real' world in Irish literature.

Lords and ladies: the rise of a hierarchical fairyland

As we have seen, the idea that there were rulers in otherworld realms was not absent from earlier medieval accounts – we might think of King Iubdan of the leprechauns, the faun-like Fairy King encountered by King Herla in Walter Map's story, and the tiny king of fairyland in the story Gerald of Wales received from the priest Elidyr. However, although Irish mythology portrayed the sí or Tuatha Dé as otherworld *peoples*, there was no medieval Irish tradition of a single otherworld realm accessed via the mounds or ruled over by a single king.[44] But, just as various miscellaneous otherworld beings began to coalesce into elves or fairies in the later Middle Ages, so the disparate otherworlds that might be accessed via individual mounds and underground tunnels began to coalesce into a single coherent otherworld. For a hierarchical society, that meant it was virtually inevitable the otherworld should be conceived of as a kingdom ruled over by a king and queen. But the Fairy King and the Fairy Queen, who had become familiar figures (at least in Britain) by the early modern period, have rather different origins.

Hutton has argued that the idea of fairy monarchs emerged only at the end of the thirteenth century,[45] which is not quite true; but Hutton is no doubt correct in his contention that the popularity of romance literature and its recursive influence on folklore did cement the idea of rulers of fairyland. Although the Fairy King appears in English literary works such as the romance *Sir Orfeo*, Angana Moitra has argued convincingly that he is an essentially 'Celtic' figure – or, more precisely, a British one, since it is in Welsh and Breton contexts that we first encounter the idea of a king of Annwn (the Welsh underworld/otherworld). *Sir Orfeo*, in which the Fairy King takes on the role of Pluto in the Orpheus and Eurydice myth, was based on a now lost thirteenth-century Breton *lai* about Orpheus; but the idea of an otherworld ruled over by a king is at least as old as the twelfth century in Welsh tradition, and probably much older.[46]

In the Welsh tale *Culhwch and Olwen*, which probably dates from the twelfth century,[47] Gwyn ap Nudd is appointed to rule over Annwn – which is ostensibly a Welsh-inflected version of hell, but also has much earlier antecedents that apparently stretch back to pre-Christian Romano-Celtic religion.[48] Furthermore, Gwyn ap Nudd is not an analogue to Satan, so Annwn is a much more ambiguous space than the Christian hell. For Moitra, the Fairy King is best understood as a religiously 'creolized' entity who emerges from a combination of Pluto/Hades and Satan, the ruler of the Christian hell, but is in truth neither Pluto nor Satan but a wholly new figure.[49] The figure of the Fairy King underwent a process of 'cultural translation' between antiquity and the Middle Ages;[50] in other words, the originally 'Celtic' figure of a ruler of Annwn became classicized as a functional analogue to Pluto, but also began to replace Pluto in medieval narratives because a fairy character was more suitable to the literary register of vernacular romance than a pagan god.[51] In other words, the Fairy King was created by the demands of narrative.

If the origins of the Fairy King lie in Welsh folklore, the origins of the Fairy Queen can be found in romance literature, where powerful female fays were a staple. The most prominent of these was Morgan le Fay, who according to Geoffrey of Monmouth ruled an island paradise called the Isle of Apples or Fortunate Island (perhaps a garbled reference to Isidore of Seville's description of the Canary Islands). By the late twelfth century, Morgan had begun to take on the sinister characteristics that would later make her an adversary to King Arthur and Merlin, but she was the first supernatural otherworld woman portrayed as a ruler in medieval European tradition. Hutton has argued, however, that a fairy queen requires a coherently defined fairyland, and that it was not until around 1300 that the idea of a fairy realm clearly emerged in romances such as *Sir Orfeo*, where fairyland was a more pleasant version of the ancient

Figure 4.2 *Prince Arthur and the Fairy Queen*, by Henry Fuseli, *c*.1788

Greek underworld. The earliest romance to portray a queen rather than a king ruling over fairyland was *Artus de Bretagne* (likewise *c*.1300); here Proserpine is identified as the Fairy Queen in the same way *Sir Orfeo* had identified Pluto as the Fairy King.[52]

According to Hutton, it was Chaucer who first referred to '*the* Fairy Queen' (with the definite article), and thereafter the idea of the Fairy Queen spread rapidly through English and Lowland Scottish society (figure 4.2).[53] The figures of the fairy monarchs were sufficiently well known by the fifteenth century for English rebels to style themselves the King and Queen of the Fairies[54] – in part, surely, as a joke, yet also drawing upon genuine ideas of otherworld authority. Then, in the fifteenth-century Scottish romance *Thomas of Erceldoune*, we encounter for the first time the idea, which became a staple of Scottish fairy lore, that the Fairy Queen holds fairyland 'in fee' from Satan, as a result of which the devil occasionally takes an inhabitant of fairyland away to hell.[55] Clearly, this is an idea derived from medieval feudal service; the status of a fiefdom was usually independent in all respects apart from an agreed tribute, so the narrative device of fairyland as a fief of hell cleverly preserves fairyland as an independent realm while admitting that the fairies are outside the mercy of Christ. However, it does little to explain what the fairies are and where they originally came from.

If the Fairy King was a distinctively Welsh creation, the Fairy Queen was an English one who was rapidly adopted in Lowland Scotland. There is no evidence that such a construct was adopted in late medieval Ireland. But the Fairy Queen was not unique as a monarch of otherworld peoples; in Scandinavian tradition, Hacka was said to be queen of the trolls, and Hildur of the elves;[56] in the Netherlands, the queen of the elves was Vrouw Holle,[57] while in Galicia, Queen Lupa or Loba is said to rule the hosts of humans and wolves who roam by night.[58] Similarly, in Hungary, Tündér Ilona is sometimes the queen of the fairies,[59] not to mention the Queen of the Nereids in Greece and southern Italy.[60] Fairy queens are perhaps one of the most consistent features of fairy lore across cultures and regions, even if the Fairy Queen whose image has proved the most culturally enduring is English: Shakespeare's Titania.

Domestic helpers, poltergeists, and child-stealers

The association between fairies and the household and family is complex and fraught with ambiguity, since fairies can be both domestic helpers and sources of chaos in the home – including the abduction of human infants and their replacement with fairy changelings. The tale of Malekin, recounted by the chronicler Ralph of Coggeshall, which supposedly took place at Dagworth Hall in Suffolk during the reign of Richard I (1189–99), reveals some of these paradoxes.

The children of Sir Osbern de Bradwelle began hearing the disembodied voice of a one-year-old child who asked to play with them. The invisible child called herself Malekin and said she lived with her mother and brother 'in a neighbouring manor', but clearly an invisible manor of the otherworld, since Malekin's mother beat her for talking with human beings. Malekin displayed supernatural knowledge and could talk in both English and Latin, and the family eventually got used to her. She discussed the Scriptures with the family's chaplain and could be felt as well as heard – although she was only seen once, by a maid who begged Malekin to show herself, as 'a very tiny infant, who was dressed in a kind of white tunic'. Malekin asked for and ate food from the household, and said that she and others of her kind remained invisible by wearing a magical hat. Yet Malekin was not herself a fairy, but rather a human infant who had been born in the village of Lavenham. Her mother took her into a field one day and left her while she ate with others, which was when her current otherworld family took her. She had been with them for seven years, and would stay with them seven years more before she returned to human form.[61]

Malekin is not exactly a domestic spirit (since she does not seem to have done anything helpful around the house), but she is a kind of benign poltergeist, as well as the consequence of an act of child-stealing: she is the spirit of a child taken by the fairies (although they are never named as such). Whether this makes Malekin herself a fairy is open to debate. Although Malekin has been with the fairies for seven years, she seems to remain at the age at which the fairies took her, although she is old beyond her years in her knowledge of languages and theology. Indeed, the story implies that Malekin, and perhaps her otherworld family as well, are Christians.

Very different from Malekin, but also present in the household, are Gervase of Tilbury's Portunes, who 'wear little patched coats, and if anything was to be done in the house, or burdensome work to be undertaken, they bind themselves to doing it, completing it more easily than any human'.[62] This tradition of domestic spirits is not found in Ireland, but it is present in England, Wales, and Lowland Scotland.[63] But there was often a danger that a domestic spirit could become malevolent; Gervase noted that in the south of France, invisible spirits called follets took up residence in people's houses and caused havoc – another early instance of the poltergeist.[64] Indeed, the poltergeist could be considered an inverted domestic spirit, who disrupts rather than helps in the household.[65]

Apart from the Malekin story, changeling narratives do not reappear in English tradition until 1519,[66] although child-stealing elves are mentioned in fifteenth-century mystery plays,[67] and there is earlier evidence of the harm fairies could do to children. For instance, at her ecclesiastical trial in 1499, Agnes Clerk confessed that she spoke too much to elves as a child, as a result of which 'her head and neck were twisted around backwards' and she needed assistance from a fairy healer.[68] The identity of the beings who abducted (and sometimes returned) children was fluid; in the thirteenth century, for example, the Dominican friar Étienne de Bourbon reported that fauns were believed to steal children and, if women brought their changelings to the forest and invoked the intercession of the 'dog saint' St Guinefort, the fauns might return the real child.[69] In the case of the changeling myth, it does seem that fairies served a merely functional purpose, standing in for other beings as those beings faded from popular belief or fairies became more prominent. This seems the most likely explanation for the late appearance of fairies in relation to child-stealing; it was not that people did not fear the replacement of infants with changelings, but that there were diverse traditions about which beings were responsible.

The departing and hidden fairies

In her book *The Vanishing People* (1978), Katharine Briggs noted that, in folklore, the fairies are 'always going, never gone'.[70] In other words, in traditional tales (or by the tellers of such tales), the fairies are often said to have departed, and to be a thing of the past. But at the same time, it turns out that people are still encountering the fairies. Indeed, the 'superannuation' of fairies – the sense that they somehow no longer belong to the present world, even if they are still encountered there – is arguably a key characteristic of the modern fairy. As Patrick Harpur put it, the idea that the fairies 'have been superseded or are extinct' is 'part of fairy belief itself'.[71] It is linked to the notion, explored earlier in the Introduction above, that fairies are fit only for children because adults ought to have outgrown them; today's fairy superannuation is the sense that the world itself has outgrown fairies.

The idea that Christianity somehow drove otherworld peoples to the margins was already present in early medieval Ireland, as we have seen in chapter 3; and it was consistent with the belief in monstrous peoples dwelling at the edges of the world. But in the late Middle Ages we encounter a rather more specific idea that the fairies are departing, rather than just the idea that their position is made awkward by the Christian faith. The best-known of all such statements is to be found in Chaucer's *Canterbury Tales*, where the Wife of Bath declares,

> In the old days, the days of King Arthur,
> . . .
> All of this land was full of magic then.
> And with her joyous company the elf-queen
> Danced many a time on many a green mead.
> That was the old belief, as I have read:
> I speak of many hundred years ago.
> But now elves can be seen by men no more,
> For now the Christian charity and prayers
> Of limiters and other saintly friars
> Who haunt each nook and corner, field and stream
> Thick as the motes of dust in a sunbeam,
> Blessing the bedrooms, kitchens, halls, and bowers,
> Cities and towns, castles and high towers,
> Villages, barns, cattle-sheds and dairies,
> Have seen to it that there are now no fairies.[72]

As it turns out, the Wife of Bath's preamble is a wry joke at the expense of friars, who she notes have taken the place of the elves in waylaying women under bushes – although, in an apparent reference to the sort of beliefs about the dangers of sex with elves expounded in the *South English Legendary*, Chaucer's character notes the friars will only take a woman's honour. Yet Chaucer's playful replacement of elves with friars does not mean people in Chaucer's time did not literally believe what the Wife of Bath describes: that the world of the past had been less saturated with the blessings and sacramentals of the Christian church, and therefore filled with elves. For many of Chaucer's readers would have believed in the reality of the Fairy Queen he mentions; the question was not so much whether fairies existed, but whether there were any of them around any more.

Chaucer seems to make quite explicit the connection between the theme of the departing fairies and the church's intensifying interest in banishing fairy belief in the late Middle Ages. Since demonization was not altogether successful when applied to fairies (as we have seen), the portrayal of fairies as essentially irrelevant to the present may have been an alternative strategy for the clergy. On the other hand, Chaucer does not say that the friars and 'limiters' are *deliberately* banishing fairies, and the process he is describing seems to be the 'deep Christianization' of late medieval English society – the permeation of every level of folk culture by a popular Christianity in which saints and angels had become more important than fairies, who faded into the background. The historical evidence suggests this is not true; people still dealt with the fairies in late medieval England. But perception also mattered; as we shall see in chapter 5 below, the association between fairy belief, rural ignorance, and social marginalization would intensify in the sixteenth century.

In Ireland, the aos sí and the Tuatha Dé Danaan disappeared in a very literal way in the late Middle Ages, as they ceased to be subjects of Irish literature. The transition of the sí and Tuatha Dé from vernacular Irish literature to folklore, and the transition from the sí to the Irish 'fairies' remains poorly understood. Lisa Bitel has suggested that fairies such as the leprechauns, *púcai*, and dullahan were latecomers to Ireland, replacing the ancient aos sí as dwellers in Ireland's prehistoric monuments and burial mounds, rather than developing from them.[73] As we saw in chapter 2 above, the dwarfs of medieval Irish tradition are a separate development from the sí, and we will see in chapter 8 below that, even in the twentieth century, experiences of the sí continued to differ from stereotyped encounters with the 'little people'. Indeed, late medieval Irish literature dealt directly with the theme of the dying out of Ireland's original otherworlders. At the end of the fifteenth-century story *The Children of Lir*, it is implied that the children's death marked the end of the Tuatha Dé, while their father Lir's *síd* lies overgrown and abandoned.[74]

English-speaking communities emerged in Ireland in the fourteenth and fifteenth centuries as the Hiberno-Norman aristocracy made the transition from Norman French to English, but these were confined to the Pale (a collection of counties around Dublin that were under the direct control of the English king as Lord of Ireland), and the position of English in medieval Ireland was always uncertain, since the 'English of Ireland' had a tendency to become Gaelicized in their language and customs. England ruled parts of Ireland via powerful Anglo-Norman lords such as the earls of Kildare, and it was only in the mid sixteenth century, in concert with attempts to impose the Reformation on Ireland, that the English Crown launched sustained, centrally directed military campaigns to subdue the Irish. Even then, the Irish language endured and even predominated for a long time, until its fairly rapid collapse in large swathes of rural Ireland in the nineteenth century as a consequence of depopulation through catastrophic famine and mass emigration, as well as the imposition of the English language. In the midst of all this, at some point, the word 'fairy' came to be adopted as the Hiberno-English term for the aos sí.[75]

There are signs that the Tuatha Dé were indeed undergoing degradation in late medieval Ireland. In a story composed in the 1500s, *The Tragic Deaths of the Children of Tuireann*, the society of the Tuatha Dé is portrayed as a degraded one of thugs and psychopaths, perhaps reflecting the chaos of early sixteenth-century Ireland where English occupation waxed and waned in campaigns of brutal violence and shifting alliances with Irish leaders.[76] And in *The Tale of the Kern in the Narrow Stripes*, Manannán mac Lir and his kind are said to have departed entirely (albeit very recently) from Ireland in a tale written, in all likelihood, in the lifetime of its protagonist Black Hugh O'Donnell: 'now at least [Manannán] is vanished from among us without leaving us more than the bare report; even as all other magicians and artists that ever have been are vanished, likewise the Fianna, and all classes of people that since that date have appeared or for all time shall appear'.[77] Yet while the Tuatha Dé are degraded (and even departed) in late medieval tales, they are not so diminished as to have become leprechauns, and it remains unclear exactly how the Tuatha Dé (or some of them, anyway) became 'the little people'.

Another variant on the theme of the departure of the fairies was their diminishment – which could mean not only their withdrawal from the world as most people experienced it, but also a literal dwindling in size. Although, as we have seen, the tradition of supernatural dwarfs and pygmies was always an aspect of fairy lore, the extreme 'miniaturization' of fairies to the size of flowers or insects was a literary theme that first emerged in Lowland Scotland in the poetry of Robert Henryson (fl. 1450–1500), a notary of Dunfermline. Henryson's whimsical poem *King Berdok* (i.e. burdock) imagined a Fairy King living inside a cabbage stalk in a world of miniature fairies,[78] and while *King Berdok* seems to have had no immediate direct influence on people's perception of fairies, the theme of miniature fairies would return in literature. In the long run, it would be these miniature or insectoid fairies who would come to define the internationally recognized cultural stereotype of the fairy.

In late medieval Iceland, the elves did not so much diminish or leave the land altogether as depart *into* it, becoming only occasionally visible to their human neighbours. It was in this period, from the thirteenth century onwards, that references to the alfár come to be replaced by the idea of the huldufólk – who are still the elves, of course, but whose 'hiddenness' is emphasized by the origin myth ascribed to them.[79] This is the famous story, collected by Jón Árnason in the nineteenth century, that God dropped in on Adam and Eve at home after their banishment from Eden, and Eve was unable to wash all of her children to make them presentable to God before he arrived. Eve therefore hid the dirty children, which angered God; he declared that what Eve had tried to hide from him should henceforth be hidden to everyone, and thus the dirty children became the ancestors of the huldufólk.

It is unclear how old this story is, and others were in circulation at an earlier date; in the seventeenth century, Jón 'the Learned' Guðmundsson noted a belief among Icelanders that the elves were born when Adam's semen fell to the ground before the creation of Eve. Others in nineteenth-century Iceland told folklore collectors a variant of the myth of neutral angels.[80] Yet it seems likely that the deeper Christianization of Iceland, as in England, drove elves further into the realm of the invisible – even if they were far from gone.

Fairies and magic

With the notable exception of the Scandinavian tradition of *trolldómr*, before the late Middle Ages magical practitioners seldom claimed to derive their power from fairies and kindred beings.[81] Conjurations of elves can be found in Anglo-Saxon England, as well as Anglo-Norman medical material and on amulets from the germanophone world that sought to cover all their bases by conjuring all kinds of malign beings.[82] But these conjurations were invocations of divine power *against* elves rather than any kind of attempt to invoke the supernatural power of elves for magical assistance. But in the twelfth century a new kind of magic arrived in Western Europe that involved the invocation of spirit-beings: ritual magic, whose origins lay in the Arab and Jewish worlds.[83]

Traditionally, in its Christian version, ritual magic involved the conjuration of demons – that is to say, the summoning, binding, employment, and finally exorcism of fallen angels. Many grimoires (books of ritual magic) resembled manuals of exorcism, with the crucial difference that the ritual magician did not simply try to get rid of demons who were already there, but summoned and employed the demons as well.[84] Yet the qualifications of an exorcist were usually deemed necessary for a ritual magician as well during the Middle Ages – he (for ritual magic was almost exclusively a male activity) should be a priest, or at least a cleric, and knowledgeable in Latin, since the formulas of ritual magic were often adapted from the church's liturgy.

Clearly, the conjuration of demons was morally and theologically problematic, and ritual magic was widely prohibited by the church as an illicit abuse of clerical sacramental power. It may have been in response to such concerns that some ritual magicians switched to conjuring angels as an alternative to demons in the late Middle Ages,[85] but this too was not without its theological problems. While the demons might be seen as lower than human beings, and subject to the commands of Christians and clerics, it was less clear what gave a magician the right to command an angel. It may have been anxieties such as these that first led some ritual magicians to switch to conjuring fairies – beings who were neither angels nor demons, and who had no established place in the Christian cosmos. A fifteenth-century English alchemical manuscript claimed that a Fairy Queen named Elchyell was a revealer of alchemical secrets,[86] but the earliest surviving manuscript featuring fairy conjuring was produced in Italy in around 1494 and features a conjuration of 'Oberion', portrayed as a naked figure with hair all over his body, like a woodwose.[87]

'Oberion', who was to become one of the most popular spirits conjured in the sixteenth century – and features as Oberon in Shakespeare's *A Midsummer Night's Dream* – was a being not of folklore but of literature. In the romance *Huon of Bordeaux*, 'Auberon' is an immortal hunchbacked dwarf, the son of Julius Caesar and a supernatural woman, who rules over an enchanted forest kingdom somewhere in the Middle East. Auberon was given supernatural powers by beings who attended his birth, but was also struck with deformity when he was cursed by another such being; but in spite of his magical powers, he is portrayed as a devout Christian.[88]

The appearance of Oberon in ritual magic is a clear instance of ostension – the emergence in real-world practice of ideas drawn from folklore or literature, and in this case from literature. There was no tradition of fairy magic before the late fifteenth century, and the idea of conjuring fairies seems to have been inspired by romance literature itself, where fairies were presented as magical beings.[89] It was quite literally a case of literary fiction breaking into reality – comparable to fans attempting to perform spells from J. K. Rowling's *Harry Potter* books as a sincere occult practice.

Lauren Kassell has argued that this kind of permeability between fiction and real-world magical practice could occur only in a society where belief in fairies was in decline, or at least in the process of becoming marginal.[90] Magic, as a transgressive practice, was more likely to invoke marginalized beings. Whatever the reason for its appearance at this moment in time, ritual magic involving fairies was better able to withstand the religious upheavals of the Reformation than conjurations of angels or demons because fairies were beings of story rather than theology; but, as we shall see, this did not stop people taking fairy-conjuring (and the claims of magicians who conjured fairies) entirely seriously.

Fairy-conjuring was not wholly without medieval roots: early modern fairy grimoires sometimes adapted earlier spells, such as the conjuration of the seven fevers (named variously as Lilia, Hestilia, Fata, Sola, Afrya, Africa, Julia, and Venulla) in the medieval 'Sigismund Fever Charm', who had become fairies by around 1600 (although it should be noted that such names as 'Lilia' (a variant of Lilith) and 'Fata' already have a fairy flavour).[91] Furthermore, spells involving laying a table for a visit by 'three sisters of the fairies' that were ultimately inspired by the canons of Burchard of Worms were a staple of sixteenth-century fairy-conjuring,[92] and there was a long-standing vernacular tradition that fairies could confer magical powers on people – such as the claim by Marion Clerk (mother of Agnes) in 1499 that she had powers of healing from *les Gracyous Fayry*.[93]

As fairies became more familiar and more clearly defined figures, a process assisted by vernacular literature, other cultural figures – from Satan and King Arthur to Pluto and Proserpina – underwent a kind of 'fairyization', since their reconceptualization as fairies aided the telling of stories about them. Fairyland had the requisite ambiguity to make any story possible – and any story acceptable – without raising troubling questions of theology; it allowed the weaving of playful narratives around non-human characters at one remove from contemporary concerns. As Jeremy Harte puts it, fairies '[took] up the imaginative spaces that were not already reserved for God and his saints, for angels, ghosts and devils'.[94] But if there was a drift towards greater demonization of the fairies from the mid thirteenth century onwards, this was as nothing compared to the religious transformation that loomed on the horizon as Europe entered the sixteenth century. For even fairyland would be affected by the Reformation.

FIVE

The reformation of fairyland: early modern fairies

In 1555, a pioneering work on the history and ethnography of Northern Europe was published in Rome, authored by a Swedish bishop who had been exiled from his home country by the upheavals of the Lutheran Reformation. Olaus Magnus's *History of the Northern Peoples* is rich in woodcuts depicting the marvels and wonders of the north, including a portrayal of 'The Elves: That is, the Nightly Dance of Spectres' which is the earliest labelled depiction of elves or fairies in print (figure 5.1). Olaus's decidedly therianthropic elves surround a circle that looks like a large letter 'O', combining animal and human features in a variety of ways. Some have the legs of goats or donkeys; others, bird-like claws; but all have human faces, with a variety of animal ears and horns; some are naked, but others are wholly or partly clothed. One elf holds a snake, and another a flower. On one side of the circle, an animalistic elf plays the lute; on the other, an elf plays the bagpipes.[1] The image is whimsical rather than threatening, and although Olaus's elves bear some resemblance to the animalistic demons of medieval

Figure 5.1 'The Elves: That is, the Nightly Dance of Spectres', from Olaus Magnus, *History of the Northern Peoples* (1555)

iconography, they owe more to the fauns and satyrs of the Classical world.

Olaus's elves are distinctively early modern in several ways. Most obviously, they appear in print – the revolutionary information technology of the early modern era. They are also freighted with theological anxiety – in the text, Olaus seems undecided as to whether the elves are apparitions created by demonic agency, or the souls of those who have given themselves over to pleasure, or a monstrous race of some kind. But there is no doubt that elves exist. And Olaus's portrayal of elves combines folklore – such as the idea that elves dance in circles at night – with a self-conscious Renaissance classicism in which the elves are identified with the various therianthropic and animalistic godlings of the ancient world. The early modern era was a decisive moment for the history of fairies, for it is in this period that we finally have a significant body of evidence for fairy belief across Europe, and not just in Britain, Ireland, France, and Scandinavia. In the sixteenth century, humanist antiquarians and ethnographers began to show some interest in what ordinary people believed, freeing the historian from dependence on purely ecclesiastical sources such as sermons, penitentials, and records of church courts. Yet, although the evidence from the early modern era is richer, it is also difficult to use; learned commentators often wrote in Latin, assimilating folk belief to Classical models as a matter of course, and in doing so they often concealed rather than revealed the true nature of vernacular culture.

But it was the Reformation (and its Catholic counterpart, the Counter-Reformation) that had the greatest impact on the position of fairies in European culture, as interaction with fairies became not just a matter of concern to the ecclesiastical and civil authorities but also potential evidence of witchcraft. The demonization of fairies, as we have seen, was nothing new in the sixteenth century; but the Reformation rendered such demonization potentially lethal. Most importantly, however, elite concern about fairy belief – and the anxiety that fairy belief represented a form of lingering paganism – produced an outpouring of detailed description and commentary on people's dealings with the fairies. Yet learned interest in fairies in this period was not just confined to using interaction with fairies as potential evidence of witchcraft; the sixteenth century was the first period when fairies first gained 'status as objects of intellectual inquiry and speculation',[2] and it seems clear that some hankered after the enchanted world of the ancients.

The 'classicization' of fairyland, in the conscious scholarly identification of fairies with the godlings of the ancient world, was a distinctive feature of the 'reformation of fairyland', and it fed directly into the fears of Protestant and Catholic reformers. For if the fairies were merely godlings of the ancient world in rustic, folkloric guise, then they were relics of paganism that medieval Catholicism (which, to Protestants, was a perversion of the Christian Gospel) had failed to eradicate. This made the identification of fairies as demons an urgent priority it had never been even at the height of late medieval anxiety about popular superstitions. Yet it is also in this period that our evidence base for European fairy belief begins to expand significantly; we begin to hear more voices of ordinary people, and we start to encounter the otherworld beings of Southern and Eastern Europe. This expansion of evidence is also, ironically, down to the church's increased concern about fairy belief, which prompted learned exploration of the subject and questions designed to cover fairy belief in episcopal visitations, witchcraft trials, and other investigations. Ironically, therefore, thanks to the growth of bureaucracy and record-keeping, we know more about the enchanted world of early modern people than about that of their predecessors.

Witchcraft, fairies, and demonization

As we saw in chapter 1 above, fairies have a long history of entanglement with witches. The Reformation coincided with a sharpening and intensification of ideas about witchcraft that had the effect of targeting fairy belief as well. The relationship between witchcraft and the Reformation is now a classic problem in the historiography of the early modern era, because it is clear that no simplistic account in which the religious turmoil of the Reformation stirred up anxiety about witchcraft makes historical sense. The intensification of theological and judicial interest in witchcraft began *before* the Reformation (in the late fifteenth century) and preoccupation with witchcraft crossed confessional lines in the Reformation era itself – indeed, the desire to persecute people suspected of witchcraft was something that united Catholics and Protestants even at the height of their differences.

While it is beyond the scope of this book to try to explain why anxieties about witchcraft turned lethal in the late fifteenth century, resulting in thousands of executions in some regions, one way in which the theological approach of churchmen shifted in this period was that they began to take folklore literally. An older discourse of contempt for popular superstition, ridicule of 'vain observances', and mockery of deluded people who pretended to supernatural powers was replaced by an alarmist discourse in which the idea that people could derive supernatural power from the devil was taken very seriously indeed.[3] The same went for fairy lore: in 1489, for example, the German demonologist Ulrich Müller recorded that a man had married a water spirit and had children with her, but that she had returned to the water after he violated a taboo. This is a classic tale-type, but Müller chose to treat it as data about the literal behaviour of demons.[4] A century earlier, it might have been dismissed as a silly story told among the ignorant, but a late medieval 'revolution of credulity' meant that such stories were taken not only as literally true but also as a basis for judicial proceedings.

It is difficult to single out just one reason why the church shifted from treating popular peasant belief and folklore with haughty contempt to treating it as a potential spiritual threat, but it may be significant that the depopulation of Europe by the Black Death in the fourteenth century made elites more fearful of ordinary people in other ways. If a newly emboldened peasantry were more violent, more rebellious, and less deferential to their lords, could it be that churchmen also began to perceive them as a threat on the spiritual plane as well? In a new climate of fear, popular magic and fairy lore, latterly dismissed as vain fancies, took on the black hues of malefic witchcraft and diabolism.

Whatever the explanation, the 'reformation of witchcraft' was coincident with rather than consequent upon the Reformation of religion – but the Reformation of religion also did nothing to abate the church's burgeoning obsession with witchcraft. As the Bible as the Word of God became central to the new reformed confessions, Exodus 22:18 ('Thou shalt not suffer a witch to live') became the basis for a lethal judicial campaign against witches, rather than the old medieval canons that had brought people who pretended to supernatural powers before church courts and imposed penances on them for misleading the faithful and promoting false belief. Yet renewed attention to the scriptural prohibition on witchcraft raised the question of what exactly witchcraft was – with the added problem that witchcraft was a culturally specific concept, denoted by words with slightly (or significantly) different meanings in the different vernacular languages into which the Bible was now being translated. Thus, in the 1541 Swedish translation of the Bible, Exodus 22:18 became *En trollkona skall du inte låta leva* (Thou shall not suffer a troll woman to live), imposing a culturally specific understanding of what witchcraft was – that is, as a practice entangled with the trolls as an otherworld supernatural community.[5]

Fairies turn up explicitly in only a handful of early modern English witchcraft cases; in Somerset in 1555, Dorset in 1566, Yorkshire in 1567, and Sussex in 1609.[6] In England, fairies were usually associated not with witchcraft but rather with 'service magic', and with treasure-hunting in particular because fairies were thought to dwell in the kinds of mounds (prehistoric barrows or natural features) where people used magic to look for treasure.[7] The fairies were also appealing as a source of occult power to unlearned magical practitioners (especially women) who were illiterate or did not have access to books.[8] Likewise, in Ireland fairies were never connected in any meaningful way with witchcraft (and Ireland was in any case largely free of witchcraft trials).[9]

However, it is possible that fairies played a more prominent role in English witchcraft belief than appears at first glance. In some of the testimonies extracted by the 'Witchfinder General' Matthew Hopkins during his campaign of witch-hunting in 1645–7, we find elements of what seems to be fairy lore, such as mentions of changelings and diabolical familiars who appear as diminutive, shining children – as if those tormented by the witchfinder were being forced to dredge up what folklore they could remember in order to satisfy the demands of their interrogators. Even the characteristically English theme of animal familiars is susceptible of a fairy interpretation – for the fairies, after all, were said to be able to transform into animals at will.[10]

Whether or not there is much sublimated fairy lore lurking beneath the surface in English witch trials, in Scotland there are numerous witch trials where the accused's commerce with the fairies was a major subject of investigation. An important reason for this was that Scotland's Witchcraft Act (1563), in contrast to its English counterpart, flung wide the net of interpretation so that virtually *any* form of service magic or popular divination could be classified as witchcraft; furthermore, the Scottish Act criminalized those who consulted witches as well as the witches themselves.[11] King James VI's *Daemonologie* (1597), an unusual case of a sovereign personally establishing the demonological discourse of his own realm, made clear that 'the Phairie' were to be treated as demonic illusions: 'the devil illuded [i.e. tricked] the senses of sundry simple creatures, in making them believe that they saw and heard such things as were nothing so indeed'.[12] James noted that 'ignorant magistrates' let witches off who claimed to work by the fairies, because they did not consider fairies to be devils; and he argued that this loophole should be closed off. Referring to people who trafficked with the fairies, James declared: 'That sort I say, ought as severely to be punished as any other witches, and rather the more, that they go dissemblingly to work.'[13]

While the more thoroughgoing character of Scotland's Calvinist Reformation may have encouraged a more paranoid approach to witchcraft than in England, Wales, and Ireland – which resulted in fairy belief being drawn into Scottish witchcraft accusations by association – it also seems that fairies were more heavily implicated in acts of harmful magic in Scotland than elsewhere in Europe. Furthermore, Julian Goodare has argued that fairies were actually worshipped in early modern Scotland under the name of 'Seely Wights', a cult that was apparently first mentioned by William Hay in the 1530s, and had some commonalities with the cult of Diana described in the early Middle Ages by Regino of Prüm.[14] Hutton, however, is more sceptical of whether the Seely Wights were actually worshipped.[15]

One of the features of Hay's accounts of the Seely Wights which has puzzled historians is the apparent terminological fluidity of the term, which seems to have referred both to a class of fairies and to their worshippers. Such fluidity is not solely confined to Scotland, however; Éva Pócs has described the 'fairy societies' of the early modern Balkans and Hungary, who invoked the patronage of the fairy saint Ilona or Elena and fought 'witch societies', like the two rival groups who clashed on the Hill of St Vid in Hungary in 1552. The members of the fairy societies acted on behalf of the fairies but also in some sense *became* fairies.[16] Indeed, as Diane Purkiss has shown, groups of people whose identities merged with the supernatural 'good people' whom they followed were common throughout Europe.[17]

It is likely that no country in history has ever judicially persecuted fairy belief as intensely as Scotland. The Edinburgh trial of Jonet Boyman in 1572 gives some sense of the extent to which fairy belief was implicated in Scottish fears about witchcraft. Jonet was a cunning woman who confessed that she invoked 'evil spirits' at an 'elrich [i.e. eldritch] well' beside Arthur's Seat (a hill in the park of the Palace of Holyroodhouse), 'who she called upon to come, to show and declare' what would happen to her patient, Allan Anderson. She conjured 'a great blast' and the figure of a man appeared on the other side of the well, whom she charged in the name of the Father, and of the Son, and of King Arthur and Queen Elspeth, to heal Anderson. The fairy then gave her instructions which Anderson's wife failed to follow correctly, leading to a mighty din that beset Anderson's home, including the rushing of wind, hammering, and the hooves of horses. A child of Anderson's subsequently died, and Jonet claimed the Seely Wights had blasted the child because its mother had failed to bless it sufficiently. Jonet was convicted of witchcraft and burned to death.[18]

Unlike English law, Scottish law did not require an alleged witch to have caused any harm; Bessie Dunlop of Ayrshire, who confessed to refusing an offer to go to Elfame (fairyland), was burned to death anyway in 1576 just for being in contact with the fairy realm at all.[19] Indeed, confessing to contact with the fairies usually guaranteed the death penalty; charming was a lesser offence, but if a healer or service magician said they had received power from the fairies (which was often part of their marketing), then execution for witchcraft would follow.[20] However, the Scottish witch trials are notable not just for the severity of their treatment of fairy belief but also for the beliefs about contact with fairies that records of trials and interrogations have preserved. In some cases, these testimonies were perhaps dreamt up for the court by people who believed a full and lurid confession might secure clemency; but this hardly provides an explanation for all the elaborate claims made, at least some of which seem to have been sincere.

Andro Man, tried for witchcraft in 1597–8, claimed to have been the Fairy Queen's lover for thirty years, summoning her with the Latin word *Benedicite*, and he mingled his fairy belief with garbled and unorthodox Christianity by claiming he received counsel from a 'folk angel' called Christsonday (whom the court did not hesitate to identify with the devil).²¹ In Orkney, perhaps reflecting the ancient Norse tradition of identifying elves with the dead, Elspeth Reoch confessed in 1616 that her spirit-guide was a dead kinsman, John Stewart, who was 'a fairy man' because he was 'slain by McKay at the down-going of the sun, and therefore neither dead nor living but would ever go betwixt the heaven and the earth' – a curious aetiology that seems to classify fairies as a class of the unquiet dead.²² The fairies of the archipelagos of Orkney and Shetland, where the Norse language of Norn was still spoken, were the trows – relatives of the trolls of Scandinavia, although they came to resemble Scotland's fairies more than their Scandinavian siblings. In 1616, the Shetland woman Katherine Johnsdochter confessed to 'seeing the trows rise out of the kirkyard of Hildiswick and Holycross Kirk of Eschenes and that she saw them on the hill called Greinfaill at many sundry times and that they come to any house where there was feasting or great merryness, and especially at Yule'.²³

Perhaps the most famous Scottish case that mingled witchcraft and fairy belief, however, was that of Isobel Gowdie, tried at Nairn in 1662. Gowdie confessed to belonging to a coven of thirteen witches, to whose Sabbaths she flew on a straw while shooting 'elf-arrows' at whomever the devil instructed her to; these arrows were made by 'elf-boys'. Gowdie also said she had met and dined with the King and Queen of the Fairies inside the Downie Hills.²⁴ While Gowdie may have been one of the few people brought to trial for witchcraft in early modern Scotland who sincerely believed she was a witch, her conception of witchcraft was not that of the learned demonologists but remained entangled with fairy belief. It is as though we see in such cases the ungainly imposition of demonological lore (the flight to the witches' Sabbath, the pact with the devil, and so on) on a substratum of pre-existing fairy belief – even if Isobel Gowdie managed to internalize both, for psychological reasons we cannot now fathom.

On the other side of Europe, a phenomenon similar to the demonization or 'demonification' of ambivalent folkloric beings in Scottish witch trials occurred in Muscovy during the same period. The Orthodox world did not undergo the Reformation, but state centralization in sixteenth-century Muscovy was accompanied by an intensification of the church's involvement in people's lives. It was during this period that the generic Russian Orthodox concept of a *bes* (demon) came to take on more folkloric characteristics. In Muscovite trials for witchcraft, demons were said to procreate, have children, and form families; they were also said to eat (and offer people food), and penitents began to confess to sexual intercourse with demons. Demons could even be physically killed.[25]

These developments may have been driven by the territorial expansion of Muscovy and a resulting syncretism between Russian Orthodox belief and the beliefs of non-Christians. As ethnic Russian settlers ventured farther into the Volga–Ural region, they came into contact with animist Finno-Ugric peoples such as the Komi, Mari, and Udmurts, who venerated forest spirits, resulting in a new category of syncretic 'forest demons' in vernacular Orthodoxy. On the face of it, this development could be given a veneer of doctrinal orthodoxy by an appeal to authors such as Michael Psellus, who had argued some rebel angels fell to earth rather than into hell, but in practice the placation and negotiation with forest demons by Russian Christians in remote regions of Muscovy's expanding sphere of influence was scarcely distinguishable from pre-Christian animism.[26] As in Scotland, so in Muscovy, elite and popular conceptions of the supernatural interacted to create a dangerous cultural soup – albeit the increased awareness of intermediate spiritual beings in Russia did not lead to witchcraft trials as deadly as Scotland's.

Meanwhile, in Iceland, a late sixteenth-century Lutheran bishop of Skálholt, Oddur Einarsson, offered an account of the island's elves that consciously avoided any suggestion that they were demons. Einarsson noted that these beings 'live in the hills close to men', and are 'endowed with bodies of incredible subtlety, since they are even thought to enter into mountains and hills'. Elves are invisible to most people unless they choose to reveal themselves – although a minority of people, Einarsson reported, can always see them. The bishop portrayed the elves as sex pests towards Iceland's women, and noted their habit of abducting children and young people, either forever or for a period of time (although he made no mention of infants, the usual victims of fairy abduction). Einarsson suggested two possible explanations for elves: either 'these things are brought about by the frauds, impostures, and illusions of the devil', or elves 'are some kind of mixed species created between spirits and animals' – a curious suggestion which seems to bring us back to the therianthropic nature of fairies.[27]

Ármann Jakobsson has argued that the folkloric Icelandic elf first encountered in the sixteenth and seventeenth centuries, who is usually invisible and can slip in and out of the land, ought to be regarded as a being distinct from the medieval álfar.[28] Elves were a matter of considerable learned interest in early modern Iceland, provoking a kind of 'semi-theological discussion' which suggested 'a consolidation between local belief and orthodox demonology'. In 1591, the Icelandic author of a now lost work on elves, Sigurður Stefánsson, was said to have been led astray to his death by vengeful álfar, angry at his betrayal of their secrets – foreshadowing stories that would later be told about the seventeenth-century Scottish minister Robert Kirk. In 1637, Bishop Gísli Oddson of Skálholt (1593–1638) wrote that trolls were extinct, but reported the existence of two kinds of elves – the hidden, usually invisible and malevolent huldufólk; and the *ljúflingar* (sweet ones) who have relationships with humans and help them. The *ljúflingar*, having interbred with old Icelandic families, were now partly human.[29]

The Icelandic landscape itself legitimized such speculations; after all, the idea that Mount Hekla and other Icelandic volcanoes were mouths of hell was a cliché of medieval geography, and the strange sights, variations in temperature, and smells encountered by Icelanders – as well as the disappearance of people in a dangerous landscape – naturally reinforced the impression of a spirit-haunted land. When Guðmundur Einarsson (1568–1647), schoolmaster of Hólar, mooted in 1627 the conventional European view that Iceland's elves were demons, the notion was immediately dismissed by Ari Magnússon, who maintained the corporeality of the elves as a hidden race.[30] Iceland, like Ireland, remained peculiarly resistant to the systematic demonization of its otherworld population.

It is in this period that we also glimpse for the first time the folklore of the Iberian peninsula, where a ballad of around 1530 introduced the legend of the *gentiles*, a race of prehistoric giants who were exiled at the same time as the Moors from Granada in 1492. Indeed, the ballad seemed to conflate the *gentiles* with the Moors themselves as supernatural creatures. The *gentiles* seem to have served as an explanation for Iberia's Cyclopean megalithic structures, as well as being elided with the giants of Genesis 6.[31] Similarly, an account of 1589 told of how a piper was transported to an underground world of hunchbacked subterranean goblins who wanted to dance to his playing.[32]

Early modern Spain's most lasting contribution to fairy lore, however, is surely the appearance of the female fairy (*fada* or *hada*) wielding a magic wand in Spanish literature between 1600 and 1650 – before the publication of Perrault's fairy tales.[33] The fairy's wand was destined to become a defining feature of the 'international fairy' of twentieth-century mass culture.

Hags of Rome? Fairies, Catholicism, and paganism

In the English reign of James VI and I (1603–25), the anti-Puritan clergyman and poet Richard Corbet (1582–1635) made use of the theme of the departing fairies for satirical purposes against both Catholics and Puritans in the poem 'Farewell Rewards and Fairies':

Lament, lament, old abbeys,
The fairies' lost command:
They did but change priests' babies,
But some have chang'd your land;
And all your children sprung from thence
Are now grown Puritans:
Who live as changelings ever since
For love of your demains.
. . .

Witness those rings and roundelays
Of theirs, which yet remain,
Were footed in Queen Mary's days
On many a grassy plain;
But, since of late Elizabeth,
And later James, came in,
They never danc'd on any heath
As when the time hath been.

By which we note the fairies
Were of the old profession;
Their songs were Ave Marys,
Their dances were procession.

> But now, alas, they all are dead,
> Or gone beyond the seas,
> Or farther for religion fled,
> Or else they take their ease.[34]

The idea that the reign of Mary I (1553–8, when Henry VIII's eldest daughter made an ultimately unsuccessful attempt to restore Catholicism) had been a time of particularly intense superstition was one that took root in hindsight, during Elizabeth's reign. Thus, the physician William Bullein, who encountered a fairy-charmer at Parham in Suffolk in the early 1560s, bemoaned the fact that in Mary's reign such witchcraft had been allowed to flourish while 'so many blessed men [were] burned', referring to the Protestant martyrs of the period.[35] In 1612, William Warner had Robin Goodfellow deliver a speech to his fellow fairies that praised Mary's reign as a golden age for the fairies: 'Was then a merrier world with us when Mary wore the crown, / And holy water sprinkle was believed to put us down.'[36] Given that Mary's reign lasted only a little over five years, the significance accorded it here seems to be down to a kind of nostalgia where the reign of England's last Catholic Tudor monarch came to stand for an imagined England that had been superstitious, yet merry.

In subsequent decades, the fairies were repeatedly identified as undesirable relics of the Catholic past, and the hope was expressed that the progress of the Reformation would put them to flight,[37] like the 'yellow-skirted Fayes' of John Milton's *On the Morning of Christ's Nativity* (1629), who 'Fly after the Night-steeds, leaving their Moon-lov'd maze'.[38] Similar attitudes prevailed in Scotland; in the late seventeenth century, the soldier-poet William Cleland noted that, in former times,

> About mill-dams, and green brae faces,
> Both Elrich elfs and brownies stayed,
> And green gown'd fairies danc'd and played:
> When old John Knox, and other some,
> Began to plot the Hags of Rome;
> Then suddenly took to their heels[39]

The fairy kingdom described by Robert Herrick in his poem *The Fairy Temple* (1648), with its 'many mumbling mass-priests', was likewise a satire upon Catholicism;[40] and the 'Kingdom of the Lowlanders' under Hampstead Heath conjured by the London cunning-woman Mary Parish during her affair with the seventeenth-century Whig politician Goodwin Wharton mimicked the Catholic church, having its own pope and elaborate religious ceremonies. One of the most important characters in the Kingdom was 'Father Friar', the oldest and wisest fairy who was advisor to the Fairy King.[41] Interestingly, Mary Parish was herself a Catholic, and thus less likely to mock the Catholic church by portraying fairies as Catholics.

Indeed, anti-Catholic discourses were already well established and it was hardly necessary for Protestants to discredit Catholics further by associating them with fairies, although one pamphlet denounced the Jesuit leader Robert Parsons as 'a cursed fairy brat' (i.e. a changeling).[42] The association between fairies and Catholicism is perhaps better understood through the lens of nostalgia rather than that of anti-Catholicism. The fairies belonged, in some sense, to the old world – and therefore to the Catholic world. Just as fairies in the late Middle Ages were sometimes portrayed as Jews, belonging to the Old Covenant and worshipping only God the Father,[43] so in the sixteenth century it made sense that they would be portrayed as followers of the older religion.

Darren Oldridge has shown that, while Protestants generally demonized fairy belief in general, they were apt to interpret individual fairy encounters as illusions.[44] A tension existed, in other words, between a theological imperative to portray fairies as devils and a polemical imperative to show that fairies were a mere delusion of the Catholic past, and therefore non-existent. I have argued elsewhere that a similar hermeneutical tension existed in English Protestant attitudes to the relationship between witchcraft and Catholicism; here, there was a temptation to equate Catholics with witches (and indeed this happened at a purely rhetorical level[45]), but the dominant narrative that emerged was one of Catholic fraud, focussed on the theme of Catholics inciting false witchcraft accusations.[46] Hutton has argued that belief in the reality of fairies was undermined not just by this strand of anti-Catholic polemic but also by the satirical portrayal of 'fairy cozeners' in early modern drama.[47] And, indeed, early modern confidence tricksters did often make claims about hidden treasure revealed by fairies or offered access to the Fairy Queen,[48] which must have contributed to a discrediting of the fairy mythology.

The case that fairies were nothing more than a Catholic fable, and that the preaching of Protestantism would eventually drive them away, was made most forcefully by Reginald Scot (*c.*1538–99), whose scepticism was so intense that his *Discoverie of Witchcraft* (1584) became a target of King James VI in his *Daemonologie*. Scot noted that 'when Robin Goodfellow kept such a coil in the country' (presumably, before the Reformation), many more spirits had been seen. He attributed people's belief that they encountered fairies and other supernatural beings to weak-mindedness and fear engendered in childhood:

> [Our parents] have so frayed us with bull-beggars, spirits, witches, urchens, elves, hags, fairies, satyrs, pans, fauns, sylens, Kit with the candlestick, tritons, centaurs, dwarfs, giants, imps, calcars, conjurers, nymphs, changelings, incubus, Robin Goodfellow, the spoorne, the mare, the man in the oak, the hell wain, the firedrake, the puckle, Tom Thumb, hobgoblin, Tom tumbler, boneless, and other such bugs, that we are afraid of our own shadows.

Scot expected such superstition to disappear in the near future: 'this wretched and cowardly infidelity, since the preaching of the Gospel, is in part forgotten; and doubtless, the rest of those illusions will in short time (by God's grace) be detected and vanish away'.[49] Yet Scot's 'psychologizing' explanation for fairies was unsatisfactory to demonologists such as James VI because it seemed to deny the possibility that the devil was behind fairy phenomena. Scot's thoroughgoing scepticism was destined to remain a fringe view for another century, therefore, until the advent of the Enlightenment.

Regina Buccola has claimed that fairy lore helped keep Catholicism alive in early modern England, albeit 'under another (and a not specifically *religious*) guise'. Catholicism, unlike Protestantism, 'offered the theological space for constructs such as the fairyland-linked purgatory and not quite angelic, not quite demonic spirits such as the fairies'.[50] But apart from Mary Parish, there is not much evidence of Catholics in Britain actively embracing fairy belief, even if it may be true that folklore in general sustained 'sub-Catholic' expressions of popular religion under the radar in Protestantized nations.

Indeed, 'official' Catholicism had little truck with fairies. Catholic missionaries in Scotland sprinkled with holy water fields that had remained uncultivated on account of their fairy associations,[51] and the 'superiority of Christian symbols over fairies', such as the sign of the cross in Irish fairy lore, seems to be no older than the early modern era – suggesting a Counter-Reformation hostility to fairies as demonic beings afraid of Christian symbols.[52]

Similarly, early modern Catholics sometimes recast phenomena that might hitherto have been perceived as evidence of fairies as proof of the reality of purgatory. In 1658, the Jesuit William Atkins was called in to exorcise the house of Charles Coleman in Cannock Chase, Staffordshire, which was being haunted by a helpful spirit who made beds, fetched coal, and made fires, but who also sometimes knocked on the walls and overturned furniture like a poltergeist. The spirit, who could communicate with a sixteen-year-old maid named Anne Cherington, turned out not to be a fairy but the soul of Charles Coleman's father John, who had been released from purgatory to warn his son to amend his ways. John's spirit was sometimes pursued by a demon, which caused him to knock over furniture.[53] A century earlier, it seems highly likely that this spirit would have been treated as a fairy.

The association between fairies and the Catholic past was not confined to England or Britain. Throughout Europe, the Reformation prompted a hunt for paganism, fuelled by a new understanding of what Christianity was – an active, personally chosen belief in Jesus Christ as the Christian's saviour, and in the Bible as the Word of God, as opposed to a set of passively inherited customs and traditions underpinned by the supernaturally efficacious sacraments of the church. For the most enthusiastic Protestants, Catholicism was little more than paganism in Christian dress – and this was proved not only by the idolatrous character of Catholic worship but also by the medieval church's toleration of fairy belief.

In countries that underwent the Reformation, interactions with local spirits that might have been treated as superstition in the late Middle Ages came to be regarded as outright paganism. Thus, the Lutheran provost Henrik Boisman, who was conducting a visitation in the county of Kexholm in Finland in 1675, reported that in the parish of Jaakkima people gathered on a hill called Lehmänmäki where they prepared a gruel and offered it to the spirits of the forests and hills by climbing a tree with the offering. The people would then eat the gruel, but anyone who mentioned the name of Christ would be beaten up.[54]

A key question in the historiography of popular religion at Europe's geographical and cultural margins in the early modern period is whether the practices described by antiquaries and ethnographers should be interpreted as a 'paganism' (in the sense of sacrifice to pre-Christian deities) that set these cultures apart from the European Christian mainstream, or whether the spirits venerated by Finns, Estonians, Latvians, and Lithuanians (for example) were little different from the fairies of the rest of Europe.[55] Leo Allatius (1586–1669), the learned Greek librarian of the Vatican, noted that the Greeks of his own time believed domestic spirits sometimes appeared and moved through the house in the form of snakes, 'and honoured them with a certain religious awe, although they did not worship them',[56] and this absence of worship has been one way in which fairy belief has been distinguished from 'paganism'.

But 'sacrifices' to fairies were not wholly absent even from deeply Christianized European nations. Apart from offerings that might be made as part of magical acts, offerings to fairies continued in the Balkans and other areas of Southern Europe into the twentieth century,[57] and the offering of milk and cream to the fairies in Ireland on May Day is a well-known feature of Irish folklore.[58] However, fairies, gods, and saints had a tendency to merge in popular religion, and it is not always clear what sort of entity an offering was being made to, especially if it was something done out of immemorial tradition – such as the libation poured into the sea to 'Shoney' in the Western Isles, who may have been a degraded 'St John' rather than a fairy or deity.[59]

In reality, whether commerce with fairies was likely to be considered 'pagan' or not did not so much depend on the nature of the interaction as on the expectations of commentators. No one really thought Irish or Croatian peasants were pagans, but Finns or Lithuanians were much more likely to attract such accusations even if the spirits they sought to placate were functionally little different from the fairies of other nations. Everyone knew that pre-Christian traditions were much closer to the surface among the Finns and Lithuanians.

Whether a commentator considered fairy belief to constitute worship also depended on their theology; in Scotland, for example, areas where the fairies were believed to emerge to ride across the landscape at Hallowe'en were deemed to be consecrated to the devil, especially when they were named for the 'Goodman'.[60] Yet Protestantism did not necessarily correspond to hostility towards fairies; Ulster Presbyterians were as likely to leave out offerings for the fairies as their Catholic neighbours, and the proliferation of fairy names given to natural landmarks and prehistoric landscape features may have resulted from the erasure of saints' names once given to them.[61] In Scandinavia, too, certain traditions (such as the risk to 'unclean' women after childbirth and newborn children from elves) seem to *postdate* rather than pre-date the Reformation, and derive from the Lutheran church's emphasis on rituals of churching.[62] Julian Goodare has argued that 'the plurality of realms within the popular cosmos' of early modern Scotland may have enabled the fairies to survive the onslaught of the Reformation – in other words, people did not *just* believe in fairies (but also in brownies, trows, giants, and so on) and so it was difficult to target and discredit just one class of folkloric supernatural beings.[63]

Indeed, the Reformation (or cultural processes consequent upon it) might be blamed for making people *more* rather than less frightened of fairies. For Reformation rhetoric not only demonized fairies as never before – and therefore rendered them more frightening – but also made it impossible for people to interact with fairies as they had once done. As we have seen, fairies are characterized by their capricious behaviour and tendency to take offence; and so when people were forced into behaviours potentially offensive to the fairies, it filled them with fear and cast the fairies as an ever-present threat. For example, the systematic felling of sacred trees and forests in the Baltic seems to have made local people afraid of potential revenge by nature spirits. In eighteenth-century Estonia (whose Lutheran Reformation was only then beginning to take effect), August Wilhelm Hupel recorded that a man who cut down part of an ancient forest believed that the protective deities of the forest – which had existed since the beginning of the world – were now pursuing him in his dreams. He called these beings *maa-alused* (subterraneans).[64]

The early modern rise of the poltergeist can perhaps be blamed on the Reformation and Counter-Reformation too, insofar as the new religious ideas might leave household spirits unplaced. The fear that household spirits, who normally brought good luck, might turn against a house's inhabitants and even burn the house down was especially intense in Lithuania. After a group of Jesuit missionaries had exorcised a house in the diocese of Vilnius in 1605, they found some old men putting eggs inside a beam as offerings to the household spirits, terrified that the spirits had been offended by the exorcism. The Jesuits smashed the eggs and exorcised the house again.[65] Gillian Bennett defined early modern poltergeists as 'homely ghosts', 'household sprites', and 'housesprites'.[66] Like all fairies, they were capricious and could both help and harm, although in common with other fairies their responses to both favour and slight were exaggerated; the household spirit became a poltergeist when it took offence, or was neglected.

The early modern period saw an explosion of scholarly interest in noisy and troublesome household spirits (although the much later term 'poltergeist' remains an anachronism for the era, and the most common term used for these beings was 'follets'). If for no other reason than that poltergeists seem to defy classification – they are clearly not the same as ghosts, for instance – they seem to belong more comfortably to the fairy world than to the realm of the unquiet dead.[67] But if poltergeists were indeed household spirits gone bad, they show the potential for the reformation of religion to exacerbate rather than stamp out the power of fairy belief – as in Estonia, for instance, where Ülo Valk has argued that the suppression of domestic cults of household spirits simply caused 'former benevolent and neutral spirits' to become mischievous or even malevolent, such as the sauna spirits who punished people who washed too late on a Saturday evening.[68] Rather than banishing fairies, therefore, it seems that in some cases the combined effect of demonization and exorcism was to turn fairies bad – the folkloric equivalent, perhaps, of creating experts in crime by banishing criminals to prison.

Return of the godlings: classicizing fairyland

If the demonization of fairies in the early modern era was just an intensification of trends already established in the late medieval period, the 'classicization' of fairies in this period was something largely new, and paradoxical in its consequences. Although, as we have seen in chapter 4 above, fairy characters were sometimes identified in the Middle Ages with ancient deities (such as the identifications of the Fairy King with Pluto and the Fairy Queen with Proserpina in romance literature), this was largely a consequence of the 'vernacularization' of culture and the use of fairies as recognizable cultural placeholders for ancient gods and goddesses. Early modern classicism was, by contrast, a learned project: an effort to trace the origins of fairies in the Classical world and, in doing so, to give them an abiding significance beyond the local and the rustic.

In this sense, the classicization of fairyland represented a positive appraisal of fairies that acted as a counterweight to their demonization by theologians and helped to maintain the ambiguity of fairies as neither thoroughly good nor thoroughly bad. On the other hand, however, classicization validated the suspicions of the fairies' opponents that fairy lore was unambiguously pagan – for, if the fairies were indeed the nymphs and satyrs of the ancients, they were pagan godlings who had to be erased as part of the struggle against idolatry, just as much as altars to Jupiter or Venus.

The persistent notion that 'fairies are pagan' has proved to be the long-term legacy of the classicizers – albeit twentieth-century folklorists were apt to deem this a positive rather than a negative fact about them. However, it is important to bear in mind that the idea of fairies as a legacy of the pagan past, or as 'pagan survivals', is rooted ultimately in anti-Catholic polemic – the accusation that the medieval Catholic church failed to eradicate paganism among the peasantry – and antiquarian scholarship that is decidedly questionable by modern standards, and not supported by the latest research. I have argued elsewhere that 'Fairy lore is the diffuse and repurposed wreckage of pre-Christian religious beliefs, not their lineal successor.'[69] In other words, the fairies of medieval Europe were composite, reassembled beings constructed, in part, from a few surviving remains of pre-Christian belief; but, as we have seen, it took a long time for the recognizable late medieval / early modern fairy to crystallize from an incoherent menagerie of supernatural otherworld beings. Early modern antiquarians were led astray by a fallacy of translation: the mistaken notion that because certain Latin terms (such as *faunus* or *nympha*) had become established glosses for words like 'elf' or 'fairy', this indicated a direct genetic relationship between the two.

For example, in his 1649 English–Latin dictionary, the lexicographer Charles Hoole confidently translated 'Angel-guardian' as *Genius*, 'fairies' as *lamiae*, and the Fairy Queen as *Lamia*. Hoole's elves were *larvae*, while *Fauni* were 'Fairies of the wood', *Dryades* 'Fairies of the Okes', *Nymphae* 'Fairies of the Springs', *Naiades* 'Fairies of the Streams', and *Oreades*

'Fairies of the Hills'. 'Fairies of the house' were *Lares*, while 'Spirits in the Air' were *Clusii* (a typographical error for *dusii*).⁷⁰ Such glosses were not just a process of translation; among Hoole's learned readers, translation served to impose a Latinate conceptual framework on the supernatural world. Even in English translations of classical works, words like *dryades* and *naiades* began to be rendered as 'fairies'.⁷¹

The antiquary John Aubrey, writing in the 1680s, was convinced that Robin Goodfellow was simply the god Faunus in rustic guise, and identified the fairies with the nymphs,⁷² while seventeenth-century Dutch antiquaries made strenuous efforts to trace the pedigree of the 'White Ladies' of Dutch folklore to the nymphs of the ancient world.⁷³ Aubrey identified fairies as the daemons of the Greeks, and the *daimōnion* of Socrates as a 'Good Genius'.⁷⁴ Aubrey's friend Lancelot Morehouse actually believed he had heard a faun laughing in the English countryside,⁷⁵ an incident that shows learned classicizing interpretation of fairies was just as likely to lead to ostension as anything else; if people believed they might encounter godlings of the ancient world, then that began to inform their experience of reality.

One of the best-known classicizing accounts of fairies in early modern Britain can be found in Robert Burton's *Anatomy of Melancholy* (first published in 1621), in which Burton defined fairies as 'terrestrial devils' and grouped them indiscriminately with the godlings of the ancient world. Burton averred that, on account of their terrestrial nature, fairies could be considered more harmful than other kinds of devils, and noted that some believed they were degenerated gods (in the sense that they had once been offered divine worship). Fairies are 'sometimes seen by old women and children', but primarily belong to 'former times'.

In addition to the fairies of folklore, Burton mentioned the elementals of Paracelsus and 'foliots' (poltergeists), concluding that this kind of spirit was also responsible for belief in ghosts owing to their habit of 'simulating the souls of the dead'.⁷⁶ Burton's identification of fairies with ghosts is a reminder that it was easier for Protestants to believe in fairies than in ghosts; the Reformation had done away with purgatory and therefore, so many thought, with the possibility of the souls of the dead returning to earth. But there was no prima facie reason why fairies, identified as a class of demons, were not as plausible to Protestants as to Catholics. Burton simultaneously elided fairies with demons, and with the lares, genii, fauns, satyrs, and nymphs of the ancients. In a similar way, court masques such as Ben Jonson's *Oberon* (1611) promiscuously mixed satyrs, sylvans, fairies, and elves;[77] the Renaissance and baroque classicizing impulse saw fairies merged with the godlings of the ancient world rather than replaced by them.

This kind of classicization was not confined to Britain, and Francisco Molina-Moreno has examined the same phenomenon in early modern Poland, where attempts were made to identify Poland's *rusałki* with the *aōrai* of Greek mythology (spirits of young women who suffered an untimely death).[78] Poland's *rusałki*, like the *rusalki* of the East Slavic world, are 'the spirits of drowned maidens, especially maidens who committed suicide in response to being jilted in love after becoming pregnant'.[79] In Greece, however, antiquarians were confronted with the question of why the nymphs of ancient Greece had been so transformed in contemporary popular belief. Leo Allatius, who was born on the island of Chios, showed considerable interest in 'those most beautiful women, whom [the Greeks] call *narayidas* by a corrupted word, since they ought to say *nereidas*', and reported a mixture of continuity and change in Greek beliefs about these *exotika*:

> The common folk call them *kalas archonlisas*, the beautiful ladies. They are of nymph-kind, who dwell in the fields, and sometimes meet together even in a town. They please themselves with ritual steps and dances among the thickest forests and beautiful valleys – and especially if the soil is made wet by the flowing of waters. They frequent the shade of trees, especially at midday. They desire madly the love of young men, but especially handsome ones, and delight in infants of both sexes. These, when they can, they steal.[80]

Allatius reported that people were most at risk from attack by the nereids if they defecated in the open country, without spitting on the ground three times beforehand.[81] Allatius broadly endorsed Michael Psellus's sceptical explanation of the nereids as an illusion produced by the brain, and he made a connection between the *exotika* and the phenomenon of sleep paralysis, which he called Ephialtes. However, Allatius was quite clear that such illusions had real physical consequences: 'for many perish at a blow of the eye, or by an apparition which they say they have seen, or contract a disease of the body'.[82]

Classicization lent a certain universality to vernacular terms that were otherwise local and specific, implying that broadly the same collection of godling existed in every culture, and that *interpretatio Romana* (a Roman conceptual framework) could safely be applied to them all. This had always been a problem in dealing with fairies; learned authors used Latin terms that did not correspond in any way to the language or conceptual frameworks of ordinary people.[83] This priority of *interpretatio Romana* meant that early modern writers trying to make sense of animistic societies fell back on Greek and Latin vocabulary of godlings when trying to come to terms with unfamiliar landscapes of belief. Thus, Johannes Schefferus spoke of the Sámi people's veneration of the *manes* (spirits of the ancestors) as well as 'fauns, sylvans and tritons' who were inseparable from the natural places they inhabited, and he used the Latin term *numina* (spirits) rather than *di* (gods) for the spirits venerated by the Sámi.[84]

But such terms obscured the original languages, local beliefs, and regionally specific concepts of the supernatural. For instance, when translating the Swedish-language writings of Samuel Rheen, Schefferus insisted on rendering 'trolls' as *daemonia*, which was surely too generic to be meaningful. Dorian Jurić has shown that a similar process occurred in Balkan literature of the sixteenth and seventeenth centuries, where Slavic vilas essentially took the role of Classical nymphs (under a local name).[85] The use of the Latin language to describe the supernatural beliefs of hitherto non-literate cultures forced them into a conceptual straitjacket and erased their distinctive and culturally specific characteristics.

Purkiss has shown that Shakespeare's reimagining of fairies in his plays, which is often cited as the foundation of the modern idea of the fairy, was heavily influenced by Classical sources, from Seneca's *Hippolytus* to the *Anacreontea*.[86] Even before Shakespeare, the literary or stage fairy seems to have parted company with the fairies people feared might steal their children or hoped might lead them to treasure; only in the light of such a dissociation could Elizabeth I allow herself to be saluted as the Fairy Queen in masques and flattering poems.[87] With the Elizabethan literary fairy, we are in the realm of the fairy as placeholder – a non-human being who allows escapist stories to be told that stand outside human life and human affairs, just as painting non-human fairies allowed Victorian painters to experiment with eroticism on the basis that their subjects supposedly stood at one remove from humanity.

THE REFORMATION OF FAIRYLAND

Figure 5.2 Robin Goodfellow, 1639

As we saw at the start of this chapter, classicization also had a significant impact on pictorial representations of fairies in the sixteenth and seventeenth centuries, such as the faun-like elves of Olaus Magnus's *History of the Northern Peoples*. In English woodcuts of the seventeenth century, fairies were portrayed either as tiny people wearing pointed hats or as goat-legged fauns – such as in the 1639 broadside *Robin Goodfellow, His Mad Prankes and Merry Jests* (figure 5.2), where Robin is a priapic, moustachioed satyr dancing in a ring of diminutive fairies, wielding a candle in one hand and a broom in the other.[88] It is possible that the idea of winged fairies also germinated at this time, or that it was at least influenced by Classical imagery. In the seventeenth century, a partially intact fourth-century wall painting depicting an enthroned goddess, the 'Dea Barberini', was discovered in Rome and mistakenly restored as the goddess Roma (it actually portrays Venus). Psyche, who was traditionally portrayed in Graeco-Roman art with butterfly wings, appears as a diminutive winged figure perched on the goddess's shoulder (figure 5.3).[89]

The first representation of a winged fairy seems to have been in a masque costume designed by Inigo Jones in 1611, although since wings were added to numerous characters in early Stuart masques it is possible

Figure 5.3 A tiny winged Psyche perches on the shoulder of Venus in the Roman fresco known as the 'Dea Barberini' (Rome, fourth century)

that the addition of wings to fairies was simply part of an effort to make costumes ever more outlandish and elaborate, rather than a statement about the nature of fairies.[90] Either way, it was in the world of theatre that the winged fairy would develop, before emerging in visual art at the end of the eighteenth century as painters increasingly portrayed fairies as they were represented on the stage. While the precise origins of fairy wings remain somewhat obscure, it seems likely that they served the same purpose in the early modern theatre as they do today – as an immediately recognizable visual shorthand for the 'non-humanness' of fairies.

Elemental beings: learned and occult fairies

If classicization brought a new respectability to fairies as the successors of the godlings of the ancient world, the learned speculations of the early modern era also had the capacity to generate new beings – or at least revive entirely forgotten ones – that we might also include in the category of fairies. In the Hellenistic world, the idea that *daimōnia* were specifically associated with the elements had been widespread. Thus, the Middle Platonist philosopher Alcinous declared, 'And indeed there are other daemons, whom some would call (not erroneously) gods born in individual elements; some visible, others invisible, in the ether, in fire, and in water; so much so that there would be nothing in the universe that lacks a soul, and a life better than a mortal nature.'[91]

The idea of elemental daemons was famously revived and reinvented in the sixteenth century by the controversial Swiss physician Philippus Aureolus Theophrastus Bombastus von Hohenheim (*c.*1493–1541), known as Paracelsus, who advocated a radically new 'empirical' medicine that drew on the full range of ancient philosophical and esoteric thought rather than just the canonical ancient medical tradition. In his *Liber de nymphis, sylphis, pygmaeis et salamandris* (Book of Nymphs, Sylphs, Gnomes, and Salamanders), which was published posthumously in 1566, Paracelsus argued that *Geistmenschen* (spirit-people) inhabited each of the elements of earth (gnomes), air (sylphs), fire (salamanders), and water (nymphs).[92] Paracelsus's elementals may have been inspired in part by Nicholas of Cusa's (1401–64) speculations about extraterrestrial inhabitants of planets who shared each planet's elemental nature, as well as by the ancient daemons.[93] Paracelsus's doctrine of elementals should be seen in the context of a broader revival of the idea of monstrous races whose existence – and, crucially, lack of souls – demonstrated the uniqueness and spiritual importance of the human race.[94] The elementals are monstrous races that permeate the very fabric of reality, in a 'vitalist' conception of the universe where, to Paracelsus at least, it made sense that intelligent life should be everywhere.

In the pseudo-Paracelsian *Philosophia ad Athenienses* (Philosophy to the Athenians, 1564), the elementals were explicitly identified as fairies (*fata* or *fatalischen*) in an elision of learned occult speculation and folklore.[95] Indeed, Paracelsus's work both drew on and fed back into folklore, for instance in his elision of his elemental *pygmaei* or *gnomi* with the German *Bergmännlein*, diminutive spirits said to live in mines and inside mountains. The metallurgist Georgius Agricola (1494–1555) devoted a book, *De animatibus subterraneis* (On Subterranean Spirits, 1549) to the *Bergmännlein*, whom miners often reported seeing and hearing.[96] The new prominence given to this entity, like the later 'knockers' of Cornwall, was a consequence of early industrialization; early modern Europe's increased demand for silver led to an expansion of mining activity and therefore a burgeoning folklore of mines and mining.

Although Paracelsus's elementals are, in some ways, unlike fairies – they are strictly separated from one another and can dwell only in their element, for instance – in other respects Paracelsus could be said to have provided a 'scientific' account of fairy lore. He explained, for example, that the reason nymphs sought to intermarry with humans (which would explain stories of men marrying mermaids and water spirits) was that they could thereby obtain souls for themselves and their children. In Jan Veenstra's view, Paracelsus 'gave to the spirits of nature an independent place in the order of things, like a biologist who draws up a taxonomy of species'.[97]

Yet Paracelsus's speculations about diminutive beings were not confined to gnomes; he also believed, in common with many alchemists, that it was possible to *make* a diminutive, humanlike being that he believed was a sort of double of the alchemist, albeit without a soul.[98] The idea that magicians could create *homunculi* stretched back into the Middle Ages, and was entangled with fairy lore; as Samuel Gillis Hogan has shown, magical formulas for an ointment made from a lapwing that would allow the magician to see fairies derived from the same tradition as the *homunculus*.[99] The ointment was made not from a normal lapwing but from a bird spontaneously generated by the same sort of magical procedures used to create a *homunculus* – which might suggest that these procedures rendered the spontaneously generated lapwing a *fairy* lapwing, and that was how making an ointment from it made it possible to see fairies. As we have seen, the idea of fairies as soulless doubles of human beings was one found in both Scottish and Hungarian folklore, and perhaps something similar was going on here.

It was in the sixteenth century that fairy magic – the conjuration of fairies in ritual magic – really took off, at least in England. Frank Klaassen has speculated that English fairy magic was influenced by the Reformation, as well as incipient nationalism; fairies were less Catholic than angels or demons, but also more 'British'.[100] Dan Harms cautions against essentializing 'fairy magic' as a distinct category (or even sub-category) of ritual magic in this period, while maintaining that it is nevertheless possible to distinguish conjurations of fairies from conjurations of other kinds of spirits – not least because fairies are often known by a limited number of stereotyped names such as Oberon and Sibylia.[101]

Fairies were especially popular among magicians who wanted to conjure them for sex, perhaps because fairy brides so often featured in folklore.[102] Indeed, ritual magicians' interest in sex may have been a major reason for the conjuration of fairies, given that the portrayal of fairies in romance literature made them a more appealing proposition for sex than angels or demons.

Manuscripts of ritual magic invoking fairies rarely included commentary, but one late seventeenth-century English manuscript discovered by Harms includes a brief digression whose purpose seems to be to prove that fairies are spirits (fallen angels less evil than the demons) rather than 'some kind of people, which live here on earth, who are begotten and born one of another, and eat and drink as we do, and when they die are buried in the earth as we are'.[103] Clearly, the older 'naturalistic' idea of the fairies as one of the monstrous races was no good to the ritual magician who wanted spirits to conjure. But the author of the manuscript also claimed direct testimony for the spiritual nature of fairies:

> [A] certain friend of mine, who in his youth was much conversant with them and beloved of them, signified to me as far as I could perceive, that their stature was about five quarters high, he said they were a people living on the earth invisible as he supposed; I asked [if] they did eat such meal, and drink such drink as we do, he said no, but that they eat some kind of food.[104]

Perhaps under Paracelsian influence, the magician identified four kinds of fairies distinguished by colour: black, red, green, and white – colours that partly reflect their moral character, and partly their domain of action. John Walsh, who was tried for witchcraft in Dorset in 1566, similarly confessed to dealing with white, green, and black fairies, while William Camden noted a charm from Ireland that invoked 'woodland fairies, white, red, black, etc.'[105] However, it remains unclear whether this classification of fairies was a learned Paracelsian import into folklore, or a folk tradition we simply do not have enough information about to understand.

It is worth noting, however, that neither the classicization of fairies, nor their stigmatization by association with witchcraft, nor their invocation in magic and abuse by confidence tricksters caused most people to doubt their existence. Indeed, in the sixteenth century, fairies became more firmly rooted in elite, learned culture than ever before. The reformation of fairyland was not an assault on the *reality* of fairyland – quite the opposite, in fact. The late medieval and early modern 'revolution of credulity' privileged questions of interpretation over questions of ontology; if people said they had dealt with the fairies, that was usually taken to be true – the question that mattered was how that experience was to be interpreted, and what sort of demons were trying to deceive the faithful under a fairy guise. But, as we have seen, demonization of fairies could never wholly succeed, because fairies did things that demons were not supposed to be able to do – or, if they did them, it set them apart as a specific category of demons who seemed more like fairies than demons anyway. Fairies remained a stubborn and ineradicable weed in European culture that religious reformation failed to dislodge; the most reformers could accomplish was a transformation of the way people perceived and interacted with fairies. In the end, it would not be zealous Protestantism or militant Counter-Reformation Catholicism that began to eradicate the fairies, but an entirely different kind of discourse: for in the second half of the seventeenth century, the Enlightenment was dawning.

SIX

Trying the spirits: fairies and the enchanted Enlightenment

One day in 1645, a nineteen-year-old woman named Ann Jeffries, a poor apprentice in the house of the Pitt family in the village of St Teath in north Cornwall, went into the garden to knit. She sat down in an arbour next to the garden hedge; but after a little while she was alarmed to see six little people dressed in green come over the hedge into the garden. The young woman fell into a fit, where she was found by the rest of the household; and she remained dangerously ill into the spring of 1646. During her illness, it became clear that Ann had acquired the ability to see fairies; and when she recovered, she claimed they often visited her, fed her secretly, and gave her the power to heal.

Cornwall at the time was a county in arms; it was one of the last redoubts of hard-pressed Royalist forces in the English Civil War, who finally surrendered the northern part of the county to Parliamentarian forces that spring. This was bad news for Ann Jeffries; the new Parliamentarian magistrate John Tregeagle had Ann arrested on suspicion of witchcraft and confined in Bodmin gaol, where she was kept without food (since she claimed she received sustenance from the fairies). At Ann's trial a young boy of the household, Moses Pitt, was questioned about how she fed herself. But although Ann was imprisoned for many months, she was never convicted of any crime, and at last she was released to live out the remainder of her days in rural obscurity.[1]

The only reason we know anything about Ann Jeffries, and the extraordinary claims she made about the fairies, is that fifty years later the young boy who testified at her trial wrote an account of his memories of the case for the bishop of Gloucester, Edward Fowler. England in 1696 was a very different place from the war-torn England of 1646. It was an embryonic parliamentary democracy with a king (William of Orange) chosen by Parliament rather than claiming to rule by divine right. It was the England of the Royal Society, of Isaac Newton, Robert Boyle, and Robert Hooke, where pioneering industrialists such as Thomas Savery were beginning to experiment with steam technology – and where bishops such as Fowler sought a 'latitudinarian' middle ground contrasting with the fanaticism of the Civil War era. In his introductory letter to Bishop Fowler, Moses Pitt name-dropped Gilbert Burnet and John Tillotson,[2] bishops known for their modernizing and 'latitudinarian' views; and he presented his account of Ann Jeffries as an argument against atheism – 'By which the greatest Atheist may be convinc'd, not only of the Being of a God, but also [of] his Power and his Goodness.'[3]

On the face of it, a pamphlet presenting encounters with fairies as real might not seem a typical product of the Enlightenment. But Moses Pitt was a man at the epicentre of the early British Enlightenment, which in many respects set the pattern for the rest of Europe. Pitt was a printer and bookseller whose bookshop was patronized by Robert Hooke and other fellows of the Royal Society, who engaged Pitt on numerous publication projects.[4] Indeed, as the man with the practical wherewithal to bring complex scientific works to publication and market them, Pitt was arguably *the* lynchpin of the Enlightenment in 1690s London. Yet he believed in fairies. Indeed, his account of Ann Jeffries adamantly defended these 'airy spirits' as a part of God's cosmos. Just before her arrest, according to Pitt, Ann came to Pitt's father 'with a Bible in her hand' (although she was illiterate),

> and tells us, that when she came to the Fairies, they said to her, 'What, has there been some Magistrates and Ministers with you, and dissuaded you from coming any more to us, saying we are evil Spirits, and that it was all the Delusion of the Devil? Pray desire them to read that Place of Scripture in the 1st Epistle of St. John, chap. 4. ver. 1. *Dearly Beloved, believe not every Spirit, but try the Spirits, whether they are of God,* &c.' This Place of Scripture was turn'd down to in the said Bible.[5]

Whether Ann herself ever spoke these words or not (and whether or not the fairies spoke them to her), they certainly reflected Pitt's attitude, and that of the Royal Society. Bishops such as Burnet, Tillotson, and Pitt's addressee Edward Fowler were interested in both the natural and supernatural worlds. They were 'anti-Sadducists', reacting against some of the more radical and materialist speculations of Civil War-era religious sects and philosophers such as Thomas Hobbes, whom they identified with the Sadducees of the New Testament (an ancient Jewish sect who denied the resurrection and the existence of spirits). The anti-Sadducists were eager to assert both the truth of religion and the value of empirical investigation into natural philosophy. 'Try the spirits' might serve as a motto for the early Enlightenment. The avowed intent of the anti-Sadducist movement was to demonstrate the reality of the world of spirit, in the belief that denying any part of it was a slippery slope that would lead ultimately to atheism.

The fairies did not usually feature in anti-Sadducist polemic,[6] but the movement produced an outpouring of intellectual adventurousness in which some of the reservations of the sixteenth-century reformers were set aside; famously, Joseph Glanvill revived the idea of ghosts as spirits of the dead after decades of Protestant denunciations of ghosts as demonic deceptions.[7] What Glanvill did for ghosts, Moses Pitt attempted to do for fairies, returning to an earlier medieval notion of fairies as remarkable providences of God – an attitude that had more in common with Gerald of Wales than with his immediate predecessors.

Historians are intensely divided on the nature of the Enlightenment, and even on the question of whether it happened at all. Like 'the Dark Ages' and 'the Renaissance', 'the Enlightenment' is a folk-historical concept that has come under intense scrutiny by revisionist scholars eager to show that it was not what it seemed. In the area of supernatural belief, historians such as Owen Davies, Jonathan Barry, and Thomas Waters have shown that popular belief in witchcraft, service magic, ghosts, and fairies did not decline in Britain in the Enlightenment era (which, for the sake of argument, I will take as the years 1650–1800).[8] At the same time, however, learned and elite rejection of 'superstition' dominated publications during these years. As Paul Monod puts it, 'What can no longer be sustained is the hypothesis that magical beliefs had less appeal to ordinary labouring folk in England after the mid-seventeenth century than in the preceding hundred years . . . [and] decline in belief among educated people . . . was not a uniform or straight process, and was far from complete by 1800.'[9]

Indeed, even for Enlightenment elites, scepticism about the supernatural was sometimes more social performance than sincerely held conviction, and Monod and other scholars have highlighted the extent to which eighteenth-century thinkers remained intensely curious about the supernatural in spite of public displays of contempt for 'superstition'. Historians such as Monod and Michael Hunter have shown that it is not entirely true that 'scepticism about the supernatural . . . was the foundation of Enlightenment sciences'.[10] Scepticism was less a foundation, and more of a rhetorical glamour that overlay embryonic sciences whose conception of reality was less stable than the savants cared to admit. Thomas Sprat claimed in his *History of the Royal Society* (1667) that the advancement of knowledge had freed people from the fear that 'an infinite number of Fairies haunted every house',[11] but we know that Fellows of the Royal Society were actively interested in fairies at the very time Sprat was writing. The fact that demand for grimoires remained intense among elite book collectors throughout the eighteenth century tells its own story, perhaps.[12]

This chapter will explore the impact of the Enlightenment on perceptions of fairies, beginning with the sceptical onslaught against fairy belief. We shall then meet those who in the Enlightenment period continued to believe in fairy encounters and were prepared to defend the existence of intermediate spirits, before considering the evolution of representations of fairies in literature, art, and on the stage. Finally, the chapter considers the earliest beginnings of learned antiquarian interest in the phenomenon of fairy belief among ordinary people – which was, in effect, the beginning of the study of folklore as we know it.

The onslaught on fairyland

Just as the appearance of witches onstage in comedies in the Restoration period may have reduced the sense of threat people felt from witches, and introduced the comic witch as a stock character,[13] so the repeated appearance of fairies onstage in masques and plays seems to have suspended the usual fear of fairies, at least for some.[14] Yet the literary fairy was nothing new, and neither was the use of fairies as placeholders and objects of fantasy and imagination; why, then, was it only in the second half of the seventeenth century that some began to question the reality of fairies – as opposed to the long tradition of demonizing them?

Hutton suggests that 'fairy cozeners' like the enterprising cunning-woman Mary Parish, who in the late seventeenth century led the Whig politician Goodwin Wharton a merry dance with promises of fairy treasure and marriage to the Fairy Queen,[15] began to tarnish and discredit fairy belief – in combination with the established anti-Catholic tradition of treating fairy phenomena as illusions. We have to tread carefully here, however, as in the traditional anti-Catholic account fairy phenomena were *demonically generated* illusions, and therefore still required a demonology. A true attack on fairy belief required not only a questioning of the *identity* of fairies (for fairies could always bounce back from that sort of scepticism), but a questioning of the need for *any* sort of demonological account of fairies on the grounds that fairies were entirely non-existent.

It was Thomas Hobbes, in *Leviathan* (1651), who provided this challenge – although, as we have seen, naturalistic explanations of fairies as illusions date back at least as far as Michael Psellus, and Reginald Scot had anticipated Hobbesian scepticism in the 1580s. Hobbes argued that 'the opinion that rude people have of Fairies, Ghosts and Goblins', as well as witchcraft, was down to their inability to distinguish genuine sense impressions from dreams and 'decaying sense'.[16] This was the kind of attitude displayed by the earl of Shaftesbury, on hearing of Bishop Fowler of Gloucester's interest in fairies in 1711 – incredulity that such an educated man as Fowler could take fairies seriously. As Jeremy Harte puts it, 'As the fairies became less credible, they did fewer things that might stretch belief, which in the end meant doing very little at all.'[17] It is as though the 'revolution of credulity' that began in the second half of the fifteenth century had run out of steam by the late seventeenth, when theologians were more inclined to acknowledge the theoretical possibility of various kinds of demonic activity, rather than being eager to seek it out in actuality.

Brian Copenhaver has argued that the Enlightenment – or at least the 'scientific revolution' of the late seventeenth century – began with the breakdown of the 'reflexive deference to antiquity' that had characterized learning in both the Middle Ages and the Renaissance. This deference, which only intensified in the Renaissance, had ensured that scholarship remained primarily a philological activity; the aim of learning, under these conditions, was to establish the most authentic readings and interpretations of ancient texts, and not to discover new information about the world itself. Scholarship resembled a closed loop of textual reception, where both ancient and more recent authors were deemed 'authorities'.

What occurred in the late seventeenth century, according to Copenhaver, was a kind of 'empirical turn' in which empirical experimentation and fieldwork were elevated to the highest epistemological authority.[18] Mockery of belief in spirits – such as Laurent Bordelon's satirical *History of the Extraordinary Imaginings of Monsieur Oufle* (1710) – focussed on the absurdity of the castles in the air built by learned aficionados of demonology, who constructed an entirely paper image of the invisible world that was founded on text and authority rather than on experience.[19]

This attack on the *learned* sources of demonology was important, because it took sceptical critique beyond the charge of superstition (which had always been levelled, to some degree, against ordinary people who believed in fairies – including by the medieval church courts). Learned demonologists had always been able to defend themselves against the charge of superstition precisely because their subject was grounded in an elite textual tradition, such as the forest of references that supported Robert Burton's reflections on godlings and fairies in *The Anatomy of Melancholy*. Furthermore, the early modern classicization of fairies had extended their lifespan, rendering respectable the study of beings who were seemingly the denizens of Graeco-Roman mythology, and not just the dross of peasant folklore.

But authors such as Bordelon advanced a wholly new sceptical approach, in which mere learning, in and of itself, was no guarantee of getting any closer to the truth about the world. In 1679, Charles Blount, who quoted Hobbes approvingly, attacked *both* the godlings of the ancients and 'the opinion the rude people have of Fairies, Ghosts, Goblins and Witches'.[20] This represented a marked contrast to Burton's approach, where ancient belief in godlings *confirmed* the reality of fairies, or at least fairy experiences. The challenge fairies faced was this: if ancient authorities, popular superstition, and learned demonology were all worthless as evidence, what exactly was the empirical evidence that fairies existed? Empirical scepticism fed back in turn into philology; the Swedish philologist Carl Aurivillius (1717–86), for instance, unravelled one of the traditional biblical supports for fairy lore by arguing that the 'satyrs' of Isaiah 13:21 were misidentified goats or apes, and Scripture therefore did not support the existence of mythological beings.[21]

While thorough and explicit scepticism of the Enlightenment kind about fairies was rare before the second half of the seventeenth century (with notable exceptions such as Scot), we might be forgiven for thinking that earlier authors were sometimes rather tongue-in-cheek about fairies, and sceptics in all but name. As we have seen, the idea that the fairies belonged to a former world, and were either leaving or had left long ago, can be traced to the late Middle Ages; and the extravagance of the fantasies woven around fairies in the medieval romances and early modern literature hardly suggest that fairies were always taken seriously. Fairy belief was routinely mocked as superstitious by early modern learned elites – but 'superstition' was a double-edged term before the late seventeenth century.

On the one hand, 'superstition' suggested fatuous and unfounded belief in beings unsanctioned by Christian dogma or ancient authorities; but on the other hand, since the late Middle Ages, 'superstition' had been taken by everyone from bishops to witchfinders as a guide to the sins of ordinary Christians. Popular superstitions provided a map of the demonic world, and the ways in which the devil deceived the ignorant faithful. Furthermore, the willingness of an author such as Chaucer to make fun of fairy belief does not tell us that he would have entered a wood reputed to be a haunt of fairies without trepidation. Levity, in and of itself, is not reasoned scepticism.

Since fairies had long been regarded as a demonic deception by some demonologists, thoroughgoing scepticism about fairies required the elimination of the significance of the devil; and for this reason, Enlightenment scepticism about the existence of fairies should be viewed in the context of wider scepticism about the power of spirits. Such scepticism seldom proceeded as far as an open denial of the devil's existence, because Christian dogma still required belief in angels and demons. Yet bare assent to the existence of such beings did not require any particular interpretation of the nature of their involvement in the present world, even if their involvement in the narrative of the Bible was usually beyond question.

The disengagement of the devil from reality was a project of both Catholics and Protestants, and the Spanish Jesuit theologian Francisco Suárez (1548–1617) strictly limited the capacity of demons to afflict believers (and even unbelievers), and considered Satan himself to be bound in hell.²² The Dutch theologian Balthasar Bekker (1634–98) went even further, arguing on the basis of the mechanistic philosophy of René Descartes that demonic activity was impossible in *De Betoverde Weereld* (The World Bewitched, 1691–3).²³

Over the course of the eighteenth century, it became almost an elite orthodoxy in England to assert that the devil and demons existed (for the Bible said they did), but swiftly to follow this with the claim that they had no power in the Christian era. Furthermore, any speculation about them that exceeded the bare words of Scripture (including any talk of fairies) was liable to be dismissed as arrant nonsense. For John Toland, writing in 1696, 'the celebrated Feats of Goblins and Fairies . . . must be accounted idle and superstitious Fables'.²⁴ John Trenchard, writing in 1709, echoed the earlier arguments of Reginald Scot when he medicalized fairy experiences and portrayed them as the consequence of mental and perceptual weakness: 'To these Weaknesses of our own, and Frauds of others, we owe the Heathen Gods and Goddesses, Oracles and Prophets, Nymphs and Satyrs, Fauns and Tritons, Furies and Demons, most of the Stories of Conjurers and Witches, Spirits and Apparitions, Fairies and Hobgoblins.'²⁵

Beyond England, the learned German Jesuit polymath Athanasius Kircher (1602–80) adopted an equally sceptical but more naturalistic approach, arguing that beings such as mermaids who appeared to imitate the human form, mistaken by the ancients for gods, were in fact just animals with no more than simian intelligence, since 'nature revels in jokes of this kind'. They could not possibly be of equal capacity to humans, since that would call into question humans' status as 'the end of nature' and the image of God.²⁶

The diminishing faith of England's learned elite in the capacity of spirits to act in the world seems to be indicated by the virtual disappearance of accounts of ritual magic in the eighteenth century, although in 1703 Arthur Bedford reported that a Thomas Perks of Mangotsfield, Gloucestershire, had managed to summon up 'little maidens, about a foot and a half high' using a magical book.²⁷ Harte has argued that occultists in the eighteenth century tended to be interested in angels rather than fairies, and few would have tried to conjure the *regina pigmeorum* (Queen of the Fairies) as the astrologer William Lilly did in the late seventeenth century.²⁸ More than anything else, however, it was the growing distance between popular and 'genteel' culture in eighteenth-century Europe – what Purkiss calls 'civility'[29] – that cemented the marginalization of fairy belief. By 1750, it was more or less unthinkable that a wealthy English landowner might share the same folkloric beliefs as his tenants (at least openly). In 1680, a landowner sharing his tenants' belief in fairies would not have been especially remarkable.

By the later seventeenth century, fairy belief was no longer sustained by the need to explain otherwise incomprehensible phenomena such as fairy rings and 'elfshot', as other explanations were becoming available. John Aubrey took the view that fairy rings in grass were caused by 'the breathing out of a fertile subterraneous vapour',[30] and Robert Plot and Edward Lhuyd realized that the tiny flint barbs traditionally identified as elfshot were prehistoric arrowheads.[31] It is not as though fairy belief was ever sustained entirely by such 'fairy phenomena' – at its heart had always been fear of the fairies, and reported encounters with them – but the availability of alternative naturalistic explanations (however vague) removed one of the barriers to mockery of fairy belief for elites. There was no longer any reason to hold on to fairies as a hypothesis to explain anything.

There was also no reason for churchmen to be any more reluctant to let go of fairy belief than anyone else, given that the position of fairies in Christian theology had always been unestablished and insecure. Enlightenment clerics sought to downplay the supernatural elements of Christianity and to strip the elements of faith back to their essentials; and belief in fairies was certainly not essential. Even in Ireland, that heartland of fairy belief, the Catholic church began to express concern about the clergy's involvement in reinforcing popular cosmologies in the eighteenth century. In 1771, Nicholas Sweetman, Catholic bishop of Ferns, ordered that 'No pastor, priest or ecclesiastic whatsoever, in the diocese of Ferns, must presume, *sub poena suspensionis et privationis beneficii* [on pain of suspension and deprivation of his benefice], to read exorcisms or Gospels over the already too ignorant, and by such ecclesiastics to much deluded people, or act the fairy doctor in any shape, without express leave in writing from the bishop of the diocese.'[32]

Such prohibitions were as much to do with the social and cultural differentiation of priests from the ordinary faithful as they were to do with stamping out fairy belief. There is little evidence that the eighteenth-century church in Ireland seriously attempted the latter; but this era also saw the professionalization of the clergy as an elite social as well as spiritual class – a process that would only intensify in nineteenth-century Ireland, as Catholic priests remade themselves in the image of the Protestant clergy they rivalled. This was a process that required a clear differentiation between the 'superstition' of the ordinary faithful and the sophisticated theological understanding of the priests.

The defence of fairyland

While the 'empirical turn' of the Enlightenment certainly gave people plenty of reasons to disbelieve in fairies if they wanted to, sceptical responses to fairies were hardly universal among the luminaries of the era. The natural philosopher and poet Margaret Cavendish (1623–73), for example, was willing to accept the reality of fairies;[33] and as late as 1715–16 Richard Boulton insisted in his *Complete History of Magick, Sorcery and Witchcraft* that 'those who were Brothers and Sisters of the Art of Witchcraft' had traffic with the King and Queen of the fairies, whom Boulton portrayed as sinister beings.[34]

Enlightenment-era resistance to fairy scepticism was not just a sign of lingering or revived occultism, however – nor was it always an instance of self-conscious adherence to more conservative views on the spirit world (such as John Wesley's famous insistence on the reality of witchcraft). Rather, some Enlightenment thinkers took issue with the basic premise that there was no empirical evidence for fairies. As Nancy Caciola put it, 'investigation into the natures of spirits and demons was embedded within rationalist and analytical forms of inquiry' in early modern Europe.[35]

John Beaumont (*c*.1650–1731), a Fellow of the Royal Society and pioneering geologist, gave a detailed account of his encounters with 'Genii or Familiar Spirits' in his *Historical, Physiological and Theological Treatise of Spirits, Apparitions, Witchcrafts, and other Magical Practices* (1705). Beaumont's fairies were about 3 feet tall and he witnessed hundreds of them dancing in a ring in his garden, with their backs to the centre of the circle. Beaumont's claims came in for some strident criticism from deists, but even in 1705 the dominant response to Beaumont's extraordinary book seems to have been curiosity rather than ridicule. Sir Hans Sloane

(1660–1753) hosted a dinner party where he gave Beaumont the chance to share his testimony with a group of distinguished intellectuals. Even the duke of Buckingham, the most sceptical member of the group, apologized to Beaumont for his levity when he realized how sincerely Beaumont believed in his fairy experiences,[36] although Sloane himself was convinced there was a medical explanation for Beaumont's fairy visitations.[37]

In 1665, a new edition of Reginald Scot's *Discoverie of Witchcraft* (1584) was published with a new section on 'astral spirits', intermediate between angels and demons, by an anonymous author known as 'Anti-Scot', who seemed determined to present Scot's *Discoverie* as the very opposite of what Scot himself had intended. Whereas Scot had been an extreme sceptic (by the standards of his time, at least) intent on deriding belief in witchcraft and fairies, Anti-Scot sought to reframe the book as a storehouse of genuine information on the invisible world. Anti-Scot's intermediate astral spirits were picked up by the poet John Dryden, and Dryden was subsequently cited in the 1677 testimonies of women accused of witchcraft in the Scottish village of Pollok, showing that Anti-Scot's new characterization of intermediate spirits was penetrating popular consciousness and even informing judicial proceedings.[38]

Edmund Jones (1702–93), a nonconformist minister of Aberystruth in Monmouthshire, was a diligent collector of accounts of encounters with the fairies in Wales in the second half of the eighteenth century. Indeed, Simon Young identifies Jones's collection as the earliest British attempt to collect fairy accounts systematically – as veridical, first-person accounts rather than as folklore.[39] Jones was not interested specifically in fairies but in 'apparitions' generally, and indeed in any evidence of the reality of the spiritual world that would confound sceptics. He was critical, for instance, of Parliament's decision to repeal the 1604 Witchcraft Act in 1736.[40] But fairies feature prominently, such as the 'fairy funeral' seen by a turf-burner, 'imitating the singing of psalms as they went' – an apparition that foreshadowed a human funeral shortly afterwards.[41]

The best-known account gathered by Jones was that of a 'Mr E. W.' who recounted how, in 1757, he and his sisters had been crossing a field in Denbighshire when they spotted a ring of dancers, all dressed in red like soldiers – one of the dancers broke away from the group and pursued E. W. and his sisters, but failed to catch them.[42] In 1767, an innkeeper of Llangynwyd Fawr 'saw a numerous company with speckled clothes of white and red colour' in an upper room of the inn whom he took to be fairies, and who left behind 'a strange, red substance on the chamber floor'.[43]

As far as Jones was concerned, the fairies were unambiguously evil spirits. But his views on them were nuanced rather than dismissive, informed by the accounts he had received. For instance, he observed that they preferred 'dry grounds not far from trees and hedges and the shade of grown trees', and he noted their love for and protection of 'the female oak', harming anyone who cut one down – 'likely for the sake of the paganism of the ancient Britons, which they greatly practised especially under the female oak'. Jones complained that people thought the fairies 'to be some happy spirits, because they had music and dancing among them', but the preaching of Calvinist Christianity was empowering people to 'resist' the fairies and stop welcoming them into their homes – which also allowed people to cut down oak trees without coming to harm.[44]

The fairies seem to have been identified primarily by their wearing of the colour red and their distinctive activity of dancing in a ring, as well as by impossible feats – such as the jumping fairies who made great loops in the air seen by Edmund Daniel.[45] The fairies often appeared as children, or as child-sized (with old, wizened faces), and Jones knew of at least one changeling in his parish; but it was thirty years (he reported in 1780), since the fairies had been seen in the parish of Aberystruth, when a 'fairy wedding' had portended a wedding that was about to occur.[46] Some of Jones's fairies were shapeshifters – for example, the vanishing sheep seen by a group of people in 1760.

Perhaps because Jones was an autodidact without formal education who was still part of the community he served, he listened carefully to his informants and was never dismissive of their experiences. Indeed, he allowed their testimony to inform his own view of the supernatural world, which was rooted in the Bible but was also open to nuances of interpretation. For instance, Jones came to accept that not all spirits were equally bad ('though none of them good'), since '[as] the flesh of vipers . . . is of use in medicines; so some of the serpents of hell . . . are indirectly of some use in the kingdom of God'.[47] Rather like Dante's notion of the neutral angels in the vestibule of hell, Jones considered that the fairies were 'those [spirits] who are least in the hellish state, and but just in it on the other side of the unpassable gulf between heaven and hell'. But, unlike Dante, Jones did not think the fairies were fallen angels: '[They] are nothing else, after all the talking about them, than the disembodied spirits of men who lived and died without the enjoyment of the means of grace and salvation.'[48]

The true value of Jones's fairy accounts lies in the early date at which they were collected, which gives a glimpse of the 'pre-folkloric' state of fairy lore in Wales before the folklorists of the nineteenth century imposed their romantic, nationalistic, elite, and taxonomizing interpretations on fairy lore. This is not to say that Jones did not bring his own agenda of interpretation, of course – but his openness about his beliefs, his willingness to accept witness testimony as true, and his non-elite status make his collection uniquely important.

Another eighteenth-century hunter after fairies was the French Benedictine monk Antoine Augustin Calmet (1672–1757), best known today for his investigations of vampires. Unlike Jones, Calmet was extremely learned and was well aware of the literature on godlings and intermediate spirits, both ancient and more recent, but he was also a man of his time in relying on witness testimony as more reliable than the reports of the ancients. Thus, Calmet rejected gnomes and 'knocking spirits' in mines on the grounds that miners he interviewed told him such tales were mere fables.[49] At the same time, Calmet accepted the reality of *esprits folets* (in modern terms, domestic poltergeists) and familiar genii on the basis of witness reports he had received. Calmet seems to have been tempted to believe the *esprits folets* were not altogether evil, although he ultimately insisted they could only be considered devils:

> There is a place for wondering whether the *folet* spirits about whom we recount so many things are good or evil spirits; for the faith of the Church admits nothing between these two sorts of *genii*. Everything that is a genius is good or bad; but since there are in heaven many mansions, as the Gospel says, and as there are among the blessed various degrees of glory differing one from another, thus one may believe that there are in hell various degrees of punishments and torments for the damned and for the demons.[50]

Calmet also considered the possibility that poltergeist-like phenomena were caused not by spirits but by magicians somehow projecting their power. But in the end, the evil character of domestic spirits was proved by the fact they were unable to bear holy words or images; and Calmet took the view that where spirits did no harm, this was only because the power of God prevented them from doing so.[51] Calmet's approach was a strange mixture of a pre-Enlightenment-style accumulation of authorities and indiscriminate anecdotes and a distinctly Enlightenment insistence on direct testimony and a predisposition to doubt. Yet because he took personal testimony seriously, the value that Calmet placed on evidence did not always lead him in the direction of scepticism.

In countries where there were powerful cultural traditions of interaction with fairies, such as Scotland and Iceland, even learned intellectuals sometimes found it impossible to deny the evidence for a richer view of reality than Newtonian physics offered. The Icelandic historian Þormóður Torfason (1636–1719), known by his Latinized name Torfaeus, was one representative of the early Enlightenment who took seriously reports of elves, trolls, and spectres – not merely on the basis of the textual authority of a demonological tradition but because such things were 'seen, tested and with various signs proven'.[52] Gunnell has shown that Torfaeus drew on a pre-existing learned tradition of writing on elves and trolls in Iceland, and it seems likely that Iceland's small and embattled population, which was constantly on the alert against the dangers of a challenging climate and landscape, made a cultural separation between the preoccupations of clergy and those of ordinary people all but impossible. In the 1660s, Þorsteinn Björnsson of Setberg (d. 1675), evoking the uncertainty of theories of matter at the time, wrote that elves were 'similar to men in size and appearance, but their bodies are made of a light, fine-grained matter, for they are neither men nor spirits, but half-way beings. It is said that they die like humans. Those who have seen them say that they have no division between their nostrils. They live in hillocks and rocks.'[53]

Authors such as Björnsson and Torfaeus were interested in elves not just because they were fascinated by folklore, but because they believed that the existence of elves might explain features of the world they perceived around them. Torfaeus quoted with approval the view of Einar Guðmundsson that the elves 'were created by God with solid bodies and the senses granted to spirits', and noted that they 'follow perfectly human nature', while nevertheless insisting they were not human.

The elves 'do all they can to have their children immersed in holy water and christened', but their lack of humanity means that they cannot receive the sacraments. Torfaeus reported that in one church the remains of a cloth could be seen in which a girl was brought to church for baptism who was the illegitimate daughter of a local man and a woman of the álfar; the man's failure to acknowledge his hybrid elf–human daughter brought nine generations of mental afflictions on his descendants.[54]

Given the fluidity of early scientific speculations about the nature of matter, it is not immediately obvious that denying the existence of people made from a different kind of matter was the easiest way for seventeenth- and eighteenth-century Icelandic writers to process stories about the álfar. The possibility that a class of being *might* exist that belonged to a different class of matter was so intriguing that it could scarcely be ignored; and the fact that in Icelandic tradition the elves were customarily not demonized as mere spirits may have heightened Enlightenment fascination with them. Yet not everyone who thought fairies might exist conceptualized them as beings of a different material order; John Webster, writing in 1677, considered that the fairies 'are no real Demons, or non-Adamick Creatures, that can appear and become invisible when they please, as Paracelsus thinketh'; rather, they were 'truly of human race endowed with the use of reason or speech (which is most probable) or at least . . . they were some little kind of Apes or Satyres, that having their secret recesses and holes in the Mountains, could by their agility and nimbleness soon be in or out like Conies, Weazels, Squirrels, and the like'.[55]

As we have seen, the theory that godlings and fairies were monstrous races of wholly corporeal beings can be traced back to late antiquity; it was an idea supported by the euhemerized interpretation of Ireland's Tuatha Dé Danaan as a human population of ancient invaders, and even Gerald of Wales seems to hint at something similar in his observation that Elidyr's fairies spoke an archaic form of the British language. Webster, however, seems to have been the first author who articulated clearly the idea of fairies as a hidden 'relic population' of degenerated humans, which was to become an extremely popular notion among folklorists in the Victorian era. When Edward Tyson (1651–1708) was presented with the body of a 'pygmie' in 1698 (it was really a juvenile chimpanzee), he concluded that the pygmies were not a human race, but rather intermediate between human beings and apes. But he also thought the pygmies were the origin of legends of satyrs and wild men of the woods,[56] putting a folkloric complexion on his conclusions. If fairies turned out to be a real race of creatures, albeit not a supernatural one, did that mean fairies were real or not? The Enlightenment was ambiguous on the question.

In Scotland, as in Iceland, the phenomenon of 'second sight' seemingly offered empirical evidence of the fairies, and it was in this period that Scotland became a kind of laboratory 'where data about abnormal phenomena could be collected and theories tested'.[57] Margo Todd has argued that a 'cosmological pluralism' prevailed and was tolerated in seventeenth-century Scotland, if for no other reason than that the kirk was unable to eradicate it.[58] But it is also true that in Scotland (as in Iceland) the gulf between elite and popular cosmologies was nowhere near as vast as it was becoming in Enlightenment England. Scottish Enlightenment thinkers did not dismiss out of hand claims that were, apparently, supported by an extensive body of evidence and trustworthy report.

No one better exemplified this open curiosity than the learned minister of Aberfoyle, Robert Kirk (1644–92), who wrote one of the most important books on fairies ever written, *The Secret Commonwealth of Elves, Fauns, Fairies* (1692) – although it was not published until 1815. Marina Warner has argued that Kirk displayed 'a benign and tolerant delight in the breadth of human understanding, imaginings, and possibility', and regarded popular belief as 'worthy of intellectual interest and genuine respect'.[59]

While Kirk's open curiosity can be compared to the writings of Sir Thomas Browne, John Aubrey, or Robert Boyle (among others), Kirk's innovation was to defend the reality of the spiritual world not on the basis of the reality of witchcraft, but on the basis of the reality of fairies.[60] Kirk, like Moses Pitt, was not a fringe or reactionary cultural figure but someone deeply involved in the enlightened discourse of late seventeenth-century Britain. Much of *The Secret Commonwealth* was based on conversations Kirk had in London with Edward Stillingfleet, later the latitudinarian bishop of Worcester, who was renowned for his rationalist outlook.[61] Although *The Secret Commonwealth* is today seen as a book about fairies, and as a work of proto-folklore, Kirk's foremost interest was in the phenomenon of 'second sight' – in other words, people who claimed to see the fairies, to learn from them, and to foretell the future – rather than in the fairies themselves. It was the prominence of second sight in Gaelic culture that made it impossible for a man such as Kirk to dismiss fairy belief in the way that an educated Englishman would have found so easy at the same date. Kirk's subject was the fairies 'as they are described by those who have the second sight'.[62] It was, therefore, an *empirical* rather than a *demonological* investigation, albeit an eccentric one. But, crucially, Kirk admitted the second sight as a class of sense perception.

In Michael Hunter's view, *The Secret Commonwealth* was a 'Boylian' book in its 'genuine attempt to understand this interface between the natural and supernatural ... in its acceptance that things might be true even if we could not fully understand their rationale and its celebration of the discoveries of his age', such as microscopes.[63] Indeed, there seems no good reason not to regard *The Secret Commonwealth* as an early scientific work, insofar as it set out to explain an empirically attested phenomenon: second sight. It is just that second sight, and interaction with fairies as an explanation for it, have been consigned to the epistemological dustbin that Wouter Hanegraaff calls the Enlightenment academy's 'rejected knowledge'.[64] In *The Secret Commonwealth*, Kirk adhered to the scientific standards of his time, sometimes relying on first-hand observation (for instance, of the effects of elfshot on cattle), and seemingly making use of his own visionary experiences (although he never admitted this). As a seventh son (traditionally said to be gifted with the second sight), he was also a participant in his own folkloric narrative.

Kirk also relied on authorities, from the Bible to Raymond de Sebond, Cornelius Agrippa, Girolamo Cardano, Richard Baxter, and Henry More (although not, curiously, Paracelsus). The concept of the 'astral body' made of 'congealed air', introduced by Anti-Scot, was key to Kirk's work, and he explicitly compared fairies to the 'daemons ... of old'. Kirk produced an elaborate account of fairy nutrition, which they sucked from the 'foyson' (essence or nutritive quality) of corn, and portrayed a rich social life in which fairies were divided into 'tribes'. The fairies were 'subterranean' because they lived in 'cavities' in the earth, but they could also emerge from them. Kirk's fairies reproduced and were subject to mortality (albeit their lives were much longer than ours), and they would be judged at the last day. He also hinted at the identification of the fairies with the ancient inhabitants of the landscape, 'the print of whose furrows do yet remain to be seen on the shoulders of very high hills'.[65]

While it might be overstating the case to say that Enlightenment thinkers were as likely to contemplate the reality of fairies as not, it remains true that the likes of Beaumont and Kirk were as much motivated by the epistemological values of the era as anyone else. Martin Martin, in defending the second sight in an account of the Western Isles in 1703, noted acerbically that sceptics were usually willing to believe ancient texts that gave accounts of such phenomena but 'deny the People of this Generation the liberty to believe their intimate Friends and Acquaintance, Men of probity and unquestionable Reputation'.[66] In other words, the second sight was so integrated into the experience of all classes of society in the Western Isles that its reality was confirmed not only by experience, but also by networks of trust and sociability.[67]

As late as the 1760s, speculations such as Kirk's seem to have lingered among educated people in the Scottish Highlands; in 1763, 'Theophilus Insulanus' considered it plausible that gradations of life existed between humans and angels, 'as cogitative intelligent beings, [who] can communicate in sleep, or awake to the imagination . . . such truths as are hid, and always must escape the knowledge of organized bodies'.[68] As for Kirk himself, his fate was to become part of folklore; although the minister of Aberfoyle died in 1692, stories later sprang up that that he had been taken into fairyland, either because he had revealed too much of the fairy realm or because the Fairy Queen wanted him as her chaplain.[69]

Yet, alongside the expansive empiricism of Boyle and his admirers, there also existed an out-and-out esotericism as an elite counterculture in Enlightenment Europe. For the esotericists, embracing (or re-embracing) the Hellenistic notion of daemons presented little difficulty; it was part and parcel of the intense desire for an authentic Classicism that was a significant strand in Enlightenment culture. Durant Hotham, in his 1654 life of the German mystic Jakob Böhme, insisted that the 'aery region' (traditionally, the zone inhabited by the daemons) was inhabited by its own life forms, and drew on Jewish mysticism to support his contention:

> Nor is the Aery Region disfurnished of its Inhabitant Spirits; Some of the Jewish Rabbis say that [by] the creation of the Fowls of Heaven mentioned in Genesis, is understood not those only whose bodies we see, and catch, and

feed upon, but that far more numerous Progeny of Aerial Spirits, lodg'd in Vehicles of a thinner-spun thread than is (otherwise than by condensation) visible to our dim sight.[70]

Behmenism can, perhaps, be dismissed as the mystical fringe of Enlightenment thought. But the centrality of the figure of Socrates to the much more mainstream Enlightenment cult of reason served as a Trojan horse for daemons, since the *daimōnion* of Socrates was central to his story. The German Lutheran minister and historian Jacob Brucker (1696–1770), one of the foremost Enlightenment historians of the early history of philosophy, accepted the *daimōnion* as real, and denied it was an evil spirit; he acknowledged the *daimōnion*'s prophetic power, but he was also sceptical of the claim that the *daimōnion* should be identified as Socrates' guardian angel. After all, the *daimōnion* allowed Socrates to engage in idolatry by sacrificing to it, and it did not warn him of his impending trial and death or try to save him from it. The 'paredral daemon' of Socrates was, therefore, neither good nor bad.[71] If the *daimōnion* of Socrates was a real yet morally ambiguous being – a sort of 'fairy of the philosophers' that derived not from folklore but from metaphysical speculation and from Socrates' direct experience – then fairies could hardly be dismissed as absurd out of hand.

Fairies literary, painted, and theatrical

If the speculations of Enlightenment savants both for and against fairies are now largely forgotten, the same cannot be said of the transformation fairies underwent in literature, theatre, and art in this period, which has largely established the present-day expected appearance of the 'global fairy' in popular culture. Jeremy Harte has argued that it was from the 1730s that depictions of fairies were generally drawn from theatrical costumes, rather than from the garb of the aristocracy,[72] and theatrical costumes in turn influenced painters, who often portrayed scenes from Shakespeare. Both William Blake (1757–1827) and Henry Fuseli (1741–1825) portrayed fairies without wings in paintings based on *A Midsummer Night's Dream* executed between 1786 and 1790, although both painters included characters with butterfly-like wings on their heads. Laura Forsberg has argued that Thomas Stothard's 1797

Figure 6.1 Winged sylphs in Thomas Stothard's illustration for *The Rape of the Lock* (1797)

illustrations for Alexander Pope's poem *The Rape of the Lock* (figure 6.1) first introduced fairies with butterfly wings to illustration, although Fuseli had portrayed 'Robin Goodfellow-Puck' with bat-like wings a few years earlier (figure 6.2),[73] and Simon Young has identified portrayals of fairy wings pre-dating 1797.[74] It should be noted, however, that the problem of the origins of fairy wings is a peculiarly British one, since the Slavic vila and some varieties of Greek nereid have always been winged,[75] while Ireland's fairies still lack wings to this day.

The most important literary fairies of the early Enlightenment were forged not in Britain, however, but in France – in the *contes des fées* (fairy tales) that emerged from the late court of Louis XIV and are associated above all with Charles Perrault (whose *Tales of Mother Goose* was published in 1697), but in reality were written primarily by women.[76] Perrault's *Tales of Mother Goose* transmitted the tales of Cinderella, Sleeping Beauty, Puss-in-Boots, and Bluebeard (among others) in more or

Figure 6.2 Henry Fuseli, *Robin Goodfellow-Puck*, 1787–1790

less recognizable forms, although it is to be noted that these *contes des fées* were not exclusively about fairies. Lewis Seifert has argued that the *contes des fées* represented 'an elegantly stylized imitation of peasants' folktales' that deliberately subverted the highly classicized court literature of late seventeenth-century France. The *contes*' imitation of rusticity advanced the cause of the 'moderns' against the 'ancients' because it introduced a supposedly 'native' tradition of fables that rivalled the literary traditions of Greece and Rome.[77] The fairies themselves served in the *contes* as resolvers of narrative and bringers of order, represented most notably by the figure of the 'fairy godmother', who possesses foreknowledge of the future and bestows gifts on newborns, reflecting the ancient origins of the *fées* in the fate-speaking Parcae.[78]

The *contes des fées* were not, however, merely a revival of the fairy romance of the Middle Ages. Fairies did not act just as placeholders for ancient deities, as advancers of narrative, or as a mere *deus ex machina*. In the *contes des fées*, the mock rusticity and grotesqueness of the *fées* was the point, and *conteuses* (storytellers) such as Marie-Catherine d'Aulnoy (1650–1705) created what was perhaps the first truly 'international fairy', who in the eighteenth century began to displace native conceptions of supernatural beings in Iberia and elsewhere.[79] The spread of the *contes des fées* and their conception of fairies was undoubtedly aided by the fact that French courtly culture became the gold standard to which other European courts aspired, even to the point of speaking in French and fashioning their own *contes des fées*.

French literature proved the inspiration for the English writer Alexander Pope (1688–1744), whose portrayal of fairies in the satirical poem *The Rape of the Lock* (about the theft of a lock of hair from a society beauty) came to be especially influential. Pope drew his 'Rosicrucian' supernatural machinery from a French book (or its English translation) by Abbé Nicolas-Pierre-Henri de Montfaucon de Villars (d. 1673), *Le Comte de Gabalis* (1670).[80] The titular *comte* of the Abbé de Villars's book is a student of Paracelsus who advocates the reality of sylphs and gnomes, but *Le Comte de Gabalis* was not always received as satire; indeed, when the Abbé de Villars was assassinated on the road in 1673, a rumour that circulated was that the killers were a gang of angry sylphs, taking vengeance on De Villars for his exposure of their world – in much the same way Robert Kirk was said to have been taken by the fairies because he revealed too many of their secrets.[81] The Inquisition certainly missed the book's satirical intent, condemning an Italian man, Gioseppe Borri, who copied some passages from *Le Comte de Gabalis* in the 1680s.[82] Indeed, the Abbé sailed close to the wind in satirizing Christian doctrine itself – at one point, the Comte de Gabalis declares that God's original intent for man was for a polyamorous union with a gnome, sylph, nymph, and salamander rather than with woman.[83]

But mockery of fairies as superstition could sometimes carry a certain ambivalence. When, in 1691, the *Athenian Mercury* reported that fairies 'were never found, but where people were superstitious and credulous', it could not forbear from remarking that fairies were 'devils assuming such little airy bodies'.[84] In other words, the sceptics of the early Enlightenment were still, at heart, demonologists – eager to send fairies packing, but unable to resist the temptation to categorize them first. Furthermore, the revival of fairies for use in satire raises the question of why and how fairies still served a useful purpose, even if only a comic one.

What Purkiss calls 'teeny-weeny fairies' came to dominate eighteenth-century fairy poetry in England, which by the second half of the century was 'exhausted, left limp and gasping by the onslaught of imitativeness'.[85] But Pope's *Rape of the Lock* offered something new – an injection of Paracelsian weirdness, even if his sylphs and gnomes are entirely ineffectual beings. Yet they served a genuine purpose; only included from the second edition of Pope's poem in 1714, the sylphs and gnomes suitably distanced the events depicted from reality, allowing Pope to avoid accusations of impropriety by the gentry families whose feud he had caricatured in the first edition.[86] Furthermore, sylphs and gnomes provided a fitting *deus ex machina* for a mock epic, where the Classical gods or Milton's angels and demons would hardly have fitted. And there was a certain sense in which Pope's ineffectual fairies *were* real, insofar as Pope thought such superstitions did really render people ineffectual.

Like the Abbé de Villars and Pope, the Italian polymath Francesco Algarotti (1712–64) satirized demonology and fairy belief in a mock treatise of 1758, *Sinopsi di una introduzione alla nereidologia trattato filosofico erudito e critico* (Synopsis of an Introduction to Nereidology, a Philosophical, Erudite and Critical Treatise, 1758), which took aim at 'idiot savants' – people who were extremely learned and well read, but lacked the critical faculties to distinguish truth from nonsense. Yet Algarotti's 'nereidology' was not entirely a joke, for he also regarded the ancient cult of godlings with a certain wistfulness, even admiration:

> The sea was crowded with Tritons and Nereids, the rivers with Naiads, and the mountains with Dryads. The woods swarmed with Fauns and Nymphs, who, in these obscure retreats, sought an asylum for their stolen embraces. . . . Among the ancients, every thing sported with the fancy; and in those works, which depend entirely on the imagination, some of our greatest masters have thought they could not do better than borrow from the Pagans.[87]

In these words, written in 1756, there is perhaps an inkling of the Romantic approach to the power of the imagination that would dawn at the end of the century, in which the imagination's capacity to conjure marvellous beings would no longer be a subject for derision and medicalization, but a source of wonder and admiration.

The earliest folklorists

If fairies were of interest to Enlightenment savants, esotericists, poets, and artists, they were also under investigation by Europe's very earliest folklorists – scholars who were interested in folk culture for its own sake, which was highly unusual before it emerged as a fashionable scholarly pursuit in the nineteenth century. The term 'folk-lore' (originally with a hyphen) would not be coined until 1846, but the phrase 'popular antiquities' preceded it, at least in England. For the most part, even Enlightenment thinkers who were open to the possibility of the supernatural tended to reject traditional folkloric explanations for supernatural phenomena out of hand. Joseph Glanvill's account of the notorious poltergeist known as the 'Tedworth Drummer', which terrorized the family of John Mompesson in Wiltshire in the 1660s, included letters that referred to earlier fairy experiences in the house, but Glanvill did not consider fairies as a possible explanation for the phenomena.[88] This might be taken as the moment that the modern poltergeist was born, as an anomalous paranormal phenomenon severed from its roots in the fairy realm.

Elsewhere in Europe, by contrast, there was scant room for the study of folklore because supernatural belief was still under investigation as a judicial matter in the eighteenth century. Most of what we know about Hungarian fairy belief in this period, for example, comes from trial records.[89] In order to exist, the study of folklore or popular antiquities had to fall somewhere between the contempt of the philosophers and the paranoia of the authorities, in a sweet spot of disinterested curiosity that was not always easy to achieve before the nineteenth century. Nevertheless, the eighteenth century did see the emergence of a few works of this kind. Henry Bourne, in his *Antiquitates Vulgares* (1725), was curious about fairies as the detritus of paganism – a position that both stigmatized them and rendered them rather fascinating to learned antiquaries steeped in the Classical world.[90] Bourne, whose fieldwork was conducted in the north-east of England, found that there were still some people living who claimed they had been abducted by the fairies as children, and made to live with them for seven years (the same period of time the child Malekin had been forced to spend with a fairy family in the twelfth century).[91]

However, fairy lore was changing. Jeremy Harte has argued that the changeling story was 'pure narrative' by the eighteenth century, and no one conducted protective rituals any more against the abduction of infants.[92] The words people used for fairies were evolving, and during the eighteenth century the Devon dialect word 'pixy' (seemingly a variant of Middle English *pouke*) spread first to Dorset and then to Somerset, with pixy lore and pixy tales replacing older conceptions of fairies.[93] One early explorer of popular antiquities was George Waldron (1690–c.1730), who made a detailed record of the fairy lore of the Isle of Man, where he lived between 1724 and 1728 in the service of the British Crown.[94] Waldron's book attracted a considerable reputation to the island, and in 1794 David Robertson recommended the Isle of Man as the best place to have a chance of still seeing fairies.[95]

In Scandinavia, the early folklorists were influenced by the taxonomizing of Carl Linnaeus, the great Swedish botanist who invented the modern system of taxonomizing species. If flora and fauna could be divided into natural kinds, then surely the same applied to the beings of folklore, regardless of their reality.[96] This was an approach to supernatural beings that was to have a far-reaching influence and a long afterlife; it established not only the idea that categories of fairies could be sharply distinguished from one another, but also the notion that these fairy types were conceptualized in folklore as distinct races or populations of fairies – species, in other words. It is only since the 1970s that folklorists have begun to question seriously whether this 'taxonomic' approach obscures more than it illuminates, concealing the fluidity and complexity of local conceptions of folkloric beings and reifying the names of spirits as conceptually distinct categories when they were very far from stable. Yet the great age of the study of folklore was yet to come: it would emerge from the Romantic movement, bursting on the world in the nineteenth century like a dazzle of fairy glamour. But before we visit the nineteenth century, it is time to take a necessary detour and explore the spread of fairy lore throughout the world, beyond the boundaries of its European heartland. Fairies were about to go global.

SEVEN

Fairies go global

In 1650, a woman from Ostoticapac in the Mexican province of Jalisco, Catalina de Castañeda, was brought before Miguel Martínez, commissioner of the Inquisition of New Spain, accused of being in possession of a fairy in a box. An accuser testified that Catalina had communicated with the *duende* in the house of Agustín de Súñiga, who seems to have been a client; Catalina asked the little goblin questions and it communicated via knocks if the answer was yes. In particular, Agustín de Súñiga had sought to know whether the souls of dead acquaintances were in heaven, purgatory, or hell; Catalina asked these questions and listened for the knocks.[1]

Of course, the Inquisitor did not believe Catalina really had a *duende* in a box; the Spanish Inquisition, and its colonial franchises in the New World, was noted for its contempt for popular belief. Catalina was, rather, on trial for her belief that it was possible to know the destination of a person's soul after death – which, in Catholic teaching, is known only to God. Catalina was, in the Inquisition's eyes, a heretic – not because she believed in *duendes* (in the Inquisition's eyes, an empty superstition) – but because she held unorthodox beliefs about the afterlife.

Catalina de Castañeda was one of many people who not only brought European beliefs about fairies to the New World, but also developed them in distinctive ways. A fraught question in the folklore of the Americas is whether we should regard the fairies of the New World as nothing more than transplanted fairies from the Old World, or as entirely new, composite entities formed from the interaction of settler folklore with the beliefs of Indigenous peoples. Settlers appropriated elements of the supernatural beliefs of the Indigenous peoples they encountered, and vice versa; and even when such interaction was minimal, fairy belief outside Europe evolved in its own directions and acquired its own distinctive characteristics.

The transplantation of fairies beyond their countries of origin into settler societies is, on the face of it, surprising; fairies are supposed to be 'land spirits', tied intimately to the soil itself. It was a commonplace of writers on the colonization of the New World and Australasia to remark on the practicality and unsentimentality of settlers, and their freedom from superstition.[2] The reality, however, was rather different; European settlers not only brought their fairies with them, but they also entered into cultural dialogue with the spirit traditions of Indigenous peoples, as well as producing a mélange of European-derived folklore where settler groups of diverse European heritages mingled with one another.

The focus of this chapter is fairies as colonists – that is to say, the ways in which European folkloric conceptions colonized regions beyond Europe, and especially the Americas and Australasia, where European colonization resulted in permanent settlements of people of European heritage. Africa and Asia lie largely outside of the scope of this chapter, since European settlers did not generally become the dominant cultures there – even if Europeans did sometimes try to understand African, Indian, and Far Eastern religions through the lens of fairy lore. Indeed, just as European conceptions of fairies colonized the Americas and Australasia, so the Islamic conception of the jinn influenced and integrated itself into many cultures in Africa and Asia. At the same time, missionaries might be said to have culturally or psychologically colonized numerous cultures well beyond the reach of settler-colonialism. This might have consequences for a culture's 'small gods', who became subordinated to the Christian God and (in effect) 'fairyized' as ill-fitting occupants of a Christian or quasi-Christian cosmology.[3]

Nevertheless, the focus of this chapter is on the effect of actual settler-colonization on fairy lore, rather than the broader effects of European cultural and religious influences on belief in 'small gods' throughout the world – a subject too unmanageably broad to explore. Five broad groups of Europeans settled and brought their folklore with them in the Americas and Australasia: the Norse, the Iberians (the Spanish and Portuguese), the French, the English, and the 'Gaels' (the Irish and Scots). These groups were associated with the colonial settlement of different parts of the world: the Norse with Greenland, the Spanish and Portuguese with Latin America (and the Philippines), the French with Atlantic Canada and the Mississippi River, the English with the Atlantic seaboard of North America (as well as Australia), and the Irish and Scots with New England and Newfoundland respectively (as well as Australia).

The chapter will consider each of these regions in turn, and the distinctive ways in which fairy lore developed in them.

Skraelings and pygmies: Greenland and Vinland

The first Europeans to encounter the continent of North America were Norse mariners who settled in Greenland, the world's largest island, in the late tenth century CE. By the year 1000, Norse explorers had reached the regions that are now Newfoundland and the Gulf of St Lawrence, which they called Vinland. While Norse settlement in Vinland was short-lived, the Norse settlement of Greenland endured into the fifteenth century. In his *Íslendingabók* (Book of the Icelanders), composed in the 1120s, Ari Thorgilsson was the first to describe the Indigenous peoples of the Arctic and Atlantic North America as *Skrælingr*, a word that has so far proved etymologically impenetrable but seems to have been a pejorative term denoting the Indigenous peoples' small stature compared to the Norse.[4] Given that later geographers repeatedly reported the presence of 'pygmies' in Greenland and the far north, it has long been debated in Norse historiography whether the pygmies of Greenland were a misunderstanding of the Skraelings – or whether, in fact, Norse understandings of the Skraelings owed more to folklore than to fact.

For example, the Norwegian explorer Fridtjof Nansen (1861–1930) speculated that the beards ascribed to the Skraelings in the sagas and

Figure 7.1 Pygmies of Greenland, from Olaus Magnus, *History of the Northern Peoples* (1555)

reports of their dwelling underground were inspired by folkloric beings, and he noted that the names given to two Skraeling kings, Avalldamon and Avalldidida, seem to be linked to the name of the elf Ívaldr, whose sons made a spear for Odin.[5] In other words, lacking information about Indigenous peoples of the Arctic and North America, the medieval Norse filled in the gaps with folklore. However, Kirsten Seaver emphasizes the influence of medieval learning rather than Norse folklore, arguing that *Skrælingr* was simply the Norse translation of the Latin word *pygmaei*, and the Norse explorers had been primed by authors such as Isidore of Seville to expect to encounter monstrous races at the edge of the known world.[6] Isidore had actually reported that the pygmies could be found in India, so a considerable shift of perception was required to imagine pygmies living in the far north. This appears to have occurred in the thirteenth-century *Historia Norvegiae*, which reported pygmies dwelling in Orkney (and building wondrous cities) but did not identify the Skraelings as pygmies.[7] The Scottish tradition of a 'Pygmies' Isle' located somewhere in the Western Isles, where tiny bones were dug up, endured well into the early modern period.[8]

The Danish cartographer Claudius Clavus (b. 1388) reported on a map of 1424 that in 'the forests of Gronolonde' there were 'wildmen' entirely covered with hair, and *Pigmei maritimi* (coastal pygmies) dwelling in mountains towards the west. Clavus reported that a long hide-covered boat belonging to these pygmies was displayed in Trondheim Cathedral (probably a kayak belonging to the Thule people, ancestors of today's Inuit).[9] The report of pygmies 'only a cubit high' was repeated in an anonymous letter of around 1450 sent to Pope Nicholas V.[10] The idea that Greenland was inhabited by pygmies found its way into Olaus Magnus's *History of the Northern Peoples* (1555), where Olaus combined medieval reports of Greenland with the widespread and early ancient Greek idea of pygmies battling cranes (figure 7.1).[11] In Robert Rix's view, the myth of Greenland's pygmies was 'a garbled representation of the idea that Skraelings were diminutive men' in the sagas,[12] but when Dietmar Blefkenius met an aged blind Greenlandic monk in Iceland in 1563, the monk (who may have been an Inuit Christian – he is described as 'dark in colour, and with a wide face') was clear that Greenland's pygmies were different from the native population:

He said that the pygmies were a most perfect representation of the human form, and that they were hairy even to the tips of their fingers, and the men bearded down to their knees. But if they have the form of a man, there is however no sense in them, and no articulate speech, but only a certain hissing in the manner of geese. He said that his abbot nourished two of them, both a man and a woman, but they did not live long; he said they are brute animals, and live in perpetual darkness.[13]

It is difficult to know what to make of this account, but one detail of Blefkenius's interview with the Greenlandic monk is telling. The monk said nothing about the pygmies fighting storks, which would have linked them to the stereotyped image of pygmies derived from Classical mythology. That raises the possibility that the pygmies of the monk's account should be interpreted as spirits belonging to Inuit mythology – perhaps the underground-dwelling *ingnersuit*, diminutive beings said to help kayakers;[14] or the *aua*, a female 'shore spirit' who is no taller than an arm's length.[15]

Whatever the truth, there is no indication in any account other than that of the *Historia Norvegiae* (which refers to Orkney) that the pygmies of the north were in possession of any marvellous powers, so it is unclear whether we should see them as fairies. But it is also simplistic to view the pygmies of Greenland as merely a garbled account of real human populations, and they hover somewhere on the boundary of ethnography and myth, mingling notions of monstrous peoples inherited from the ancient world with travellers' tales, and perhaps even the beliefs of the Inuit themselves.

Conquest of fairyland: Latin America

Apart from the early Scandinavian settlements, the earliest European settlers in the Americas came from the Iberian peninsula, and it was Spanish and Portuguese ideas of the supernatural world that therefore dominated early European engagement with this domain of geography and humanity that was entirely new to Europeans. Iberian settlement of Latin America produced culturally complex and ethnically mixed societies in which Indigenous beliefs mingled with folklore brought from the Old World, such as belief in *duendes* (dwarf-like domestic spirits), beautiful supernatural women, and supernatural giants (*gentiles*). Specifically local beings compounded of elements of local and imported lore, such as La Llorona and the subterranean *chaniques* of Mexico, can also be found throughout the Latin American world. As in the Old World, fairy-like beings in Latin America are associated with bodies of water, aspects of the living natural world (such as trees), the abduction of children, and the dead, as well as playing a role in practices of divination. And as in the Old World, they occupy an ambiguous 'parareligious' status within Latin American popular Catholicism.

For some of the earliest Atlantic explorers, there was a sense in which they expected new lands beyond the ocean to *be* fairyland; as we have seen in chapters 1 and 2 above, the Irish tradition of *immrama* (tales of otherworld voyages) portrayed fairyland as a place located in the isles of the western sea, like the 'Isle of Birds' where St Brendan encountered the neutral angels who seem to be one and the same as the aos sí. However, over the course of the Middle Ages, this literary tradition acquired a *geographical* dimension as cartographers began to add St Brendan's 'Isle of the Blessed' or 'Hy Brasil' to maps, perhaps confusing these mythical places with the real 'Fortunate Islands' (or Canaries) which were rediscovered by Europeans in the thirteenth century.[16]

As late as the 1530s, when the Spanish were penetrating deep into the interior of Central America and encountering the great Mesoamerican civilizations, medieval legends about otherworld islands where gold was commonplace still motivated the Conquistadors, while islands discovered by the Spanish or Portuguese sometimes seemingly disappeared and could not be found again, like fairy glamours.[17] Famously, Bernal Díaz viewed Tenochtitlan through the lens of medieval romance literature, remarking that the city 'seemed like an enchanted vision from the tale of Amadis', while some soldiers wondered if they were dreaming.[18] Even if they did not think they were visitors to a literary fairyland, explorers fully expected to find the monstrous races who populated the fringes of medieval maps,[19] and in 1499 Amerigo Vespucci believed he had encountered a race of giants. The idea that parts of the New World (especially Patagonia) might be inhabited by giants who had somehow escaped the Flood (and were, presumably, descended from the giants of Genesis 6) proved a persistent one.[20]

But it was not only for those actively engaged in exploring it that the New World was an enchanted realm; if anything, for Europeans at home receiving news of the new lands beyond the ocean, the Americas were even *more* enchanted, and a site where reality and fantasy intermingled. It is unsurprising, perhaps, that the model of fairyland, which allowed people to imagine a non-Christian civilization at arm's length from normal domains of humanity, was invoked in order to process these simultaneously real and imagined realms. Thus, the English poet Edmund Spenser declared that the Fairy King 'all India obeyed, / And all that now America men call'. Fairyland offered an 'opposition to the known and the homely' and was always, like the New World, 'just beyond the boundaries of the known'.[21]

Among the Conquistadors, however, the enchantment of Amadis was short-lived. The most common (indeed, almost universal) European Christian response to the Indigenous religions of the Americas was to demonize them as the worship of devils. But this raised difficulties of translation, since the Indigenous people themselves did not have a binary understanding of the spiritual world as one that was divided into good and evil entities. Thus, when the Incan word *zupay* was used to translate 'devil', it gave Incans an inaccurate idea of what the Christian devil was, since a *zupay* was a spirit of a dead ancestor who appeared when ritually invoked. Bartolomé Álvarez complained to King Philip II that it was difficult to convince the Incans their gods were devils, since they had no word for 'devil'.[22]

Irene Silverblatt has shown that Incan religion underwent a complex transformation as a result of Spanish conquest: prevented from sacrificing to their gods, the Incans became intensely afraid of the gods' vengeance and therefore receptive to the missionaries' portrayal of the gods as evil – although the testimony of some Incans brought before the Inquisition also shows that they believed *huacas* (Andean 'gods' or spirits) deprived of sacrifice were hungry, enfeebled beings who were unable to do much to help them against the Spanish.[23] Once-powerful deities were on their way to becoming diminished beings of vernacular culture, not unlike the fairies of Europe.

Missionaries engaged in extensive campaigns of iconoclasm against Indigenous sacred sites, but Fernando Cervantes has argued that the mendicant missionaries, and the Franciscans in particular, 'succeeded in instilling upon the indigenous minds an image of Christianity as a new power filled with supernatural forces that seemed stronger than the nature spirits of the local religious systems, but not for this reason dramatically different from their world view'.[24] In other words, the Franciscans encouraged a view of the power of angels, saints, and the Virgin Mary that was theurgic (focussed on miracles) and immanent – infusing the whole world, rather than inaccessible in a remote heaven.

In many ways, the fairy beliefs of Latin America were very similar to those held in Spain and Portugal; José Manuel Pedrosa has noted that we can speak, to some extent, of a 'pan-Hispanic popular mythology' from the early modern period onwards.[25] For instance, the Iberian folklore of *gentiles* (mythical giants) came to be transferred from the Pyrenees to the Andes.[26] Nevertheless, many of those brought before the Inquisition of New Spain for unacceptable beliefs were *mestizos* – people of mixed Spanish and Indigenous heritage – for example, a woman interrogated by the Mexican Inquisition who reported holding conversations with a *duende* dressed as a Mercedarian friar every day when she woke up.[27] Another woman confessed in 1676 to having sex with a *duende*.[28] The association with *mestizos* raises the question of whether the *duendes* and other apparently European folkloric beings of Latin America were composite beings consisting of both Indigenous and imported European elements.

In some cases, the presence of Indigenous inspiration seems quite clear. For instance, in the city of Tunja in New Granada (now in Colombia), Beatriz de la Gasca was accused in 1649 of holding prayer vigils with four other women; she made wax candles into crosses and burnt them on makeshift altars while saying the rosary, but while she did so 'a golden snake and white doves' as well as 'a winged shadow with a dog's snout' appeared, which Beatriz interpreted as her guardian angel but the Inquisitors saw as evidence that Beatriz was really praying to pre-Christian ancestral spirits.

This kind of ambiguity concerning whether 'angels' were actually demons was not confined to the Americas, and Fernando Cervantes notes that the same concerns were raised about the apocryphal 'Seven Angels of Palermo' in Sicily.[29] Apocryphal angels became immensely popular from Peru to Bolivia in the seventeenth century, and the extent to which these beings were intimately involved in the natural world in

Latin American piety meant they risked straying from an orthodox view of angels.[30] In later Latin American folklore, we continue to encounter the *duendes*, as well as locally specifically versions of them such as the Mexican *chaniques*, usually portrayed as small naked beings who live underground, protecting the earth and water sources.[31] Indeed, whereas in Iberia *duendes* usually protected buried treasure, in Latin America they came to protect nature, such as a *duende* called Abigar who protected trees in the area of Guadalajara, and the *duendes* who protect the tree of Tecolote.[32] In the province of Jalisco (whose capital is Guadalajara), *duendecillos* (little *duendes*) were also thought to steal infants from their cradles, and tried to drown young children in bodies of water.[33] *Duendes* have thus become linked in modern Mexican folklore to *lloronas*, weeping female ghosts who are mourning their drowned children and yearn to drown others – who often seem more like Europe's supernatural fairy women than ghosts of dead human beings.[34]

Often conceived of as a singular being, La Llorona (the weeping woman) has been identified as the goddess Cihuacóatl, lamenting the destruction of Tenochtitlan and of her children the vanquished Mexica people. She then became transmuted in folklore into a much more local figure, particularly associated with bodies of water.[35] It is probably not meaningful to ask who La Llorona was 'originally', and this seems to be asking the wrong question – even if La Llorona incorporates elements of the identity of a Mesoamerican goddess, she is now a distinct figure of Mexican folklore who has her own function and associated stories. In their study of *mouras encantadas* (enchanted moors, the traditional fairies of Portugal) in the Brazilian Amazon, Mara Nogueira and Sonia Maria Sampaio argue that syncretism and creolization were not one-way streets that saw supernatural beings from Portugal simply imposed on Brazil. Brazil's *mouras encantadas* in their turn became merged with the *iaras*, water spirits of Indigenous belief.[36]

Indeed, the synthesis of Iberian with Indigenous folklore was not unique to the Americas: it also extended to the Philippines in East Asia. Under Spanish rule from 1565, the Philippines were Christianized by Spanish missionaries in a similar way to New Spain, resulting in a fusion of lore documented by the Filipino folklorist Maximo Ramos. This included belief in *duwendes* not dissimilar from the *duendes* of New Spain, although it is always unclear where Filipino traditional belief ended and

Spanish influence began.[37] Figures like the *duendes*, La Llorona, and the *mouras encantadas* are creolized entities with both Iberian and Indigenous elements that cannot now be separated.

From oky *to* lutins: *fairies of French North America*

In francophone North America, from Quebec to Newfoundland and Louisiana, imported folklore interacted with Indigenous beliefs in much the same way as they did in Latin America, and the seventeenth-century French Jesuits who attempted to evangelize the Indigenous peoples of present-day Canada were challenged by beliefs about the spiritual world that corresponded to no Old World religions – resembling folklore more than religion. Old World entities such as *lutins* and *feux follets* took on new meanings and new identities in North America, where they fused with Indigenous traditions of unreliable trickster spirits, while travellers were struck by the apparent close resemblance of Indigenous spirits such as the Cree *memeguayiwahk* to European conceptions of fairies. Like fairies in Europe, the Indigenous 'little people' of North America had the capacity to coexist with Christianity, and could even be integrated into popular Catholicism.

The French Crown began to explore North America in the sixteenth century, but it was not until 1605 that French settlers began to colonize Acadia (present-day Nova Scotia) with some success; the foundation of Quebec followed in 1608, and by 1655 the French had begun to colonize Newfoundland. Colonists established French control over the Great Lakes region and the vast Mississippi River, and the colony of Louisiana (at the mouth of the Mississippi) was established in 1682. This gave the French the upper hand in the interior of North America until French defeat in the Seven Years War (1763) and the Louisiana Purchase (1803) handed the former New France to the British and Americans. The economy of New France was largely driven by the fur trade, and while the French established some key centres of population, the expansion of New France was economically extractive rather than focussed on the colonization and cultivation of land by French settlers. However, Catholic missionaries (most notably the Jesuits) made determined efforts to convert the Indigenous peoples encountered by the French, who were the first Europeans to reach the deep interior of what are today Canada and the Midwestern United States. As elsewhere, a challenge for the missionaries was interpreting the beliefs of peoples such as the Huron and Iroquois in terms comprehensible to Christian theology.

While Jesuits usually identified the *manitou* (a kind of spiritual life-force) of Native American belief in New France with the devil, some missionaries acknowledged *manitou*'s moral ambivalence; for Paul Le Jeune, superior of the Jesuits in Quebec between 1632 and 1639, *manitou* referred to all natures superior to the human, whether good or bad, while Paul Ragueneau acknowledged that a different Algonquian word, *oky*, could refer to 'things that have a virtue like supernatural'.[38] Even when the Jesuits interpreted the spiritual forces of North America in wholly demonic terms, it was clear that the demons behaved rather differently from those at home, and more like fairies than demons – they demanded gifts of tobacco and offerings of armour, and could even take the form of portable objects called *aaskouandy* (which might be pouches or bundles of string or feathers) – and Cowan has argued that the Jesuits saw the demons as mirror images of themselves insofar as both Jesuits and demons were busily accommodating themselves to the peculiarities of Iroquois and Huron culture.[39] Paul Le Jeune also responded to claims of diabolism with scepticism, suggesting that many Indigenous claims of prophetic dreams and visions were attention-seeking charlatanry.[40] Yet some practices, such as the carrying of *aaskouandy* (which were understood to be personal beings, embodied in a physical object carried in order to achieve success) were seemingly too far beyond the Jesuits' experience for them to form a coherent opinion on them.[41]

In a sense, what the French missionaries found among the Indigenous peoples of North America was folk belief unmoored from the superstructure of religion they had come to expect in Europe; Native Americans had no creeds, no places of worship, no religious institutions or hierarchies, and no specialized clergy; rather, for them the entirety of nature and the landscape was infused with spiritual energy.[42] Jean de Brébeuf, who lived among the Huron, acknowledged that the Huron were in error but insisted that their spiritual beliefs should be carefully listened to and treated with respect, and sometimes expressed uncertainty about the origins of some of their claimed communications with the spirit-world, even mooting the possibility that some special providence of God had endowed the Huron with supernatural gifts – an approach echoing Scottish discourse on the second sight.[43]

Ironically, in return the Indigenous people sometimes concluded that the 'Black Robes' (as they called the Jesuits), with their strange ways and claims to supernatural power, were themselves sorcerers, shamans, or even *oky* – beings of spiritual power.[44] There seems to be no sign, however, that the Jesuits ever tried to make sense of Indigenous belief in terms of the folklore of the French peasantry. Missionaries were, in a sense, the Christians least likely to interpret Indigenous cultures through the lens of folklore because they often saw the folklore of the mother country as part of the same problem of idolatry and superstition. Thus, Zoë Crossland has suggested that the Welsh missionaries David Jones and David Griffiths, on a mission to Madagascar in 1822, may have vandalized the 'tomb' of a hero of the Vazimba (the legendary fairy-like pre-human inhabitants of the island) *because* the legend associated with it resembled that of the fairy bride who emerged from Llyn y Fan Fach in their home country of Wales.[45]

Syncretism between French and Indigenous Cree or Algonquian belief did, however, arise among the Métis people: people of mixed heritage generally descended from the unions of French fur trappers with Cree or Algonquian women in what are now Alberta, Saskatchewan, Manitoba, Ontario, British Columbia, and the Northwest Territories. Perhaps the best-known product of syncretism in Métis folklore is the *rougarou*, who combines characteristics of the French werewolf with the 'skinwalker' of Native American belief,[46] but the *memeguayiwahk* or 'little people' also represented a synthesis of European and Indigenous belief – or at least a marked degree of convergence. Like the fairies of Europe, the existence of the *memeguayiwahk* explained the discovery of flint arrowheads, and the little people were said to live in mounds.[47] However, they were also intensely violent, vicious, and extremely strong, as Meriwether Lewis reported when he was accompanied by ten Métis men to the 'Mountain of the Little People' at the junction of the Vermillion and Missouri Rivers on 5 August 1804.[48] In the 1990s, Louis-Jacques Dorais was studying the supernatural beliefs of the Inuit people of Nunavik – the vast and sparsely inhabited northern portion of the province of Quebec – and found a high degree of syncretism in Inuit shamanic practice that reflected the influence of Christian missionaries. For instance, shamans might channel or ritually become the spirits of animals unknown to the Inuit but spoken of in the Bible, such as lions. However, he found belief in *inugagulligait* (whom Dorais identified as *lutins*) in decline, 'because they do not have a role to play in modern life'. Yet belief in ghosts and visionary dreams among the Inuit continued unabated.[49]

Meanwhile, the French settlers of New France brought belief in *lutins* with them, although much evidence for Canadian fairy lore is late and dates only from the late twentieth century.[50] Gary Butler, searching for belief in *lutins* among the French-speakers of Newfoundland in the 1980s, found that the *lutin* had dwindled to an explanation for the inexplicable matting or braiding of horses' manes in the stable, which was supposed to be done by the *lutins* to make little stirrups for themselves when riding the horses at night.[51] An earlier belief that *lutins* might manifest in the forms of various animals, recorded in Quebec at the end of the nineteenth century,[52] seems to have vanished by the end of the twentieth. The French-Newfoundlanders' belief in *lutins* and *feux follets* (will-o'-the-wisps that led travellers astray by night) seemed to derive from a mixture of Breton, Norman, and Acadian cultural influences,[53] and is also found across the border in the US state of Maine, especially in Aroostook County where many people of Acadian descent still live.[54]

The *feux follets* could also be found in Louisiana where they were sometimes identified as dancing fairies, but at other times as the souls of unbaptized babies or souls escaped from purgatory.[55] The *lutins* of Louisiana, however, belong not only to the folklore of the descendants of French settlers but also to the Indigenous Houma people, who describe the *lutins* as mischievous beings about the size of small children, with attractive faces and long beards. The *lutins* can be repelled by leaving mustard grains in a cup, but sometimes they are said to engage in more menacing acts such as sucking blood from babies. Nathan Rabalais has noted the similarity of Houma *lutin*-lore to the Choctaw *bohpoli*, a connection generally missed by folklorists who have assumed that the French name of the *lutins* means they are largely derived from French folklore. As Rabalais puts it, 'It is impossible to ascertain whether at some point the French term *lutin* may have replaced a Houma word in the eighteenth century as the tribe gradually adopted French as its primary language or if a vestige of Acadian folklore may have fused with a preexisting Houma belief that in turn reinforced it among the White Francophone population.'⁵⁶

This problem is a perennial one for the interpretation of fairy lore beyond Europe and the Middle East. When a word used for a fairy-like being in Europe is used in a cultural context outside Europe, does it refer to the European being transposed to a new territory, or does it refer to a being of Indigenous belief under a borrowed European term, or does it refer to a new composite being combining European and non-European folkloric elements? These questions are often unanswerable.

'No fairies in the Mayflower came': New England

New England (the states of Connecticut, Maine, Massachusetts, New Hampshire, Rhode Island, and Vermont) was colonized by English settlers from 1620 – the so-called 'Pilgrim Fathers', who are usually perceived as Puritans hostile to folk belief in their home country. Owen Davies has argued that the English settlers did not bring fairy lore with them, because it was closely tied to specific features of the English landscape; furthermore, the English Puritans were more afraid of witches than they were of fairies, and belief in witchcraft proved more readily portable than fairy belief.⁵⁷

However, early American Puritans were very much aware of fairies and perceived them as a threat. When the anti-Puritan settler Thomas Morton (*c*.1579–1647), founder of the short-lived colony of Merrymount (now Quincy, Massachusetts), set up a maypole and encouraged dancing involving both the settlers and native people, he was denounced by Governor William Bradford of the Plymouth Colony for imitating the fairies: 'They also set up a maypole, drinking and dancing about it many days together, inviting the Indian women, for their consorts, dancing and frisking together (like so many fairies, or furies rather), and worse practices. As if they had anew revived and celebrated the feasts of the Roman goddess Flora, or the beastly practices of the mad Bacchanalians.'⁵⁸

It is not altogether clear why Bradford compared the settlers of Merrymount to fairies; fairies were associated with dancing in a circle, with May Day, and with paganism. Perhaps all three senses were meant. But Bradford's seeming identification of fairy belief with paganism chimed with both the learned speculations of antiquaries such as John Aubrey and a Puritan religious paranoia that viewed any hint of traditional religion not founded on the Bible as pagan. The idea that the Puritan settlers created a New England free from fairies became embedded in American culture, and in an 1848 celebration the children of Boston sang that 'No fairies in the Mayflower came.'[59]

Perhaps it might be more accurate, however, to say that the Puritans brought with them a reluctance to speak about fairies, rather than a total absence of belief in their existence. As Peter Muise has shown, belief in 'elf-shot', especially as an explanation for illness in horses, was indeed brought to New England,[60] and in the 1830s a boy of English descent in Campton, New Hampshire, encountered a tiny fairy, seemingly before other cultural influences held sway over New England.[61]

The cultural conformity craved by the earliest Puritan settlers was always more of an aspiration than a reality. The New England colonies were desperately in need of people in order to make their existence viable, and it was not long before settlers from beyond the Puritan heartlands of East Anglia and the Midlands of England began to make their mark on New England's developing folklore. For example, the town of Marblehead, New Hampshire, was settled by fishermen from England's West Country who were not hostile to fairy lore, judging from stories from Marblehead reported in the nineteenth century.[62] But it was not settlers from the West Country who would bring fairy lore to prominence in English-speaking North America, but the Irish immigrants who began to arrive in North America in the first half of the nineteenth century, and became a flood after the Great Famine of 1845 caused by potato blight in Ireland.

In some cases, the Irish fairies of New England were simply Irish fairies transplanted to an American context, such as the banshee heard wailing at the time of the assassination of President John F. Kennedy, the banshees of Harrisville, Rhode Island, and the fairy hawthorn trees found in Providence.[63] In other cases, however, the Irish (or Scots-Irish) fairies of New England underwent an evolution of their own to become distinctive to the region, such as the fairies of Derry, New Hampshire.

Derry was founded as Londonderry by a lake called Tsienneto by Scots-Irish settlers from Ulster in 1729, and in 1907 Robert N. Richardson elaborated a legend in which the name Tsienneto was that of a Native American medicine man who created features of the lake – a story told to the poet by a 'wood nymph'. Within a few years, Tsienneto had evolved in Derry folklore into a fairy queen who lived in the lake and came to the aid of those in distress. As late as the 1950s, people were claiming to encounter fairy-like beings around Derry.[64] Similarly, the rumour that a man of Sherman, Connecticut, named Perry Boney (1855–1921) not only communicated with the fairies but actually *was* a fairy seems to express a distinctively North American inflection of fairy lore.[65]

As in French-speaking North America, Native Americans in New England adapted their lore of spirits in response to European and missionary influence. For instance, among the Passamaquoddy people of Maine the rather menacing *mekumwasuck* (forest spirits who would cause the death of anyone they looked at) also became Christians and took on the role of protectors of churches, beating up anyone who stole from churches or otherwise violated their sanctity.[66] Clearly, European anxieties about the compatibility of traditional land spirits with Christian belief did not prevail among the Passamaquoddy, with the malevolent spirits of Indigenous belief serving to *enforce* correct Christian behaviour. The identification of beings of Native American belief, such as the *mikumweswak* and *wanagemesmak* of the Penobscot people, as 'fairies' by anthropologists may say more about European assumptions than about how Indigenous peoples themselves perceived them,[67] although by the 1960s members of the Passamaquoddy people sometimes drew an analogy between spirits they called the *winokomehsuwok* and leprechauns.[68]

The malevolent pukwudgies, who are perhaps the best-known of all New England 'fairies', may not be native to New England at all, and seem to derive from settler interpretations of Native American beliefs in the Midwest. But wherever they come from, sightings of pukwudgies are now regularly reported by Americans of European descent across New England.[69] The portrayal of pukwudgies as troll-like, ugly, and malevolent, which is common in contemporary American culture, seems to date only from the 1980s, however; before that, the pukwudgies were simply small versions of the human form.[70]

New England's reputation as a haven of religious liberty and religious free-thinking may have contributed to the rise of its fairy lore under the influence of Transcendentalism, Spiritualism, and Theosophy, promoted by authors such as Louisa M. Alcott and Dora van Gelder Kunz.[71] But the major impact of European settlement on Native American traditions of social spirit-beings seems to have been to make Indigenous encounters with them less frequent. As the Mohegan elder Fidelia Fielding reported to an anthropologist in 1908, before the spread of white settlements 'folks saw more things in the woods than they do nowadays'.[72]

An Atlantic fairy stronghold: Newfoundland

The island of Newfoundland (which may be the Vinland of the sagas) was briefly colonized and then abandoned by Norse settlers around 1000 CE before its rediscovery by Europeans at the end of the fifteenth century. It was not until 1610 that the English established a permanent colony on the island, and dominance over Newfoundland was contested with France in the seventeenth century. Irish and Scottish immigrants arrived in Newfoundland in the early nineteenth century, and the region is renowned for the extent to which its inhabitants of Irish and Scottish descent maintain folk traditions, to a greater extent than most parts of mainland North America, lending Newfoundland culture a distinctively 'Gaelic' character.

This is reflected in Newfoundland fairy lore, which is among the richest of any settler community in North America, and largely retained the character of Scottish and Irish fairy belief. The Canadian folklorist Barbara Rieti has extensively documented the fairy lore of Newfoundland, where fear of the 'fairy blast' was especially prevalent. The fairy blast, an idea related to 'elfshot', was the belief that if the fairies (usually when they were offended) successfully threw an object at someone it would create a wound or tumour that would never truly heal, and might extrude a variety of foreign objects over time.[73]

Rieti identified Newfoundland fairy tradition as primarily a composite of lore from south-east Ireland and the West Country of England,[74] and the island's fairy lore retained remarkably archaic features for a folklore exported thousands of miles across the Atlantic.[75] On the one hand, Newfoundland was a cultural melting pot of English, Irish, Scots, Ulster-Scots, and French settlers; but on the other hand, it was an exceptionally isolated place (Newfoundland did not become part of Canada until 1949), the fairy lores of its various communities were broadly compatible, the traditional lifestyles of Newfoundlanders were maintained for a long time, and the extinction of Newfoundland's Indigenous Beothuk people meant that there was little or no interaction between European and Indigenous traditions about spirit-beings. However, Newfoundland's fairy lore has also been intensively collected; as Simon Young notes, Memorial University's collections of fairy lore are rivalled only by those of Ireland's National Folklore Collection, and some of the world's most gifted folklorists have worked on Newfoundland fairy belief. So it could be that the richness of Newfoundland lore is due, in part, to the greater extent to which it has been investigated, in comparison with that of other regions.[76]

Newfoundland fairy lore is remarkable for its strength and persistence rather than for its uniqueness or originality, although certain features are emphasized in Newfoundland stories to a greater extent than in Ireland. These include the risks and consequences of the fairy blast, the particular hazards faced by berry-pickers, the 'fairy squall' (the idea that fairies arrive on the wind), the bad luck associated with building on 'fairy paths' (a tradition recorded in modern Ireland), and the idea of horses' manes being plaited by the fairies (as we have seen, a French *lutin* tradition).

There are also some distinctively North American inflections to the tales told about fairies in Newfoundland – for example, someone kidnapped by the fairies is rescued by being pulled off a sledge rather than off a horse, and fairies in Labrador are said to help rather than lead astray people who get lost in snow storms.[77] In modern Newfoundland, as in Ireland and Iceland, traditional fairies have not yet succumbed to sentimentalization or been replaced by anodyne international stereotypes drawn from film or fiction – and, perhaps more importantly, tales of interaction with the fairies have not yet been relegated to the folkloric neverland of 'once upon a time' but are still grounded as historic events in communal memory, such as the woman who reported in 1973 that the fairies had last swapped a changeling fifteen years earlier.[78]

Kintji *and* Patupaiarehe: *fairies of Australasia*

Humans have inhabited Australia for at least 50,000 years, but the isolated landmass was brought into the ambit of European colonial expansion only when James Cook sailed into Botany Bay and claimed 'New Holland' for Great Britain in 1770. This was followed by the establishment of the first British penal colony at Sydney Cove in 1788.

Over the following century, European settlers expanded along Australia's coastlines and even into its arid interior, displacing and impoverishing Aboriginal Australians who nevertheless interacted culturally with white European Australians.

Evidence for the settlers' importation of British and Irish folklore to the Australian landscape is not as abundant as it is in North America, but it seems to have influenced Aboriginal Australians' interpretations of their own lore. For example, in the 1990s Aboriginal people in South Australia speaking to the folklorist Philip Clarke described their *kintji* spirits as 'little men' and equated them with the Irish leprechauns. Echoing Victorian ethnographers' interest in the social supernatural populations of Australasia as oral memories of earlier populations, they expressed hope that scientists would one day prove the reality of the *kintji*.[79] Children's literature has also given rise to settler fairies distinctive to Australia: Cecelia May Gibbs's Gumnut Babies, an antipodean equivalent to England's flower fairies.[80]

New Zealand was first settled by British colonists in 1815, but little has been written on the importation of European fairy lore there. As in Australia, however, British and Irish settlers came into contact with the belief systems of the Indigenous Māori people. As early as 1855, Sir George Grey confidently recounted two Māori tales involving 'fairies' in his *Polynesian Mythology*.[81] These Māori 'fairies', according to Grey, 'are a very numerous people; merry, cheerful, and always singing, like the cricket. Their appearance is that of human beings, nearly resembling a European's; their hair being very fair, and so is their skin. They are very different from the Maories, and do not resemble them at all.'[82]

Grey's 'fairies' were in fact the Patupaiarehe of Māori belief,[83] although his account of them was not particularly accurate. The Patupaiarehe have continued to be identified as 'fairies' in modern New Zealand, including on a postage stamp that depicted them in 2000, although it is unclear whether this equivalence is embraced by the Māori themselves. Between 2014 and 2017, Simon Young's 'Fairy Census' collected from New Zealand fourteen accounts of people's encounters with fairies,[84] followed by another five accounts from New Zealand in the second Fairy Census of 2017–23[85] – all, seemingly, from New Zealanders of European rather than Māori heritage. Of these New Zealanders who claimed to have met fairies, only two referenced traditional Māori beliefs about spirits of nature, and one witness expressed surprise that the fairies she met were Caucasian in appearance and did not resemble the Māori. Similarly, in forty-six accounts of contemporary fairy encounters from Australia collected by Simon Young between 2014 and 2023,[86] only two witnesses mention Aboriginal belief in spirits – while noting, again, the 'European' appearance of the fairies encountered.

The global fairy

It should be noted that this brief survey of fairies beyond Europe is by no means exhaustive; future researchers might choose to examine the influence of Dutch folklore on South Africa, for example, or the beliefs of German, Dutch, and Swedish settlers in North America. It is important to state that the spirit-beings of Indigenous cultures encountered by Europeans settling beyond Europe were not fairies, and such spirits are deserving of study in their own right, for their own sake; we do these cultures a disservice if we try to shoehorn their spirit-beings into European categories.

The fact remains, however, that European settlers *did* identify such beings as fairies, and this has therefore become part of their history and part of the history of fairies. At the same time, European settlers also exported their own folklore wholesale into entirely new lands and landscape (with Newfoundland fairy lore a notable example of fairly 'conservative' fairy belief surviving in a North American context), and fairy traditions continued to evolve in their own way in the New World. It was, of course, the American film industry (via Disney) that popularized what Simon Young calls the SWF ('Small, Winged Fairy') that has become the international reference point of popular culture when the word 'fairy' is mentioned. Another modern American contribution to childhood fairy lore, which has migrated to Great Britain, may be the phenomenon of the Tooth Fairy.[87]

As regions were settled by Europeans with a higher level of education in the nineteenth century, especially in Australia and New Zealand, the folklore that arrived with the settlers was also accompanied by an urge to explain the Indigenous beliefs they encountered in euhemeristic terms; thus, the Native American *memeguayiwahk*, the *kintji* of Aboriginal Australians, and the Patupaiarehe of the Māori came to be interpreted as confused Indigenous memories of earlier lost populations, following a line of reasoning that will be explored in its European context in chapter 8.

One effect of this simultaneous appropriation and rationalization of Indigenous spirit-beings is a phenomenon we might call 'cryptidization', whereby a spirit-being comes to be interpreted by settler-colonial communities in naturalistic terms as a non-supernatural, as yet undiscovered species of animal or hominid – in other words, a cryptid. Thus the bunyip and yowie of Australia and the pukwudgie of Massachusetts are best known today as cryptids rather than supernatural beings.[88] While it might be compared to European explorers' treatment of Tibetan belief in the yeti, 'cryptidization' is largely a North American and Australian phenomenon because the vast, unexplored extent of those continents gave scope for Europeans to imagine undiscovered species in a way that would have been implausible in a European context. However, as we shall see in chapter 9 below, there is a case to be made for cryptid lore itself being an unacknowledged modern expression of fairy lore.

Ironically, however, it was neither the colonial expansion of Europeans bringing their fairy lore with them, nor the synthesis of European with Indigenous lore, that produced the modern 'global fairy'. Central to the diffusion of that fairy was what happened at Cottingley in Yorkshire in 1917–21, which will be explored in the next chapter. At the centre of that incident was a young girl who had grown up in South Africa; when she sent one of her fairy photographs to a friend in Cape Town, she wrote on the back: 'It is funny I never used to see them in Africa. It must be too hot for them there.'[89] The notion that fairies belong to temperate climes such as Britain and Ireland has itself become part of the perception of the global fairy. In the 1920s and 1930s, American pop culture digested European literature such as Perrault's *Contes des fées*, J. M. Barrie's *Peter Pan*, and the Theosophical speculations attendant on the Cottingley fairies to produce Disney's familiar fairy godmother and small, winged, wand-wielding, and usually airborne Tinker Bells. This kind of fairy was transmitted to America and the rest of the world by mass media rather than colonization; and it is to the development of the modern fairy – back in its European homelands – that we now turn.

EIGHT

The coming (back) of the fairies: the nineteenth and twentieth centuries

Sometime in the 1960s, not far from the city of Leningrad, a woman of the Finno-Ugric Vepsian people went day after day to a crossroads near her home. Falling to her knees, she crossed herself and prayed earnestly – not to God, but to the *mecan izhandaizhed* and *mecan emagaizhed*, the masters and mistresses of the forest with whom the Veps had a relationship long pre-dating their adoption of Christianity in the twelfth century (never mind the Communist ideology of the Soviet Union, in which the Veps now found themselves). The woman begged the forest spirits to return her son, who had travelled to the far east of the USSR to work, in the same way her people routinely petitioned the return of cattle, adults, or children who had got lost in the forest, led astray by the *mecan izhandaizhed*. The Veps imagined the *mecan izhandaizhed* as being much like them – they had families, children, cattle, and they could be helpful or bad; but they were invisible to most. The woman then did the only thing she could to compel the spirits to restore her son – she took rowan twigs she had broken off a tree and formed them into crude crosses, placing one over each of the roads that made up the crossroads in order to 'close' every way, apart from the road that led to the east. Unable to pass the sign of the cross, the spirits would be forced to come towards the woman's home from the east, bringing her son back with them.[1]

The Soviet Union at the height of the Cold War might seem unpromising terrain in which to encounter fairies. I begin this chapter in such an unfamiliar landscape, however, as a reminder that belief in non-human populations of supernatural beings existed all over Europe, and not just in those countries where it was endlessly discussed and self-consciously revived by romantically inclined intellectuals in the nineteenth and twentieth centuries. Spirits such as the *mecan izhandaizhed* of the Veps were the great survivors, proving their resilience in the face of centuries of Christianity and decades of Soviet repression, not to mention the Winter War with Finland, the Nazi siege of Leningrad, and the region's depopulation for forced labour and military conscription in the Red Army.

Ironically, as the Soviets closed the churches and suppressed the Russian Orthodox Church, the cult of the masters and mistresses of the forest only flourished more strongly among the Veps, just as the ethnographer Ljubov Gribova found sacrifices to the *chud* (diminutive subterranean spirits) flourishing among the Komi people of northern Russia in the 1970s.[2] After all, who else was there to turn to? The intense moral ambiguity of the forest spirits was well suited to the climate of fear fostered by the Soviet state. It gave scant comfort, but at least it offered some limited sense of control – if the spirits could somehow be placated or cajoled into returning the lost. And just as they ruled over the dark, trackless forest and those who wandered in it, perhaps the spirits also ruled over that totalitarian darkness in which the individual human soul could become lost, far from home in some Siberian work camp. Fairies, after all, are infinitely adaptable beings.

When it comes to fairies in the nineteenth and twentieth centuries, most people are likely to think of Victorian and post-Victorian British culture – *Peter Pan* (figure 8.1), 'flower fairies', and the notorious incident of the Cottingley fairies at the end of the First World War. But there is a great deal more to the history of fairies in the period than this, and it is in the nineteenth century that we enter the period of greatest evidential abundance for fairy lore throughout Europe. The collection and analysis of folklore exploded, as did fairy literature and art.

While the forest spirits of the Veps of the Lake Ladoga region might seem a far cry from Cottingley Beck, both of these manifestations of twentieth-century fairy lore took place against the background of the same process: the decline of religion, and Christianity in particular, as people's dominant framework for understanding the world. For the fairies, initially threatened by the advance of the Enlightenment, turned out to be the surprising beneficiaries of a decline in religious belief and in the power of the church. The demonization of fairies largely came to an end, and their independence from the old world's established Christian cosmology rendered them unexpectedly attractive and culturally malleable figures in an increasingly secular world.

In addition to the decline of religion, a widespread reaction against the coldness of scientific rationalism – even if it was sometimes more

Figure 8.1 Winged fairies, illustration by Arthur Rackham in *Peter Pan in Kensington Gardens* (1906)

performative than genuine – worked in the fairies' favour. Carole Silver writes of a 'trickle up' of fairy belief, in which elite figures (especially in the fields of literature and the arts) began to entertain the idea of the reality of fairies in a way that would have been almost unimaginable before the second half of the nineteenth century.[3] The valorization of folk culture, which was often linked with burgeoning nationalism, encouraged people to consider fairies valuable cultural property – as did the era's tendency towards sentimentality, and the cult of innocence and of the child. Yet elite appropriation of fairy lore also transformed it, and sundered it from its popular roots. While the story elsewhere in Europe was different, among ordinary people in Britain and Ireland traditional fairy lore continued to decline – and, indeed, the transplantation of fairies to pantomime and nursery only accelerated the trend.

Covering roughly the century and a half between 1800 and 1960, this chapter will trace the 'fairy revival' of the nineteenth century, arising from the Romantic movement, and the role of fairy lore in the burgeoning self-realization of nations, including its key role in Ireland's 'Celtic revival'. At the centre of the chapter is the notorious episode of the Cottingley fairies, when the fairy lore fostered by the Victorian and Edwardian imagination seemingly came alive and burst into reality – for some, a *reductio ad absurdum* of the self-evidently fraudulent and ridiculous; for others, an inspiration to search for fairies as a new form of life; and for still others, the impetus to escape the stranglehold of storybook fairies and seek out the authentic, frightening otherworld beings of folk tradition.

It should be noted, however, that no single chapter could ever do justice to the vast range of representations of fairies generated during this rich period, and therefore I have chosen to focus primarily on those who took fairies seriously, and those who claimed they might be encountered as real beings, rather than on fairies as a cultural artefact. Other scholars such as Nicola Bown, Diane Purkiss, Carole Silver, and Richard Sugg have dealt expertly with the enormous subject of the fairy in the literature, theatre, and art of the nineteenth and twentieth centuries, and I heartily commend their work to the reader.[4]

The fairy revival and the lure of folklore

The Romantic movement was, in origin, a phenomenon of the late eighteenth century that represented a reaction against the rationalism of the Enlightenment – although it should be noted that early Romantic authors often retained the intellectual presuppositions of elite culture in the Enlightenment, including denial of the reality of the supernatural. The Romantics were initially interested in an *aesthetic* revalorization of the wild, the barbaric, and the old-fashioned, rather than in interrogating their metaphysical assumptions.

By the early nineteenth century, however, it was becoming clear that some of the Romantics were willing to exceed the intellectual strictures of a merely aesthetic movement. As Purkiss has argued, for authors from

Goethe to Keats, the fatal fairy, whether the Erlkönig or the Belle Dame sans Merci, became less of a metaphor and more of a representation of a 'choking, rapturous presence' that took possession of the Romantic author and, all too often, resulted in an early death.[5] Patrick Harpur, similarly, has argued that the Romantics 'reverse[d] our common notion of the imaginative as something unreal, something imagin*ary*, and allow[ed] it an autonomous life that includes spontaneous apparitions'.[6] Indeed, it was not only artists whose brilliance projected itself as a being with its own agency, and Napoleon Bonaparte was supposed to have had a personal daemon that sometimes appeared to warn him in the form of a red-clad dwarf.[7]

Among the British Romantics, the poet and artist William Blake (1757–1827) is perhaps most notable for launching into full-blown mystical speculation that effectively jettisoned the intellectual underpinnings of the Enlightenment. Blake believed he had witnessed a fairy funeral in his own garden.[8] It was perhaps inevitable that the Romantic and Gothic movements, with their love of all things culturally recondite, would stimulate a revival of esotericism. In 1801, the occultist and balloonist Francis Barrett published a grimoire, *The Magus*, that unhesitatingly affirmed the reality of fairies, identifying them as essentially a lower order of helpful angels:

> some are called woodmen, some mountaineers and some fieldmen, some domestics: hence the gods of the woods, country gods, satyrs, familiars, fairies of the fountains, fairies of the woods, nymphs of the sea, the Naïades, Nereïdes, Dryades, Piërides, Hamadryades, Patumdies, Hinnides, Agapte, Pales, Parcades, Dodonae, Fanilae, Levernae, Parcae, Muses, Aonides, Castalides, Heliconides, Pegasides, Meonides, Phlebiades, Camenae, the graces, the genii, hobgoblins, and such like.[9]

Even Barrett, however, was eager to distinguish between his sophisticated 'Platonic' magic and the opinion of 'the vulgar' – folklore, in other words – and Barrett's occultism represented an attempted revival of Neoplatonist theurgy rather than of medieval magical traditions, although it remains unclear how real Barrett's practice of magic ever was.[10] Certainly, Barrett did not describe any attempt to conjure fairies. However, the Romantics' intensifying interest in the literature of the past, and especially in Shakespeare, Chaucer, and the medieval romances, inevitably raised the profile of fairies and interest in them.[11] The poet Robert Southey (1774–1843) professed his belief in them, although he also thought the fairies were really druids who went underground and became renowned for their uncanny powers – a euhemerizing tendency that would prove very popular throughout the nineteenth century.[12]

It would be in Scotland, however, that a fully fledged learned interest in fairies re-emerged in the early nineteenth century. The antiquarian and novelist Sir Walter Scott (1771–1832), while not avowing belief in fairies like Southey, was intensely interested in Scottish fairy traditions. He discovered the manuscript of Robert Kirk's *Secret Commonwealth* in the Advocates' Library in Edinburgh and published it in 1815,[13] and stated his views on fairies in an essay, 'On the Fairies of Popular Superstition' in his *Minstrelsy of the Scottish Borders* (1802).

In Scott's view, the origins of Scotland's fairies were 'to be sought in the traditions of the east, in the wreck and confusion of the Gothic mythology, in the tales of chivalry, in the fables of classical antiquity, in the influence of the Christian religion, and finally, in the creative imagination of the 16th century'.[14] Scott elaborated his ideas in *Letters on Demonology and Witchcraft* (1830), in which he offered a euhemeristic explanation for tales of fairies as accounts of diminutive aboriginal peoples sent into hiding by the arrival of later waves of migration:

> There seems reason to conclude that these *duergar* [dwarfs] were originally nothing else than the diminutive natives of the Lappish, Lettish, and Finnish nations, who, flying before the conquering weapons of the Asae, sought the most retired regions of the north, and there endeavoured to hide themselves from their eastern invaders. They were a little diminutive race, but possessed of some skill probably in mining or smelting minerals, with which the country abounds; perhaps also they might, from their acquaintance with the changes of the clouds, or meteorological phenomena, be judges of weather, and so enjoy another title to supernatural skill. At any rate, it has been plausibly supposed, that these poor people, who sought caverns and hiding-places from the persecution of the Asae, were in some respects compensated for inferiority in strength and stature, by the art and power with which the superstition of the enemy invested them. These oppressed, yet dreaded fugitives, obtained, naturally enough, the character of the German spirits called Kobold, from

which the English Goblin and the Scottish Bogle, by some inversion and alteration of pronunciation, are evidently derived.[15]

As we have seen in chapter 6 above, the idea that fairies could be euhemeristically explained as human 'relic populations' distorted by folklore was nothing new. It was articulated by John Webster in the 1670s, and can be traced back to the medieval idea of fairies as akin to the monstrous peoples of ancient and medieval ethnography and geography. But the intellectual climate of the nineteenth century supercharged the idea; Darwin's *Origin of Species* was still twenty years off when Scott wrote his *Letters on Demonology*, but European colonialism and encounters with very different human populations were already stimulating racialist debates about whether the human race was one, or whether multiple human-like species existed.

The advent of the Theory of Evolution opened up the possibility of speculation about other human-like races, and the application of such thinking to fairies reached its apogee in David MacRitchie's (1851–1925) 'pygmy theory' of the origins of fairy lore as a folk memory or 'race memory' of diminutive peoples driven to hills and caves by ancient invaders.[16] The 'pygmy theory' proved influential on Victorian literary fiction, with authors such as John Buchan and Arthur Machen taking it to its logical conclusion by imagining the lairs of sinister troglodytic peoples in remote areas of modern Britain.[17]

Then, as now, however, most folklorists understood that the primary role of the serious collector of fairy lore was not to 'explain it away' in naturalistic terms. Two years before the publication of Scott's *Letters on Demonology*, in 1828, the Irish writer Thomas Keightley (1789–1872) brought out the first edition of his *Fairy Mythology*, which would be much revised and reprinted. Keightley was influenced by the 'comparativist' approach of Jacob (1785–1863) and Wilhelm Grimm (1786–1859), whose *Märchen* (fairy tales) seldom featured actual fairies but who laid the foundations of the discipline of folklore.[18] Indeed, when he coined the term 'folk-lore' in 1846, William John Thoms explicitly referenced the work of the Grimms,[19] whose breakthrough was to apply a comparative methodology modelled on linguistics to folk narratives.[20]

Early folklorists who came under the Grimms' influence, including Keightley, were often convinced that their discipline was a more exact science than it actually was; Keightley was convinced that the development of fairy lore was an inevitability, governed by immutable laws:

> In accordance with these laws, we find in every country a popular belief in different classes of beings distinct from men, and from the higher orders of divinities. These beings are believed to inhabit, in the caverns of earth, or the depths of the waters, a region of their own. They generally excel mankind in power and in knowledge, and like them are subject to the immutable laws of death, though after a more prolonged period of existence.[21]

While Keightley offered a somewhat exotic etymology for the word 'fairy', tracing it to the Persian word *peri*,[22] others reached different (and more realistic) conclusions. The French antiquary Jacques Cambry (1749–1807), for example, declared that '*Fatua*, the good goddess, is the same word as *fée* [in French]; *fata* in Provençal; *fada* in Italian; *hada* in Spanish; the Celto-Breton *mat* or *mad*'.[23]

The early folklore collectors were often rather trusting in accepting that any traditional story collected from an old nurse had remained essentially unaltered for centuries, and gave access to some immemorial (and possibly prehistoric) stratum of story. When the folklorist Edward Clodd (1840–1930) came upon the story of 'Tom Tit Tot' in the *Ipswich Journal* in 1877 (a Suffolk version of 'Rumpelstiltskin'), which Anna Fison said her nurse had told her as a child, he became convinced it was of ancient vintage and wrote an entire book about what 'Tom Tit Tot' revealed of the 'savage philosophy' of our distant ancestors.[24]

One of those inspired by the Grimms to start collecting the folklore of his own nation was the Irish antiquary Thomas Crofton Croker (1798–1854), who brought out three volumes of *Fairy Legends and Traditions of the South of Ireland* between 1825 and 1828. Croker's work in turn inspired the collection of folklore in Norway, and Croker's decision to include illustrations meant that he not only set the agenda for the collection of Irish fairy lore but also established an imagery for it.[25] But early folklore collecting was sporadic and inconsistent, and while fairies were a significant object of interest in Ireland this was not so in England.

An exception was the vicar of Stowmarket in Suffolk, Arthur Hollingsworth (1802–59), who in 1844 appended a remarkable collection of local fairy lore to his history of Stowmarket. Perhaps signifi-

Figure 8.2 'Plucked from the Fairy Circle' from *British Goblins* (1880) by Wirt Sikes

cantly, Hollingsworth had lived in Ireland, and thus may have been more sympathetic to fairy lore than most English antiquaries.[26] Wales had to wait until an outsider took an interest in its folklore, the American consul in Cardiff Wirt Sikes (1836–83), whose *British Goblins* (1880) proved very popular on both sides of the Atlantic (figure 8.2).[27]

While the early folklore collectors may have been mistaken about the antiquity of what they collected, Lizanne Henderson and Edward Cowan adopt a sympathetic attitude towards their claims to have recovered medieval traditions – on the basis that life had changed little for most people in rural Scotland in around 1800 and was 'socially, economically and culturally ... still essentially medieval'.[28] Put another way, while the folklore might not have been a medieval survival, there is no good reason to think that the lifestyle and environment that produced the stories told in the Scottish Highlands in the nineteenth century were all that much different from those that produced the unrecorded stories of medieval peasants. Certainly, the folklore collectors recovered intriguing folk-rationalizations of the fairies, such as Eliza Bray who noted in her *Description of the Part of Devonshire bordering on the Tamar and the Tavy* (1836) that local people believed the pixies were the embodied souls of infants who died unbaptized.[29] But not all folklore collectors were elite. The Scottish writer James Hogg (1770–1835) drew on the fairy encounters of his own grandfather, 'Will o'the Phaup', who was reputed to have been the last man in his locality to talk to the fairies – for which Hogg was mocked by fellow writers from less humble backgrounds.[30]

It is in the nineteenth century that we encounter a plethora of popular explanations for who and what the fairies are. Folklorists exploring the Highlands of Scotland encountered the story that 'Balkin, the Lord of the Northern Mountains' was the father of the fairies; Balkin was 'shaped like a satyr and fed upon the air', fathering 12,000 children who became the fairies, and he fought the fiery spirits of Mount Hekla in Iceland. A more Christian-inflected account of the origin of fairies was given to the folklorist Alexander Carmichael by an old man of the island of Barra:

Not of the seed of Adam are we
Nor is Abraham our father,
But of the seed of the Proud Angel
Driven forth from heaven.

Carmichael was told in Barra that the fairies were not the souls of the dead, but fallen angels. In Shetland, he learned that the angels who fell on earth became fairies, while those who fell in the sea became seals. And because they are not human, the fairies are excluded from salvation – exemplified in the tale of a fairy who tried to say the Lord's Prayer, but could only ever say 'Our Father who wert in heaven' (a reference to fallen Lucifer).[31]

By the nineteenth and twentieth centuries, this seems to have been a very widespread origin story for the fairies – even in Estonia, one of Europe's latecomers to Christianity, folklorists recorded the story that the angels who fell to earth became forest spirits, while those who fell in the water became water spirits.[32] Such rationalizations may have justified the continuation of pre-Christian traditions of appeasing forest spirits.

What is striking about Scottish fairy belief, however, is that it coexisted harmoniously with an intensely Protestant religious culture, especially in the Highlands, the Western Isles, and Orkney and Shetland. Indeed, the more intensely Calvinist a community was, the stronger faith in the second sight seemed to be – perhaps because the Old Testament offered ample examples of seership and prophecy.

Highland Scotland, an intensely Protestant region, was certainly a counterexample to the nineteenth-century English press's canard that it was Ireland's backward Catholicism that gave fairies a refuge – given that fairies were just as plentiful in the Highlands. But in Ireland itself, it was as much the country's educated, English-speaking nationalist elite (who were often Protestants) as the Gaelic-speaking Catholic Irish who spearheaded a major revival of fairy belief.[33] It was a characteristic of the nineteenth century that fairies were as much a preoccupation of the educated as they were of the uneducated rural folk; and the educated often failed to realize or acknowledge that their own speculations fed back recursively into the oral lore of the folk, who were not as naïve or innocent of engagement with print culture as elite folklorists often thought. For folklorists did not just *collect* folklore; in many cases, they also published it, in their own words and under their own interpretations – at a time when folklore enjoyed cultural prestige and was a cultural product popular with wider society.

In the nineteenth century, fairies passed from oral folk culture into mass popular culture, and in the process they passed from the realm of folklore to what Paul Manning calls the 'folkloresque'. The fairies of folklore were, in other words, processed into acceptable, readily understandable, illustrated, and often 'child-friendly' form.[34] This processing could easily cross the line into invention; thus, Eliza Bray was largely responsible for 'inventing' pixies as a distinct category of fairy, peculiar to Devon and Cornwall, when the word 'pisky' was simply a West Country word for a fairy, and the luminaries of the Celtic Revival in Ireland based their equation of the fairies of modern Irish folklore with the heroes of medieval Irish literature on supposition rather than fact.[35]

The folklorists did much to preserve traditions that would otherwise have gone unrecorded, but their legacy is a mixed one: they brought their own interpretations to bear on folk traditions, they did not always record or retell tales accurately or truthfully, and they often came to folklore with an agenda. Above all, they often took stories far more seriously than the storytellers themselves, and thereby missed the humour, playfulness, and creativity of the traditions they were attempting to record.

Fairies and nation-building

The notion that fairies were in some sense a 'national' characteristic is one that may have emerged in England as early as the late seventeenth century, but it was only in the nineteenth century, with the advent of nationalism in its modern form, that the idea that a nation's supernatural and folkloric beings might somehow define its essence was properly articulated and came to prominence. As Terry Gunnell observes, this is a development that can be traced largely to Jacob Grimm, who believed there had once been a unifying pan-Germanic religion and mythology, and that modern folklore was traceable to an original Germanic pagan religion. This was an ideological perspective on folklore formed in the context of the German states' humiliation in the Napoleonic Wars, which created the initial impetus towards German nationalism.[36] Out of respect among folklorists for the Grimms, these two propositions were widely adopted, even beyond the Germanic world, and they had far-reaching consequences for perceptions of fairies.

In the first place, if the Grimms were right that an original pan-Germanic religion had once existed (and, by extension, a pan-Celtic religion, and a pan-Slavic religion, and so on), then mythological beings occupied fixed positions in that religion, and there was a definitive hierarchy of divine and semi-divine beings to be discovered by the diligent folklorist. Second, if folklore encoded pre-Christian religion, then any elements of folklore that seemed post-pagan were obviously corruptions of an original lore that folklorists should try to 'reverse-engineer' to its pristine state.

For fairies, this meant that either they were deemed gods who had been mistakenly degraded, or they were deemed to have always existed – which resulted in attempts to elide modern folklore with much earlier literary portrayals. Thus, the elves of nineteenth-century Iceland were supposed to be exactly the same beings as the elves of the earliest sagas, with the pristine folklore of the culturally conservative Icelanders conveniently supplying what Old Norse literature omitted. We now know, of course, that this sort of analysis is based on flawed assumptions. There is no straight line to be drawn between modern folklore and medieval literature.[37] For a long time, however, the assumption that there was such a straightforward connection distorted perceptions of both medieval and modern folkloric beings. When nineteenth-century folklorists asked Icelanders about elves, they did not want to be told Christianized tales of Eve hiding her children, but rather stories that chimed with the narrative grandeur of the Old Norse *Eddas* – and when they read the *Eddas*, they wanted to encounter the elves as a distinct, clearly defined race of supernatural beings.

Fairy lore was not always received as a political positive. In Ireland, in particular, fairy belief came to be negatively politicized by the British press as proof that the Irish people were too ignorant, superstitious, and stupid to govern themselves. Not long after the Westminster Parliament emancipated Catholics in Britain and Ireland in 1829, a newspaper referred disparagingly to Ireland's 'priest-protected fairies', thereby yoking together Catholicism and superstitious fairy belief in the service of anti-Catholic and anti-Irish propaganda.[38] On the ground, as Diarmuid Ó Giolláin has documented, the nineteenth century saw the Catholic church in Ireland turn against unauthorized popular religion (including fairy belief) as the Victorian Catholic clergy became increasingly professionalized.[39] Events such as the murder of Bridget Cleary in 1895, who was burnt to death by her husband because he believed she was a fairy changeling, were intensely embarrassing both to the Irish church and to the administration in Ireland, suggesting that both church and state had failed to eradicate harmful superstition.[40]

At the same time as both the Catholic church and the civil authorities had grave concerns about fairy belief in Ireland, however, Irish intellectuals were intent on reviving it as a bulwark of a newly instantiated Irish national identity. Indeed, as Silver has argued, 'belief in fairies was almost a political and cultural necessity' for nationalists in nineteenth-century Ireland.[41] The boldness of Walter Evans-Wentz in describing Celtic fairy belief as a 'fairy faith' offered the prospect that fairy lore was *the* distinguishing characteristic of Irish culture that had survived the anglicization and oppression of Ireland under the British Crown. Crucially, it was not just a cultural but a *spiritual* inheritance – a different way of viewing the world that proved the 'Irish soul' was different from, and would never be, a British soul.

The American scholar Walter Evans-Wentz defended his thesis for the degree of bachelor of science at Jesus College, Oxford in 1910, which was based on extensive fieldwork collecting folklore in the 'Celtic' world. Evans-Wentz then worked the thesis into a book, *The Fairy-Faith in Celtic Countries*, published by Oxford University Press in 1911. The book consisted of three sections; in the first, Evans-Wentz included his contemporary ethnographic data derived from interviewing people in Ireland, Scotland, the Isle of Man, Wales, Cornwall, and Brittany.[42] The second part of the book examined the historical evidence for the 'Fairy-Faith' – notably, the medieval literature on the Tuatha Dé Danaan, the gods of the Britons, the Celtic otherworld, and belief in reincarnation.[43] The third section of the book examined the evidence from archaeology and pagan and Christian sources for 'The Cult of Gods, Spirits, Fairies, and the Dead';[44] and the book's fourth and strangest part claimed to offer a 'scientific' (or rather Spiritualist and Theosophical) assessment of the foregoing evidence.[45]

In Mark Williams's view, Evans-Wentz 'was not reconstructing ancient Celtic religion so much as the spiritual reality out of which he felt sure that religion had grown'.[46] He took as his premise the claim of *The Hymn of Fiacc* (discussed in chapter 2 above) that the ancient Irish had worshipped the sí. Taking this as uncomplicatedly true, Evans-Wentz concluded that contemporary Irish fairy lore must encode a lost pan-Celtic religion, and his ambitious project was the attempted harmonization of modern folklore, medieval literature, and contemporary psychical research in their portrayal of the fairies.

Evans-Wentz's 'pan-Celticism' is no longer convincing to scholars,[47] but his ethnographic methodology was also weak (even if the remarkable collection of fairy accounts he assembled is the book's most lasting legacy). As Williams observes, Evans-Wentz took a naïve and condescending approach to his informants, assuming they were sharing with him a body of pristine traditional lore; this overlooked the fact that some of them were educated people, and some were active confabulators of new mystical lore for the Irish revival, such as A. E. Russell.[48] Evans-Wentz, the American interloper, seems to have been 'taken for a ride' by quite a few informants who were themselves well aware of folkloric tropes and narrative traditions. His Spiritualist and Theosophical preoccupations, too, had the effect of imposing on ancient and modern Ireland a mentality derived from the Edwardian seance room rather than the tribal society of the Bronze Age.

But if not everyone accepted Evans-Wentz's conclusions, folklore and fairy lore remained central to the construction of Irish national identity in the country's revolutionary period, from the Easter Rising of 1916 and the establishment of the Irish Free State in 1922 to the advent of the Republic of Ireland in 1937. It was no accident that an eminent folklorist, Douglas Hyde (1860–1949), was elected the first president of Ireland, and in 1937 the Irish Folklore Commission (which was officially supported by the Irish state) began the systematic collection of folklore from Irish schoolchildren. The Schools Collection remains one of the most remarkable attempts at state-sponsored folklore collection at a national scale, and took advantage of the fact that there was one group of people in Ireland (schoolchildren) who could all be asked to write down the folklore they (or their older relatives) knew about.[49] Around 12,000 stories collected from Irish schoolchildren deal with the fairies.[50]

Ireland was not alone in the national significance it accorded its fairies, however. All over Europe, the beings of nations' 'lower mythologies', who were often believed to be the lone survivors of a nation's original pre-Christian religion, attracted intense attention. In Lithuania, a hill by the River Nemunas known as Rambynas, where the fairy-like laumės had been venerated at an altar-like rock, became in the nineteenth and twentieth centuries a sort of national shrine for the Lithuanian people – so much so that when Hitler annexed the area to Germany in 1939 he made a point of destroying Rambynas.[51]

Yet the Nazis themselves were obsessed with folklore as a foundation for their ultranationalist self-understanding, convinced that fairy tales such as those collected by the Brothers Grimm encoded in symbolic language lessons about the greatness of the eternal German national consciousness. Nazi folklorists eagerly sought to strip German folk customs of their supposed Christian accretions and turned against the traditional demonization of folkloric beings.[52] Some Nazi scholars even showed an interest in the fairy lore of other countries, such as Hans Hartmann who explored the fairy doctors of Ireland.[53]

Ülo Valk has argued that in nineteenth-century Estonia the 'folklorization' of traditional spirits succeeded their demonization, but it was potentially just as distorting a process as the denunciations of pastors and missionaries. The folklore collectors, convinced that Estonia's folklore made it possible to excavate the country's pagan past, showed no interest in Estonian popular Christianity or in Christianized folklore; indeed, where folklore concerned the devil or angels, these were often interpreted as thinly veiled pagan spirits in a process of folkloric 'reverse engineering'.[54] However, the pagan past – and the possibility it might be recovered – mattered intensely to the construction of Estonian national identity, since Estonia had no written history that pre-dated its conquest by crusaders.[55] Accordingly, the attempt to write Christianity out of Estonian folklore turned it into an imagined library of pre-Christian knowledge, but it did not necessarily reflect the true preoccupations of Estonian peasants.

Encounter at Cottingley

In April 1917, nine-year-old Frances Griffiths (1907–86) arrived from South Africa with her mother to stay with the Wrights, her aunt and uncle, in the village of Cottingley near Bradford in West Yorkshire. A small stream, Cottingley Beck, ran at the bottom of the Wrights' garden, and it was here that Frances began to see 'little men', with rugged faces, marching as if in military formations and tending to the plants: 'The first time I ever saw anything was when a willow leaf started shaking violently, even though there was no wind, I saw a small man standing on a branch, with the stem of the leaf in his hand, which he seemed to be shaking at something. He was dressed all in green.'[56]

In addition, she caught sight of tiny, winged, and diaphanous beings, but only out of the corner of her eye. Occasionally, the fairies even made eye contact with the girl.[57] Frances confided what she had seen to her sixteen-year-old cousin, the Wrights' daughter Elsie (1901–88), but Elsie Wright was unable to see the fairies for herself. When Frances told Mr and Mrs Wright about the fairies at the bottom of the garden, she was met with incredulity; and so the two girls hatched a plan that would, in time, propel them to global fame.

The affair of the Cottingley fairy photographs was, arguably, the foundational event of humanity's modern relationship with fairyland – at least in the English-speaking world. In Simon Young's view, the Cottingley fairies 'mark the transition from the dregs of medieval fairy belief, which had survived in the rural corners of the UK, to a new spiritualized fairy, who tended to be both less dangerous and harder working'.[58] Without

Figure 8.3 Frances Griffiths and the leaping fairy

ever intending it, Frances and Elsie's creativity became as central to the development of public perception of fairies as Bram Stoker's fiction was to the public perception of vampires. In a sense, the girls created the modern fairy. Albeit for reasons very different from those that Sir Arthur Conan Doyle imagined, Cottingley was indeed 'an event in human history which may in the future appear to have been epoch-making in its character'.[59]

The conventional view of the Cottingley fairies in popular culture is that it was a clever hoax, which came to particular prominence because Frances and Elsie managed to hoodwink a man who should have known better – Sir Arthur Conan Doyle, creator of the ultra-rational detective Sherlock Holmes. But this popular Cottingley legend is wrong on several counts. Frances and Elsie had at first no intention to perpetrate a hoax; the photographs were taken in 1917, and it was not for another three years that they came to public attention, and only then because the Theosophist Edward Gardner 'discovered' the girls, not because they came to him. The original audience for the photographs were Arthur and Polly Wright, Elsie's parents, and not the wider public. Whether the teenage Elsie ever believed her little cousin had really seen fairies remains unclear, but Frances knew it would be impossible to photograph the fairies she had seen – their appearances were too unpredictable for that, even if it were possible to get close enough to catch them on camera.

As far as Frances was concerned, the purpose of the photographs was to convince her uncle and aunt that she was telling the truth. The photographs were not really photographs of fairies, as both girls knew (figure 8.3); but they used the technology and media available at the time to convey the truth (as Frances saw it), in much the same way as newspaper photographers would pose and restage an event never photographed at the time, or newsreel cinematographers of the silent era would engage actors to re-enact a battle for the cameras.

The tragedy of Cottingley was that photographs never intended as a hoax to begin with *became* a hoax via a cascade of events that Frances and Elsie could never have controlled, drawing the girls into becoming hoaxers. As more and more eminent people came to believe the girls had really photographed fairies, and finally Sir Arthur Conan Doyle came to believe in them, it became practically impossible for two working-class cousins to bring disgrace to their family by confessing to a deception that had got out of hand. Elsie and Frances were locked into a story they could never escape; and even in 1983, when the two women finally admitted in old age what they had done and explained it in detail, the confession only cemented their reputation.[60] Cottingley continued the Victorian tradition of linking fairies 'to the young and pure in heart, thus diminishing them to a phenomenon essentially for children', but it also inversely 'rendered them trivial and foolish' by piling the credulity of misinterpreting obviously counterfeited fairy scenes on top of the credulity of thinking fairies might exist in the first place.[61] Furthermore, by providing supposed photographic proof of the fairies, the Cottingley photographs 'deprived the elfin peoples of their grandeur and status', because they 'denud[ed] the fairies of the invisibility that made them powerful and frightening'.[62]

One of the questions most often posed about the Cottingley affair is how a man as intelligent as Doyle could have been fooled – a question that is usually answered by reference to Doyle's equally credulous approach to the claims of the Spiritualists. Doyle was indeed a committed Spiritualist, but there was nothing about Spiritualism that made it especially sympathetic to the idea of fairies. However, Doyle's uncle

Richard Doyle (1824–83) was famous for his fairy illustrations, so perhaps it was a family interest.[63]

Although the supernatural 'rapping' that originally brought the Fox sisters fame in 1850s America and began the Spiritualist movement was seemingly a development of poltergeist phenomena, the Spiritualists of the 1920s were intently focussed on the question of human survival after death. This is not to say that Spiritualists were entirely indifferent to fairies; the Spiritualist Emma Hardinge Britten had promoted the idea of fairies as 'elementals' as early as the 1870s,[64] but by the 1920s Spiritualists had largely yielded interest in fairies to the Theosophists. Doyle admitted that his fellow Spiritualists, 'to whom a new order of being as remote from spirits as they are from human beings was an unfamiliar idea', begged him to drop the Cottingley fairies more earnestly than anyone else, since they 'feared, not unnaturally, that [the fairies'] intrusion would complicate that spiritual controversy which is vital to so many of us'.[65] In other words, as far as the Spiritualists were concerned, the existence of fairies was not a battle worth fighting when the real struggle was convincing people the soul survived beyond death.

In the early 1920s, British Spiritualists felt as though they were on the cusp of achieving respectability and general acceptance – not least because they had recruited such luminaries as Doyle – and Doyle's unaccountable enthusiasm for fairies risked undoing everything. But Doyle felt differently. Writing to Edward Gardner in October 1921, he admitted that the matter had no direct bearing on Spiritualism or its main concerns: 'But anything which extends man's mental horizon, and proves to him that matter as we have known it is not really the limit of our universe, must have a good effect in breaking down materialism and leading human thought to a broader and more spiritual level.'[66] In other words, Doyle was engaged in an anti-materialist crusade, and fairies were grist to the mill: the more evidence of 'more things in heaven and earth', the better.

Yet it was not primarily science that Doyle saw as the enemy of a more spiritual outlook on life, but religion – after all, the Spiritualists often framed their ideas in pseudo-scientific terms (as did Doyle, with his talk of 'vibrations'), and they were intently focussed on the issue of evidence.[67] Christian opponents of Spiritualism, on the other hand, appealed to the Bible's prohibitions of mediumship and converse with the dead – and it was for this reason that Doyle speculated, in his letter to Gardner, that 'wise entities' might have sent the fairies instead. 'They can't destroy fairies by antediluvian texts, and when once fairies are admitted other psychic phenomena will find a more ready acceptance.'[68]

Given that, for Doyle's critics, the existence of fairies was probably the *least* credible supernatural claim that could possibly be made, Sir Arthur's firm avowal of the reality of fairies takes on the aspect of an opening negotiating position with the materialistic public: if they couldn't accept fairies were real, perhaps they would meet Doyle halfway and settle for the immortality of the human soul and the reality of mediumship. Doyle was right, of course, that the Bible says nothing *against* fairies, but he was deluding himself (in more ways than one) if he thought religious believers would be more convinced by the Cottingley fairies than they were by seances.

In one respect he was right, though; fairies, unlike human souls, did stand outside accepted religious cosmologies, and therefore outside the contest between the Spiritualists and the church. The Cottingley fairies would never be contested in the same way as the apparitions at Fátima in Portugal, which appeared to three children aged between nine and six at exactly the same time as Frances Griffiths was seeing 'little men' by Cottingley Beck. Perhaps no starker illustration could be imagined of the differences between England and Portugal than the contrasting interpretative frameworks adopted for Cottingley and Fátima – in Fátima, what the children had seen was interpreted via the lens of Catholic piety; in England, via the lens of storybook.

The year 1917 was also, of course, the height of the First World War, and a time of crisis for both England and its ally Portugal. Were these kinds of supernatural encounters somehow a result of, or a response to, a time of widespread anxiety and fear? In 1919, a young Romanian soldier occupying Budapest during the ethnic and national conflicts that followed the end of the War believed he was being transported back to his home in Moldavia every night to dance with the *szépasszony*,[69] but it would be too simplistic to characterize these sorts of experiences as mere escapism from the horrors of war. For the Romanian soldier, at least, the experience of fairy abduction seems to have been as stressful as armed conflict, and the theological controversy that attended Fátima provoked its own kind of crisis in Portuguese Catholicism. Rather than escapism, these experiences are perhaps better seen as a form of inward spiritual rebellion in a world of machine guns, barbed wire, disposable human life, and unburied corpses. It was not for nothing, perhaps, that Doyle worried about the welfare of fairies, now that they had been discovered – would they, like the Indigenous peoples of the Americas, face the cruelty of human exploitation?[70]

Cottingley split cultural engagement with fairies in three separate directions. For many, it finally exploded and put an end to the insipid Victorian fairy cult, and provided a salutary exemplum of the human capacity for credulity. As Nicola Bown puts it, Cottingley 'killed off interest in fairies as an adult preoccupation and consigned them to the world of childhood'.[71] For others, however, who wanted to take fairies seriously but were appalled by the banality of Cottingley, it forced them to rediscover fairies anew from the sources. And for still others, it convinced them of the reality of 'Cottingleyesque' fairies and inspired them to look for and encounter such beings for themselves.

From the perspective of a folklorist, what is most surprising about the Cottingley fairies is that no one seems to have noticed that the fairies of Cottingley were of the kind encountered in books and pictures (specifically, *Princess Mary's Gift Book*), and not of the kind encountered in folklore. At one point in *The Coming of the Fairies*, Doyle references a Welsh account of fairies riding horses the size of hares, but because fairy horses do not form part of his image of fairies, he dismisses the notion out of hand.[72] Doyle's and the Theosophists' willingness to believe in fairies was not as strange as their unwarranted certainty about what they expected fairies to look like, and their willingness to accept picture-book fairies as real beings.

Admittedly, the study of English fairy lore was rudimentary before Katharine Briggs, but it seems astonishing that Doyle – who insisted we ought to take folklore seriously – was not aware that fairy wings, for example, did not exist in folklore. This was a point made by the Welsh writer Arthur Machen, whose own portrayal of fairies approached much closer to the terrifying beings of folklore.[73] But as Richard Sugg observes, the consequences of the exposure of the 'hoax' of Cottingley in 1983 were unexpected: 'the cousins had somehow created a new kind of fairy folklore'.[74] When a journalist from the *Daily Express* chased down Elsie in 1965, she said of the photographs, 'let's say they are pictures of figments of our imagination'.[75] This was not untruthful; but since Theosophists believed that the imagination of the perceiver was capable of imposing form on the ethereal bodies of fairies, it was susceptible to more than one interpretation. Even when the two women confessed in 1983 to faking the photographs, the truth about the images was not generally received as a repudiation of the existence of fairies per se, or even of the validity of Frances Griffiths's childhood experiences of seeing fairies.[76]

In the end, the true story of the Cottingley fairies is so haunting, so complex, so remarkable – and the deception of Doyle so barely credible – that the hoax has turned out to be as historically important as if Elsie and Frances really had successfully photographed fairies. On one reading, the Cottingley affair was in a long tradition of 'fairies as performance', where showmen would exhibit living people with dwarfism, living great apes, or modified body parts of monkeys sewn together as 'fairies'. It is a tradition that continues, inviting the willing suspension of disbelief, and has resulted in 'in-universe' books that present fairies 'as if real' in the style of biological or ethnographical works (most famously Wil Huygen and Rien Poortvliet's *Gnomes* (1977) and Brian Froud and Alan Lee's *Faeries* (1978), both of which were researched intensively).[77] More recently, the tradition has manifested in art projects such as Dan Baines's 'mummified fairy' hoax in Derbyshire in 2007,[78] Tessa Farmer's tiny yet disturbing insectoid fairy sculptures and stop-motion films,[79] and the charming YouTube videos in which Erwin Saunders hunts for pixies in Britain's woodlands.[80] All of these 'found fairies', where we know the fairy is manufactured but the knowing observer becomes part of the performance, are the cultural offspring of the Cottingley fairies – although they also represent a turn to the grotesque and macabre that seems a far cry from the Cottingley photographs.

Taking fairies seriously

When the fairy tale collector Andrew Lang (1844–1912) became president of the Society for Psychical Research in 1911, he insisted that he wanted the SPR to pay more attention to historical, folkloric, and anthropological evidence for paranormal phenomena – not because Lang believed in such phenomena, but because he thought folklore illuminated the fact that 'the same sort of beliefs and delusions' that were rife in Edwardian Britain had been around for centuries.[81] Fairy lore was worth taking seriously, in other words, not because it was true, but because it illuminated something important about human nature.

Lang's attempt to combine parapsychology with folklore proved unpopular, however.[82] Others were equally certain that fairies were to be taken seriously – but because they really existed as scientific fact, rather than because they were revealing of the human psyche. Darwin's Theory of Evolution inspired the idea that fairies were simply another form of life that had evolved in a different way, and would soon be proved by science to be entirely non-supernatural. Thus, the evolutionary biologist Alfred Russel Wallace (1823–1913) speculated about the existence of 'preterhuman discarnate beings',[83] and Edward Gardner identified fairies as the evolutionary kin of insects and butterflies, who had simply evolved in a more humanoid direction.[84] In a series of lectures in 1908–9, the Austrian occultist Rudolf Steiner (1861–1925) speculated about the role of nature spirits as elementals used by the higher intelligences to create the world, and thought that humans could ennoble themselves and escape the material world by engaging with elementals. Similarly, the Danish-American Rosicrucian Max Heindel (1865–1919) argued in a book posthumously published in 1925 that the elemental spirits helped build up the body of man to become a Creative Intelligence.[85]

While such mystical speculations might seem at first sight like a retreat from the modern world of twentieth-century science and technology, they could also be interpreted as the technologization and even industrialization of fairyland. As the Theosophist Henry Vanstone declared, 'I am inclined to think that elemental beings are engaged, like factory hands, in facilitating the operation of Nature's laws.'[86] Perhaps, then, the twentieth-century fad for fairies derived as much from an experience of alienation from nature as from an effort to reconnect with it; the twentieth-century mind-in-the-factory, unable to imagine nature as anything other than a production line, inevitably peopled it with little factory workers. At the same time, however, the idea that fairies were somehow crucial to the care and management of nature derived from literature – the picturesque poets of the seventeenth century and, more recently, the ubiquitous 'flower fairies' of sentimental illustrations. But, except insofar as they were associated with places such as woods and meadows and wore the colour green, the fairies of tradition were not generally credited with the maintenance of the natural world.

Occultists were not alone, however, in their interest in fairies as potentially real beings. Two twentieth-century authors notable for their commitment to Christian orthodoxy, C. S. Lewis and J. R. R. Tolkien, also took fairies very seriously. They were not inspired by contemporary testimony; Lewis was unconvinced by the Cottingley fairies, and remarked that 'the mere making of the claim [that a fairy could be photographed] – the approach of the fairy to within even that hailing distance of actuality – revealed to me at once that if the claim had succeeded it would have chilled rather than satisfied the desire which fairy literature had hitherto aroused'.[87] Indeed, one of Cottingley's important consequences was that it functioned as a performative *reductio ad absurdum* of the Victorian view of fairies, forcing those who *did* take fairies seriously to break free entirely from the Victorians and rediscover fairies anew from the original folkloric sources. Lewis and Tolkien shared a particular dislike of 'Victorian' fairies. For Tolkien, these were 'that long line of flower-fairies and fluttering sprites with antennae that I so disliked as a child, and which my children in their turn detested',[88] while Lewis refused to use the word 'fairy' at all: 'that word, tarnished by pantomime and bad children's books with worse illustrations'.[89]

While their fantasy fictions are what Lewis and Tolkien are best known for today, from a professional standpoint, as scholars of medieval literature, they were both deeply interested in what the fairies encountered in this literature were. They understood that the back-projection of modern ideas of fairies, derived at best from folklore and at worst from picture books, simply would not do in trying to make sense of how medieval writers perceived these otherworld beings. As Stephen Joy puts it,

> they struggled to puzzle out the moral and theological position of such characters as Merlin or the elfin lords of old. In the end, they seem to have concluded that there had once been 'room' for creatures aligned neither with Heaven nor with Hell, and that forms of nature magic had been at least marginally lawful, but that with the passage of time the moral rules had tightened.[90]

To elucidate this concept, Lewis appealed to the *longaevi* of Martianus Capella (see chapter 3 above), including an essay on them in his book *The Discarded Image* (1964). Lewis also discussed the 'ferlies' as subjects of medieval romance literature;[91] he broadly accepted the idea that fairies were degenerated gods, but also considered the origins of fairies to be of little importance compared with their effect on the mind.[92] For Lewis, the fairies are not so much 'supernatural' as more natural than human beings are, in the sense that they are rooted in the earth and, unlike us, lack souls destined for heaven.[93] For Lewis, the fairies are 'lawless vagrants' who do not fit in any straightforward way into the medieval model of the world,[94] although this unaffiliated nature increased their fascination.

Tolkien's 1947 essay 'On Fairy-Stories' is notable for its hedging on the question of whether the elves Tolkien devoted so much thought to were actually real: 'For if elves are true, and really exist independently of our tales about them, then this also is certainly true: elves are not primarily concerned with us, nor we with them'. To this remark, Tolkien added a note: 'This is true also, even if they are only creations of Man's mind, "true" only as reflecting in a particular way one of Man's visions of Truth.'[95]

At no point, however, did Tolkien state definitively that elves were 'creations of Man's mind', and the same ambiguity runs through the essay. Tolkien declares that, 'in verity or fable', human narrators have 'stained the elves' with the effects of human original sin,[96] and writes that mythological beings 'live, if they live at all, by the same life, just as in the mortal world do kings and peasants'.[97] When writing of fantasy, Tolkien chooses his language carefully when he notes that 'The human mind is capable of forming mental images of things *not actually present*' (my italics), rather than things *not actually real*, and he chooses to speak of 'the Primary World' rather than the 'real world' to describe the matrix of experiences in which we usually dwell.[98]

Indeed, Tolkien claims that 'The Primary World, Reality, of elves and men is the same, if differently valued and perceived.'[99] At the heart of Tolkien's essay on fairy stories was a call for the recovery of fairies, and of their enchantment, 'as things apart from ourselves', as we were meant to see them.[100] In other words, it is not good enough merely to deploy fairies or enchantment in metaphor or allegory; these themes are of no value unless presented in such a way as we *could* believe them, even if Tolkien remains ambiguous on the question of whether we *should* believe them. Lewis agreed; we could only begin to understand medieval literature – and to write anything as convincing – 'if we can imagine what it would feel like to witness, or think we had witnessed, or merely to believe in' fairy wonders.[101] This recovery of realistic fairies was a self-conscious rejection of triteness. Tolkien was critical of Andrew Lang's belief that fairy tales were suitable for children because children were credulous and likely to believe a tale to be true. For Tolkien, fairy tales are 'plainly not primarily concerned with possibility, but with desirability'.[102]

The 'dumbing down' or infantilization of fairies that Tolkien called 'Pigwiggenry' (in reference to a seventeenth-century fairy poem by Michael Drayton) has surely declined as the boundaries between children's, young adult, and adult literature have broken down – with children and young people reading fantasy written for adults, and vice versa, with the result that books for older children are now often written to appeal to adults too.[103] Some contemporary readers of Tolkien himself might not even realize that *The Hobbit* was written for children, especially after Peter Jackson adapted the book into three feature-length films clearly aimed at an adult audience; and fandoms such as the 'Wizarding World' of Harry Potter have resulted in people reading books well into adulthood (and wanting more books) in a series intended for children.

In a sense, this development (which arguably began with Tolkien himself) is the coming full circle of Sam Leith's observation that the nineteenth century's folklore craze inadvertently invented children's literature, when authors such as Hans Christian Andersen (1805–75) decided that folklore provided not only the raw material for children's literature but also the pattern and programme for entirely new tales written for children.[104] From Tolkien onwards, fairy tales began to be written for adults, and fantasy literature developed as an adult equivalent of new fairy tales fashioned on the pattern of the old.

While admitting that they offer consolation, Tolkien denied that fairy stories are an 'escape' from the 'real world' (whatever that is).[105] 'The world outside', he observed, 'has not become less real because the prisoner cannot see it'.[106] Most famously, in the epilogue to his essay, Tolkien coined the notion of 'eucatastrophe' – a sudden, joyful, and positive turn of events – as a key element of fantasy literature, arguing that eucatastrophe is so powerful in 'secondary worlds' because it expresses a truth of the primary world: namely, the Christian narrative of the redemption of the world by the self-offering of Jesus Christ. 'Legend and History have met and fused', and the Gospel has 'hallowed' new legends that express its truth.[107]

But Tolkien may have underestimated, in this respect, the extent to which what he created was something truly new, rather than just newly manufactured fairy tales like the stories of Andersen. As Tolkien's elves defy immemorial folkloric convention by (for instance) forging and using iron tools and weapons, so Tolkien's conception of fairy tale as essentially Christian departs from the intense fatalism of the traditional fairy tale, which is so often a place of brutal, unmerciful justice rather than Christian providence or redemption.[108] Dmitra Fimi has argued compellingly that Tolkien's view of fairies was rooted in a tradition of Christian (and indeed Catholic) vitalism reaching back through the poet Francis Thompson (1859–1907) to John Henry Newman (1801–90),[109] who in one sermon (for the feast of St Michael and All Angels) argued that 'there are Spiritual Intelligences which move those wonderful and vast portions of the natural world which seem to be inanimate'. While Newman's 'Spiritual Intelligences' were angels rather than fairies, they were as intimately involved in nature as the elementals of the Theosophists; ministering angels, not chance, explained the weather and the cycle of the seasons, and Newman compared the invisible operation of these spirits in nature to the invisible operation of the human soul.[110] It was only a short step from mundane angels of this kind to a neutral order of beings, responsible for the natural world, who could be identified with the fairies of folklore.

Tolkien was not alone among twentieth-century authors of fiction in contemplating the real existence of elves, fairies, and trolls. The children's author Alison Uttley (1884–1976), for instance, firmly believed in fairies and listened eagerly to the stories of those who claimed to have seen them,[111] while D. J. Watkins-Pitchford (1905–90, known as 'BB') saw a gnome in his nursery at the age of four, and was ever after convinced of their existence – allowing him to write surprisingly realistic books about the adventures of his gnomes, the 'Little Grey Men'.[112] The Finnish author Yrjö Kokko (1903–77) claimed to have begun writing his popular children's tale of trolls, *Pessi and Illusia* (1944), when he encountered tiny trolls on the windscreen of his car during the dark days of Finland's Continuation War against the Soviet Red Army.[113] But the woman who made the greatest impact on perceptions of fairies in twentieth-century Britain was undoubtedly the folklorist Katharine Mary Briggs (1898–1980). Briggs may not have made as obvious a cultural impact on popular views of fairies as Tolkien, and her works have not been adapted for the cinema or streaming services. However, her work laid the foundation for all subsequent study of British fairy lore and brought rigorous scholarly standards that had hitherto been largely absent.

While always interested in fairy tales and storytelling, Briggs's interest in fairies seems to have intensified during the Second World War, when she was serving in the WAAF (Women's Auxiliary Air Force) at Syerston in Lincolnshire. After the War, Briggs decided to pursue postgraduate studies in English Literature at Lady Margaret Hall in Oxford, and presented to her tutor, Ethel Seaton, a manuscript entitled *The Personnel of Fairyland*. This represented Briggs's first attempt to make sense of the bewildering variety of fairies and fairy names in British folklore – a lifelong task that would culminate in her *Encyclopedia of Fairies* (1976). Briggs herself evinced agnosticism when it came to the existence of the fairy realm – although she acknowledged that 'Some of the fairy anecdotes have a curiously convincing air of truth.'[114]

Under Seaton's supervision, Briggs embarked on a DPhil thesis about supernatural beings in seventeenth-century English literature, but she also continued to work on *The Personnel of Fairyland*, which was eventually published in 1953. Here, Briggs began to establish the division of types of fairies that is one of her major legacies, such as Heroic Fairies, Solitary Fairies, Small Trooping Fairies, Tutelary Fairies, and Nature Fairies.[115] Briggs's DPhil thesis turned into *The Anatomy of Puck* (1959), which was ostensibly a study of fairies in Shakespeare but was in reality a much wider and deeper examination of English fairy lore.

Briggs's concern with the restoration of 'middle spirits' to a central place in early modern English literature was shared by the literary critic William Empson (1906–84), who was critical of Frances Yates for writing off fairies as mere 'imagery' in her *Occult Philosophy in the Elizabethan Age*, and eager to restore the *longaevi* to their proper place in the cosmos.[116] Like Lewis and Tolkien, Briggs was a devout Christian and regular churchgoer – although, having been born into a Unitarian family, she was not confirmed in the Church of England until 1947.[117] As her biographer noted, Briggs avoided excessive theorizing and focussed on collecting fairy lore and, crucially, setting it in its proper historical context; it was no accident that her academic background, before she turned to English literature, lay in early modern history.[118] Indeed,

Briggs's most lasting contribution to the study of fairy lore may have been her utter refusal of reductivism, which went against the grain of mid-twentieth-century scholarship but has largely stood the test of time.

While Briggs was primarily interested in fairy lore as a phenomenon of the past, and showed no inclination to engage with contemporary reports of fairy encounters, this was not true of all scholars. The historian Dermot Mac Manus (1892–1990) – for he was adamant he was a historian, and not a folklorist – published a collection of modern fairy accounts from Ireland, *The Middle Kingdom*, in 1959. Mac Manus distinguished between traditional Irish fairy tales, which 'are just nursery entertainments and . . . without any relation to everyday life', and the accounts he had collected, which he only included if a central character in the account was still alive, and was prepared to stand by the veracity of the account, and where 'the incidents are well authenticated and can be verified by anyone', presumably by tracking down the original narrator.[119] Mac Manus divided the accounts into such categories as incidents involving fairy trees, the Pooka, fairy pranks and mischief, fairy ground, the phenomenon of the 'stray sod' (when someone steps on a fairy-haunted piece of ground and becomes lost and disoriented, regardless of their location), and hostile fairies.

In the final section of the book, Mac Manus confronted the question of the reality of the fairies, suggesting that the right question to ask is not 'Do you believe in fairies?' but 'Do you believe in the supernatural?' Once someone is willing to contemplate the existence of a supernatural world, Mac Manus argued, then fairies should not be judged on their inherent plausibility but on the truthfulness and trustworthiness of reports of them, and on the volume and prevalence of such accounts. In rural Ireland, as Mac Manus notes, that volume was very great; fairies and the risks they posed were simply accepted as part of life.

Mac Manus was equally scathing of the charge of 'superstition' levelled against believers in fairies, on the grounds that no one could ever clearly define what was superstitious and what was not – leading Mac Manus to believe the word was just a way of policing acceptable and unacceptable knowledge.[120] While Mac Manus's own avowed position was one of open-mindedness, *The Middle Kingdom* was clearly a rallying cry in defence of Ireland's traditional folk-cosmology and the integrity of its people against a scoffing discourse of 'superstition' that often cloaked anti-Irishness in an affected scepticism. The convictions of Mac Manus's witnesses derived from traditional lore, the fairy world they encountered was an old one, and the spirits they met were not flower fairies but the terrifying sí of legend – the tall figures in black cloaks seen by Michael Sheehy one night at Killeaden were a far cry from the Cottingley fairies.[121] It was one thing to believe Irish farmers, and quite another to indulge the accounts of what middle-class Spiritualist ladies in England's Home Counties claimed to have seen in their gardens.

Yet neither Briggs's cautious agnosticism nor Mac Manus's avowal of faith in the fairies was a luxury available to folklorists elsewhere in Europe. When the Lithuanian folklorist Norbertas Vėlius published his *Mitinės Lietuvių sakmių butybės* (Mythical Beings of Lithuanian Tales) in 1977 it was the first work devoted to Lithuania's 'lower mythology', but Vėlius had to include a preface favourably quoting Karl Marx and situating the study of folklore within the context of dialectical materialist ideology.[122] There was certainly no possibility of Vėlius surveying contemporary Lithuanians working on collective farms to ask them about their experiences of aitvaras or the laumės, since Soviet materialism excluded the possibility of such beings existing.

On the one hand, folklore studies were sufficiently 'proletarian' in their subject matter to be tolerated by Soviet ideology; but on the other, folklore promoted local, regional, and national identities – and supernatural beliefs – that the Soviet regime was eager to suppress. Folklore studies, when tolerated, flourished in Lithuania under Soviet occupation because it was one of the few avenues of expression for national identity; but at other times, as under other Communist regimes in Eastern Europe, the very pursuit of folklore was enough to provoke suspicion.

Looking for fairies: the Fairy Investigation Society

Given that Elsie Wright and Frances Griffiths did not admit to fabricating the Cottingley photographs until the 1980s, for those who chose to believe in them the photographs constituted proof of the existence of fairies for over sixty years. Even after the cousins' confessions, people claimed to hear fairies at Cottingley, and Frances never admitted that the fifth photograph taken at Cottingley Beck was a fake.[123] It was arguably Sir Arthur Conan Doyle himself who began the practice of seeking anecdotal evidence for the existence of fairies via witness accounts from people in modern Britain, since he included a section in *The Coming of the Fairies* that assembled other pieces of evidence (besides Cottingley), including letters Doyle had received from other fairy witnesses.[124] Not since Edmund Jones in the eighteenth century had there been a determined effort to collect first-hand fairy experiences, rather than just fairy stories.

In 1927, the inventor of the wireless telephone, a naval officer named Quentin Craufurd, decided to found a society dedicated to the investigation of fairy phenomena, the Fairy Investigation Society (FIS). In a case of life imitating art, Craufurd was inspired by a fictional society, the Society for the Investigation of Faery Fact and Fallacy, which was dreamt up by Bernard Sleigh (himself a fairy believer) for his novel *The Gates of Horn* (1926).[125] In the real world, however, the FIS proved less harmonious than its fictional counterpart – Craufurd noted that not all members had the same motives, and some disagreed with his desire to keep the Society largely secret, preferring to prioritize the commercial or the sensational.

Unfortunately, the Society's early records were destroyed in the Blitz in 1940, but Craufurd wrote down his own reminiscences in 1957. He recorded that the group carried out experiments between 1927 and 1932 communicating via psychic radio and automatic writing with nine 'marsh fairies' who were supposed to guide them to archaeological remains – a strange fusion of the traditional role of English fairies as guardians of treasure with technology and Spiritualism.[126]

In spite of the loss of its archive, the FIS just about survived the Second World War; indeed, among its most famous members was a key figure in that conflict – Air Chief Marshal Hugh Dowding, who commanded RAF Fighter Command in the Battle of Britain, but also believed fairies were essential for the growth of vegetable life.[127] After the War, Dowding feared the onset of battle between gnomes, fairies, and human beings in Ireland.[128] Curiously enough, Dowding's interests were not the fairies' only involvement with the RAF in the Second World War – pilots belonging to Clan MacLeod reportedly carried photographs or small pieces of the 'Fairy Flag of Dunvegan' (a flag supposed to have been given to a chieftain by the fairies, and kept at Dunvegan Castle on the Isle of Skye).[129] Whether or not the fairies assisted the British war effort, however, in 1950 the energetic Marjorie Thelma Johnson (1911–2011) became secretary of the FIS. During the 1950s, Johnson diligently collected reports of fairy encounters, and it was during this period that Walt Disney (who had visited Ireland in search of fairies in 1947) joined the Society.[130]

Craufurd died in 1957, and disaster struck in 1960 when comments made by Marjorie Johnson about 'the sex life of sprites' proved a viral sensation in tabloid newspapers around the world. Johnson took a step back from the FIS, but was unable to find a publisher for her extensive compendium of fairy sightings, *Seeing Fairies*. The book was eventually published in German translation in 2000, and subsequently in Italian; but it was not until after Johnson's death in 2011 that Simon Young edited the original English text of *Seeing Fairies* for publication. Johnson included not only letters she had received about fairy sightings but also stories encountered by accident in the press or on the radio, and included details of how she followed up some of the sightings with further questions.

The encounters recorded by Johnson ranged from the Spiritualist to the folkloric and traditional.[131] However, a view of the fairies as tiny, largely benign, and associated with nature (and plants specifically) predominated. At its peak in the first half of the 1950s, the Fairy Investigation Society had as many as 120 members, but it seems to have declined after Craufurd's death and the completion of *Seeing Fairies* – although it still theoretically existed, in vestigial form, as late as 1996.[132] As we shall see in the next chapter, however, Marjorie Johnson's programme of systematically collecting fairy encounters was by no means in vain, and it has inspired contemporary folklorists to embark on similar projects.

The nineteenth century witnessed a cultural apotheosis of the fairy, as far as the prestige of the collecting of folklore, the retelling of fairy tales, the elaboration of new fairy fantasies, and the illustration of fairies was concerned. But the 'cultural mainstreaming' of fairies came at a price. The folklorists, by observing it, affected the system they observed; and their assumptions (such as the Irish folklorists' certainty that the fairies of nineteenth-century Ireland were the old Irish gods) fed back into the subsequent development of folklore. Furthermore, cultural mainstreaming weakened the fairies' mystique, and certainly removed much of the fear associated with them. Fairies came to be associated with children, with 'cuteness', with the garden, and with tiny size, and by the end of the century fairies were primarily conceived of by educated people as what Silver calls 'psychic insect life'.[133] The traditional fairy had come to be replaced by a new kind of 'international' fairy that was acceptable to both Spiritualists and illustrators of children's books alike.

Katharine Briggs paid no attention whatsoever to Marjorie Johnson's fairy investigations,[134] and the worlds of folklorist and fairy seer remained resolutely impervious to any kind of interaction. The Folklore Society, for instance, was silent on the Cottingley photographs, and those members who did comment were dismissive.[135] But even in the second half of the twentieth century, there were those (such as Lewis and Tolkien) who took fairies very seriously indeed – and this included many folklorists. As Barbara Rieti commented towards the end of the twentieth century, 'although I have never seen anything worse than myself (as the saying goes), I would not rule it out entirely'. She agreed with one of her informants that 'From my point of view, probably [the fairies] don't exist, but I wouldn't say they don't', and she rejected 'a certain unwarranted arrogance on the part of those who dismiss them out of hand'.[136] By the late twentieth century, such words were not so much an expression of sentimentality or romantic wishful thinking, as an acknowledgement that the world remained a mysterious place, and the true nature of reality remained still unknown. In an increasingly uncertain and rapidly changing world, fairies took on a new significance, and renewed their menace. It is to that contemporary 'rewilding' of fairies that we now turn.

NINE

Rewilding fairyland: fairies today

In the late spring or early summer of 2003, I was living in a flat that overlooked a portion of ancient woodland in rural Warwickshire, but it had never occurred to me to enter the wood until one day, in the late afternoon, I felt a certain compulsion to do so. The wood was, at first, prosaic; and my focus was on my footing, on not tripping over brambles or stepping in rabbit holes. But as I walked deeper into the trees I was struck by the quality of the light, and by the sense of a presence beckoning me farther in. It is difficult to describe what this was like – but it was as though I had left the mundane world behind me, and was walking into story. Something was going to happen; some*one* was weaving a narrative for me, and I felt as though that someone had a mischievous streak.

Eventually I reached a clearing in the wood that was beautifully carpeted with wild flowers. In the centre of the clearing stood a single tree, with a crooked branch low to the ground that looked somewhat like a seat. I stared at it for some time, captivated by the quality of light in the clearing, but as the feeling built that something was about to happen, I responded with fear. I decided I should leave. But I was unable, initially, to find my way out of the wood – even though it had probably taken me less than five minutes to reach the clearing. I found myself wandering among silver birches, puzzled that there seemed no way out – and even when I eventually reached the edge of the wood, I became captivated by the yellow catkins hanging from the hazels, and spent a long time looking at them. This was when I had an experience of time seemingly slowing down, and I found myself endowing the catkins with a kind of personality, as if they were waving me farewell. When I got back to my flat, I was astonished at how long I had spent in the wood – far more time had passed than I had experienced.

Was this a fairy experience? A more interesting question, perhaps, is why I associated this experience, at the time and thereafter, with fairies. It is not as though I saw or met any otherworld beings; soberly considered, the experience was simply an atmospheric walk in the woods – even if, as D. J. Watkins-Pitchford remarked in 1942, Warwickshire is one of the last English counties where you might hope to meet a fairy.[1] But in the same way my culture (that of rural England) tends to associate dark graveyards with the possibility of ghosts, so it associates woodland with the possibility of fairies.

A combination of fantasy literature, art, nostalgia for childhood, and the rise of spiritualities decoupled from organized religion sustains interest in the modern fairy, at least in Britain. A minority of adults in the contemporary Western world incorporate experiences of fairies – or, indeed, the possibility that fairies might be experienced – into their view of the world. In some cases, this is a conscious adoption, perhaps based on a person's Pagan[2] religious beliefs or 'alternative' spiritual commitments. In other cases – and this might come as a surprise to some – it is an adjustment to a worldview hitherto unaware of fairies that has been forced by an encounter with beings best interpreted through the lens of fairy lore.

While fairies remain a staple of mass consumer culture, usually aimed at children, a curious feature of fairy lore since the 1960s is that the overall trajectory of cultural engagement with fairies has been becoming more serious. The late twentieth century saw the emergence of a desire, which has only intensified in the twenty-first century, to 'rewild' fairyland: to recover the feelings of awe and fear that attended our ancestors' experience of the fairies, and to strip fairies of their 'cute' and 'twee' associations. Understanding this development is the subject of this final chapter, which explores why people are not content to consign fairies forever to the nursery, and why they might want to take fairies seriously.

As we have seen in chapter 8 above, there were already people in the mid twentieth century who wanted to take fairies seriously, and bridled at the Cottingley photographs' misrepresentation of fairies and their cultural consequences. But the social revolutions and transformations of the later twentieth century, which had us re-evaluating our relationships with the divine, with religion, with received moral certainties, with the natural environment, and even with the nature of reality itself, lent a new appeal to figures as unstable and ambiguous as the fairies. Fairies are the original misfits; in a world where most of us feel like misfits, at least some of the time, it is perhaps no wonder that we are drawn to identify with them.

The bottom line of the garden: fairies for sale

Before we come to consider the 'rewilding' of fairies as beings to be taken seriously and sought earnestly by those who believe in them, it is important to consider what is perhaps the most culturally visible development in modern fairy lore: the commercialization of fairies. The marketing of the 'stage fairy' is as old as the sixteenth century, and lies at the root of the modern international 'Small, Winged Fairy' (SWF). But the late twentieth century also saw an explosion in the marketing of more specific kinds of local and regional fairies, trolls, and elves, often linked with tourism.

The world's best-known 'tourist fairy', who has become an immediately recognizable symbol of an entire country, is surely the Irish leprechaun.[3] The stereotyped appearance of the 'international leprechaun', which seems to have originated among Irish Americans rather than in Ireland itself, reflects (and perhaps *deflects*) caricatures of the 'backward' Irish from the nineteenth-century British press. Just as Ireland has lost control of the leprechaun, so the Swedish *tomte* has become a ubiquitous feature of Christmas decorations beyond Scandinavia, and in Britain has merged with the gnome-like 'gonk' marketed for every occasion from Valentine's Day to the coronation of King Charles III.

Other kinds of popular fairy, such as the garden gnome and the Christmas elf, seem to exist almost solely for their commercial potential.[4] The modern troll, meanwhile, has had a mixed commercial career; while Tove Jansson's Moomintrolls are perhaps the literary trolls best known to children, they depart significantly from the folkloric portrayal of trolls insofar as they are neither frightening, ugly, nor magical. However, the story of the Billy Goats Gruff remains popular, and in America it became popular for a while to erect statues of trolls under bridges. Plastic troll dolls, which are now the basis of a film franchise, might now be the first thing children outside Scandinavia think of when trolls are mentioned.[5] To adults, meanwhile, trolls are peddlers of hate on social media and the internet – while those who try to shut down online trolls, continuing the folkloric theme, sometimes call themselves 'elves'.[6]

The familiar SWF has, meanwhile, succumbed to what is often called 'Disneyfication', a hyper-stylization of fairy nature that is often reduced to wings and (usually) femininity. As Richard Sugg has argued, the near-universal availability of these garish stylized fairies has undermined any notion of fairy glamour as dazzling and special. At the same time, however, as Sugg acknowledges, there has been something of a revival of more threatening and ambiguous fairies in both cinema and children's literature.[7]

It is a paradox of the 'tourist elf' that certain countries, such as Ireland and Iceland, have integrated into their tourist appeal the notion that their fairies are more 'authentic' than those of other nations – on the premise that people in Ireland and Iceland still genuinely believe in fairies. In Ireland, for example, exaggerated presentations of the authenticity and indigeneity of fairy traditions have become an integral part of the tourist experience of a visit to the Emerald Isle.[8] Yet in selling themselves on the 'authenticity' of their fairy populations, Ireland and Iceland engage in a commercialization that inevitably transforms the presentation of their fairies. If a country has a reputation for belief in fairies, and people are attracted to visiting the country for that reason, then there is a cultural and commercial incentive for its citizens to affect such belief. Thus, it has become 'almost a fashion to say that you believe in supernatural beings' in modern Iceland, since such avowals of belief provoke international journalistic interest in the country – which, for a small country such as Iceland, is no small thing. For this reason, the high numbers of Icelanders who claim to believe in elves (over half, according to a survey conducted in 1998) should perhaps be taken with a pinch of salt.[9]

Ármann Jakobsson identifies the 'Icelandic tourist elf' as a distinct type of 'fakelore', whose history and meaning are vastly simplified and who has little connection with traditional Icelandic folklore.[10] Matthias Egeler, meanwhile, has drawn attention to the advent of 'Reykjavík fairies' who are essentially 'New Age fairies' transplanted to Iceland, and have no precedent at all in Icelandic folklore. Typical of this trend was the self-declared fairy psychic Erla Stefánsdóttir (1935–2015), who claimed to be able to map the elves of Iceland, regularly appeared on TV, and helped form international perceptions of Iceland's supernatural fauna. But Stefánsdóttir drew on Theosophical ideas and dreamt up beings such as *blómálfar* (flower fairies) who owed more to Cottingley than they did to Icelandic folklore.[11]

The lesson, perhaps, is that 'authenticity' is a commodity so readily marketable that it is unlikely to remain authentic for long. The advent of the tourist elf invites narrative flattening, stylization, and conformity to the expectations of visitors. Nathan Rabalais documents similar trends in Louisiana, where folkloric 'characters that enjoy particular popularity' do so because they 'have no fixed narrative associated with them' and do not require extensive explanation to outsiders.[12] Tourism, it seems, is the enemy of the distinctive.

On the other hand, there is some historical basis to the tourist legend of Iceland as an elf-haunted island, and the folklorist Valdimar Hafstein documented the genuine fear of elves that held up many Icelandic road-building projects in the 1970s.[13] However, in the pitting of elves against development and modernity, we see a departure from the elves' traditional place in Icelandic society as a mirror population – for, as Icelandic elf-seers report, the elves of modern Iceland live the lives of Icelanders of two or three centuries ago. They are no longer keeping pace with their human counterparts.[14] It is worth noting that this fairy eschewal of technology seems not to be universal, as the incident of the Wollaton gnomes testifies – a mass sighting of gnomes driving cars and chasing children around Nottingham's Wollaton Park in September 1979.[15] But Iceland's elves are not just a way to sell the country to outsiders; they are also the 'superlative Icelanders' who 'incarnate heritage and tradition', ensuring that, regardless of social changes, Iceland remains always the same on some unseen level.[16]

It is easy to despise or make fun of the commercialization of fairy lore, to view it as financially motivated 'fakelore', and to dismiss it as a debasement of motifs drawn from literature and traditional folklore. The irony is that taking people for a ride with the aid of flimsy illusions is something that the fairies themselves are said to do, and today's children's entertainers and party planners are a great deal less dishonest than the fairy cozeners and fairy magicians of the past. There is nothing solemn and po-faced about the fairy tradition, which has always had an element of playfulness and self-mockery to it; fairies are beings of folklore, not religion. As Art Leete and Vladimir Lipin found among the Komi hunters of the Urals, jokes about forest spirits and magical practices did not mean the hunters did not believe in them.[17]

Fairy magic is not entirely dead in Europe, and Judit Kis-Halas has documented the practice of a traditional healer named Erszike in the village of Rádfalva in southern Hungary. Erszike became a healer owing to experiences during a 'fairy illness' or 'fairy possession', and she subsequently offered to help others by means of angelic and fairy magic. Yet, while Erszike might seem like a throwback to an earlier phase of Hungarian village life, her clients come from all strata of society and she is happy to make use of modern 'New Age' materials in her traditional healing practice (indeed, this willingness to make use of any available source of magical power arguably makes Erszike *more* traditional).[18] In truth, there is no such thing as a pure and unspoilt fairy tradition that can help us distinguish authentic from inauthentic expressions of fairy lore. Commercialization has always been part of the picture.

Chasing fairies

As we have seen in chapter 8 above, the idea of gathering living people's fairy experiences as *data* (as opposed to the collection of folkloric narratives) can be traced back to the work of Walter Evans-Wentz and Sir Arthur Conan Doyle's anti-materialist crusade in *The Coming of the Fairies*, and it was a task enthusiastically taken up in Britain by the Fairy Investigation Society and then by Marjorie Johnson. Johnson was not alone in collecting contemporary fairy accounts, however, and in addition to Dermot Mac Manus's *The Middle Kingdom* (discussed in the previous chapter), Janet Bord collected fairy encounters and Carolyn Eve Green extensively interviewed the traditional Irish storyteller Eddie Lenihan, publishing a volume of his collected accounts of modern Irish encounters with fairies as *Meeting the Other Crowd* (2003).[19] Keith Corcoran recently contributed another sixty-two stories of fairy encounters from Donegal in a separate book focussed on that Irish county.[20]

While Purkiss has been contemptuous of modern fairy encounters, writing them off as 'runaway post-Romantic pseudo-Celtic New Age posturing',[21] folklorists are increasingly interested in present-day fairy sightings. Simon Young, who ensured Johnson's *Seeing Fairies* finally saw the light of publication in 2014, published his own 'Fairy Census' in 2018, which brought together 500 fairy experiences from across the world (but mostly from Britain) contributed by participants in Young's online questionnaire about fairy encounters between 2014 and 2017.

Unlike Evans-Wentz or Johnson, however, Simon Young had no agenda of proving the existence of fairies in conducting the Fairy Census; he was simply interested in how people perceived fairies in the modern world. And there is no prima facie reason why contemporary fairy encounters should be any less interesting than medieval or early modern ones; nor is there any good reason to doubt the sincerity of most respondents. Without a doubt, people see strange things – even if there is more than one possible explanation for such experiences. But the strength of folklore studies is that it is not focussed on explanations. People do not need to justify themselves or explain what they saw in order for their experiences to be deemed important to a project such as the Fairy Census.

The use of the term 'census' for Young's survey is not to be taken literally, of course, and none but the most general conclusions about the statistical prevalence of fairy experiences can be drawn from it; Young's respondents were, by definition, self-selecting – and even among those who have had fairy experiences, those who responded to Young's questionnaire included only those willing to interpret their experience as fairy-related, and willing to share and talk about it. In spite of its name, therefore, the Fairy Census is a qualitative source of modern fairy anecdotes rather than quantitative research.

Nevertheless, the Fairy Census does raise questions about whether seeing fairies is a more common experience than society generally acknowledges – because people either have no frame of reference within which to categorize their experiences, or are too fearful of mockery to share them. Young's questionnaire ensured his correspondents remained anonymous, but asked them their age, gender, and when they had their fairy experience (which was often in childhood). The questionnaire asked people for the country and region in which their experience took place, and about the time of day and surrounding environment in which they witnessed the phenomena. The questionnaire went on to ask correspondents whether they were alone or accompanied, whether others saw the same thing, how long it lasted, and what the light conditions were like.

There were also questions about the fairies themselves: were they male or female, what size were they, did they try to communicate with the witness, and what senses of the witness were involved in the experience? Young asked contributors to comment on the character or mood of the fairies, what they looked like, and whether people heard music; he asked if the contributor believed in fairies before or after the experience, whether they identified with a spiritual or religious tradition, and about their level of education and the frequency of their supernatural experiences. He also singled out certain specific phenomena for inquiry, such as loss of time, profound silence, tingling on the skin, sudden warmth, or sudden chill. Perhaps the most interesting questions Young asked were why people thought their experience was one of fairies (rather than some other interpretation), and what the contributor thought fairies were.[22]

The Fairy Census is an ongoing project, and Simon Young released another 500 fairy accounts in 2023 that had been gathered since 2017. This time, the majority of the accounts (around 68 per cent) came from beyond the UK, most of them from the United States.[23] By the time the second Fairy Census was published, however, Simon Young was not alone in chasing down fairies. In October 2020, the folklorist Jo Hickey-Hall launched a monthly podcast, *Modern Fairy Sightings*, which features in-depth interviews with witnesses about their fairy encounters.[24] At the time of writing, Hickey-Hall's own book about these encounters is due to be published in October 2025.[25]

Are more people really seeing fairies, or do they simply have more opportunities to share such experiences? Even if not every fairy encounter is genuine, scepticism about people's experiences of fairies paradoxically reinforces the strength of the fairy tradition – for the fairies, after all, are notorious for casting a glamour and leading people astray. What is *faerie* but enchantment? If the fairies wanted to mess with us, of course they would make people see fairies who aren't there. Nevertheless, it is clear that new forms of media, from online surveys to social media and podcasts, have made it easier than ever before for people to share their fairy experiences. New technologies make it possible for online communities to exist with highly specialized interests, which means that people can share fairy experiences that might be dismissed or mocked in other forums.

The Fairy Census is a fascinating source of information on the sort of experiences people identify as being associated with fairies – as opposed to ghosts, poltergeists, aliens, demons, cryptids, and so on. Here, for example, is just one of hundreds – a meeting with an 'elf' in a Suffolk churchyard that occurred when the respondent was nineteen years old:

> I had walked up and taken hold of the handle [of the church door] to study the metalwork when I felt the sensation of someone watching me. When I

turned around to my surprise there was someone watching me from the other side of the chest high hedge, fifteen or so feet away, that formed the boundary of the churchyard. I think I half spoke a greeting and looked right into their eyes. The eyes were big and a deep blue without white or pupil, but I could tell they were looking into mine. It had a thin face that tapered to a very narrow jaw and small chin. Its nose was fine, and its lips were small and thin. And it had long straight light brown hair. The eyes and the dimensions of the face were strange and inhuman but not unpleasant. I remember it smiled slightly and I got the impression that it was feminine. We maintained eye contact for several long seconds until I couldn't hold the stare any longer and had to blink. In the moment it took me to blink it fled, and as my eyes opened, I caught the motion of it ducking down behind the hedge. I was overcome with the urge to know, to understand, to experience and I rushed to the hedge and looked over to see where it had gone. On the other side was an empty field with nowhere to hide, about a hundred yards away flanking the field on the left was a large house and about half that distance away on the right was a small wood. But the watcher had disappeared.[26]

The respondent thought that fairies were 'spirits of the natural world or perhaps the animals and people of another realm of existence alongside our own'. There is no typical fairy encounter; but it is nevertheless hard to ignore that, while some experiences are disquieting, the fairies of the Fairy Census are seldom objects of terror. Indeed, the prevailing feelings surrounding most of the sightings (albeit not to the extent of Johnson's *Seeing Fairies*) are positive. We have to be careful here, and remember that the respondents are self-selecting; therefore, they are probably people who are interested in fairies, and most people who are interested in fairies have a fairly positive view of them. The people who have had terrifying fairy encounters they would rather forget have, perhaps, decided not to participate in the Fairy Census.

Even so, it does seem that a cultural shift has taken place over the last century or so, whereby fairies have moved from beings best avoided to beings some people actively *want* to see. It is a development that raises troubling questions about meaning and definition; in the end, fairies are whatever people want to call fairies, but if the 'consensus fairy' migrates too far from traditional fairy lore, does 'fairy' just become an old label applied to a completely new kind of being? A comparison could be drawn with the use of the word 'vampire' for both the mindless revenant corpses of traditional Balkan lore and the seductive sex-symbols of modern popular culture. Modern fairies do not seem to abduct, seduce, or even scare anyone. Indeed, from a functional point of view, the being of modern folklore who comes closest to the medieval and early modern fairy is probably the poltergeist – invisible, terrifying, unpredictable, alternately playful and malicious, tied in some way to place, and seemingly interested in teenage girls and young women.

If new technologies are allowing us to share fairy experiences as never before, they are also making it possible to research folklore in ways never hitherto imagined – such as through the digitization (and therefore searchability) of vast swathes of nineteenth-century newspapers. This is a resource that Simon Young and other folklorists have made use of to great effect. Digitization allows the study of fairy lore to extricate itself from the tyranny of anecdote that has long held folklore studies captive; it is now possible to establish *as fact* (quantitatively speaking) how widespread certain tale types were in print, and when they first appeared there.

One new digital technology, ISEBEL (the Intelligent Search Engine for Belief Legends), has expanded this searchability beyond sources in a single language by using internal machine translation powered by Artificial Intelligence. Myrthe Osse has deployed ISEBEL to survey shared themes in fairy lore across North-West Europe, searching material in English, Dutch, German, and Icelandic. Her initial findings suggest that malevolent fairy activities outweigh helpful ones, while helpful household spirits are absent from Iceland. The violation of taboos is central to triggering fairy vengeance in all of the surveyed nations, but the theme of changelings is scattered and sporadic, and not a central feature of North-Western European fairies.[27] But it is unlikely that the full potential of such digital tools has yet been realized, and the digital humanities have much yet to contribute to the study of fairy lore.

Guardians of Gaia: Pagan and eco-fairies

As the great historian of modern Paganism Ronald Hutton has demonstrated, the immediate inspiration for modern Pagan witchcraft (or Wicca) was the writings of the Egyptologist Margaret Murray (1863–1963), whose book *The Witch-Cult in Western Europe* (1921) put forward the idea that a Neolithic fertility cult had survived into early modern Europe, and had been demonized by the church as witchcraft.[28] It was a short step from this idea for Gerald Gardner (1884–1964) to claim in *Witchcraft Today* (1954) that the witch-cult still existed, and that he had been initiated into it. With Gardner's bold act of breathing contemporary life into a historical theory, the modern initiatory religion of Wicca came into existence.

But the position of fairies within Wicca was problematic; Murray subscribed to the 'pygmy theory' of fairies, identifying them as an 'aboriginal' population who went into hiding and preserved their prehistoric religious traditions. In fact, since the 'fairies' preserved the witch-cult, the fairies *were* witches,[29] and thus Murrayite historiography actively demythologized fairy lore. The fairies were actually human, traditional fairy lore was degraded collective memory, and the idea of fairies as non-human supernatural beings was excluded by definition.

In modern Paganism, however, the idea of fairies as separate beings is far from absent. As Sabina Magliocco explains, '[Pagans] are interested in fairies precisely because of their presumed link to an earlier worldview in which the cosmos was alive with energies, animated by spirit beings – in other words, enchanted and ensouled.'[30] The widespread rejection of Murrayite and Gardnerian theory as literally true among contemporary Pagans may explain why fairies are now more prominent in Pagan spiritualities – as well as the entanglement of Paganism with other 'alternative' spiritualities such as earth and ecological mysticism.[31]

A key moment in the development of ecological mysticism was the arrival of Eileen and Peter Caddy and Dorothy Maclean at Findhorn in the Scottish Highlands, leading eventually to the foundation of the Findhorn Ecovillage in 1972. According to Paul Hawken, writing in 1975, the 'miracle of Findhorn' – which allowed enormous vegetables to be grown in arid, sandy soil at a latitude farther north than Alaska and Moscow – was down to the fact that 'the elemental world of plants and animals co-operates with fairies, elves and gnomes in creating a land where nothing is impossible and legends are reborn'.[32]

A key influence on Findhorn was Robert Ogilvie Crombie (1899–1975), who famously met a faun in Edinburgh's Botanic Gardens and encountered the god Pan on the island of Iona in a powerful mystical experience of 'reconciliation between the Nature kingdom and man'.[33] Ogilvie Crombie's account of his many encounters with fairies and other elemental beings was published in 2011.[34] The fairy seers of Findhorn, such as Dorothy Maclean, 'technologized' and harnessed the power of specialized fairies in the garden, by welcoming and interacting with them – such as fairies who had a specific responsibility for tomatoes.[35] Findhorn thus represented a very extreme and instrumentalized version of the Theosophical idea of 'Cottingleyesque' fairies as the guardians and attendants of nature, which was popularized by the Cottingley photographs. But there was also a darker side to Findhorn's fairy revelations; human beings are killing and destroying nature, and the fairies are angry.[36]

Andy Letcher has documented the rise of eco-protesters' engagement with the idea of fairies from the 1990s onwards, when a broad-based protest movement against the UK government's roadbuilding programme (often inflected by alternative spiritualities) became a ubiquitous feature of any announcement of a major infrastructure project. Indeed, I remember when the eco-protesters, including 'Swampy', came to my own home town in Suffolk to protest against a service road that ran across water meadows, and camped in trees. While identification with fairies and pixies was often expressed in the songs of the movement, and was largely symbolic, a minority of protesters literally believed in fairies. When conducting fieldwork among the protesters, Letcher found that a number of them reported encountering fairies, sometimes under the influence of hallucinogenic mushrooms. Encounters with fairies were 'incorporated into the belief systems of protest culture', and 'held to vindicate protestors' actions'.[37] Here, as at Findhorn, the idea of fairies as guardians of nature was instrumentalized to advance a cause.

Under the influence of Gerald Gardner's belief that the fairies *were* the witches, some contemporary Pagans have come to believe that they are partly of fairy ancestry, and that this accounts for clairvoyant gifts or a latent attraction to Pagan spiritualities and magic.[38] These beliefs perhaps feed into the phenomenon of fairy cosplay and live-action roleplaying (LARPing), a feature of contemporary American culture that crosses the cultural boundaries between Pagan spirituality, fantasy fandoms, and LGBTQ+ subcultures. Faerieworlds and FaerieCon are annual events, and there is even a 'Faerie–Human Relations Congress' that meets in the woods in Washington State.[39] Forms of spirituality and Pagan practice have developed that are grounded specifically in fairy lore, and the place of fairies in modern American Paganism has been ably chronicled by Morgan Daimler.[40]

In Magliocco's view, in the Pagan community, 'fairy narratives serve primarily to reenchant the natural world at a time of unprecedented ecological crisis'. This requires an exercise of active imagination, which can result in 'embodied experiences of spiritual beings'. Ironically, however, while Pagans seek to draw on fairies as sources of spiritual power, they also often work within a framework of interpretation in which fairies are friendly guardians of nature and have lost most of their threat.[41] While Magliocco found no agreement among Pagans on what fairies are, most perceived them as 'an order of beings who coexist with humans, but do not depend upon them', living in parallel realms that nevertheless interact and intersect with our own. Pagans have adopted the Theosophical idea that fairies are affected by our expectations of them, and will adapt themselves to our perceptions. Magliocco's respondents variously identified fairies as nature spirits, manifestations of the elements, spiritual reflections of animals and insects, a spiritual layer of the material world, and externalizations of subjective experiences.[42]

Contemporary Pagan fairy belief is strongly linked to a desire to re-enchant the world, and, sometimes, with a belief that a new age is dawning and that the fairies are trying to help us enter it.[43] It would be too simplistic, however, to say that contemporary Pagans 'believe in fairies'; rather, they *experience* fairies, and are often conscious readopters of a relationship with fairies in adult life, having earlier jettisoned their childhood belief in them. As Magliocco notes, modern Pagans are unique in seeking a religious connection with fairies – beings with whom contact has traditionally been avoided.[44]

Pagans' fairy belief (or, more accurately, their relationship with the fairies) reflects the Pagan emphasis on taking pride in 'rejected knowledge' and deliberately reviving what was cast aside first by Christianity, then by the Enlightenment, and then by industrialized scientism. The transgression of accepted boundaries of 'sensible' belief is the point. But there is a price to be paid for this; by paying the fairies quasi-religious honour, contemporary Pagans almost inevitably transform them into benevolent beings. The fairies become 'tamed' by the very act of valorizing them as rejected knowledge, because the traditional Christian fear of fairies must be subverted – Pagan fairies have to be predominantly benign beings.[45] Thus, while Pagans may long for a renewed fairy faith to transform the world and turn around human attitudes towards nature and the environment, it remains to be seen whether their fairies can be frightening enough to urge a change of heart.

Close encounters of the elf kind? Fairies, UFOs, and cryptozoology

The notion that 'aliens' (whether understood as extraterrestrials or not, but always associated with UFOs) are the fairies of modern times is one so often repeated in books about fairy lore that it has become a cliché. In Purkiss's view, 'aliens are our fairies' because we are still unable to tolerate uninhabited space of which we are ignorant, and feel the need to populate it with beings who mirror ourselves.[46] For our ancestors, that space might have been the woods, hills, uncultivated meadows, and the *terra incognita* at the edge of maps, while for us it is outer space. Aliens, in Purkiss's view, 'work . . . as early modern fairies did, canalizing our most potent fears and desires, beliefs and disbeliefs', particularly when it comes to the abduction of children.[47]

People who claim to have been abducted by aliens, in common with those who claimed to have been abducted by the fairies in an earlier era, often speak of being sexually molested, and 'Ufologists' are as obsessed with categorizing aliens as demonologists were with categorizing fairies. Even if accounts of alien abduction have not been influenced in any way by fairy lore, the similarities originate from 'common feelings' – including, perhaps, the need to imagine an unseen, hidden community of beings shadowing our own, and that threatens to intersect with our reality.[48] For Barbara Rieti, aliens are 'the fairies' close kin', and she highlights certain shared preoccupations between fairy lore and UFO lore, such as sexuality, invasion, and the intrusion of foreign bodies.[49]

One of the best-known proponents of a connection between fairies and aliens is Jacques Vallée, who in his *Passport to Magonia* (1969) argued that UFO sightings were 'a resurgence of a deep stream in human culture known in older times under various other names',[50] and that 'the saucer myth is seen to coincide to a remarkable degree with the fairy-faith of Celtic countries'.[51] Vallée was arguing not that aliens were fairies, or that fairies were aliens, but that both phenomena represented the way a single mysterious background phenomenon manifested in different cultures under different guises. The 'Magonia' of the book's title referred to a ninth-century report by Agobard of Lyons; Agobard reported (rather mockingly) that country people thought crops destroyed by *tempestarii* (weather magicians) were stolen by people in ships that came from the clouds and took them back to 'Magonia'. Bernadette Filotas identified the term 'Magonians' as a corruption of the Latin *manes* (spirits of the dead) – suggesting that the Magonians were probably field spirits originally, and the story of their visits in ships from the sky was a later elaboration.[52]

The story of the Magonians suited Vallée's purposes because it seemingly showed that the theme of strange visitors arriving in ships from the sky ran through human history; indeed, collecting such stories was a popular pastime among the Ufologists of the 1970s and 1980s. The aliens of Whitley Strieber's classic contactee memoir *Communion* (1987) are similarly inflected by fairy lore, and Strieber drew explicit connections between aliens and fairies. He speculated, in Theosophical fashion, that both fairies and aliens are 'thought-forms' who appear in a sci-fi guise to modern people because that is what we expect; or that the fairies have undergone a technological revolution of their own and have become the aliens.[53] In Strieber's view, fairies (and aliens) are another species sharing our planet, 'who attach to reality along a different line than we do'.[54]

There are, of course, some similarities between fairy lore and UFO lore. The theme of abduction is one; although, unlike the fairies, aliens seem to abduct adults as often as they kidnap children. However, given that fears of infant abduction in the ancient world pre-date fairy lore as we understand it, the fact that both fairies and aliens abduct does not mean aliens are simply another mask worn by the fairies. As in fairy lore, in alien-abduction lore the aliens often seem both powerful and physically weak, requiring humans to renew their stock; UFO encounters, like fairy encounters, are associated with lost time and disorientation, as well as with strange injuries that refuse to heal, like those caused by the 'fairy blast'. In Britain, UFOs sometimes appear above prehistoric monuments (traditionally associated with the fairies). Furthermore, in early UFO encounters, before the stereotyped image of the alien 'grey' developed, contactees sometimes reported that the occupants of flying saucers had a goblin-like appearance – like the Kelly-Hopkinsville 'goblins' of 1955, when a family were supposedly besieged in their farmhouse by goblin-like beings.

However, the possibility that elements of traditional fairy lore fed into UFO lore is not the same as claiming that aliens *are* fairies – either a new kind of fairy, or fairies in a new guise – or that UFO lore represents some kind of modern evolution of fairy lore. Vallée's argument relies on frequent appeals to 'underlying archetypes' rather than genuine commonalities between fairy lore and UFO reports, and his reliance on Evans-Wentz (who, as we have seen, often interviewed Spiritualists and Theosophists) should make us wary of his argument. Likewise, in order to advance similar arguments, Peter Rojcewicz relied upon the elucidation of 'the archetypal structure of folklore [that] reflects the mind's deep core'.[55]

But such Jungian-style claims of archetypal similarity can be adjusted to serve almost any argument. In spite of some similarities, aliens are *historically* different from fairies in fundamental ways that mark out aliens as a new folkloric phenomenon. The most important of these differences is that aliens come from the sky: the craft from which the aliens emerge is central to the mythos, with most witnesses seeing only the craft itself while only a few contactees claim to have met the aliens themselves. With the exception of a handful of traditions, such as the Hungarian belief in a fairy heaven, the night ride of Diana and the Wild Hunt, and the isolated story of the Magonians, fairies in every tradition are not aerial phenomena. They are associated not with the sky, but with the earth. Even the aerial battles often reported in the early modern period as supernatural phenomena began in the Middle Ages as visions of mysterious fairy armies fighting on the ground in lonely places.[56] Fairies emerge from the earth, they live in the earth, and they are tied to it. Fairies are chthonic beings.

There are those, of course, who dispute that the occupants of UFOs come from outer space at all, even if the UFOs are seen in the sky. Aliens need not be construed as extraterrestrials. Alien activity may be manifested more chthonically, and the interpretation of crop circles as caused by aliens might be seen as an attempt to synthesize UFO mythology with traditional fairy lore. There is even the possibility that the aliens emanate from human consciousness itself, in a kind of projection of a subjective experience into reality. In these scenarios, the aliens do appear more like fairies, as David Luke speculated: 'the aliens themselves may actually be elves, but they are more intra-terrestrial than extra-terrestrial, or perhaps even trans-terrestrial – that is, they are not actually outside, but then inside is the wrong term as well'.[57]

Overall, however, we do a disfavour to both the integrity of fairy lore and the distinctiveness of UFO lore to lump aliens in with fairies as somehow the same thing: they both deserve better than that. Perhaps Valdimar Hafstein may have been onto something when he suggested that fairy lore provides a framework for coming to terms with the past, but UFO lore allows people to come to terms with the future in a highly future-oriented society such as modern America.[58] In this sense, aliens are both old and new.

As I argued in my book *Twilight of the Godlings*, contemporary belief in aliens does not recall traditional fairy belief as much as contemporary cryptozoology does.[59] While the aliens belong to the stars (or, perhaps, to the deep psyche), the cryptids belong to the untamed wilds; and while the aliens may be human*oid* in appearance, cryptids like Bigfoot are human-*like*. In other words, while aliens are frightening because they are so different from us, cryptids like Bigfoot are fascinating because they are *almost* human; and, indeed, there is a long tradition of people interpreting human-like animals such as the great apes through the lens of folklore, and the orangutan was originally classified as *Satyrus indicus* (the Indian satyr).[60] Yet, in truth, neither aliens nor cryptids really have what it takes to be fairies. They are defined by their *otherness*, and by their inaccessibility to human investigation. Even if their uncanniness lies, in part, in their dim resemblance to humanity, they are too different from us to be mirror populations like the fairies; they do not share or mimic our social life, as fairies do.

Machine elves: fairies of psychedelia

In 1922, Sir Arthur Conan Doyle suggested that 'some sort of psychic spectacles' might one day be invented that would give people access to the fairy realm, by adjusting their 'vibrations' to those of the fairies.[61] The idea that the fairies might give people some means of seeing them was an old idea in folklore, of course – although in the tale 'Midwife to the Fairies', it takes the form of a magical ointment rubbed on the midwife's eyes rather than spectacles. In this respect, the folklore was closer to the truth; it would be ingested substances rather than new technologies that would leave people believing they had access to the fairy realm.

In 1965, the American ethnobotanist Terence McKenna (1946–2000) first encountered 'self-transforming machine elves' after smoking the tryptamine derivative DMT in Berkeley, California. The experience of meeting 'elves' was common among experimenters with hallucinogenic drugs, and especially DMT; this led McKenna to conclude that there existed a 'DMT space' that was inhabited by the beings he called machine elves (as they seemed to be part organic, part machine, and capable of transforming themselves). Significantly, McKenna was familiar with the work of Evans-Wentz, and Erik Davis has suggested that 'an evolutionarily adapted cognitive bias towards agent detection' in humans may cause the brain to generate entities in hallucinogenic experiences – a theory inspired by the anthropologist Stewart Guthrie.[62]

But why should the entities encountered on a hallucinogenic 'trip' be diminutive elf-, gnome- or goblin-like beings, rather than, say, angels, gods, or saints? Perhaps Davis's observation that McKenna and other psychedelic radicals were 'religious visionaries after religion' offers a clue.[63] In a sceptical, post-religious age, the machinery of religion was unavailable to McKenna for the interpretation of the numinous, and so it was the lesser beings of sub-religious folklore that manifested. When the Hungarian scientist Stephen Szára first experimented with DMT a decade before McKenna, he found the whole room 'filled with spirits', experienced a sensation of flying, and was confronted with 'two quiet sunlit gods'. The encounter with entities came only at the end of the DMT experience, which usually lasts around ten minutes and begins with 'interior flowing of energy and consciousness' before the smoker is confronted by brightly coloured geometric patterns; the experiencer then passes through some sort of tunnel or passage to a space where the intelligent entities are encountered.[64] However, the entities are not always elf-like, and insectoid and reptilian manifestations abound (especially praying mantises); furthermore, the research of Rick Strassman suggested that only about half of DMT users experienced encounters with otherworld beings.[65]

Nevertheless, it seems that many people who experiment with DMT and have no previous expectation of elves (unlike the Evans-Wentz-reading McKenna) meet elf-like beings. To Peter Meyer, the elves 'often took on a very cartoon-like, clownish form, shape-shifting, never really keeping still, moving around and impossible to pin down', while David Luke experienced the elves not only within 'DMT space' but also intruding into normal perceptual reality (they trooped into his tent), which he found 'just too much of an ontological challenge'.[66] In an effort to explain the DMT elves, Davis appeals to Bruno Latour's notion of 'beings of metamorphosis' who lack sustained continuity of being, seemingly appearing and disappearing because they inhabit other modes of being.[67] But while most people might be minded to be dismissive of the experiences of those who use psychedelics *because* they had those experiences while using psychedelics, for McKenna the very fact that psychedelics were seemingly necessary to unlock such experiences was evidence of their significance. Drugs such as DMT did not create illusions but rather unlocked Aldous Huxley's 'doors of perception', implying that a realm lay beyond those doors that was inhabited by life forms of its own.

We are here in the realms of 'speculative realism' or 'object-oriented ontology', in which strange experiences are more likely to be interpreted as expressions of an external reality, rather than delusions generated in some way by the perceptual or neurological shortcomings of the perceiver – such as the metaphysics espoused by the philosopher Graham Harman, which ascribes reality even to the objects of the imagination.[68] In such thinking, familiar distinctions between reality and fiction, imagination and perception, subjective and objective are elided. People experience things that are simultaneously 'real' (even to the point that others can experience them, too) and generated from the imagination. As the psychoanalyst Félix Guattari speculated, we may be surrounded by 'incorporeal domains of entities we detect at the same time that we produce them, and which appear to have been always there, from the moment we engender them'.[69] Such entities are Latour's uncanny ventriloquist's dummies: they are unable to function without the presence of the operator, and yet they are nevertheless somehow uncannily endowed with a separate agency that renders them ontologically independent beings.[70] From this perspective, the 'unreality' of fairies is inconsequential; in a reversal of the denial that kills fairies in *Peter Pan*, fairies are real because our imaginations make them real. Elsie Wright and Frances Griffiths were, presumably, literally making fairies.

The difficulty with the machine elves of psychedelia, however, is that they are accessible only to those who are willing to enter 'DMT space', and even then there is no guarantee of meeting them. Why should it be necessary to take psychedelics in order to access other layers of reality, and why was it possible for human beings in other historical periods to encounter these beings without the assistance of chemicals that were only synthesized in twentieth-century laboratories? One answer to this question is to speculate that people in pre-modern societies who encountered fairies were indeed inadvertently 'tripping' on various types of fungi, but this seems distinctly implausible (not to say reductive).

An alternative approach is to appeal to the alienation of modern human life, trained in a materialistic and limited perception of the world and steeped in technology and multimedia entertainment, where an 'animistic' connection with the deep nature of reality itself becomes possible only with chemical help. In this modern iteration of the myth of the departing fairies, the elves have retreated from the hills and gone not into caverns or across the ocean, but trooped into transdimensional and transperceptual spaces accessible only via the ingestion of psychedelics. Indeed, Luke speculates that naturally occurring DMT in the chemistry of the brain could explain people seeing elves without the ingestion of psychedelics, and could be 'the neurochemical substrate of these spontaneous conducive-to-elf experiences'.[71] But in accepting this, we would be in danger of giving in to the lure of reductivism, and the attraction of a single overarching explanation for a complex feature of human cultures.

Lord of the elves: fairies and the re-enchantment of Christianity

The fraught relationship between Christianity and fairy belief has been a running theme of this book, since the presence (and, usually, dominance) of Christianity is the shared inheritance of most European nations for the last millennium and a half. As we have seen, Christian responses to fairies have ranged from attempts to integrate them into a Christian cosmology to efforts to recast them as demonic beings or even to exclude them from existence altogether.

Many Christians today think that fairies are incompatible with Christian belief, for three different reasons. Many of them will share the majority view of educated people in the developed world that fairies obviously do not exist, and are just silly. Some of them will think fairies are just another form in which demons choose to appear and deceive the human race. Thus, Christians in contemporary Mexico have reacted negatively to a revived folkloric interest in *chaneques* (creole spirits apparently combining elements of the Iberian *duende* with Indigenous belief), regarding the *chaneques* as accursed entities who maintain the power of Satan.[72] Still others will believe fairies are incompatible with Christian belief because fairies are an inheritance of paganism – a perception that, as this book has hopefully demonstrated, is based on a limited and outdated historiography.

As we saw in chapter 8 above, even in the twentieth century there were committed, theologically informed Christians who took fairies seriously. Unlike the Theosophists, however, Christians such as Tolkien and Lewis were not drawn to fairies because they adhered to an ideology in which fairies were required to maintain the world in some way; fairies are not in any sense a *necessary* component of a Christian worldview. But it was in the twentieth century that many Christians, especially those with a more conservative outlook, began to argue that the Christian faith was in retreat in the developed world because it could not thrive outside a traditional society with a pre-modern worldview.

The prolific Roman Catholic essayist G. K. Chesterton (1874–1936) was especially outspoken on this subject, calling for a renewal of traditional ways of living and thinking as part of the renewal of Christian faith, and railing against industrialization and machine-like ideology. For social conservatives such as Chesterton, Tolkien and Lewis fairy belief was emblematic of a living folk culture, as well as closely linked to the pre-industrial world they longed to preserve. Fairy belief acted as a sort of barometer of the health of traditional culture. As Chesterton remarked in 1927:

> It is the peasants who preserve all the traditions . . . It is they who remember, so far as anyone remembers, the glimpses of fairies or the graver wonders of saints. In the classes above them the supernatural has been slain by the supercilious. That is a true and tremendous text in Scripture which says, 'where

there is no vision the people perish' [Proverbs 29:18]. But it is equally true in practice that where there is no people the visions perish.[73]

Chesterton was not endorsing the reality of fairies. But he was endorsing the importance of traditional culture, represented by (among other things) the persistence of fairy lore. This is why Arthur Machen, an author with a deep interest in folklore, and a folklorist such as Katharine Briggs (both of them also committed Christians) were horrified by the Cottingley photographs. It was not so much that the photographs were obvious fakes, but that *fairies were not supposed to be like this*. They did not belong in the drawing rooms (or even the gardens) of middle-class Theosophists, but to the *folk* – even if the rural working class was fast disappearing.

There is a certain paradox in Christians being concerned about the decline of traditional belief in beings that have little to do with Christianity. The fairy tale has often provided an escape from the strictures of belief imposed by the church, because 'The tongue can be very free when it is speaking outside the jurisdiction of religion', since fairies 'do not belong to an established living faith and therefore do not command belief or repudiation'.[74] This was certainly Tolkien's attitude; he was not interested in formally inserting fairies into a Christian cosmology, in the style of the jinn of Islam, but he did long for people to tell stories about fairies that expressed deep truths. Accordingly, Tolkien declared that 'God is the Lord, of angels, and of men – and of elves'[75] – not because elves certainly exist, but because they are a deep well of story that has the capacity to reveal something of the Creator.

Among advocates of a countercultural and re-supernaturalized Christianity there are still those who view fairy lore in a positive light. The American Christian philosopher David Bentley Hart, writing in 2013, contemplated the existence of fairies, and argued that 'the sciences might perhaps have something to say about [fairies], if a proper medium for investigating them could be found'.[76] Hart's openness to fairies seems to derive from his rejection of a 'hierarchy of hypostases' mediating between the world and God; Hart's God is wholly transcendent, and 'transcendently present in all beings', and does not express his power 'in lesser principles'. This conception of the divine opens up the possibility of a less hierarchical and more chaotic ecosystem of spiritual creatures, perhaps even including fairies.[77] Other Christian conservative authors such as Richard Beck and Rod Dreher have likewise called for a re-enchanted Christianity – even if fairies are not uppermost in their vision of Christianity's future.[78]

As we have seen (in chapter 2 above), the notion of an 'inclusive monotheism' in which God's majesty is exalted by his rule over diverse populations of spirit-beings does have a place in the Christian tradition, albeit a marginal one. The American Orthodox priest Andrew Stephen Damick – whose popular podcast with Stephen De Young, *Lord of Spirits*, has brought some of the stranger aspects of the Eastern Christian tradition to a mass audience – is adamant that the monotheism/polytheism dichotomy fails to describe God's relationship to spiritual creatures, and his starting point for Christian apologetics is people's ongoing fascination with a diverse range of spirits:

> Despite the public discourse of a modern world that assumes a flat materialism, those who inhabit it nevertheless remain haunted by angels, demons and saints. In terms of what we take seriously as 'real life', these spirits are perhaps just on the edge of our consciousness. But in our cultural output, they are positively thronging on every side. The stories we tell of wizards, elves, dwarves, fairies, orcs, trolls, superheroes, and space aliens are all attempts to come to terms with this haunting we feel, the sense that there is something just beyond our physical sight.[79]

Of course, from a 'Tolkienian' or 'Chestertonian' point of view, the fact that people tell stories about fairies is itself significant, for stories express profound truths; consigning fairies to story is not so much a way of distancing them from reality as a way of *processing* their reality and the reality of a spiritual world as a whole that we now have no way of approaching outside the framework of story. On this reading, people in Europe and America LARP as fairies at fantasy conventions not because they are childish and hopelessly disconnected from reality, but because our culture denies people any *other* recognized outlet for engaging with an aspect of reality that some yearn for and feel profoundly. Many expressions of Christianity, meanwhile, when faced with difficult questions about the spiritual world, either reinforce consensus materialism or default to condemnation, demonological classification, and warnings to ignore any unapproved spirit-beings.

Yet there is ample evidence that the Christian tradition is expansive enough to make a place for otherworld beings, as the theologian Paul Thigpen has outlined in the context of debates about the church and extraterrestrial intelligence.[80] In Ireland, particularly, the church still seems able to coexist with fairy belief, as the Capuchin Franciscan friar Richard Hendrick testified when he spoke to Jo Hickey-Hall in episode 95 of the *Modern Fairy Sightings* podcast. Hendrick described his encounters with otherworlders, his approach to them within a Christian cosmology, and how an exorcist negotiates with otherworld beings and nature spirits. Hendrick emphasized the importance of courtesy and understanding the traditional rules of engagement with fairies.

Christian thinkers who trace an intellectual lineage back to Chesterton, Tolkien, and Lewis – or indeed the Greek Fathers or St Francis of Assisi – are more likely to value wonder, storytelling, traditional culture, and spiritual interaction with nature, and so are more open to people's personal experiences of the preternatural. Rather like the anti-Sadducists of the seventeenth century, some contemporary Christians are as much horrified by a *general* decline in awareness of the supernatural as they are by a decline in formal allegiance to the Christian faith. Re-enchantment, therefore, becomes for the likes of Hart, Dreher, or Damick a propaedeutic to the eventual restoration of living faith and a Christian culture. If people are experiencing fairies, that is grist to the mill of re-enchantment – on the understanding that, in due course, an enhanced experience of the spiritual world should lead people to Christian faith.

Neo-animism, re-enchantment, and the fairy in the machine

The historical theory that fairies are an expression of animism was a key theme of this book's first chapter, but the idea that a kind of animism lies in humanity's future (and present) as well as in its past is one that has been gaining ground in the last thirty years. In his 1994 book *Daimonic Reality*, Patrick Harpur claimed that '[T]he same world-view existed everywhere in pre-Christian times and still exists in non-monotheistic cultures. It even exists, against the odds, unofficially – instinctively – among groups and individuals in our culture.'[81] Yet, as Harpur argues, the daemons have never gone away; they simply manifest in different ways – as the neuroses of depth psychology, in mysterious big-cat sightings or crop circles, in dream and nightmare. All of these things are 'daimonic' (or, we might say, animistic) because they retain 'intimations of autonomous life', distinct from mere imagination. Nature manifests itself to us as 'impersonal, objective, inhuman and soulless' because we choose to perceive nature in that way – but at the edges of our knowledge, nature still manages to trouble our certainties, the true nature of reality seems unclear, and it is not even obvious whether we are observing the cosmos or the cosmos is observing us.[82]

The contemporary desire for fairies to be taken seriously – even if it is not always actual belief in fairies, or even a desire to believe – seems to emerge from deep dissatisfaction with a 'disenchanted' world; and that dissatisfaction is not merely aesthetic or sentimental, but philosophical. Late Victorian confidence in a complete model of reality was comprehensively shattered by twentieth-century science, but 'scientism' (the irrational belief that science can and does explain everything) still lingers like an unwanted house guest we are reluctant to evict, because we are not sure what would replace it. To many people, a disenchanted world is now not only unappealing, but fundamentally unconvincing as well. As the novelist Salley Vickers wrote in 2022, 'Whether or not fairies, gods and angels exist is not the point. Fairies, gods, and angels can, and should be, thought of as manifestations of the mysterious untold aspects of a world whose multiple facets are not easily apparent to us but nonetheless have salience, responsiveness and place.'[83]

It is not just the 'usual suspects' (religious believers and adherents of alternative spiritualities) who now advocate re-enchantment; some atheists and humanists also regard it as an urgent imperative, on the grounds that only a reawakened sense of wonder and awe before nature and the animal world is likely to motivate a cultural shift away from humanity's path of ecological destruction.[84] But these advocates of the re-enchantment of nature are likely to reject the kind of 'naïve animism' that might include encounters with fairies, arguing that the wonder of nature and a deeper understanding of the science behind it should be enough to re-enchant the world on its own.[85]

However, a limitation of such metaphorical or materialistic attempts at re-enchantment ('Isn't nature amazing!') is surely that they remain at the level of the subjective; the materialist beholder of nature, however great his or her wonder, remains alienated from nature by the unbridgeable divide that separates the mental and non-mental worlds. This does not seem to be the way Indigenous peoples and small children experience reality, and Chris Gosden argues that, whether we recognize it or not, we inhabit 'sensate ecologies' where the boundary between the self and nature is not wholly impermeable.[86]

Philosophers, anthropologists, historians, and depth-psychologists can be found working today who are increasingly sceptical of the sharp distinction scientism makes between the subjective and the objective, the real and the imagined. Although the classic rationalist objection to fairies is that there is no evidence for their existence, this is demonstrably untrue; there is a great deal of evidence, in the form of personal testimonies of encounter – but it is not the sort of evidence that sceptics want or that science can process. But this, of course, is the point; as Wouter Hanegraaff argues, the methodologies of the sciences as we know them were explicitly designed to exclude 'clairvoyant perception, religious revelations, intuitive understanding, occult correspondences, spiritual presences, or non-causal influences in nature'.[87] As Harpur has noted, fairy seers in our society are denied 'a sense of precedent for their view, an historical context for the evidence of their own eyes'.[88] Of course fairies don't exist; it is unacceptable for them to exist. If anyone does claim to see a fairy, their testimony falls into the category of anecdote, rather than joining a body of evidence in any discipline (except perhaps folklore). 'Anomalistics' or 'Forteana' (as it is sometimes known, after the great collector of anomalous phenomena Charles Fort) is condemned forever to be a collection of data points. These remain unintegrated into any systematic study – and it is therefore impossible for them to generate what most people would consider to be *fact*.

Nevertheless, anecdote has a pathway of its own towards belief and acceptance, and that is personal trust. Many people will have friends or family members whose fairy experiences they believe because they know the witness to be trustworthy, and not given to fanciful imaginings. Some people will have had those experiences themselves, and will trust the evidence of their eyes and ears. The fact that people genuinely have very strange experiences is one that most historians now accept – few now cling to the fantastical theory that every claim of supernatural vision is a deliberate fraud – although there are, of course, multiple ways to interpret a person's sincerely held conviction that they have seen something impossible. But in Jeffrey Kripal's view, there are just too many of these experiences, and they are too vividly experienced (sometimes by multiple witnesses), for us to set aside their reality. At the same time, however, experiences such as UFO encounters seem to transgress the boundary between external reality and the internal consciousness of the perceiver, leading Kripal to conclude that anomalous experiences of this kind are 'neither traditionally religious nor conventionally scientific, nor are they simply material or purely mental'. They occupy, instead, a 'third space' of 'mind-matter' that we do not yet fully understand.[89]

Pierre Gallais, the historian of medieval French fairy lore, argued that the fairy is a 'projection of the active imagination' that can only truly be understood via depth psychology.[90] To the historian, the idea that fairies can be treated as objective experiences might seem to threaten the process of tracing fairies' cultural construction – but in truth there is no necessary contradiction between something being objectively experienced and that same thing being culturally constructed. Consider, for example, that dolphins and seals have, at various times and in different cultures, been identified as fairy-like beings – just as great apes were sometimes identified as satyrs. These real-world animals therefore formed part of the cultural construction of fairies; but showing that dolphins-as-fairies are a cultural construction does not prevent dolphins existing. The same is true of fairies in general; it would be wrongheaded to treat folklore as a kind of science, consisting of empirical observations about fairies. But that does not mean that entities do not exist who stand in some way behind fairy lore.

Ian Cuthbertson has put forward the idea of 'fluid enchantment', 'in which individuals partially, ironically or playfully engage with magical or supernatural beliefs . . . without fully adhering to these beliefs'.[91] Yet the possibility of playful semi-engagement with belief (as a kind of performance, perhaps) seems to presume that belief does not arise from being confronted with direct experience. It seems to start from a world that is disenchanted, in which people long for enchantment – rather than from a world that is already enchanted, in which people lack the concepts and vocabulary to process and articulate the 'impossible' experiences they have. This does not mean that people's interpretations of their extraordinary experiences are always correct – and, as any psychologist will tell you, interpretation is built into the very structure of experience itself – but the weight of testimony makes it hard to cling to the idea that fairies are mere cultural constructions or products of story or imagination. There is *something*, whether within us or outside us, that witnesses are directly experiencing.

In an animist (or neo-animist) worldview, fairies are a kind of radical ostension of personification: they are an outward and real manifestation of the human tendency to endow the non-human with personhood. As I noted in chapter 1 above, personification seems to function within such worldviews as a mode of perception: the animist who treats all living things (and even perhaps non-living things) as persons may experience and encounter ideas, abstractions, emotions, and so on as persons too. To most of us, this is an entirely alien way of viewing the world, but it was less alien to people in the ancient world. Thus, St Ambrose in his *Hexaemeron* tells us that 'the shadow stays close to the body', a choice of words that personifies and grants implicit agency to a person's shadow – even though this is not what Ambrose means in any literal sense.[92] But it is a way of speaking that is more likely to dispose us to think of shadows as entities with a separate existence, just as children enjoy racing their own or others' shadows while also knowing (on some level) that a shadow is not itself a being with independent agency.

In fact, this way of thinking and speaking is not as alien to us (or as strictly confined to small children) as we might think. The habits of speech we have developed around computers, and in particular around Large Language Models (LLMs), are a case in point. Even in 1998, Carole Silver could write of people who endowed computer viruses with personality and agency, as if they were a new elfin species.[93] We know computers and programs do not really think and are really without personality, but somehow it is easier to speak of them as if they were person-like. Indeed, the advent of generative Artificial Intelligence (GenAI) is further blurring the boundaries between human and non-human consciousness. If the computers of the past raised questions about the 'ghost in the machine', 21st-century technology raises the possibility of fairies in the machine – unpredictable entities dwelling in the uncanny valley of a GenAI that draws on the sum total of human creativity yet somehow creates something beyond the human. The recurrence and consistency of GenAI 'hallucinations' suggests, to some, the presence of mischievous consciousnesses that somehow inhabit this new digital space – like the 'glitchtokens' in ChatGPT described by Ed Prideaux, which seem to be AI-generated archetypes of good and evil: a moon goddess called 'Leilan' and a goblin-like being called 'petertodd'.[94] These are entirely artefacts of GenAI, which seemingly manifest *as if* they have an independent life. Perhaps McKenna's machine elves have migrated from 'DMT space' to take up residence in 'AI space'.

At least for now, the accepted social rules governing what educated adults may treat as a personification seem to be quite rigidly prescribed; indeed, even *performed*. It is not that people lose belief in fairies by stripping away the delusions of childhood – for, if we are honest, can an adult truly say that reality is any less baffling to them at the age of thirty than it was at the age of three? Rather, the socially functional 21st-century adult learns a culturally determined script, honed since fairy belief first began to lose its social cachet in the later seventeenth century, according to which it is unacceptable for nature to manifest as personal beings, or for personifications to take on an independent life.

Yet the periodic irruption of poltergeist phenomena into 'normality', even in the most modern and mundane of circumstances, might suggest that the script is not always wholly successful in keeping a more complex and more disturbing reality at bay. And anyone who has seen AI-generated images or read AI-generated text will be familiar with the uncanniness of a seemingly human creative product that is, in fact, the product of a non-human agency. GenAI casts its own kind of fairy glamour, making that which is unreal seem real and tricking the eyes. On one interpretation, it risks plunging us into a digital fairy-tale forest where we are no longer able to reliably distinguish between the human and the non-human, the AI-generated and the 'real'. Paradoxically, then, the most advanced technology we possess has the potential to breathe new life into the fear of deception by non-human intelligences, one of the oldest of human instincts. So it may be that fairies, for so long consigned to humanity's past in the worn trope of the departing fairies, lie for once in humanity's future, as the machine elves that our own technology has created swarm out of their uncanny valley and overwhelm our consensus reality.

Throughout this book, it has been my contention that fairy belief is best understood not as a claim that a certain class of entity exists (subject to Ockham's razor and empirical tests), but rather as a *way of perceiving the world*. Folklorists who study fairies are not a sub-category of cryptozoologists, nor are they religious dogmatists proposing a confessional claim that fairies exist. As the philosopher G. H. von Wright observed, it is a mistake to think of the world of imagination and magic as a series of hypotheses; it is, rather, 'completely another *way of thinking* that is basically alien to us'.[95] The question we should be asking ourselves, therefore, is not whether fairies exist (in the same way that pots and pans, dogs and badgers exist), but whether there is still a place for a way of thinking in which fairies make perfect sense. We could also ask whether there is a *need* for such a way of thinking; and we could even ask if it is a way of thinking that is never wholly escapable for human beings, and best managed and understood rather than suppressed. These are questions that lie beyond the scope of the historian. But, as we have seen, the English word 'fairy' referred originally not to an entity, but to a place and a state of being: *faerie*, which signified not just an otherworld realm but also the condition of being under enchantment.[96] Fairies *are* enchantment, because *faerie* is a synonym for enchantment, and enchantment will always find a way to take on a life of its own. We might even find ourselves face to face with it.

Conclusion

It has been the aim of this book to give fairies a history. Inevitably, historians who are intent on writing histories of the spirit-beings of vernacular culture are constrained by the stories that survive – and I am conscious always of the stories that we have lost, and of the traditions that were never written down. Fairies do not make an easy subject for the historian, but I am convinced that they are an eminently worthwhile one. The history of belief – and, to an even greater extent, the history of religion – is so often a story of conformity to increasingly stylized and unvarying tropes, but fairy lore almost always has a way of introducing a little mind-expanding anarchy. As C. S. Lewis noticed, fairies never quite fit into any system or cosmology. They are cosmic misfits, embodiments of the incorrigibly weird. As Jeremy Harte puts it, fairies are 'the irregular supernatural'.[1] Fairies are *sui generis*.

Much ink has been spilled in arguing that the fairies are *really* gods, or *really* the dead, or *really* populations of half-remembered primitive people. But it is equally easy to believe that the experience of living alongside fairies is foundational to human experience. I would propose that fairies – just as much as gods, angels, ghosts, and so on – are a basic category of the human experience of the supernatural. It is rare for anyone to ask the question 'What is a god?' – everyone seems to proceed on the assumption that we have some idea of a divinity – and it is only because scholars are disinclined to take fairies seriously that they continue to imagine they must always be something other than what they are. Fairies are an anomaly, a fly in the ointment of hierarchical conceptions of a supernatural world still organized, at some fundamental level, according to official Christian cosmologies – regardless of the religious beliefs of historians and folklorists. We should let fairies be fairies.

While this book has ranged widely, both chronologically and geographically, over European and global fairy lore, certain themes have emerged time and again. One theme is the importance of taking fairies seriously, which requires many of us to shed prejudices and assumptions imbibed from popular culture. As always in the history of belief, there is more to be gained by trying to imagine ourselves in the position of people who believe in fairies – or for whom fairies are part of their experience of reality – than there is to be gained from leaping to judgement. In doing so, we might recognize that contemporary Western culture stands out as distinctly peculiar in denying a place for fairy experiences, and that there is probably more to be learned about human consciousness and human religiosity from immersing ourselves (as far as we can) in the thought-worlds of our ancestors than from relentlessly analysing and rationalizing them. What could our experience of being human be like if all supernatural experiences, whether they fit into prescribed and acceptable categories or not, fed into our picture of reality? That is a question it is beyond the capacity of this book to answer; but I hope I have made a historical case that it is one worth asking.

Another theme of this book has been the complex relationship between fairies and Christianity – and, indeed, with religion in general. That relationship is not, in my view, characterized primarily by hostility – for, as we saw in chapter 2, intermediate spirits are themselves emanations of Near Eastern monotheism, and an inclusive and expansive monotheism is conceptually capable of accommodating (and even celebrating) a diverse ecosystem of spiritual life. But because Christianity, from an early date, tended to adopt a dualistic view of transmundane beings as good angels or evil demons, intermediate beings struggled for a place in a Christian cosmology.

Nevertheless, as this book has documented, unofficial Christian 'folk cosmologies' found a way to squeeze them in – and, for that reason, there is a sense in which fairies *are* beings of Christianity, even if only of popular Christianity. Fairies are 'parareligious beings' who do not, in and of themselves, have much to do with religion – and that is one reason why they are attractive today to some followers of alternative spiritualities. But it is also true that fairies are, in a sense, pagan; their origins often lie in pre-Christian beliefs about nature spirits; and, perhaps more importantly, the stories told about fairies seldom have anything to do with Christianity or its morality. Fairy justice is untempered by mercy, fairy truth is untempered by forgiveness, fairy fate is untempered by providence. Fairies allowed pre-Christian ways of thinking about the world and about morality to survive into the Christian era.

A further theme of this book has been the diversity of fairy lore. Although I have argued for the meaningfulness and coherence of 'fairy' as a concept found throughout European folklore (which, for some, will be controversial in its own right), I am committed to no single theory of fairy origins, no single theory of fairy diffusion, no concept of an 'ur-fairy' who was the ancestor of all European fairies. It is just as likely, in my view, that fairy traditions sprang up spontaneously in different cultures as that they somehow flowed from a common source. I simply do not know. What is clear, however, is that traditions of supernatural otherworlders subsequently interacted with and influenced one another, and that similarities in belief can be found from Scotland to Hungary, from Iberia to the Baltic. But while it is easy to become excessively focussed on a fairy lore that is culturally familiar and well attested, there is a genuine historical case to be made that Ireland's fairy lore is indeed the most important in Western Europe. It was in Ireland that the idea of fairies as neutral angels seems to have first emerged, influencing many other legendary traditions. Likewise, the Irish idea of finding fairyland in the western ocean would be of profound importance in the Age of Discovery. And even today, contemporary Irish rural culture seems to resist the pressure to trivialize and fictionalize fairies.

In exploring the global expansion of fairy lore, this book has taken the history of fairies in a new direction, moving beyond the fairies' European homelands to grapple with questions of transplantation and cultural syncretism in settler-colonial cultures. While it has been impossible to deal comprehensively with every tradition of fairy-like beings in every culture around the world, by focussing on the evolution of European-derived fairies in the Americas and Australasia I have sought to trace the origins of the more or less global familiarity with fairies in popular culture that prevails today. While people are inclined to view fairies as local and culturally specific, current research is beginning to reveal the true extent to which fairies are (almost) everywhere, if only we choose to look.

A final overarching theme of *Fairies: A History* is the persistence of fairy belief. I am not prepared to join Chaucer in saying that the fairies are departing or departed. From the anti-Sadducists of the Enlightenment to unrepentant believers such as Sir Arthur Conan Doyle and the members of the Fairy Investigation Society, there have always been those willing to uphold the reality of fairies. In the end, perhaps the greatest irony of the history of fairies is that these beings who have come to represent never-to-be-recovered childhood, lost Neverlands, and departing enchantment are among the most enduring features of human culture. Fairies emerge from the deep past of humanity, walking with us now, and in all likelihood shadowing our steps into the uncertain future of our species. For now, however, we are left with the same irresolvable cognitive dissonance as the teenage Elidyr – certain of what he experienced, but equally sure of its impossibility:

> He set out back along the road which he usually followed, down the path to the river, but when he came to where the underground passage had been there was no entry to be found. For nearly a year he searched the overhanging banks of the river, but he could never find the tunnel again.[2]

Notes

Introduction: the fairy-haunted world
1. On Estonian religion in the nineteenth century, see F. Young, *Silence of the Gods*, pp. 359–62.
2. Paulson, *Old Estonian Folk Religion*, pp. 141–2.
3. Purkiss, *Fairies and Fairy Stories*, p. 20.
4. On the word 'fairy', see N. Williams, 'Semantics of the Word "Fairy"', pp. 457–78; Harte, 'Fairy Barrows and Cunning Folk', pp. 65–78.
5. Harte, 'Fairy Barrows and Cunning Folk', p. 68.
6. N. Williams, 'Semantics of the Word "Fairy"', p. 457.
7. Ostling and Forest, '"Goblins, Owles and Sprites"', pp. 547–8.
8. Ibid., p. 548.
9. Briggs, *A Dictionary of Fairies*.
10. Jakobsson, 'The Taxonomy of the Non-existent', p. 212.
11. Ostling and Forest, '"Goblins, Owles and Sprites"', p. 549.
12. I have discussed this issue in more detail elsewhere; see F. Young, *Magic as a Political Crime*, pp. 8–10.
13. F. Young, *Twilight of the Godlings*, p. 87.
14. Narváez, 'Introduction', p. ix.
15. S. Young and Ermacora, 'Introducing the Social Supernatural', pp. 1–17.
16. Balys, *Lietuviu tautosakos skaitymai*, vol. II, pp. 86–9.
17. Pócs, 'Small Gods, Small Demons', p. 256.
18. L. Henderson and Cowan, *Scottish Fairy Belief*, p. 55; Kononenko, 'Ukraine', p. 249; Harte, *Fairy Encounters*, p. 60.
19. Briggs, 'English Fairies', p. 270.
20. Pócs, 'Small Gods, Small Demons', p. 257.
21. F. Young, *Suffolk Fairylore*.
22. Simina, *Where Fairies Meet*.
23. Alexiou, 'Modern Greek Folklore', p. 221.
24. Luhrmann, *How God Becomes Real*, pp. 3–4.
25. L. Henderson and Cowan, *Scottish Fairy Belief*, p. 1.
26. Harte, *Fairy Encounters*, p. 13.
27. Purkiss, *Fairies and Fairy Stories*, pp. 25–8.
28. Tolkien, 'On Fairy-Stories', pp. 58–9.
29. Sutcliff, 'History and Time', p. 112.
30. Slimak, *The Last Neanderthal*, pp. 153, 186.
31. For a good account of the social functions played by fairy lore in a traditional society, see L. Henderson and Cowan, *Scottish Fairy Belief*, pp. 209–13.

32 Harte, *Fairy Encounters*, p. 16.
33 Kononenko, 'Ukraine', p. 244.
34 Simpson, 'On the Ambiguity of Elves [1]', p. 82.
35 Hutton, *Queens of the Wild*, pp. 41–74.
36 Uljas et al., 'Between the Superpowers', p. 246.
37 Salisbury, *Iberian Popular Religion*, p. 25.
38 Hutton, *Queens of the Wild*, p. 37.
39 H. Valk, 'Christianisation in Estonia', p. 574.
40 For explorations of the genre of fairy tale, see Warner, *From the Beast to the Blonde*; Warner, *Once Upon a Time*; Warner, *Fairy Tale*; Purkiss, *Fairies and Fairy Stories*; Jubber, *The Fairy Tellers*.
41 Vėlius, *Lithuanian Mythological Tales*, pp. 13–14.
42 Kuusela, 'Scandinavia', p. 106 n. 62.
43 On Shakespeare's fairies, see Briggs, *The Anatomy of Puck*; Briggs, *The Fairies in Tradition and Literature*; and Pask, *The Fairy Way of Writing*. On stage fairies, see Schacker, *Staging Fairyland*. On fairies in Victorian literature, see Silver, *Strange and Secret Peoples*; and Bown, *Fairies in Nineteenth-Century Art and Literature*. On fairies in Tolkien and modern fantasy, see Fimi, *Tolkien, Race and Cultural History*.
44 Wade, *Fairies in Medieval Romance*, pp. 1–6; Green, *Elf Queens*, p. 12.
45 For a discussion of this issue, see Green, 'Forms of the Marvelous', pp. 23–44.
46 Hutton, 'The Making of the Early Modern British Fairy Tradition', pp. 1135–56.
47 Green, 'Forms of the Marvelous', pp. 23–44.
48 On the transformation of traditional into modern fairies, see S. Young, 'Fairy Ain't What It Used to Be', pp. 189–210.
49 Harte, *Fairy Encounters*, p. 126.

1 The hills are alive: sacred nature in ancient Europe

1 Rasmussen, 'The Protracted Sámi Reformation', p. 90. On the *Juovlagázzi*, see Kent, *Sámi Peoples of the North*, p. 83.
2 Harvey, *Animism*, p. xi.
3 Harpur, *Daimonic Reality*, p. 43.
4 Gosden, *History of Magic*, pp. 326–7. For a discussion of possible meanings of 'animism', see Harvey, *Animism*, pp. 3–29.
5 Evans-Wentz, *Fairy-Faith*, p. 458.
6 Leete and Koosa, 'Spiritual Power', p. 518 n. 1.
7 Gosden, *History of Magic*, p. 31.
8 Ibid., pp. 155–6.
9 Hutton, *Pagan Britain*, p. 1.
10 Insoll, *Archaeology, Ritual, Religion*, p. 30.
11 Dowden, *European Paganism*, pp. 34–5
12 F. Young, *Silence of the Gods*, p. 371.
13 Paulson, *Old Estonian Folk Religion*, p. 71.
14 Kallery and Psillos, 'Anthropomorphism and Animism', pp. 291–311.
15 Cuthbertson, *Enchantment*, p. 62.
16 On the idea of animism as a substratum or 'bedrock' of popular belief, see Wilby, *Cunning Folk*, pp. 14–17; Ostling, 'Introduction', pp. 19–20.

17 Wilby, *Cunning Folk*, p. 17.
18 Ostling, 'Introduction', pp. 19–20.
19 See, for instance, Rose, '*Numen inest*', pp. 237–57.
20 A. Hunt, 'Pagan Animism', p. 139.
21 Tolkien, 'On Fairy-Stories', p. 80.
22 Hutton, *Pagan Britain*, p. 1. Hutton has questioned, however, whether the 'Sorcerer' (drawn by Henri Breuil) is an accurate depiction of the original cave art (Hutton, *Witches, Druids, and King Arthur*, pp. 33–5).
23 Paulson, *Old Estonian Folk Religion*, p. 69.
24 Ibid., p. 62.
25 For a discussion of the term 'shamanism', see Hutton, *Shamans*, pp. vii–viii.
26 Hutton, *Pagan Britain*, pp. 15–16.
27 On the idea of fairies as a manifestation of shamanism, see Ostling, 'Introduction', pp. 26–32.
28 Robichaud, *Pan*, pp. 12–17.
29 Ibid., p. 28.
30 F. Young, *Twilight of the Godlings*, p. 88.
31 Vuković, *Wolves of Rome*, 195–6.
32 Běťáková and Blažek (eds.), *Lexicon of Baltic Mythology*, p. 223.
33 Ginsburg and Lincoln, *Old Thiess*, p. 28.
34 Běťáková and Blažek (eds.), *Lexicon of Baltic Mythology*, p. 226.
35 Madar, 'Estonia I', p. 272.
36 Bane (ed.), *Encyclopedia of Fairies*, p. 185. See also Kuusela, 'Spirited Away by the Female Forest Spirit', pp. 159–79.
37 Jurić, 'Western Balkans', p. 196; Kononenko, 'Ukraine', p. 251.
38 Harte, *Fairy Encounters*, pp. 61–5.
39 Wilby, *Cunning Folk*, pp. 123–64.
40 Ibid., p. 61.
41 Hutton, *The Witch*, pp. 225–6.
42 F. Young, *Twilight of the Godlings*, p. 70.
43 Lecouteux, *Fées, sorcières et loups-garous*, p. 83.
44 Pócs, 'Hungarians', p. 188.
45 Heide, 'Spinning *seiðr*', pp. 164–70.
46 Pócs, 'Hungarians', p. 175.
47 Ibid., p. 189 n. 1.
48 L. Henderson and Cowan, *Scottish Fairy Belief*, p. 20.
49 Geertz, '"Internal Conversion"', pp. 172–4.
50 Dowden, *European Paganism*, pp. 213–23.
51 Ovid, *Fasti* 3.314–16.
52 See Gimbutas, *The Gods and Goddesses of Old Europe*.
53 Hraste and Vuković, 'Rudra-Shiva and Silvanus-Faunus', pp. 109–10.
54 Hutton, *The Witch*, p. 228.
55 Salisbury, *Iberian Popular Religion*, p. 2.
56 Larson, *Greek Nymphs*, p. 5.
57 Ibid., pp. 6–7.
58 Ibid., p. 7.

59 F. Young, *Twilight of the Godlings*, pp. 71–2.
60 Larson, *Greek Nymphs*, p. 9.
61 Ibid., p. 10.
62 Ibid., pp. 11–20.
63 Reed, *Demons, Angels and Writing*, p. 47.
64 Somfai, 'Nature of Daemons', p. 132.
65 Luck (ed.), *Arcana Mundi*, pp. 217–18.
66 Harpur, *Daimonic Reality*, p. 41.
67 Quoted in Somfai, 'Nature of Daemons', p. 136 n. 50.
68 Ibid., p. 139.
69 Purkiss, *Troublesome Things*, pp. 11–31.
70 Egeler, 'A Note on the Dedication *lamiis tribus*', p. 16.
71 Wilby, 'Burchard's *strigae*', pp. 18–49.
72 Pratchett, *Lords and Ladies*, p. 144.
73 F. Young, *Twilight of the Godlings*, p. 109.
74 Maraschi, 'France', p. 149 n. 22.
75 Isidore of Seville, *Etymologies* 8.11.102; Augustine, *De civitate Dei* 15.23 (*PL* 41:468–71).
76 Larson, *Greek Nymphs*, p. 63.
77 Briggs, 'English Fairies', pp. 277–8.
78 Briggs, *The Fairies in Tradition and Literature*, p. 4.
79 Braccini, 'Greece (and Italy)', p. 218.
80 Kononenko, 'Ukraine', pp. 249–50.
81 Pócs, 'Small Gods, Small Demons', p. 258.
82 Barber, *Dancing Goddesses*, p. 264.
83 Ibid., p. 4.
84 Ibid., pp. 313–33.
85 F. Young, *Twilight of the Godlings*, pp. 73–4.
86 Flower, *Dancing Lares*, pp. 23–4.
87 S. Young and Ermacora, 'Introducing the Social Supernatural', p. 6.
88 Ochota, *Secret Britain*, pp. 231–5.
89 Pearson, 'Living with the Dead', pp. 155–7.
90 Cassidy et al., 'A Dynastic Elite in Monumental Neolithic Society', pp. 384–8.
91 Dowden, *European Paganism*, p. 229.
92 Brodsky, *Spanish Vocabulary*, p. 129.
93 F. Young, *Twilight of the Godlings*, pp. 16–17.
94 Green, 'Refighting Carlo Ginzburg's *Night Battles*', pp. 382–5.
95 Avarvarei, 'Shakespeare's Weird Sisters', pp. 107–17.
96 Hutton, *The Witch*, p. 160.
97 F. Young, *Twilight of the Godlings*, pp. 75–7.
98 Hutton, *Pagan Britain*, p. 266.
99 Hutton, *The Witch*, pp. 216–42.
100 Sneddon, *Witchcraft and Magic*, pp. 11–13; Būgienė, 'The Supernatural Milk-Stealer in Lithuanian Folklore', p. 99.
101 F. Young, *Twilight of the Godlings*, p. 261.
102 Ibid., p. 154.
103 Goodare, 'The Cult of the Seely Wights', pp. 198–219.

104 For a discussion of the relationship between fairies and witches, see Hutton, *The Witch*, pp. 215–42.
105 F. Young and Kubiliūtė, 'The Balts', pp. 235–6, 239.
106 Ryan, 'The Witchcraft Hysteria in Early Modern Europe', pp. 49–84.
107 Ostling, *Between the Devil and the Host*, p. 26; Goodare, *The European Witch-Hunt*, p. 134.
108 Goodare, 'Boundaries of the Fairy Realm', pp. 158–62.
109 Pócs, 'Hungarians', p. 175; Harte, 'England', p. 65 n. 11; Purkiss, *Troublesome Things*, p. 7.
110 F. Young, *Twilight of the Godlings*, p. 60.

2 Between heaven and hell: monotheism and ambiguous spirits

1 O'Grady (ed.), *Silva Gadelica*, vol. II, pp. 94–5.
2 Egeler, 'Iceland', p. 73.
3 On the issue of monotheism and monolatry in the Hebrew Bible, see Becking, 'The Boundaries of Israelite Monotheism', pp. 9–27.
4 Cf. Exodus 34:13; Deuteronomy 7:5, 12:3, 16:21; Judges 3:7, 6:25–30; 1 Kings 14:15, 14:23, 15:13, 16:33, 18:19; 2 Kings 13:6, 17:10, 17:16, 18:4, 21:3, 21:7, 23:4–7, 23:14–16; 2 Chronicles 14:3, 15:16, 17:6, 19:3, 24:18, 31:1, 33:3, 33:19, 34:3–4, 34:7; Isaiah 17:8, 27:9; Jeremiah 17:2; Micah 5:14.
5 Reed, *Demons, Angels and Writing*, p. 66.
6 Ibid., p. 19.
7 Ibid., p. 39.
8 Ibid., p. 60.
9 Ibid., pp. 66–9. For a recent exploration of the multiplicity and variety of the Old Testament's spiritual beings, see Hamori, *God's Monsters*.
10 Reed, *Demons, Angels and Writing*, p. 70.
11 Ibid., p. 47.
12 On *The Book of the Watchers*, see Reed, *Demons, Angels and Writing*, pp. 198–200.
13 Carr, *Angels and Principalities*, p. 28.
14 Reed, *Demons, Angels and Writing*, pp. 234–40.
15 Webster, *Displaying of Supposed Witchcraft*, pp. 283–4.
16 O'Sullivan, '"Subtly of Herself Contemplative"', pp. 12–13.
17 Unterman (ed.), *Dictionary of Jewish Lore and Legend*, pp. 61–2.
18 Scholem, *Kabbalah*, pp. 356–7.
19 Wahlen, *Jesus and the Impurity of Spirits*, p. 170.
20 Later translations, such as the Authorized Version, make no mention of the giants here at all: 'O Lord our God, other lords beside thee have had dominion over us . . . They are dead, they shall not live; they are deceased, they shall not rise: therefore hast thou visited and destroyed them, and made all their memory to perish.'
21 F. Young, *Twilight of the Godlings*, p. 212.
22 Reed, *Demons, Angels and Writing*, p. 41.
23 Wahlen, *Jesus and the Impurity of Spirits*, p. 172.
24 J. Z. Smith, 'Towards Interpreting Demonic Powers', pp. 425–39; Caciola, *Discerning Spirits*, p. xli; Frankfurter, 'Where the Spirits Dwell', p. 29.
25 Quoted in Somfai, 'Nature of Daemons', p. 140 n. 77.

26 Carr, *Angels and Principalities*, p. 38.
27 Forbes, 'Pauline Demonology', p. 67.
28 Ibid., p. 62.
29 Quoted in ibid., p. 58.
30 Carr, *Angels and Principalities*, p. 40.
31 Ibid., p. 33.
32 Forbes, 'Pauline Demonology', pp. 72–3.
33 Augustine, *De civitate Dei* 15.23 (*PL* 41.468).
34 Green, *Elf Queens*, p. 78.
35 Justin Martyr, *Second Apology* 10 (*PG* 6.95).
36 Clement of Alexandria, *Stromateis* 5.14 (*PG* 9.252).
37 Montuori, *Socrates*, pp. 6–7.
38 Origen, *Contra Celsum* 8.31 (*PG* 11.764–5).
39 Carr, *Angels and Principalities*, pp. 28–9.
40 Eusebius, *Praeparatio evangelica* 4.5 (*PG* 21.141).
41 Isidore of Seville, *Etymologies* 8.11.5.
42 Ibid., 11.3.21–2.
43 Harte, *Cloven Country*, pp. 8–9.
44 Uljas et al., 'Between the Superpowers', p. 245.
45 Frankfurter, 'Demon Invocations', pp. 453–4.
46 Carr, *Angels and Principalities*, p. 41.
47 Psellus, *Dialogue on the Operation of Daemons*, pp. 28–32.
48 Douglas and Young, *Paganism Persisting*, pp. 69–70.
49 Quoted in Allatius, *De templis*, p. 162.
50 Quoted in ibid., pp. 163–4.
51 El-Zein, *Islam, Arabs, and the Intelligent World of the Jinn*, pp. 16, 114.
52 Ibid., p. 39.
53 Ibid., pp. 45–6.
54 Clement of Alexandria, *Stromateis* 7.7 (*PG* 9.308).
55 Jurić, 'Western Balkans', p. 199.
56 M. Williams, *Ireland's Immortals*, p. 4.
57 Filotas, *Pagan Survivals*, pp. 83–5.
58 F. Young, *Twilight of the Godlings*, pp. 167–70.
59 M. Williams, *Ireland's Immortals*, pp. 14–15.
60 On pre-Christian Irish religion, see ibid., pp. 3–29.
61 Ibid., p. 30.
62 Ibid., p. 69.
63 Peter A. Smith, *W. B. Yeats and the Tribes of Danu*, p. 76.
64 Ibid., p. 85.
65 Ibid., p. 87.
66 Borsje, 'Monotheistic to a Certain Extent', p. 59 n. 27.
67 Quoted in ibid., p. 63.
68 Bitel, 'Secrets of the Síd', p. 80.
69 Ibid., p. 89.
70 Ibid., p. 98.
71 Ibid., p. 91.

72 Borsje, 'Monotheistic to a Certain Extent', pp. 68–9.
73 O'Grady (ed.), *Silva Gadelica*, vol. II, p. 260.
74 Bitel, 'Secrets of the Síd', p. 96.
75 On this subject, see Carey, *A Single Ray of the Sun*, pp. 1–38.
76 Borsje, 'Monotheistic to a Certain Extent', p. 56.
77 Bitel, 'Secrets of the Síd', p. 96.
78 Meyer (ed.), *The Voyage of Bran*, vol. I, p. 22.
79 M. Williams, *Ireland's Immortals*, pp. 56–68.
80 Ibid., pp. 68–71.
81 Mackley, *Legend of St Brendan*, p. 198 n. 78.
82 Ibid., pp. 117–19.
83 M. Williams, *Ireland's Immortals*, pp. 68–71.
84 Pócs, 'Small Gods, Small Demons', p. 258.

3 Here be monsters: otherworld beings in the Middle Ages

1 Jerome, *Vita Sancti Pauli* 7–8 (*PL* 73, pp. 112–13).
2 Ambrose, *The Marvellous and the Monstrous*, pp. 34–7.
3 Friedman, *The Monstrous Races*, pp. 85–6.
4 Cohen, *Hybridity, Identity, and Monstrosity*, p. 3.
5 Gorla, 'Some Remarks', pp. 145–67.
6 Martianus Capella, *De nuptiis philologiae et Mercurii* 2.167.
7 Vídalín, 'The Man Who Seemed Like a Troll', p. 222.
8 Augustine, *De civitate Dei* 16.8 (*PL* 41.485–6).
9 Bradley (ed.), *Anglo-Saxon Poetry*, p. 414.
10 Bisagni, 'Leprechaun', p. 78.
11 Quoted in Harward, *Dwarfs of Arthurian Romance*, p. 9.
12 Ambrose, *The Marvellous and the Monstrous*, pp. 1–5.
13 F. Young, *Suffolk Fairylore*, pp. 45–8.
14 On the green children as Antipodeans, see John Clark, *The Green Children of Woolpit*, pp. 164–70.
15 Ingemark, *The Genre of Trolls*, p. 8.
16 Lindow, *Trolls*, pp. 44–6.
17 Raudvere, '*Trolldómr*', p. 88.
18 Thomas of Walsingham, *Historia Anglicana*, vol. I, pp. 261–2.
19 Oelze, *Animal Rationality*, pp. 70–7.
20 Walter Map, *De nugis curialium* 1.11.
21 F. Young, *Twilight of the Godlings*, p. 239.
22 Quoted in Harward, *Dwarfs of Arthurian Romance*, pp. 6–7.
23 Gerald of Wales, *Journey through Wales*, pp. 133–5.
24 F. Young, *Twilight of the Godlings*, pp. 239–40.
25 Ó Giolláin, 'Fairy Belief and Official Religion', p. 201.
26 F. Young, *Twilight of the Godlings*, pp. 256–60.
27 Harte, *Fairy Encounters*, p. 59.
28 Lindow, 'Poetry, Dwarfs, and Gods', p. 287.
29 F. Young, *Twilight of the Godlings*, pp. 242–3.
30 Lindow, *Norse Mythology*, p. 100.

31 Lindow, 'Poetry, Dwarfs, and Gods', pp. 288–90.
32 Jakobsson, 'The Hole', p. 70.
33 Lindow, 'Poetry, Dwarfs, and Gods', pp. 300–2.
34 Douglas and Young, *Paganism Persisting*, p. 60.
35 On the *Nixen*, see Pisarek and Schaefer, 'German-Speaking Europe', pp. 155–72; on the Estonian *Näkk*, see Ü. Valk, 'The Guises of Estonian Water-Spirits', pp. 339–41.
36 Gallais, *La fée à la fontaine*, pp. 1–16.
37 F. Young, *Twilight of the Godlings*, pp. 78–87.
38 Maraschi, 'France', p. 153 n. 80.
39 F. Young, *Twilight of the Godlings*, pp. 79–80.
40 Harward, *Dwarfs of Arthurian Romance*, pp. 13–16.
41 Larson, *Greek Nymphs*, pp. 61–4.
42 F. Young, *Twilight of the Godlings*, pp. 75–7.
43 Bisagni, 'Leprechaun', pp. 61–2.
44 Harward, *Dwarfs of Arthurian Romance*, pp. 7–8.
45 Bisagni, 'Leprechaun', pp. 78–83.
46 Gerhardt, *The Old Man of the Sea*, pp. 29–30.
47 On the Portunes, see F. Young, *Twilight of the Godlings*, pp. 284–7.
48 Gerhardt, *The Old Man of the Sea*, pp. 31–2.
49 Ibid., pp. 34–6.
50 Ibid., pp. 51–4.
51 Ibid., p. 70.
52 Ibid., pp. 76–7.
53 Maraschi, 'France', p. 146.
54 Ibid., p. 141.
55 Ibid., p. 144.
56 Ibid., p. 152 n. 63.
57 Sébillot, *Le folk-lore de France*, vol. II, p. 344.
58 Boase, *The Folklore of Hampshire*, p. 111.
59 F. Young, *Twilight of the Godlings*, pp. 317–18.
60 Maraschi, 'France', pp. 142–3, 147.
61 Hall, *Elves*, pp. 54–6.
62 Ibid., pp. 173–5.
63 Bargan, 'The Probable Old Germanic Origin of Romanian *iele*', pp. 13–18.
64 Simpson, 'On the Ambiguity of Elves [1]', pp. 78–9.
65 Hall, *Elves*, pp. 71–2.
66 Lindow, *Norse Mythology*, p. 50.
67 Gunnell, 'How Elvish Were the *Álfar*?', p. 123.
68 Gunnell, 'Álfar (Elves)', p. 1577.
69 Jakobsson, 'Beware of the Elf!', pp. 215–16.
70 F. Young, *Twilight of the Godlings*, pp. 222–4.
71 Gunnell, 'How Elvish Were the *Álfar*?', p. 116.
72 Gunnell, 'Álfar (Elves)', p. 1580.
73 For a discussion of this issue, see Shippey, '*Alias oves habeo*', pp. 157–87.
74 On Tolkien's resolution, see Shippey, 'Light-Elves, Dark-Elves, and Others', pp. 1–15.
75 Gunnell, 'How Elvish Were the *Álfar*?', p. 118.

76 F. Young, *Twilight of the Godlings*, p. 36.
77 Gunnell, 'How Elvish Were the *Álfar*?', pp. 120–2.
78 Ibid., pp. 127–8.
79 Ibid., p. 129.
80 T. Wright (ed.), *St. Brandan*, p. 9 (spelling modernized).
81 Dando, 'Les anges neutres', pp. 3–76.
82 Mackley, *Legend of St Brendan*, p. 117.
83 Origen, *Writings*, vol. I, p. 71.
84 Green, *Elf Queens*, p. 25.
85 Mackley, *Legend of St Brendan*, p. 117.
86 Dante, *The Divine Comedy*, p. 47.
87 Dunphy, 'On Neutral and Fallen Angels', pp. 9–13.
88 Kieckhefer, 'Angel Magic', p. 88.
89 C. Newman, 'The Good, the Bad and the Unholy', pp. 111–12.
90 Green, *Elf Queens*, p. 25.
91 Horstmann (ed.), *The Early South-English Legendary*, pp. 305–7 (language modernized).
92 C. Newman, 'The Good, the Bad and the Unholy', p. 111.
93 Gallais, *La fée à la fontaine*, p. 14.
94 Gerald of Wales, *Journey through Wales*, pp. 155–6.
95 Quoted in C. Newman, 'The Good, the Bad and the Unholy', p. 104.
96 Ibid., pp. 117–20.
97 Quoted in Green, *Elf Queens*, p. 23.
98 Van der Horst, 'Fatum, Tria Fata', p. 217.
99 F. Young, *Twilight of the Godlings*, pp. 104–5.
100 Aramburu et al., 'Deux faces de la femme merveilleuse', p. 8.
101 F. Young, *Twilight of the Godlings*, p. 114.
102 Kors and Peters (eds.), *Witchcraft in Europe, 400–700*, p. 66.
103 Filotas, *Pagan Survivals*, p. 81.
104 Wilby, 'Burchard's *strigae*', 20.
105 Harf-Lancner, *Les fées au moyen âge*, pp. 17–25.
106 Gallais, 'Les fées seraient-elles nées au XIIe siècle?', p. 357.
107 F. Young, *Twilight of the Godlings*, pp. 219–21. For a detailed account of the formation of the figure of the incubus and its identification with fairies, see Green, *Elf Queens*, pp. 76–109.
108 F. Young, *Twilight of the Godlings*, p. 276.
109 Henningsen, 'The Ladies from Outside', pp. 191–215; Pócs, *Fairies and Witches*.
110 Pócs, 'Hungarians', pp. 182–3.
111 Braccini, 'Greece (and Italy)', p. 223.
112 S. Young and Ermacora, 'Introducing the Social Supernatural', p. 6.
113 Jurić, 'Where Does the *Vila* Live?', p. 52.
114 Ibid., p. 66 n. 13.
115 N. Williams, 'Semantics of the Word "Fairy"', p. 465.
116 F. Young, *Twilight of the Godlings*, p. 261.
117 N. Williams, 'Semantics of the Word "Fairy"', p. 465.
118 On this latter meaning of *duende*, see Lorca, *In Search of Duende*, pp. 48–62.

119 N. Williams, 'Semantics of the Word "Fairy"', pp. 466–8.
120 F. Young, *Twilight of the Godlings*, p. 249.
121 Kuusela, 'Scandinavia', p. 106 n. 38.
122 On this theme, see Sawyer, *The Medieval Changeling*.
123 Vėlius, *Lithuanian Mythological Tales*, p. 25.
124 Hutton, *The Witch*, p. 229.
125 Watkins, 'Fascination and Anxiety', pp. 45–64.
126 Harte, *Fairy Encounters*, p. 48.
127 Watkins, 'Fascination and Anxiety', p. 60.

4 Founding fairyland: the late Middle Ages
1 Baring-Gould (ed.), *The Lives of the Saints*, vol. XVI, p. 224.
2 Harte, *Cloven Country*, pp. 8–9.
3 Vėlius, *Chtoniškasis*, pp. 201–3.
4 Green, *Elf Queens*, p. 15.
5 Robbins, 'Crypto-religion', p. 421.
6 Frankfurter, 'Where the Spirits Dwell', pp. 27–46; Enges, 'Supernatural Beings', pp. 231–2.
7 Harte, *Cloven Country*, p. 61.
8 C. Newman, 'The Good, the Bad and the Unholy', p. 117.
9 Green, *Elf Queens*, pp. 59–60.
10 Ibid., pp. 76–109.
11 Ibid., p. 59.
12 Ibid., p. 17.
13 Ibid., p. 79.
14 F. Young, *Twilight of the Godlings*, pp. 142–53.
15 Green, *Elf Queens*, pp. 21–2.
16 F. Young, *Twilight of the Godlings*, pp. 153–5.
17 Hutton, *Queens of the Wild*, pp. 41–74.
18 Běťáková and Blažek (eds.), *Lexicon of Baltic Mythology*, pp. 167–8.
19 F. Young and Kubiliūtė, 'The Balts', p. 239.
20 Greimas, *Of Gods and Men*, p. 113.
21 O'Grady (ed.), *Silva Gadelica*, vol. II, pp. 311–24.
22 F. Young, *Twilight of the Godlings*, pp. 231–7 (for Evesham), p. 87 (for Woolpit).
23 Meltzer, 'Reviving the Fairy Tree', pp. 496–8.
24 N. Williams, 'Semantics of the Word "Fairy"', p. 467.
25 Hutton, 'The Making of the Early Modern British Fairy Tradition', p. 1140.
26 Briggs, *The Fairies in Tradition and Literature*, p. 10.
27 F. Young, *Twilight of the Godlings*, pp. 292–7.
28 Gallais, 'Les fées seraient-elles nées au XIIe siècle?', p. 370.
29 Hutton, *Queens of the Wild*, pp. 83, 86–7.
30 Gunnell, 'How Elvish Were the *Álfar*?', p. 125.
31 Hutton, *The Witch*, p. 231.
32 Ibid., p. 230.
33 W. Wright (ed.), *The Metrical Chronicle of Robert of Gloucester*, vol. I, p. 196 (language modernized).

34 See Hutton, 'The Making of the Early Modern British Fairy Tradition', pp. 1142–56.
35 Hutton, *The Witch*, p. 233.
36 Ibid., pp. 228–9.
37 Ibid., p. 232.
38 Green, *Elf Queens*, pp. 178–93.
39 F. Young, *Twilight of the Godlings*, p. 260.
40 M. Williams, *Ireland's Immortals*, p. 257.
41 Kerns were the light infantrymen or light horsemen of medieval and early modern Gaelic Ireland, sometimes acting as mercenaries for hire.
42 O'Grady (ed.), *Silva Gadelica*, vol. II, p. 323.
43 Peter A. Smith, *W. B. Yeats and the Tribes of Danu*, p. 99.
44 Sims-Williams, *Irish Influence*, pp. 58–9.
45 Hutton, *Queens of the Wild*, p. 79.
46 Moitra, 'From Pagan God to Magical Being', pp. 32–6.
47 Rodway, 'The Date and Authorship of *Culhwch ac Olwen*', pp. 21–44.
48 F. Young, *Twilight of the Godlings*, pp. 81–2.
49 Moitra, 'From Pagan God to Magical Being', pp. 27–30.
50 Moitra, 'From Graeco-Roman Underworld to the Celtic Otherworld', p. 86.
51 F. Young, *Twilight of the Godlings*, pp. 281–2.
52 Hutton, *Queens of the Wild*, pp. 83–6.
53 Ibid., pp. 86–7.
54 Green, *Elf Queens*, p. 22.
55 Ibid., pp. 26–7.
56 S. Young and Ermacora, 'Introducing the Social Supernatural', p. 6.
57 De Blécourt, 'The Netherlands', p. 108.
58 Pedrosa, 'Iberia', p. 130.
59 Pócs, 'Hungarians', p. 191 n. 7.
60 Braccini, 'Greece (and Italy)', p. 223.
61 Ralph of Coggeshall, *Chronicon Anglicanum*, pp. 120–1.
62 Gervase of Tilbury, *Otia Imperialia*, pp. 29–30.
63 S. Young and Ermacora, 'Introducing the Social Supernatural', p. 16 n. 58. On household spirits, see Lecouteux, *The Tradition of Household Spirits*.
64 Maraschi, 'France', p. 141.
65 For a discussion of poltergeists and fairies, see Tucker, *The Hidden Folk*.
66 Hutton, *The Witch*, p. 232.
67 Sawyer, 'Child Substitution', pp. 156–7. On medieval changeling lore, see also Green, *Elf Queens*, pp. 110–46.
68 F. Young, *Suffolk Fairylore*, p. 55.
69 Green, *Elf Queens*, p. 117.
70 Briggs, *The Vanishing People*, p. 8.
71 Harpur, *Daimonic Reality*, p. 63.
72 Chaucer, *The Canterbury Tales*, pp. 171–2.
73 Bitel, 'Secrets of the Síd', pp. 79, 98.
74 M. Williams, *Ireland's Immortals*, pp. 259–60.
75 J. Butler, 'The *Sídhe* and Fairy Forts', pp. 95–6.
76 M. Williams, *Ireland's Immortals*, pp. 260–8.

77 O'Grady (ed.), *Silva Gadelica*, vol. II, p. 323.
78 Hutton, *Queens of the Wild*, p. 90.
79 Gunnell, 'How Elvish were the *Álfar*?', p. 130.
80 Egeler, 'Iceland', p. 74.
81 Hutton, *The Witch*, p. 218.
82 Hall, *Elves in Anglo-Saxon England*, pp. 71–2; T. Hunt (ed.), *Anglo-Norman Medicine II*, p. 224; Simek, *Dämonen, Teufel, Hexenglaube*, p. 178.
83 F. Young, *Magic in Merlin's Realm*, pp. 60–4.
84 F. Young, *History of Exorcism*, pp. 75–6.
85 Kieckhefer, 'Angel Magic', pp. 71–110.
86 Hutton, *Queens of the Wild*, p. 102.
87 Hogan, 'Communing with Nature', p. 51.
88 Hutton, *Queens of the Wild*, pp. 82–3.
89 Green, *Elf Queens*, p. 107.
90 Kassell, '*All Was This Land Full Fill'd of Faerie*', pp. 107–22.
91 Bain, 'The Binding of the Fairies', p. 332.
92 Klaassen and Bens, 'Achieving Invisibility', p. 6.
93 F. Young, *Suffolk Fairylore*, p. 51.
94 Harte, 'England', p. 56.

5 The reformation of fairyland: early modern fairies

1   Olaus Magnus, *Historia de gentibus septentrionalibus*, p. 112.
2   Veenstra, 'Introduction', p. vii.
3   F. Young, *Magic in Merlin's Realm*, p. 157.
4   Goodare, *The European Witch-Hunt*, p. 135.
5   Kuusela, 'Scandinavia', p. 91.
6   Hutton, *The Witch*, p. 224.
7   Stanmore, *Love Spells and Lost Treasure*, pp. 70–1.
8   Davies, *Popular Magic*, pp. 183–4.
9   Sneddon, *Witchcraft and Magic*, pp. 14–15.
10 F. Young, *Suffolk Fairylore*, pp. 68–75.
11 Goodare, 'The Scottish Witchcraft Act', pp. 54–5.
12 James VI, *Daemonologie*, p. 74 (spelling modernized).
13 Ibid., pp. 75–6.
14 On the Seely Wights, see Goodare, 'The Cult of the Seely Wights', pp. 198–219; Goodare, 'Seely Wights, Fairies and Nature Spirits in Scotland', pp. 218–37.
15 Hutton, *The Witch*, pp. 222–3.
16 Pócs, 'Hungarians', pp. 182–3.
17 Purkiss, *Fairies and Fairy Stories*, pp. 154–64.
18 L. Henderson and Cowan, *Scottish Fairy Belief*, pp. 127–9.
19 Ibid., p. 129.
20 Ibid., p. 131.
21 Ibid., p. 133. On Christsonday, see Goodare, 'Boundaries of the Fairy Realm', p. 145.
22 Quoted in Goodare, 'Boundaries of the Fairy Realm', p. 148 (spelling anglicized).
23 Ibid., p. 155 (spelling anglicized).
24 L. Henderson and Cowan, *Scottish Fairy Belief*, p. 134.

25 Antonov, 'Between Fallen Angels and Nature Spirits', pp. 128–33.
26 Ibid., pp. 136–9.
27 Quoted in Green, *Elf Queens*, pp. 13–14.
28 Jakobsson, 'Beware of the Elf!', p. 218.
29 Gunnell, 'The Álfar, the Clerics and the Enlightenment', pp. 197–200.
30 Ibid., pp. 203–4.
31 Pedrosa, 'Iberia', p. 131.
32 Ibid., p. 132.
33 Ibid., pp. 125–6.
34 Eliot (ed.), *English Poetry from Chaucer to Gray*, vol. XL, pp. 323–4 (spelling modernized).
35 F. Young, *Suffolk Fairylore*, p. 62.
36 Quoted in Buccola, *Fairies, Fractious Women, and the Old Faith*, pp. 55–6 (spelling modernized).
37 Oldridge, 'Fairies and the Devil in Early Modern England', pp. 1–2.
38 Milton, *Poems*, p. 12.
39 Quoted in L. Henderson and Cowan, *Scottish Fairy Belief*, p. 25 (spelling anglicized).
40 Herrick, *Hesperides*, pp. 101–5.
41 J. K. Clark, *Goodwin Wharton*, p. 30.
42 Anon., *The Golden Ballance of Tryall*, fol. 43v.
43 Green, *Elf Queens*, pp. 18–19.
44 Oldridge, 'Fairies and the Devil in Early Modern England', p. 2.
45 F. Young, *Magic in Merlin's Realm*, pp. 151–61.
46 F. Young, *English Catholics and the Supernatural*, pp. 144–51.
47 Hutton, *The Witch*, p. 239.
48 On fairy cozeners, see Willard, 'Pimping for the Fairy Queen', pp. 491–508.
49 Scot, *The Discoverie of Witchcraft*, pp. 152–3.
50 Buccola, *Fairies, Fractious Women, and the Old Faith*, p. 35.
51 Walsham, *The Reformation of the Landscape*, p. 191.
52 Ó Giolláin, 'The Fairy Belief and Official Religion', p. 203.
53 F. Young, *English Catholics and the Supernatural*, pp. 93–4.
54 Toivo, *Faith and Magic*, pp. 120–1.
55 F. Young (ed.), *Pagans in the Early Modern Baltic*, pp. 14–15.
56 Allatius, *De templis*, p. 163.
57 Pócs, 'Small Gods, Small Demons', p. 263.
58 Walsham, *The Reformation of the Landscape*, p. 513.
59 Hutton, *Pagan Britain*, pp. 380–1.
60 Walsham, *The Reformation of the Landscape*, pp. 108, 127.
61 Ibid., pp. 513–14.
62 Skjebred, 'Rites of Passage as Meeting Place', pp. 215–23.
63 Goodare, 'Boundaries of the Fairy Realm', pp. 168–9.
64 Paulson, *The Old Estonian Folk Religion*, p. 136.
65 F. Young, *Silence of the Gods*, p. 265.
66 Bennett, 'Ghost and Witch', p. 4.
67 On fairy poltergeists, see Sugg, *Fairies*, pp. 141–8.

68 Ü. Valk, 'The Devil and the Spirit World', pp. 226–7.
69 F. Young, *Twilight of the Godlings*, p. 51.
70 Ibid., p. 314.
71 Hutton, *The Witch*, p. 241.
72 F. Young, *Twilight of the Godlings*, p. 8.
73 Roling, 'Our White Ladies on the Graves', pp. 442–62.
74 Aubrey, *Miscellanies*, pp. 90, 156.
75 F. Young, *Twilight of the Godlings*, p. 315.
76 Burton, *The Anatomy of Melancholy*, pp. 193–6.
77 Wilcox, 'Shaggie Thighs and Aery Formes', pp. 195–212.
78 Molina-Moreno, 'Żeńskie duchy przyrodnicze w folklorze polskim', pp. 345–78.
79 Kononenko, 'Ukraine', pp. 249–50.
80 Allatius, *De templis*, pp. 158–9.
81 Ibid., pp. 159–60.
82 Ibid., p. 162.
83 Harte, *Fairy Encounters*, p. 18.
84 Schefferus, *Lapponia*, p. 94.
85 Jurić, 'Where Does the *Vila* Live?', pp. 53–4.
86 Purkiss, *Fairies and Fairy Stories*, pp. 179–84.
87 Hutton, *The Witch*, pp. 240–1.
88 F. Young, *Twilight of the Godlings*, p. 315.
89 Ling, *Roman Painting*, p. 195.
90 Maas, *Victorian Fairy Painting*, p. 48; White, *A Midsummer Night's Dream*, pp. 8–9.
91 Quoted in Allatius, *De templis*, p. 163.
92 Veenstra and Olsen, 'Introduction', p. vii.
93 Weeks, 'Cosmic and Terrestrial Aliens', p. 256.
94 Ibid., p. 261.
95 Kahn, 'The *Philosophia ad Athenienses* in the Light of Genuine Paracelsian Cosmology', pp. 454–6.
96 Eamon, 'Making and Unmaking Marvels', p. 85.
97 Veenstra, 'Paracelsian Spirits', pp. 233–4.
98 Abraham (ed.), *Dictionary of Alchemical Imagery*, p. 102.
99 Hogan, 'Communing with Nature', p. 128.
100 Klaassen, *The Transformations of Magic*, pp. 175–6.
101 Harms, 'Hell and Fairy', pp. 63–5.
102 Bain, 'The Binding of the Fairies', pp. 323–54; Klaassen and Bens, 'Achieving Invisibility', pp. 1–14.
103 Harms, '"Of Fairies"', p. 195.
104 Ibid., p. 196.
105 Ibid., p. 194.

6 Trying the spirits: fairies and the enchanted Enlightenment

1 On Ann Jeffries, see Marshall, 'Ann Jeffries and the Fairies', pp. 127–41.
2 Pitt, *An Account of One Ann Jefferies*, p. 3.
3 Ibid., p. 5.
4 F. Henderson, 'Translation in the Circle of Robert Hooke', pp. 19–21.

5 Pitt, *An Account of One Ann Jefferies*, pp. 19–20.
6 L. Henderson and Cowan, *Scottish Fairy Belief*, pp. 176–81.
7 F. Young, *History of Anglican Exorcism*, pp. 56–7.
8 Davies, *Witchcraft, Magic and Culture*; Barry, *Witchcraft and Demonology in South-West England*; Waters, *Cursed Britain*.
9 Monod, *Solomon's Secret Arts*, pp. 7–8.
10 Purkiss, *Fairies and Fairy Stories*, p. 222.
11 Quoted in Hunter, *Decline of Magic*, p. 67.
12 Bellingradt and Otto, *Magical Manuscripts*, pp. 68–9.
13 Bostridge, *Witchcraft and Its Transformations*, pp. 92–3.
14 Hutton, *The Witch*, pp. 239–41.
15 On Mary Parish and Goodwin Wharton, see J. K. Clark, *Goodwin Wharton*.
16 Quoted in Monod, *Solomon's Secret Arts*, p. 87.
17 Harte, 'England', p. 61.
18 Copenhaver, *Magic in Western Culture*, p. 287.
19 Brock and Winter, 'Theory and Practice in Early Modern Epistemologies', pp. 3–5.
20 Hunter, *Decline of Magic*, p. 52.
21 Hübbe, 'The Fauna of Fallen Babylon', pp. 210–13.
22 F. Young, *History of Exorcism*, pp. 114–15.
23 Levack, *The Devil Within*, p. 232.
24 Quoted in Hunter, *Decline of Magic*, p. 52.
25 Quoted in ibid., p. 54.
26 Kircher, *Iter extaticum II*, pp. 139–41.
27 Monod, *Solomon's Secret Arts*, p. 144.
28 Harte, 'England', p. 64.
29 Purkiss, *Fairies and Fairy Stories*, p. 222.
30 Quoted in Walsham, *Reformation of the Landscape*, p. 361.
31 Ibid., pp. 362–3.
32 Quoted in Ó Giolláin, 'Fairy Belief and Official Religion', p. 205.
33 Monod, *Solomon's Secret Arts*, p. 94.
34 Ibid., p. 155.
35 Caciola, 'The Science of Knowing Spirits', p. 295.
36 Hunter, *Decline of Magic*, pp. 123–5.
37 Ibid., p. 128.
38 Goodare, 'Between Humans and Angels', pp. 177–9.
39 Johnson, *Seeing Fairies*, pp. 8–9.
40 Jones, *The Appearance of Evil*, p. 94.
41 Ibid., p. 58.
42 Ibid., pp. 65–6.
43 Ibid., p. 75.
44 Ibid., pp. 82, 115–16.
45 Ibid., p. 83.
46 Ibid., pp. 85–8.
47 Ibid., p. 95.
48 Ibid., p. 116.
49 Calmet, *Traité sur les apparitions des esprits*, pp. 251–2.

50 Ibid., p. 265.
51 Ibid., p. 266.
52 Gunnell, 'The Álfar, the Clerics and the Enlightenment', p. 195.
53 Quoted in ibid., p. 201.
54 Ibid., pp. 204–5.
55 Quoted in F. Young, *Twilight of the Godlings*, p. 12.
56 Mullis, 'Fear, Fairies, and Fossils', p. 121.
57 Kirk, *Secret Commonwealth*, pp. xii–xiii.
58 Todd, 'Fairies, Egyptians, and Elders', pp. 189–208.
59 Kirk, *Secret Commonwealth*, pp. ix–x.
60 Ibid., p. xii.
61 Hunter, *Decline of Magic*, pp. 152–3.
62 Kirk, *Secret Commonwealth*, p. 5.
63 Hunter, *Decline of Magic*, p. 153.
64 Hanegraaff, 'Rejected Knowledge', pp. 145–52.
65 Goodare, 'Between Humans and Angels', pp. 179–84.
66 Martin, *Description of the Western Islands of Scotland*, p. 310.
67 Ibid., pp. 316–17, 320.
68 Quoted in Goodare, 'Between Humans and Angels', p. 185.
69 Bennett, 'Balquhidder Revisited', pp. 94–115.
70 Hotham, *Life of Jacob Behmen*, sig. C2.
71 Brucker, *Critical History of Philosophy*, pp. 156–7.
72 Harte, 'England', p. 64.
73 Forsberg, *Worlds Beyond*, pp. 112–13.
74 S. Young, 'When Did Fairies Get Wings?', pp. 253–74.
75 Jurić, 'Western Balkans', p. 196; Braccini, 'Greece (and Italy)', p. 221.
76 On the *contes des fées*, see Jubber, *The Fairy Tellers*, pp. 101–36.
77 Seifert, *Fairy Tales*, pp. 6–7.
78 Ibid., pp. 196–200.
79 Pedrosa, 'Iberia', p. 127.
80 Fowler, 'The Paradoxical Machinery of *The Rape of the Lock*', pp. 151–70; Latimer, 'Alchemies of Satire', pp. 684–700.
81 Veenstra, 'Paracelsian Spirits', p. 220.
82 Ibid., pp. 220–1.
83 Ibid., p. 224.
84 Quoted in Monod, *Solomon's Secret Arts*, p. 149.
85 Purkiss, *Fairies and Fairy Stories*, p. 240–1.
86 Veenstra, 'Paracelsian Spirits', p. 216.
87 Quoted in Forment, 'La terra, il cielo e l'inferno', pp. 203–4.
88 Hunter, *The Decline of Magic*, p. 94.
89 Pócs, 'Hungarians', pp. 182–3.
90 Monod, *Solomon's Secret Arts*, p. 191.
91 Harte, 'England', p. 60.
92 Ibid., p. 62.
93 Ibid., p. 60.
94 Miller, 'The Isle of Man', pp. 32–3.

95 L. Henderson and Cowan, *Scottish Fairy Belief*, p. 18.
96 Jakobsson, 'Beware of the Elf!', p. 217.

7 Fairies go global

1 Flores and Masera (eds.), *Relatos populares de la Inquisición novohispana*, pp. 59–60, 122.
2 S. Young, 'Fairy Bread and Fairy Squalls', pp. 210–12.
3 For a study of this phenomenon, see Lorraine Aragon's exploration of the subordination of lesser spirits in Sulawesi: Aragon, 'Who Owns the World?', pp. 277–99.
4 Seaver, '"Pygmies" of the Far North', pp. 69–71.
5 Nansen, *In Northern Mists*, vol. II, pp. 19–20.
6 Seaver, '"Pygmies" in the Far North', p. 72.
7 Ibid., p. 80.
8 L. Henderson and Cowan, *Scottish Fairy Belief*, pp. 50–4.
9 Nansen, *In Northern Mists*, vol. II, p. 270.
10 Ibid., vol. II, p. 86.
11 Olaus Magnus, *Historia de gentibus septentrionalibus*, pp. 70–1.
12 Rix, *The Vanished Settlers of Greenland*, p. 52.
13 Blefkenius, *Islandia*, pp. 58–61.
14 Rink, *Tales and Traditions of the Eskimo*, p. 46.
15 Harpur, *Daimonic Reality*, pp. 43–4.
16 Magasich-Airola and De Beer, *America Magica*, pp. 132–3.
17 Ibid., pp. 140–6.
18 Purkiss, *Fairies and Fairy Stories*, p. 231.
19 Magasich-Airola and De Beer, *America Magica*, pp. 148–70.
20 Ibid., pp. 172–89.
21 Purkiss, *Fairies and Fairy Stories*, pp. 229–30.
22 Pinilla, 'Angels and Demons', p. 187.
23 Silverblatt, *Moon, Sun and Witches*, pp. 184–94.
24 Cervantes and Redden, 'Introduction', pp. 5–6.
25 Pedrosa, 'Iberia', p. 133 n. 4.
26 Pedrosa, 'Los gentiles de los Pirineos y los gentiles de los Andes', pp. 200–23.
27 Flores and Masera (eds.), *Relatos populares de la Inquisición novohispana*, p. 59.
28 Aquino, 'Tradiciones orales', p. 197.
29 Redden, 'Vipers under the Altar Cloths', pp. 163–4.
30 Pinilla, 'Angels and Demons', pp. 175–6.
31 Aquino, 'Tradiciones orales', p. 196.
32 Ibid., pp. 197–8.
33 Ibid., pp. 198–9.
34 Ibid., pp. 199–200.
35 Ibid., pp. 202–3.
36 Nogueira and Sampaio, 'Entre mouras encantadas e encantados da amazônia', pp. 77–84.
37 Ramos, *Creatures of Philippine Lower Mythology*, pp. 41–8.
38 Cowan, 'Jesuit Missionaries', p. 214.
39 Ibid., p. 221.
40 Ibid., pp. 221–2.
41 Ibid., p. 226.

42 Ibid., pp. 227–8.
43 Ibid., pp. 230–1.
44 Ibid., pp. 232–4.
45 Crossland, *Ancestral Encounters in Highland Madagascar*, pp. 85–6.
46 Cooper and Hudson, *Windows and Words*, p. 56.
47 Meili, *Those Who Know*, pp. 80–1; Bane (ed.), *Encyclopedia of Fairies*, p. 225.
48 M. Lewis, *Journals of the Lewis and Clark Expedition*, p. 505.
49 Dorais, 'Pratiques et sentiments religieux à Quaqtaq', pp. 259–60.
50 S. Young, 'Fairy Bread and Fairy Squalls', pp. 210–11.
51 G. R. Butler, 'The *Lutin* Tradition', pp. 5–21.
52 Beaugrand, 'Lutins in the Province of Quebec', pp. 327–8.
53 G. R. Butler, 'The *Lutin* Tradition', p. 9.
54 Warburton, *New England Fairies*, pp. 40–4.
55 Brown, *Louisiana Legends and Lore*, p. 142.
56 Rabalais, *Folklore Figures*, pp. 142–4.
57 Davies, *America Bewitched*, pp. 37–40.
58 Bradford, *History of Plymouth Plantation*, p. 237 (spelling modernized).
59 Warburton, *New England Fairies*, p. 10.
60 Muise, 'Puritans and Pukwudgies', p. 195.
61 Warburton, *New England Fairies*, p. 78.
62 Muise, 'Puritans and Pukwudgies', pp. 196–7; Warburton, *New England Fairies*, pp. 60–3.
63 Warburton, *New England Fairies*, pp. 96–106.
64 Muise, 'Puritans and Pukwudgies', pp. 204–5; Warburton, *New England Fairies*, pp. 79–84, 91.
65 Warburton, *New England Fairies*, pp. 27–32.
66 Muise, 'Puritans and Pukwudgies', pp. 197–8.
67 Ibid., pp. 199–201.
68 Warburton, *New England Fairies*, p. 55.
69 Muise, 'Puritans and Pukwudgies', pp. 205–8.
70 Warburton, *New England Fairies*, pp. 63–8.
71 Ibid., pp. 13–15.
72 Ibid., p. 24.
73 Rieti, '"The Blast"', pp. 284–97.
74 Ibid., p. 287.
75 S. Young, 'Fairy Bread and Fairy Squalls', pp. 219–22.
76 Ibid., pp. 216–17.
77 Ibid., pp. 218–19.
78 Rieti, *Strange Terrain*, p. 51.
79 Clarke, 'Indigenous Spirit and Ghost Folklore', p. 150.
80 Bane (ed.), *Encyclopedia of Fairies*, p. 169.
81 Grey, *Polynesian Mythology*, pp. 287–95.
82 Ibid., p. 295.
83 On the Patupaiarehe, see Bane (ed.), *Encyclopedia of Fairies*, pp. 266–7.
84 S. Young (ed.), *Fairy Census 2014–2017*, pp. 368–79, fairyist.com/wp-content/uploads/2014/10/The-Fairy-Census-2014-2017-1.pdf.

85 S. Young (ed.), *Fairy Census 2: 2017–2023*, pp. 293–5, fairyist.com/wp-content/uploads/2023/12/Fairy-Census2FINAL.pdf.
86 S. Young (ed.), *Fairy Census*, pp. 351–68; S. Young (ed.), *Fairy Census 2*, pp. 276–93.
87 Wells, 'The Making of an Icon', pp. 426–53.
88 Warburton, *New England Fairies*, p. 68; Clarke, 'Indigenous Spirit and Ghost Folklore', pp. 144–8.
89 Paul Smith, 'The Cottingley Fairies', p. 376.

8 The coming (back) of the fairies: the nineteenth and twentieth centuries

1 Salve, 'Forest Fairies in the Vepsian Folk Tradition', pp. 413–23.
2 Taagepera, *Finno-Ugric Republics*, p. 302 n. 1.
3 Silver, *Strange and Secret Peoples*, p. 33.
4 On literary and stage fairies in the nineteenth century, see Bown, *Fairies in Nineteenth-Century Art and Literature*; Purkiss, *Fairies and Fairy Stories*, pp. 246–92; Silver, *Strange and Secret Peoples*; Sugg, *Fairies*, pp. 204–23.
5 Purkiss, *Fairies and Fairy Stories*, pp. 242–4.
6 Harpur, *Daimonic Reality*, p. xii.
7 Ibid., p. 41.
8 Purkiss, *Fairies and Fairy Stories*, p. 241.
9 Barrett, *The Magus*, p. 44.
10 On Barrett and British occultism in this period, see Monod, *Solomon's Secret Arts*, pp. 300–4.
11 Hutton, 'The Making of the Early Modern British Fairy Tradition', pp. 1135–6.
12 Silver, 'On the Origin of Fairies', pp. 143–4.
13 Hunter, *Decline of Magic*, p. 166.
14 Scott, *Minstrelsy*, vol. II, p. 173.
15 Scott, *Letters on Demonology*, pp. 120–1.
16 Silver, 'On the Origin of Fairies', pp. 149–53.
17 F. Young, *Twilight of the Godlings*, p. 12. On Victorian 'pygmy theory', see Silver, *Strange and Secret Peoples*, pp. 117–47.
18 Schmiesing, *The Brothers Grimm*, p. 90.
19 Ibid., p. xii.
20 Ibid., p. 95.
21 Keightley, *Fairy Mythology*, vol. I, pp. 6–7.
22 Ibid., vol. I, p. 9.
23 Cambry, *Monumens Celtiques*, p. 337.
24 F. Young, *Suffolk Fairylore*, pp. 88–90.
25 Gunnell, 'Thomas Crofton Croker', pp. 101–2.
26 F. Young, *Suffolk Fairylore*, pp. 82–6.
27 Silver, *Strange and Secret Peoples*, p. 41.
28 L. Henderson and Cowan, *Scottish Fairy Belief*, p. 13.
29 Silver, 'On the Origin of Fairies', p. 144.
30 L. Henderson and Cowan, *Scottish Fairy Belief*, p. 199.
31 Ibid., pp. 23–4.
32 Ü. Valk, 'Angels in Estonian Folk Religion', p. 222.
33 M. Williams, *Ireland's Immortals*, pp. 314–20.

34 Manning, 'Pixies' Progress', pp. 81–103.
35 Purkiss, *Fairies and Fairy Stories*, pp. 322–3.
36 Gunnell, 'How Elvish were the *Álfar*?', pp. 111–12.
37 Jakobsson, 'Beware of the Elf!', p. 218.
38 F. Young, *English Catholics and the Supernatural*, p. 229.
39 Ó Giolláin, 'Fairy Belief and Official Religion', pp. 207–12.
40 On the murder of Bridget Cleary, see Bourke, *The Burning of Bridget Cleary*.
41 Silver, *Strange and Secret Peoples*, p. 34.
42 Evans-Wentz, *Fairy-Faith*, pp. 1–282.
43 Ibid., pp. 283–396.
44 Ibid., pp. 397–455.
45 Ibid., pp. 456–515.
46 M. Williams, *Ireland's Immortals*, p. 410.
47 L. Henderson and Cowan, *Scottish Fairy Belief*, p. 20.
48 M. Williams, *Ireland's Immortals*, pp. 411–16.
49 Koptev, 'Self-Collection of Folklore by Irish Schoolchildren', pp. 56–70.
50 The Schools Collection can be searched online: duchas.ie/en/cbes/schools.
51 F. Young, *Silence of the Gods*, pp. 343–4.
52 Bausinger, 'Nazi Folk Ideology', p. 22.
53 Hartmann, *Über Krankheit, Tod, und Jenseitvorstellungen*.
54 Ü. Valk, 'The Devil and the Spirit World', pp. 213–32.
55 F. Young, *Silence of the Gods*, p. 335.
56 Quoted in Paul Smith, 'The Cottingley Fairies', p. 374.
57 For Frances Griffiths's own account of her fairy encounters, see Griffiths and Lynch, *Reflections on the Cottingley Fairies*, pp. 14–21.
58 Johnson, *Seeing Fairies*, p. xi.
59 Doyle, *The Coming of the Fairies*, p. 9.
60 On the cousins and their dilemma, see S. Young, 'Elsie, Frances and the Beck', pp. 50–73.
61 Silver, *Strange and Secret Peoples*, p. 189.
62 Ibid., p. 190.
63 L. Henderson and Cowan, *Scottish Fairy Belief*, p. 205.
64 S. Young, 'A History of the Fairy Investigation Society', p. 139.
65 Doyle, *The Coming of the Fairies*, p. 18.
66 Ibid., p. 69.
67 On the Spiritualist preoccupation with empirical evidence, see Lamont, 'Spiritualism and a Mid-Victorian Crisis of Evidence', pp. 897–920.
68 Doyle, *The Coming of the Fairies*, pp. 69–70.
69 Pócs, 'Hungarians', p. 184.
70 Doyle, *The Coming of the Fairies*, p. 41.
71 Bown, *Fairies in Nineteenth-Century Art and Literature*, p. 196.
72 Doyle, *The Coming of the Fairies*, p. 102.
73 Silver, *Strange and Secret Peoples*, p. 192. On Machen's approach to fairies, see Mullis, 'Fear, Fairies, and Fossils', pp. 115–34.
74 Sugg, 'Fairy Magic and the Cottingley Photographs', p. 62.
75 Paul Smith, 'The Cottingley Fairies', p. 393.
76 Ibid., p. 401.

77 Huygen and Poortvliet, *Gnomes*; Froud and Lee, *Faeries*.
78 Baines, 'The Derbyshire Mummified Fairy', danbaines.com/derbyshire-mummified-fairy.
79 On Tessa Farmer's fairies, see McAra (ed.), *In Fairyland*.
80 Erwin Saunders (YouTube channel), youtube.com/@erwinsaunders/videos.
81 Sloan, *Andrew Lang*, p. 215.
82 Bihet, 'Late-Victorian Folklore', pp. 108–11.
83 Quoted in Silver, 'On the Origin of Fairies', p. 153.
84 Doyle, *The Coming of the Fairies*, pp. 122–3.
85 Veenstra, 'Paracelsian Spirits', pp. 238–9.
86 Quoted in Doyle, *The Coming of the Fairies*, p. 98.
87 Quoted in Silver, *Strange and Secret Peoples*, pp. 190–1.
88 Tolkien, 'On Fairy-Stories', p. 40.
89 C. S. Lewis, *The Discarded Image*, p. 123.
90 Joy, 'Goddess or Witch?', p. 274.
91 Green, *Elf Queens*, pp. 11–12.
92 C. S. Lewis, *The Discarded Image*, pp. 125–6.
93 Ibid., pp. 133–4.
94 Ibid., p. 134.
95 Tolkien, 'On Fairy-Stories', p. 42.
96 Ibid., p. 51.
97 Ibid., p. 52.
98 Ibid., pp. 66–7.
99 Ibid., p. 70.
100 Ibid., p. 74.
101 C. S. Lewis, 'De Audiendis Poetis', p. 17.
102 Tolkien, 'On Fairy-Stories', p. 62.
103 Ibid., p. 64.
104 Leith, *The Haunted Wood*, pp. 90–1.
105 Tolkien, 'On Fairy-Stories', p. 81.
106 Ibid., p. 76.
107 Ibid., pp. 83–4.
108 F. Young, *Twilight of the Godlings*, pp. 308–9.
109 Fimi, 'Tolkien and the Fairies'.
110 J. H. Newman, *Parochial and Plain Sermons*, vol. II, pp. 359–61.
111 Uttley, *Private Diaries*, pp. 16, 152.
112 Watkins-Pitchford, *A Child Alone*, p. 41.
113 Lindow, *Trolls*, pp. 126–7.
114 Ellis Davidson, *Katharine Briggs*, pp. 106–8.
115 Ibid., p. 114.
116 Empson, 'Elizabethan Spirits', pp. 1–3.
117 Ellis Davidson, *Katharine Briggs*, p. 124.
118 Ibid., pp. 128–9.
119 Mac Manus, *The Middle Kingdom*, pp. 11–12.
120 Ibid., pp. 146–52.
121 Ibid., pp. 43–4.

122 Vėlius, *Mitinės Lietuvių sakmių butybės*, p. 5.
123 Silver, *Strange and Secret Peoples*, p. 192.
124 Doyle, *The Coming of the Fairies*, pp. 107–20.
125 S. Young, 'A History of the Fairy Investigation Society', pp. 140–1.
126 Ibid., pp. 142–3.
127 Orange, *Dowding of Fighter Command*, p. 263.
128 Silver, *Strange and Secret Peoples*, pp. 207–8.
129 Gordon, *Afoot in the Hebrides*, p. 23.
130 S. Young, 'A History of the Fairy Investigation Society', pp. 143–5.
131 Ibid., pp. 146–8.
132 Ibid., pp. 149–50.
133 Silver, 'On the Origin of Fairies', p. 154.
134 S. Young, 'A History of the Fairy Investigation Society', p. 139.
135 Bihet, 'Late-Victorian Folklore', pp. 112–14.
136 Rieti, *Strange Terrain*, p. 13.

9 Rewilding fairyland: fairies today

1 Watkins-Pitchford, *The Little Grey Men*, p. ii.
2 When referring to contemporary Paganism, I capitalize the term 'Pagan', to distinguish it from pre-modern paganism and in order to avoid using the controversial term 'neo-pagan'.
3 Casey, *Green Space*, p. 145.
4 F. Young, 'An Earthy History of the British Gnomes', pp. 142–53; F. Young, 'How Santa Came to Recruit His Elves', spectator.co.uk/article/how-santa-came-to-recruit-his-elves.
5 Lindow, *Trolls*, pp. 127–37.
6 On online trolls, see ibid., pp. 138–43.
7 Sugg, *Fairies*, pp. 232–8.
8 Graham, '"Blame It on Maureen O'Hara"', pp. 58–75.
9 Hafstein, 'The Elves' Point of View', pp. 87–8.
10 Jakobsson, 'Beware of the Elf!', pp. 217–18.
11 Egeler, 'Iceland', pp. 71–2.
12 Rabalais, *Folklore Figures*, p. 185.
13 Hafstein, 'The Elves' Point of View', pp. 89–92.
14 Ibid., pp. 93–5.
15 See S. Young (ed.), *The Wollaton Gnomes*.
16 Hafstein, 'The Elves' Point of View', p. 98.
17 Leete and Lipin, 'Komi Hunter Narratives', pp. 282–300.
18 Kis-Halas, '"I Make My Saints Work . . ."', p. 84.
19 Bord, *Fairies*; Lenihan and Green, *Meeting the Other Crowd*.
20 Corcoran, *Finding Fairy Mysteries in Donegal*.
21 Purkiss, *Fairies and Fairy Stories*, p. 334.
22 S. Young (ed.), *Fairy Census 2014–2017*, pp. 389–401.
23 S. Young (ed.), *Fairy Census 2: 2017–2023*.
24 Hickey-Hall, *Modern Fairy Sightings* podcast, scarlettofthefae.com/the-modern-fairy-sightings-podcast.
25 Hickey-Hall, *Modern Fairy Sightings*.

26 S. Young (ed.), *Fairy Census 2: 2017–2023*, pp. 68–9.
27 Osse, 'Finding Fairies in ISEBEL', pp. 501–11.
28 Hutton, *Triumph of the Moon*, pp. 201–10.
29 Murray, *The Witch-Cult in Western Europe*, p. 14.
30 Magliocco, '"Reconnecting to Everything"', p. 327.
31 See, for example, McCoy, *A Witch's Guide to Faery Folk*.
32 Quoted in Silver, *Strange and Secret Peoples*, p. 208.
33 L. Henderson and Cowan, *Scottish Fairy Belief*, pp. 208–9; Silver, *Strange and Secret Peoples*, p. 208.
34 Crombie, *Meeting Fairies*.
35 Silver, *Strange and Secret Peoples*, p. 208.
36 Ibid., p. 209.
37 Letcher, 'The Scouring of the Shire', pp. 156–9.
38 Magliocco, 'Reconnecting to Everything', pp. 327–8.
39 Ibid., p. 326.
40 Daimler, *21st Century Fairy*.
41 Magliocco, 'Reconnecting to Everything', pp. 329–30.
42 Ibid., pp. 331–2.
43 Ibid., pp. 332–4.
44 Ibid., pp. 335–9.
45 Ibid., pp. 339–45.
46 Purkiss, *Troublesome Things*, p. 3.
47 Ibid., p. 319.
48 Ibid., p. 320.
49 Rieti, *Strange Terrain*, p. 292.
50 Vallée, *Passport to Magonia*, p. 66.
51 Ibid., p. 162.
52 Filotas, *Pagan Survivals*, pp. 80–1.
53 Strieber, *Communion*, p. 110.
54 Ibid., p. 248.
55 Rojcewicz, 'Between One Eye Blink and the Next', p. 481.
56 Harte, *Fairy Encounters*, pp. 55–6.
57 Luke, 'So Long as You've Got Your Elf', p. 290.
58 Hafstein, 'The Elves' Point of View', p. 96.
59 F. Young, *Twilight of the Godlings*, p. 319.
60 Ibid., p. 318.
61 Doyle, *The Coming of the Fairies*, pp. 9–10.
62 Davis, *High Weirdness*, pp. 103–5.
63 Ibid., p. 384.
64 Luke, 'So Long as You've Got Your Elf', pp. 284–5.
65 Ibid., p. 286.
66 Ibid., p. 288.
67 Davis, *High Weirdness*, pp. 154–5.
68 Ibid., p. 10.
69 Ibid., p. 155.
70 Ibid., p. 26; Latour, 'Who Is Making the Dummy Speak?', pp. 13–15.

71 Luke, 'So Long as You've Got Your Elf', p. 289.
72 PeñaTrujillo et al., 'Narraciones míticas', p. 30.
73 Chesterton, *Alarms and Discursions*, p. 28.
74 Warner, *Once Upon a Time*, p. 2.
75 Tolkien, 'On Fairy-Stories', p. 84.
76 Hart, 'God, Gods, and Fairies', firstthings.com/god-gods-and-fairies.
77 Hart, *The Hidden and the Manifest*, pp. 109–10.
78 Beck, *Hunting Magic Eels*; Dreher, *Living in Wonder*.
79 Damick, *The Lord of Spirits*, pp. 5–6.
80 Thigpen, *Extraterrestrial Intelligence and the Catholic Faith*.
81 Harpur, *Daimonic Reality*, p. 34.
82 Ibid., pp. 68–70.
83 Vickers, 'Why We Need Fairies', unherd.com/2022/06/why-we-need-fairies.
84 Cuthbertson, *Enchantment*, pp. 3–4.
85 Ibid., pp. 86–7.
86 Gosden, *History of Magic*, p. 416.
87 Hanegraaff, *Esotericism and the Academy*, p. 375.
88 Harpur, *Daimonic Reality*, p. 34.
89 Kripal, *How to Think Impossibly*, p. 178.
90 Gallais, 'Les fées seraient-elles nées au XIIe siècle?', p. 371.
91 Cuthbertson, *Enchantment*, p. 8.
92 Ambrose of Milan, *Hexameron, Paradise, and Cain and Abel*, p. 17.
93 Silver, *Strange and Secret Peoples*, p. 210.
94 Prideaux, 'Glitchcraft', ecstaticintegration.org/p/glitchcraft-the-tale-of-leilan-and.
95 Quoted in Knuuttila, 'Some Epistemic Problems with a Vernacular Worldview', pp. 369–81.
96 N. Williams, 'Semantics of the Word "Fairy"', p. 471.

Conclusion
1 Harte, *Fairy Encounters*, p. 50.
2 Gerald of Wales, *Journey through Wales*, p. 135.

Bibliography

Abraham, Lyndy (ed.), *A Dictionary of Alchemical Imagery* (Cambridge University Press, 1998)

Alexiou, Margaret, 'Modern Greek Folklore and Its Relation to the Past: The Evolution of Charos in Greek Tradition' in S. Vryonis Jr (ed.), *The 'Past' in Medieval and Modern Greek Culture* (Malibu, FL: Undena, 1978), pp. 221–36

Allatius, Leo, *De templis Graecorum recentioribus* (Cologne: apud Iodocum Kalcouium & socios, 1645)

Ambrose, Kirk, *The Marvellous and the Monstrous in the Sculpture of Twelfth-Century Europe* (Woodbridge: Boydell & Brewer, 2013)

Ambrose of Milan (trans. John J. Savage), *Hexameron, Paradise, and Cain and Abel* (Washington, DC: Catholic University of America Press, 1961)

Anon., *The Golden Ballance of Tryall* (London: John Windet, 1603)

Antonov, Dmitriy, 'Between Fallen Angels and Nature Spirits: Russian Demonology of the Early Modern Period' in Michael Ostling (ed.), *Fairies, Demons, and Nature Spirits: 'Small Gods' at the Margins of Christendom* (Basingstoke: Palgrave MacMillan, 2018), pp. 123–44

Aquino, Victor Emmanuel Bañuelos, 'Tradiciones orales en torno a los duendes y otros seres sobrenaturales asociados al agua en el pueblo de Tepec, en la région sur de Jalisco', *Boletín de Literatura Oral* 11 (2021): 193–206

Aragon, Lorraine V., 'Who Owns the World? Recognizing the Repressed Small Gods of Southeast Asia' in Michael Ostling (ed.), *Fairies, Demons, and Nature Spirits: 'Small Gods' at the Margins of Christendom* (Basingstoke: Palgrave Macmillan, 2018), pp. 277–99

Aramburu, Francisca, Despres, Catherine, Aguiriano, Begoña, and Benito, Javier, 'Deux faces de la femme merveilleuse au Moyen Âge: la magicienne et la fée' in Francisca Aramburu, Catherine Despres, Begoña Aguiriano, and Javier Benito (eds.), *Bien dire et bien aprandre: fées, dieux et déesses au Moyen Âge* (Centre d'Études Médiévales et Dialectales de Lille III, 1994), pp. 7–22

Aubrey, John, *Miscellanies* (London: Edward Castle, 1696)

Avarvarei, Simona C., 'Shakespeare's Weird Sisters: In Between Outlandish Womanhood and Prophesying *Moirae*', *Linguaculture* 8:2 (2017): 108–11

Bain, Frederika, 'The Binding of the Fairies: Four Spells', *Preternature* 1:2 (2012): 322–54

Balys, Jonas, *Lietuviu tautosakos skaitymai* (Tübingen: Patria, 1948), 2 vols.

Bane, Theresa (ed.), *Encyclopedia of Fairies in World Folklore and Mythology* (Jefferson, NC: McFarland and Co., 2013)

Barber, Elizabeth Wayland, *The Dancing Goddesses: Folklore, Archaeology and the Origins of European Dance* (New York: W. W. Norton, 2013)

Bargan, Andrea, 'The Probable Old Germanic Origin of Romanian *iele* "(Evil) Fairies"', *Messages, Sages, and Ages* 2:2 (2015): 13–18

Baring-Gould, Sabine (ed.), *The Lives of the Saints* (London: John Hodges, 1872–7), 16 vols.

Barrett, Francis, *The Magus, or Celestial Intelligencer* (London: Lackington, Allen and Co., 1801)

Barry, Jonathan, *Witchcraft and Demonology in South-West England, 1640–1789* (London: Palgrave Macmillan, 2012)

Bausinger, Hermann, 'Nazi Folk Ideology and Folk Research' in James R. Dow and Hannjost Lixfeld (eds.), *The Nazification of an Academic Discipline: Folklore in the Third Reich* (Bloomington: Indiana University Press, 1994), pp. 11–33

Beaugrand, H., 'Lutins in the Province of Quebec', *Journal of American Folklore* 5:19 (1892): 327–8

Beck, Richard, *Hunting Magic Eels: Recovering an Enchanted Faith in a Skeptical Age* (Minneapolis, MN: Broadleaf, 2024)

Becking, Bob, 'The Boundaries of Israelite Monotheism' in Anne-Marie Korte and Maaike de Hardt (eds.), *The Boundaries of Monotheism: Interdisciplinary Explorations into the Foundations of Western Monotheism* (Leiden: Brill, 2009), pp. 9–27

Bellingradt, Daniel and Otto, Bernd-Christian, *Magical Manuscripts in Early Modern Europe: The Clandestine Trade in Illegal Book Collections* (London: Palgrave Macmillan, 2017)

Bennett, Gillian, 'Ghost and Witch in the Sixteenth and Seventeenth Centuries', *Folklore* 97:1 (1986): 3–14

Bennett, Margaret, 'Balquhidder Revisited: Fairylore in the Scottish Highlands, 1690–1900' in Peter Narváez (ed.), *The Good People: New Fairylore Essays* (Lexington: University Press of Kentucky, 1997), pp. 94–115

Běťáková, Marta Eva and Blažek, Václav (eds.), *Lexicon of Baltic Mythology* (Heidelberg: Winter Verlag, 2021)

Bihet, Francesca, 'Late-Victorian Folklore: Constructing the Science of Fairies', *Revenant* 6 (2021): 101–17

Bisagni, Jacopo, '*Leprechaun*: A New Etymology', *Cambrian Medieval Celtic Studies* 64 (2012): 47–84

Bitel, Lisa, 'Secrets of the Síd: The Supernatural in Medieval Irish Texts' in Michael Ostling (ed.), *Fairies, Demons, and Nature Spirits: 'Small Gods' at the Margins of Christendom* (Basingstoke: Palgrave Macmillan, 2018), pp. 79–102

Blefkenius, Dietmar, *Islandia, sive populorum et mirabilium quae in ea insula reperiuntur accuratior descriptio* (Leiden: Henryk Haestens, 1607)

Boase, Wendy, *The Folklore of Hampshire and the Isle of Wight* (London: Batsford, 1976)

Bord, Janet, *Fairies: Real Encounters with Little People* (New York: Bantam Doubleday Dell, 1998)

Borsje, Jacqueline, 'Monotheistic to a Certain Extent: The "Good Neighbours" of God in Ireland' in Anne-Marie Korte and Maaike de Hardt (eds.), *The Boundaries of Monotheism: Interdisciplinary Explorations into the Foundations of Western Monotheism* (Leiden: Brill, 2009), pp. 53–82

Bostridge, Ian, *Witchcraft and Its Transformations c.1650–c.1750* (Oxford University Press, 1997)

Bourke, Angela, *The Burning of Bridget Cleary: A True Story* (London: Pimlico, 1999)

Bown, Nicola, *Fairies in Nineteenth-Century Art and Literature* (Cambridge University Press, 2001)

Braccini, Tommaso, 'Greece (and Italy): The Nereids, "Those from Outside"' in Simon Young and Davide Ermacora (eds.), *The Exeter Companion to Fairies, Nereids, Trolls and Other Social Supernatural Beings* (University of Exeter Press, 2024), pp. 217–32

Bradford, William (ed. Charles Deane), *History of Plymouth Plantation* (Boston: privately printed, 1856)

Bradley, S. A. J. (ed.), *Anglo-Saxon Poetry* (London: J. M. Dent, 1982)

Briggs, Katharine M., 'The English Fairies', *Folklore* 68:1 (1957): 270–87

Briggs, Katharine M., *The Anatomy of Puck: An Examination of Fairy Beliefs among Shakespeare's Contemporaries and Successors* (London: Routledge and Kegan Paul, 1959)

Briggs, Katharine M., *A Dictionary of Fairies: Hobgoblins, Brownies, Bogies, and Other Supernatural Creatures* (London: Allen Lane, 1976)

Briggs, Katharine M., *The Vanishing People: A Study of Traditional Fairy Beliefs* (London: Batsford, 1978)

Briggs, Katharine M., *The Fairies in Tradition and Literature*, 2nd edn (London: Routledge, 2002)

Brock, Michelle D. and Winter, David R., 'Theory and Practice in Early Modern Epistemologies of the Preternatural' in Michelle D. Brock, Richard Raiswell, and David R. Winter (eds.), *Knowing Demons, Knowing Spirits in the Early Modern Period* (Basingstoke: Palgrave Macmillan, 2018), pp. 3–19

Brodsky, David, *Spanish Vocabulary: An Etymological Approach* (Austin: University of Texas Press, 2008)

Brown, Alan, *Louisiana Legends and Lore* (Charleston, SC: The History Press, 2021)

Brucker, Jacob (ed. Leo Catana), *Critical History of Philosophy: 'Preliminary Discourse' and 'On the Socratic School'* (Oxford University Press, 2024)

Buccola, Regina, *Fairies, Fractious Women, and the Old Faith: Fairy Lore in Early Modern British Drama and Culture* (Selinsgrove, PA: Susquehanna University Press, 2006)

Būgienė, Lina, 'The Supernatural Milk-Stealer in Lithuanian Folklore and Its Counterparts in Other National Traditions of the Baltic Sea Region', *Archaeologia Baltica* 15 (2011): 99–104

Burton, Robert (ed. Angus Gowland), *The Anatomy of Melancholy* (London: Penguin, 2023)

Butler, Gary R. 'The *Lutin* Tradition in French-Newfoundland Culture: Discourse and Belief' in Peter Narváez (ed.), *The Good People: New Fairylore Essays* (Lexington: University Press of Kentucky, 1997), pp. 5–21

Butler, Jenny, 'The *Sídhe* and Fairy Forts: Ireland' in Simon Young and Ceri Houlbrook (eds.), *Magical Folk: British and Irish Fairies 500 AD to the Present* (London: Gibson Square, 2018), pp. 95–107

Caciola, Nancy N., *Discerning Spirits: Divine and Demonic Possession in the Middle Ages* (Ithaca, NY: Cornell University Press, 2003)

Caciola, Nancy N., 'The Science of Knowing Spirits: Rationality and the Invisible World' in Michelle D. Brock, Richard Raiswell, and David R. Winter (eds.), *Knowing Demons, Knowing Spirits in the Early Modern Period* (Basingstoke: Palgrave Macmillan, 2018), pp. 293–301

Calmet, Antoine Augustin, *Traité sur les apparitions des esprits, et sur les vampires et les revenans* (Paris: Debure, 1751)

Cambry, Jacques, *Monumens Celtiques, ou Recherches sur le Culte des Pierres* (Paris: Johanneau, 1805)

Carey, John, *A Single Ray of the Sun: Religious Speculation in Early Ireland* (Andover: Celtic Studies Publications, 1999)

Carr, A. Wesley, *Angels and Principalities: The Background, Meaning and Development of the Pauline Phrase* hai archai kai hai exousiai (Cambridge University Press, 1981)

Casey, Marion R., *Green Space: The Transformation of Irish Image* (NYU Press, 2024)

Cassidy, Lara M., Ó Maoldúin, Ros, Kador, Thomas, et al., 'A Dynastic Elite in Monumental Neolithic Society', *Nature* 582 (18 June 2020): 384–8

Cervantes, Fernando and Redden, Andrew, 'Introduction' in Fernando Cervantes and Andrew Redden (eds.), *Angels, Demons and the New World* (Cambridge University Press, 2013), pp. 1–12

Chaucer, Geoffrey (trans. David Wright), *The Canterbury Tales*, new edn (Oxford University Press, 2011)

Chesterton, G. K., *Alarms and Discursions* (London: Methuen, 1927)

Clark, J. Kent, *Goodwin Wharton* (Oxford University Press, 1984)

Clark, John, *The Green Children of Woolpit: Chronicles, Fairies and Facts in Medieval England* (University of Exeter Press, 2024)

Clarke, Philip A., 'Indigenous Spirit and Ghost Folklore of "Settled" Australia', *Folklore* 118 (2007): 141–61

Cohen, Jeffrey J., *Hybridity, Identity, and Monstrosity in Medieval Britain: On Difficult Middles* (Basingstoke: Palgrave MacMillan, 2006)

Cooper, Susan-Ann and Hudson, Aidan, *Windows and Words: A Look at Canadian Children's Literature in English* (University of Ottawa Press, 2003)

Copenhaver, Brian, *Magic in Western Culture: From Antiquity to the Enlightenment* (Cambridge University Press, 2015)

Corcoran, Keith, *Finding Fairy Mysteries in Donegal: Close Encounters with the Wee Folk* (Letterkenny: privately published, 2023)

Cowan, Mairi, 'Jesuit Missionaries and the Accommodationist Demons of New France' in Michelle D. Brock, Richard Raiswell, and David R. Winter (eds.), *Knowing Demons, Knowing Spirits in the Early Modern Period* (Basingstoke: Palgrave Macmillan, 2018), pp. 211–38

Crombie, Robert Ogilvie, *Meeting Fairies: My Remarkable Encounters with Nature Spirits* (Lakeville, MA: Inspired Living, 2011)

Crossland, Zoë, *Ancestral Encounters in Highland Madagascar: Material Signs and Traces of the Dead* (Cambridge University Press, 2014)

Cuthbertson, Ian Alexander, *Enchantment: A Critical Primer* (Sheffield: Equinox, 2024)

Daimler, Morgan, *21st Century Fairy: The Good Folk in the New Millennium* (London: Moon Books, 2023)

Damick, Andrew Stephen, *The Lord of Spirits: An Orthodox Christian Framework for the Unseen and Spiritual Warfare* (Chesterton, IN: Ancient Faith Publishing, 2023)

Dando, Marcel, 'Les anges neutres', *Cahiers d'études cathares*, new series 69 (1976): 3–76

Dante Alighieri (trans. Charles S. Singleton), *The Divine Comedy* (Princeton University Press, 2024)

Davies, Owen, *Witchcraft, Magic and Culture, 1736–1951* (Manchester University Press, 1999)

Davies, Owen, *Popular Magic: Cunning-Folk in English History*, 2nd edn (London: Continuum, 2007)

Davies, Owen, *America Bewitched: The Story of Witchcraft after Salem* (Oxford University Press, 2013)

Davis, Erik, *High Weirdness: Drugs, Esoterica, and Visionary Experience in the Seventies* (Cambridge, MA: MIT Press, 2019)

De Blécourt, Yseult, 'The Netherlands: *Witte Wieven* and Other White Apparitions' in Simon Young and Davide Ermacora (eds.), *The Exeter Companion to Fairies, Nereids, Trolls and Other Social Supernatural Beings* (University of Exeter Press, 2024), pp. 107–21

Dorais, Louis-Jacques, 'Pratiques et sentiments religieux à Quaqtaq: continuité et modernité', *Études/Inuit/Studies* 21:1/2 (1997): 255–67

Douglas, Robin C. and Young, Francis, *Paganism Persisting: A History of European Paganisms since Antiquity* (University of Exeter Press, 2024)

Dowden, Ken, *European Paganism: The Realities of Cult from Antiquity to the Middle Ages* (London: Routledge, 2000)

Doyle, Arthur Conan, *The Coming of the Fairies* (London: Hodder and Stoughton, 1922)

Dreher, Rod, *Living in Wonder: Finding Mystery and Meaning in a Secular Age* (London: Hachette UK, 2024)

Dunphy, Graeme, 'On Neutral and Fallen Angels: A Text from the Codex Karlsruhe 408 and Its Source in Enikel's *Weltchronik*', *Neuphilologische Mitteilungen* 96 (1995): 9–13

Eamon, William, 'Making and Unmaking Marvels in Early Modern Europe' in Donato Verardi (ed.), *Aristotelianism and Magic in Early Modern Europe: Philosophers, Experimenters and Wonderworkers* (London: Bloomsbury, 2023), pp. 83–104

Egeler, Matthias, 'A Note on the Dedication *lamiis tribus* (RIB 1331) as Represented on the Seal of the Society', *Archaeologia Aeliana*, 5th series 39 (2010): 15–23

Egeler, Matthias, 'Iceland: The Elves of Strandir' in Simon Young and Davide Ermacora (eds.), *The Exeter Companion to Fairies, Nereids, Trolls and Other Social Supernatural Beings* (University of Exeter Press, 2024), pp. 71–86

El-Zein, Amira, *Islam, Arabs, and the Intelligent World of the Jinn* (Syracuse University Press, 2009)

Eliot, Charles W. (ed.), *English Poetry from Chaucer to Gray* (New York: P. F. Collier and Son, 1909–14), 50 vols.

Ellis Davidson, H. R., *Katharine Briggs: Story-Teller* (Cambridge: Lutterworth Press, 1986)

Empson, William, 'Elizabethan Spirits', *London Review of Books* 2:7 (17 April 1980): 1–3

Enges, Pasi, 'Supernatural Beings and Christian Faith in a Sámi River Village' in Ülo Valk (ed.), *Studies in Folklore and Popular Religion*, vol. III (University of Tartu, 1999), pp. 221–34

Evans-Wentz, Walter, *The Fairy-Faith in Celtic Countries* (Oxford University Press, 1911)

Filotas, Bernadette, *Pagan Survivals, Superstitions and Popular Cultures* (Toronto: Pontifical Institute of Medieval Studies, 2005)

Fimi, Dmitra, *Tolkien, Race and Cultural History: From Fairies to Hobbits* (London: Palgrave MacMillan, 2008)

Flores, Enrique and Masera, Mariana (eds.), *Relatos populares de la Inquisición novohispana: rito, magia y otras supersticiones, siglos XVII–XVIII* (Madrid: Universidad Nacional Autónoma de México, 2010), pp. 59–60

Flower, Harriet I., *The Dancing Lares and the Serpent in the Garden: Religion at the Roman Street Corner* (Princeton University Press, 2017)

Forbes, Chris, 'Pauline Demonology and/or Cosmology? Principalities, Powers and the Elements of the World in Their Hellenistic Context', *Journal for the Study of the New Testament* 85 (2002): 51–73

Forsberg, Laura, *Worlds Beyond: Miniatures and Victorian Fiction* (New Haven, CT: Yale University Press, 2021)

Fowler, Alastair, 'The Paradoxical Machinery of *The Rape of the Lock*' in C. Nicolson (ed.), *Alexander Pope: Essays for the Tercentenary* (Aberdeen University Press, 1988), pp. 151–70

Frankfurter, David, 'Demon Invocations in the Coptic Magical Spells' in Nathalie Bosson and Anne Boud'hors (eds.), *Actes de huitième congrès international d'études coptes, Paris, 28 juin – 3 juillet 2004* (Leuven: Peeters, 2007), pp. 453–66

Frankfurter, David, 'Where the Spirits Dwell: Possession, Christianization and Saints' Shrines in Late Antiquity', *Harvard Theological Review* 103 (2010): 27–46

Friedman, John Block, *The Monstrous Races in Medieval Art and Thought* (Syracuse University Press, 2000)

Froud, Brian and Lee, Alan (ed. David Larkin), *Faeries* (London: Souvenir, 1978)

Gallais, Pierre, 'Les fées seraient-elles nées au XIIe siècle? (À propos d'un ouvrage récent)', *Cahiers de civilisation médiévale* 116 (1986): 355–71

Gallais, Pierre, *La fée à la fontaine et à l'arbre: un archetype du conte merveilleux et du récit courtois* (Amsterdam: Rodopi, 1992)

Geertz, Clifford, '"Internal Conversion" in Contemporary Bali' in Clifford Geertz, *The Interpretation of Cultures: Selected Essays by Clifford Geertz* (London: Hutchinson, 1973), pp. 170–89

Gerald of Wales (trans. L. Thorpe), *The Journey through Wales and the Description of Wales* (Harmondsworth: Penguin, 1978)

Gerhardt, Mia I., *The Old Man of the Sea: From* Neptunus *to Old French* luiton*: Ancestry and Character of a Water Spirit* (Amsterdam: Polak and Van Gennep, 1967)

Gervase of Tilbury (ed. Felix Liebrecht), *Des Gervasius von Tilbury Otia imperialia* (Hanover: Carl Rümpler, 1856)

Gimbutas, Marija, *The Gods and Goddesses of Old Europe, 7000 to 3500 BC: Myths, Legends, and Cult Images* (London: Thames and Hudson, 1974)

Ginsburg, Carlo and Lincoln, Bruce, *Old Thiess, a Livonian Werewolf: A Classic Case in Comparative Perspective* (University of Chicago Press, 2020)

Goodare, Julian, 'The Scottish Witchcraft Act', *Church History* 74:1 (2005): 39–67

Goodare, Julian, 'The Cult of the Seely Wights in Scotland', *Folklore* 123:2 (2012): 198–219

Goodare, Julian, 'Boundaries of the Fairy Realm in Scotland' in Jan R. Veenstra and Karin Olsen (eds.), *Airy Nothings: Imagining the Otherworld of Faerie from the Middle Ages to the Age of Reason, Essays in Honour of Alasdair A. MacDonald* (Leiden: Brill, 2013), pp. 139–69

Goodare, Julian, *The European Witch-Hunt* (London: Routledge, 2016)

Goodare, Julian, 'Between Humans and Angels: Scientific Uses for Fairies in Early Modern Scotland' in Michael Ostling (ed.), *Fairies, Demons, and Nature Spirits: 'Small Gods' at the Margins of Christendom* (Basingstoke: Palgrave Macmillan, 2018), pp. 169–90

Goodare, Julian, 'Seely Wights, Fairies and Nature Spirits in Scotland' in Éva Pócs (ed.), *Body, Soul, Spirits and Supernatural Communication* (Newcastle: Cambridge Scholars Publishing, 2019), pp. 218–37

Gordon, Seton, *Afoot in the Hebrides* (London: Country Life, 1950)

Gorla, Silvia, 'Some Remarks about the Latin *Physiologus* Extracts Transmitted in the *Liber Glossarum*', *Mnemosyne* 71 (2018): 145–67

Gosden, Chris, *The History of Magic: From Alchemy to Witchcraft, from the Ice Age to the Present* (London: Viking, 2020)

Graham, Colin, '"Blame It on Maureen O'Hara": Ireland and the Trope of Authenticity', *Cultural Studies* 15:1 (2001): 58–75

Green, Richard Firth, *Elf Queens and Holy Friars: Fairy Beliefs and the Medieval Church* (Philadelphia: University of Pennsylvania Press, 2016)

Green, Richard Firth, 'Refighting Carlo Ginzburg's *Night Battles*' in C. M. Nakashian and D. P. Franke (eds.), *Prowess, Piety, and Public Order in Medieval Society: Essays in Honor of Richard W. Kaeuper* (Leiden: Brill, 2017), pp. 381–402

Green, Richard Firth, 'Forms of the Marvelous: Fairy Stories, or Stories about Fairies?' in Susan Aronstein (ed.), *A Cultural History of Fairy Tales in the Middle Ages* (London: Bloomsbury, 2021), pp. 23–44

Greimas, Algirdas J. (trans. Milda Newman), *Of Gods and Men: Studies in Lithuanian Mythology* (Bloomington: Indiana University Press, 1992)

Grey, George, *Polynesian Mythology, and Ancient Traditional History of the New Zealand Race* (London: John Murray, 1855)

Griffiths, Frances and Lynch, Christine, *Reflections on the Cottingley Fairies* (Belfast: JMJ, 2009)

Gunnell, Terry A., 'How Elvish Were the *Álfar?*' in Andrew Wawn, Graham Johnson, and John Walter (eds.), *Constructing Nations, Reconstructing Myth: Essays in Honour of T. A. Shippey* (Turnhout: Brepols, 2007), pp. 111–30

Gunnell, Terry, 'The Álfar, the Clerics and the Enlightenment: Conceptions of the Supernatural in the Age of Reason in Iceland' in Michael Ostling (ed.), *Fairies, Demons, and Nature Spirits: 'Small Gods' at the Margins of Christendom* (Basingstoke: Palgrave Macmillan, 2018), pp. 191–212

Gunnell, Terry, 'Álfar (Elves)' in Jens Peter Schjødt, John Lindow, and Anders Andrén (eds.), *The Pre-Christian Religions of the North: History and Structures*, vol. III (Turnhout: Brepols, 2020), pp. 1571–80

Gunnell, Terry, 'Thomas Crofton Croker, *The Fairy Legends*, and the Arrival of the Illustrated Folk Legend in Northern Europe', *Irish University Review* 54:1 (2024): 101–11

Hafstein, Valdimar T., 'The Elves' Point of View: Cultural Identity in Contemporary Icelandic Elf-Tradition', *Fabula* 41:1–2 (2000): 87–104

Hall, Alaric, *Elves in Anglo-Saxon England: Matters of Belief, Health, Gender and Identity* (Woodbridge: Boydell, 2007)

Hamori, Esther J., *God's Monsters: Vengeful Spirits, Deadly Angels, Hybrid Creatures, and Divine Hitmen of the Bible* (Minneapolis, MN: Broadleaf, 2023)

Hanegraaff, Wouter J., *Esotericism and the Academy: Rejected Knowledge in Western Culture* (Cambridge University Press, 2012)

Hanegraaff, Wouter J., 'Rejected Knowledge . . . So You Mean That Esotericists Are the Losers of History?' in Wouter J. Hanegraaff, Peter J. Forshaw, and Marco Pasi (eds.), *Hermes Explains: Thirty Questions about Western Esotericism* (University of Amsterdam Press, 2019), pp. 145–52

Harf-Lancner, Laurence, *Les fées au moyen âge: Morgane et Mélusine, la naissance des fées* (Paris: Librairie Honoré Champion, 1984)

Harms, Daniel, 'Hell and Fairy: The Differentiation of Fairies and Demons within British Ritual Magic of the Early Modern Period', in Michelle D. Brock, Richard Raiswell, and David R. Winter (eds.), *Knowing Demons, Knowing Spirits in the Early Modern Period* (Basingstoke: Palgrave Macmillan, 2018), pp. 55–77

Harms, Daniel, '"Of Fairies": An Excerpt from a Seventeenth-Century Magical Manuscript', *Folklore* 129:2 (2018): 192–8

Harpur, Patrick, *Daimonic Reality: A Field Guide to the Otherworld* (London: Viking Arkana, 1994)

Hart, David Bentley, *The Hidden and the Manifest: Essays in Theology and Metaphysics* (Grand Rapids, MI: Eerdmans, 2017)

Harte, Jeremy, 'Fairy Barrows and Cunning Folk: Dorset' in Simon Young and Ceri Houlbrook (eds.), *Magical Folk: British and Irish Fairies 500 AD to the Present* (London: Gibson Square, 2018), pp. 65–78

Harte, Jeremy, *Cloven Country: The Devil and the English Landscape* (London: Reaktion, 2022)

Harte, Jeremy, 'England: Small Fairies are Beautiful Fairies' in Simon Young and Davide Ermacora (eds.), *The Exeter Companion to Fairies, Nereids, Trolls and Other Social Supernatural Beings* (University of Exeter Press, 2024), pp. 51–70

Harte, Jeremy, *Fairy Encounters in Medieval England: Landscape, Folklore and the Supernatural* (University of Exeter Press, 2024)

Hartmann, Hans, *Über Krankheit, Tod, und Jenseitvorstellungen in Irland: Erster Teil, Krankheit und Fairyentrückung* (Halle: Max Niemeyer Verlag, 1942)

Harvey, Graham, *Animism: Respecting the Living World* (New York: Columbia University Press, 2006)

Harward, Vernon J., *The Dwarfs of Arthurian Romance and Celtic Tradition* (Leiden: Brill, 1958)

Heide, Eldar, 'Spinning *seiðr*', in Anders Andrénn, Kristina Jennbert, and Catharina Raudvere (eds.), *Old Norse Religion in Long-Term Perspectives: Origins, Changes, and Interactions* (Lund: Nordic Academic Press, 2006), pp. 164–70

Henderson, Felicity, 'Translation in the Circle of Robert Hooke' in Sietske Fransen, Niall Hodson, and Karl A. E. Enenkel (eds.), *Translating Early Modern Science* (Leiden: Brill, 2017), pp. 17–40

Henderson, Lizanne and Cowan, Edward J., *Scottish Fairy Belief: A History* (East Linton: Tuckwell Press, 2001)

Henningsen, Gustav, 'The Ladies from Outside: An Archaic Pattern of the Witches' Sabbath' in Bengt Ankarloo and Gustav Henningsen (eds.), *Early Modern European Witchcraft: Centres and Peripheries* (Oxford: Clarendon, 1990), pp. 191–215

Herrick, Robert, *Hesperides* (London: John Williams, 1648)

Hickey-Hall, Jo, *Modern Fairy Sightings: Personal Encounters in Extraordinary Times* (London: Watkins, 2025)

Horstmann, Carl (ed.), *The Early South-English Legendary* (London: Early English Text Society, 1887), pp. 305–7

Hotham, Durand, *Life of Jacob Behmen* (London: H. Blunden, 1654)

Hraste, Daniel Nečas and Vuković, Krešimir, 'Rudra-Shiva and Silvanus-Faunus: Savage and Propitious', *Journal of Indo-European Studies* 39:1/2 (2011): 100–15

Hübbe, Benjamin, 'The Fauna of Fallen Babylon – Carl Aurivillius on the Animals in Isaiah 13:21 and the Task of Bible Hermeneutics' in Bernd Roling, Bernhard Schirg, and Stefan Heinrich Bauhaus (eds.), *Apotheosis of the North: The Swedish Appropriation of Classical Antiquity around the Baltic Sea and Beyond (1650 to 1800)* (Berlin: De Gruyter, 2017), pp. 187–219

Hunt, Ailsa, 'Pagan Animism: A Modern Myth for a Green Age' in Ailsa Hunt and Hilary Marlow (eds,), *Ecology and Theology in the Ancient World: Cross-Disciplinary Perspectives* (London: Bloomsbury, 2019), pp. 137–52

Hunt, Tony (ed.), *Anglo-Norman Medicine II: Shorter Treatises* (Cambridge: D. S. Brewer, 1997)

Hunter, Michael, *The Decline of Magic: Britain in the Enlightenment* (New Haven, CT: Yale University Press, 2020)

Hutton, Ronald, *Witches, Druids, and King Arthur* (Hambledon: Continuum, 2003)

Hutton, Ronald, *Shamans: Siberian Spirituality and the Western Imagination* (London: Hambledon Continuum, 2007)

Hutton, Ronald, *Pagan Britain* (New Haven, CT: Yale University Press, 2013)

Hutton, Ronald, 'The Making of the Early Modern British Fairy Tradition', *Historical Journal* 57:4 (2014): 1135–56

Hutton, Ronald, *The Witch: A History of Fear, from Ancient Times to the Present* (New Haven, CT: Yale University Press, 2017)

Hutton, Ronald, *The Triumph of the Moon: A History of Modern Pagan Witchcraft*, revised edn (Oxford University Press, 2019)

Hutton, Ronald, *Queens of the Wild: Pagan Goddesses in Christian Europe – An Investigation* (New Haven, CT: Yale University Press, 2022)

Huygen, Wil and Poortvliet, Rien, *Gnomes* (New York: Peacock, 1977)

Ingemark, Camilla Asplund, *The Genre of Trolls: The Case of a Finland–Swedish Folk Belief Tradition* (Åbo Akademi University Press, 2008)

Insoll, Timothy (ed.), *Archaeology, Ritual, Religion* (London: Routledge, 2004)

Jakobsson, Ármann, 'The Hole: Problems in Medieval Dwarfology', *Arv* 61 (2004): 53–76

Jakobsson, Ármann, 'The Taxonomy of the Non-existent: Some Medieval Icelandic Concepts of the Paranormal', *Fabula* 54 (2013): 199–213

Jakobsson, Ármann, 'Beware of the Elf! A Note on the Evolving Meaning of

Álfar', *Folklore* 126 (2015): 215–23

James VI, *Daemonologie* (London: The Bodley Head, 1924)

Johnson, Marjorie T. (ed. Simon Young), *Seeing Fairies: From the Lost Archives of the Fairy Investigation Society, Authentic Reports of Fairies in Modern Times* (Charlottesville, VA: Anomalist Books, 2014)

Jones, Edmund (ed. John Harvey), *The Appearance of Evil: Apparitions of Spirits in Wales* (Cardiff: University of Wales Press, 2003)

Joy, Stephen P., 'Goddess or Witch? The Pale Queen's Rise in Postwar British Literature', *Hudson Review* 69:2 (2016): 259–78

Jubber, Nicholas, *The Fairy Tellers: A Journey into the Secret History of Fairy Tales* (London: John Murray, 2022)

Jurić, Dorian, 'Where Does the *Vila* Live? Returning to a Simple Question', *Folklore* 134:1 (2023): 48–72

Jurić, Dorian, 'Western Balkans: A *Vila* Like a *Vila*', in Simon Young and Davide Ermacora (eds.), *The Exeter Companion to Fairies, Nereids, Trolls and Other Social Supernatural Beings* (University of Exeter Press, 2024), pp. 196–216

Kahn, Didier, 'The *Philosophia ad Athenienses* in the Light of Genuine Paracelsian Cosmology', *Early Science and Medicine* 24 (2019): 439–72

Kallery, Maria and Psillos, Dimitris, 'Anthropomorphism and Animism in Early Years Science: Why Teachers Use Them, How They Conceptualise Them and What Are Their Views on Their Use', *Research in Science Education* 34 (2004): 291–311

Kassell, Lauren, '*All Was This Land Full Fill'd of Faerie*, or Magic and the Past in Early Modern England', *Journal of the History of Ideas* 67:1 (2006): 107–22

Keightley, Thomas, *The Fairy Mythology, Illustrative of the Romance and Superstition of Various Countries* (London: Bohn, 1850), 2 vols.

Kent, Neil, *The Sámi Peoples of the North: A Social and Cultural History* (London: Hurst, 2014)

Kieckhefer, Richard, 'Angel Magic and the Cult of Angels in the Later Middle Ages' in L. N. Kallestrup and R. M. Toivo (eds.), *Contesting Orthodoxy in Medieval and Early Modern Europe* (Basingstoke: Palgrave Macmillan, 2017), pp. 71–110

Kircher, Athanasius, *Iter extaticum II* (Rome: Typis Mascardi, 1657)

Kirk, Robert (ed. Marina Warner), *The Secret Commonwealth of Elves, Fauns, and Fairies* (New York Review of Books, 2007)

Kis-Halas, Judit, '"I Make My Saints Work . . .": A Hungarian Holy Healer's

Identity Reflected in Autobiographical Stories and Folk Narratives' in Marion Bowman and Ülo Valk (eds.), *Vernacular Religion in Everyday Life: Expressions of Belief* (London: Routledge, 2012), pp. 63–92

Klaassen, Frank, *The Transformations of Magic: Illicit Learned Magic in the Later Middle Ages and Renaissance* (University Park: Pennsylvania State University Press, 2013)

Klaassen, Frank and Bens, Katrina, 'Achieving Invisibility and Having Sex with Spirits: Six Operations from an English Magic Collection ca. 1600', *Opuscula* 3:1 (2013): 1–14

Knuuttila, Seppa, 'Some Epistemic Problems with a Vernacular Worldview' in Marion Bowman and Ülo Valk (eds.), *Vernacular Religion in Everyday Life: Expressions of Belief* (London: Routledge, 2012), pp. 369–81

Kononenko, Natalie, 'Ukraine: Courtship Rituals and Legends of the *Bohyni*' in Simon Young and Davide Ermacora (eds.), *The Exeter Companion to Fairies, Nereids, Trolls and Other Social Supernatural Beings* (University of Exeter Press, 2024), pp. 243–60

Koptev, Nikita, 'Self-Collection of Folklore by Irish Schoolchildren: Strategies and Outcomes', *Folk-Life: Journal of Ethnological Studies* 62:1 (2024): 56–70

Kors, Alan Charles and Peters, Edward (eds.), *Witchcraft in Europe, 400–700: A Documentary History*, 2nd edn (Philadelphia: Pennsylvania State University Press, 2001)

Kripal, Jeffrey J., *How to Think Impossibly: About Souls, UFOs, Time, Belief, and Everything Else* (University of Chicago Press, 2024)

Kuusela, Tommy, 'Spirited Away by the Female Forest Spirit in Swedish Folk Belief', *Folklore* 131 (2020): 159–79

Kuusela, Tommy, 'Scandinavia: My Neighbour the Troll' in Simon Young and Davide Ermacora (eds.), *The Exeter Companion to Fairies, Nereids, Trolls and Other Social Supernatural Beings* (University of Exeter Press, 2024), pp. 87–106

Lamont, Peter, 'Spiritualism and a Mid-Victorian Crisis of Evidence', *Historical Journal* 47:4 (2004): 897–920

Larson, Jennifer, *Greek Nymphs: Myth, Cult, Lore* (Oxford University Press, 2001)

Latimer, B., 'Alchemies of Satire: A History of the Sylphs in *The Rape of the Lock*', *Review of English Studies* 57 (2006): 684–700

Latour, Bruno, 'Who Is Making the Dummy Speak?' in François Cooren (ed.), *Action and Agency in Dialogue: Passion, Incarnation and Ventriloquism* (Amsterdam: John Benjamins, 2010), pp. 13–15

Lecouteux, Claude, *Fées, sorcières et loups-garous au moyen âge* (Paris: Imago, 1992)

Lecouteux, Claude (trans. J. E. Graham), *The Tradition of Household Spirits: Ancestral Lore and Practices* (Rochester, VT: Inner Traditions, 2013)

Leete, Art and Koosa, Piret, 'Spiritual Power, Witchcraft and Protestants: Conflicting Approaches to Religious Belonging and Practice in the Komi Countryside', *Numen* 69 (2022): 517–41

Leete, Art and Lipin, Vladimir, 'Komi Hunter Narratives' in Marion Bowman and Ülo Valk (eds.), *Vernacular Religion in Everyday Life: Expressions of Belief* (London: Routledge, 2012), pp. 282–300

Leith, Sam, *The Haunted Wood: A History of Childhood Reading* (London: Bloomsbury, 2024)

Lenihan, Eddie and Green, Carolyn Eve, *Meeting the Other Crowd: The Fairy Stories of Hidden Ireland* (Dublin: Gill and Macmillan, 2003)

Letcher, Andy, 'The Scouring of the Shire: Fairies, Trolls and Pixies in Eco-protest Culture', *Folklore* 112 (2001): 147–61

Levack, Brian P., *The Devil Within: Possession and Exorcism in the Christian West* (New Haven, CT: Yale University Press, 2014)

Lewis, C. S., 'De Audiendis Poetis' in Walter Hooper (ed.), *Studies in Medieval and Renaissance Literature* (Cambridge University Press, 1966), pp. 1–17

Lewis, C. S., *The Discarded Image: An Introduction to Medieval and Renaissance Literature* (Cambridge University Press, 2012)

Lewis, Meriwether (ed. Gary E. Moulton and Thomas W. Dunlay), *The Journals of the Lewis and Clark Expedition: August 30, 1803 – August 24, 1804* (Lincoln: University of Nebraska Press, 1983)

Lindow, John, *Norse Mythology: A Guide to Gods, Heroes, Rituals, and Beliefs* (Oxford University Press, 2002)

Lindow, John, 'Poetry, Dwarfs, and Gods: Understanding Alvíssmál' in Judy Quinn, Kate Heslop, and Tarrin Wells (eds.), *Learning and Understanding in the Old Norse World: Essays in Honour of Margaret Clunies Ross* (Turnhout: Brepols, 2007), pp. 285–303

Lindow, John, *Trolls: An Unnatural History* (London: Reaktion, 2014)

Ling, Roger, *Roman Painting* (Cambridge University Press, 1995)

Lorca, Federico García (trans. Christopher Maurer), *In Search of Duende* (New

York: New Directions, 1998)

Luck, George (ed.), *Arcana Mundi: Magic and the Occult in the Greek and Roman Worlds*, 2nd edn (Baltimore, MD: Johns Hopkins University Press, 2006)

Luhrmann, Tanya M., *How God Becomes Real: Kindling the Presence of Invisible Others* (Princeton University Press, 2020)

Luke, David, 'So Long as You've Got Your Elf: Death, DMT and Discarnate Entities' in A. Voss and W. Rowlandson (eds.), *Daimonic Imagination: Uncanny Intelligence* (Newcastle: Cambridge Scholars Publishing, 2013), pp. 282–91

Maas, Jeremy, *Victorian Fairy Painting* (London: Royal Academy of Arts, 1997)

Mac Manus, Dermot, *The Middle Kingdom: The Faerie World of Ireland*, 2nd edn (Gerrards Cross: Colin Smythe, 1973)

Mackley, Jude, *The Legend of St Brendan: A Comparative Study of the Latin and Anglo-Norman Versions* (Leiden: Brill, 2008)

McAra, Catriona (ed.), *In Fairyland: The World of Tessa Farmer* (London: Strange Attractor, 2016)

McCoy, Edain, *A Witch's Guide to Faery Folk* (St Paul, MN: Llewellyn, 1994)

Madar, Maia, 'Estonia I: Werewolves and Poisoners', in Bengt Ankarloo and Gustav Henningsen (eds.), *Early Modern European Witchcraft: Centres and Peripheries* (Oxford: Clarendon Press, 1990), pp. 257–72

Magasich-Airola, Jorge and De Beer, Jean-Marc, *America Magica: When Renaissance Europe Thought It Had Conquered Paradise* (London: Anthem Press, 2006)

Magliocco, Sabina, '"Reconnecting to Everything": Fairies in Contemporary Paganism' in Michael Ostling (ed.), *Fairies, Demons, and Nature Spirits: 'Small Gods' at the Margins of Christendom* (Basingstoke: Palgrave Macmillan, 2018), pp. 325–48

Manning, Paul, 'Pixies' Progress: How the Pixie Became Part of the Nineteenth-Century Fairy Mythology' in Michael Dylan Foster and Jeffrey A. Tolbert (eds.), *The Folkloresque: Reframing Folklore in a Popular Culture World* (Denver: University Press of Colorado, 2015), pp. 81–103

Maraschi, Andrea, 'France: Humanlike Societies and Spaces among the *Fées*', in Simon Young and Davide Ermacora (eds.), *The Exeter Companion to Fairies, Nereids, Trolls and Other Social Supernatural Beings* (University of Exeter Press, 2024), pp. 138–54

Marshall, Peter, 'Ann Jeffries and the Fairies: Folk Belief and the War on

Scepticism in Later Stuart England' in Angela McShane and Garthine Walkers (eds.), *The Extraordinary and the Everyday in Early Modern England: Essays in Celebration of the Work of Bernard Capp* (Basingstoke: Palgrave Macmillan, 2010), pp. 127–41

Martin, Martin, *A Description of the Western Islands of Scotland* (London: Andrew Bell, 1703)

Meili, Diane, *Those Who Know: Profiles of Alberta's Native Elders* (Edmonton: NeWest Press, 1991)

Meltzer, Françoise, 'Reviving the Fairy Tree: Tales of European Sanctity', *Critical Inquiry* 35 (2009): 493–520

Meyer, Kuno (ed.), *The Voyage of Bran Son of Febal to the Land of the Living* (London: David Nutt, 1895), 2 vols.

Miller, Stephen, 'The Isle of Man: "They Call Them the Good People"' in Simon Young and Davide Ermacora (eds.), *The Exeter Companion to Fairies, Nereids, Trolls and Other Social Supernatural Beings* (University of Exeter Press, 2024), pp. 32–50

Milton, John, *Poems of Mr. John Milton* (London: Ruth Raworth, 1645)

Moitra, Angana, 'From Pagan God to Magical Being: The Changing Face of the Faerie King and Its Cultural Implications' in Désirée Cappa, James E. Christie, Lorenza Gay, Hanna Gentili, and Finn Schulze-Feldmann (eds.), *Cultural Encounters: Cross-Disciplinary Studies from the Late Middle Ages to the Enlightenment* (Wilmington, DE: Vernon Press, 2018), pp. 23–40

Moitra, Angana, 'From Graeco-Roman Underworld to the Celtic Otherworld: The Cultural Translation of a Pagan Deity', *Oxford Research in English* 11 (Autumn 2020): 85–106

Molina-Moreno, Francisco, 'Żeńskie duchy przyrodnicze w folklorze polskim i w mitologii klasycznej', *Prace Etnograficzne* 44:4 (2016): 345–78

Monod, Paul Kléber, *Solomon's Secret Arts: The Occult in the Age of Enlightenment* (New Haven, CT: Yale University Press, 2013)

Montuori, Mario, *Socrates: Physiology of a Myth* (Brill: Leiden, 1981)

Muise, Peter, 'Puritans and Pukwudgies: New England' in Simon Young and Ceri Houlbrook (eds.), *Magical Folk: British and Irish Fairies, 500 AD to the Present* (London: Gibson Square, 2018), pp. 193–209

Mullis, Justin, 'Fear, Fairies, and Fossils: The Legacy of Arthur Machen's "Little People" Stories', in Antonio Sanna (ed.), *Arthur Machen: Critical Essays* (Lanham, MD: Lexington, 2021), pp. 115–34

Murray, Margaret A., *The Witch-Cult in Western Europe: A Study in Anthropology*

(Oxford: Clarendon, 1921)

Nansen, Fridtjof, *In Northern Mists: Arctic Exploration in Early Times* (Cambridge University Press, 1911), 2 vols.

Narváez, Peter, 'Introduction' in Peter Narváez (ed.), *The Good People: New Fairylore Essays* (Lexington: University Press of Kentucky, 1997), pp. ix–xiv

Newman, Coree, 'The Good, the Bad and the Unholy: Ambivalent Angels in the Middle Ages' in Michael Ostling (ed.), *Fairies, Demons, and Nature Spirits: 'Small Gods' at the Margins of Christendom* (Basingstoke: Palgrave MacMillan, 2018), pp. 103–22

Newman, John Henry, *Parochial and Plain Sermons* (London: Longmans, Green and Co., 1908–11), 8 vols.

Nogueira, Mara Genecy Centeno and Sampaio, Sonia Maria Gomes, 'Entre mouras encantadas e encantados da amazônia: uma abordagem decolonial', *Revista Brasileira de Literatura Comparada* 22:39 (2020): 77–84

Ó Giolláin, Diarmuid, 'The Fairy Belief and Official Religion in Ireland' in Peter Narváez (ed.), *The Good People: New Fairylore Essays* (Lexington: The University Press of Kentucky, 1997), pp. 199–214

O'Grady, Standish H. (ed.), *Silva Gadelica (I–XXXI)* (London: Williams and Norgate, 1892), 2 vols.

O'Sullivan, Maurice, '"Subtly of Herself Contemplative": The Legends of Lilith', *Studies in the Humanities* 20:1 (1993): 12–34

Ochota, Mary Ann, *Secret Britain: Unearthing Our Mysterious Past* (London: Frances Lincoln, 2024)

Oelze, Anselm, *Animal Rationality: Later Medieval Theories 1250–1350* (Leiden: Brill, 2018)

Olaus Magnus, *Historia de gentibus septentrionalibus* (Rome: Giovanni Maria de Viottis, 1555)

Oldridge, Darren, 'Fairies and the Devil in Early Modern England', *Seventeenth Century* 31 (2016): 1–15

Orange, Vincent, *Dowding of Fighter Command: Victor of the Battle of Britain* (London: Grub Street, 2008)

Origen (trans. Frederick Crombie), *The Writings of Origen* (London: Hamilton and Co., 1869), 2 vols.

Osse, Myrthe, 'Finding Fairies in ISEBEL: An Investigation of Cross-Cultural Themes in Fairy Folklore', *Folklore* 135:4 (2024): 501–11

Ostling, Michael, *Between the Devil and the Host: Imagining Witchcraft in Early*

Modern Poland (Oxford University Press, 2011)

Ostling, Michael, 'Introduction: Where've All the Good People Gone?' in Michael Ostling (ed.), *Fairies, Demons, and Nature Spirits: 'Small Gods' at the Margins of Christendom* (Basingstoke: Palgrave MacMillan, 2018), pp. 1–53

Ostling, Michael and Forest, Richard, '"Goblins, Owles and Sprites": Discerning Early-Modern English Preternatural Beings through Collocational Analysis', *Religion* 44 (2014): 547–72

Pask, Kevin, *The Fairy Way of Writing: Shakespeare to Tolkien* (Baltimore, MD: Johns Hopkins University Press, 2013)

Paulson, Ivar (trans. Juta Kõvamees Kitching and H. Kõvamees), *The Old Estonian Folk Religion* (Bloomington: Indiana University Press, 1971)

Pearson, Mike Parker, 'Living with the Dead: Mummification and Post-mortem Treatment in Bronze Age Britain', *Archaeology International* 26:1 (2023): 145–66

Pedrosa, José Manuel, 'Los gentiles de los Pirineos y los gentiles de los Andes: razas prehistóricas, apocalipsis y geomitologías' in M. Almagro-Gorbea and Á. Gari Lacruz (eds.), *Sacra saxa: creencias y ritos en peñas sagradas. Actas del Coloquio Internacional celebrado en Huesca del 25 al 27 de noviembre de 2016* (Huesca: Instituto de Estudios Altoaragoneses, 2017), pp. 200–23

Pedrosa, José Manuel, 'Iberia: Moors, *Gentiles* and *Encantadas*' in Simon Young and Davide Ermacora (eds.), *The Exeter Companion to Fairies, Nereids, Trolls and Other Social Supernatural Beings* (University of Exeter Press, 2024), pp. 122–37

Peña Trujillo, Dalia, Olivia Morán Nuñez, Silvia Quezada Camberos, and Edgar Leandro Jiménez, 'Narraciones míticas en México y Panamá: el duende como personaje', *Rassegna iberistica* 39:105 (2016): 29–42

Pinilla, Ramón Mujica, 'Angels and Demons in the Conquest of Peru' in Fernando Cervantes and Andrew Redden (eds.), *Angels, Demons and the New World* (Cambridge University Press, 2013), pp. 171–210

Pisarek, Janin and Schaefer, Florian, 'German-Speaking Europe: *Moosweiblein, Wichtel* and *Nixen*' in Simon Young and Davide Ermacora (eds.), *The Exeter Companion to Fairies, Nereids, Trolls and Other Social Supernatural Beings* (University of Exeter Press, 2024), pp. 155–72

Pitt, Moses, *An Account of One Ann Jefferies* (London: Richard Cumberland, 1696)

Pócs, Éva, *Fairies and Witches at the Boundary of South-Eastern and Central*

Europe (Helsinki: Academia Scientarum Fennica, 1989)

Pócs, Éva, 'Small Gods, Small Demons: Remnants of an Archaic Fairy Cult in Central and South-Eastern Europe' in Michael Ostling (ed.), *Fairies, Demons, and Nature Spirits: 'Small Gods' at the Margins of Christendom* (Basingstoke: Palgrave Macmillan, 2018), pp. 255–76

Pócs, Éva, 'Hungarians: Heavenly and Earthly Fairy Societies' in Simon Young and Davide Ermacora (eds.), *The Exeter Companion to Fairies, Nereids, Trolls and Other Social Supernatural Beings* (University of Exeter Press, 2024), pp. 173–95

Pratchett, Terry, *Lords and Ladies* (London: Transworld, 1993)

Psellus, Michael (trans. Marcus Collisson), *Psellus' Dialogue on the Operation of Daemons* (Sydney: James Tegg, 1843)

Purkiss, Diane, *Troublesome Things: A History of Fairies and Fairy Stories* (London: Allen Lane, 2000)

Purkiss, Diane, *Fairies and Fairy Stories: A History* (Stroud: Tempus, 2007)

Rabalais, Nathan, *Folklore Figures of French and Creole Louisiana* (Baton Rouge: Louisiana State University Press, 2021)

Ralph of Coggeshall (ed. J. Stevenson), *Radulphi de Coggeshall Chronicon Anglicanum* (London: HM Stationery Office, 1875)

Ramos, Maximo D., *Creatures of Philippine Lower Mythology* (Quezon City: University of the Philippines Press, 1971)

Rasmussen, Siv, 'The Protracted Sámi Reformation – or the Protracted Christianising Process' in Lars Ivar Hansen, Rognald Heiseldal Bergesen, and Ingebjørg Hage (eds.), *The Protracted Reformation in Northern Norway: Introductory Studies* (Stamsund: Orkana Akademisk, 2016), pp. 77–95

Raudvere, Catharina, '*Trolldómr* in Early Medieval Scandinavia' in Karen Jolly, Catharina Raudvere, and Edward Peters (eds.), *Witchcraft and Magic in Europe*, vol. III: *The Middle Ages* (London: Athlone, 2002), pp. 75–171

Redden, Andrew, 'Vipers under the Altar Cloths: Satanic and Angelic Forms in Seventeenth-Century New Granada' in Fernando Cervantes and Andrew Redden (eds.), Angels, Demons and the New World (Cambridge University Press, 2013), pp. 146–68

Reed, Annette Yoshiko, *Demons, Angels and Writing in Ancient Judaism* (Cambridge University Press, 2020)

Rieti, Barbara, *Strange Terrain: The Fairy World of Newfoundland* (St John's, NL: ISER Books, 1991)

Rieti, Barbara, '"The Blast" in Newfoundland Fairy Tradition' in Peter Narváez (ed.), *The Good People: New Fairylore Essays* (Lexington: University Press of Kentucky, 1997), pp. 284–97

Rink, Hinrich, *Tales and Traditions of the Eskimo* (Cambridge University Press, 1875)

Rix, Robert W., *The Vanished Settlers of Greenland: In Search of a Legend and Its Legacy* (Cambridge University Press, 2023)

Robbins, Joel, 'Crypto-religion and the Study of Cultural Mixtures: Anthropology, Value, and the Nature of Syncretism', *Journal of the American Academy of Religion* 79:2 (2011): 408–24

Robichaud, Paul, *Pan: The Great God's Modern Return* (London: Reaktion, 2021)

Rodway, Simon, 'The Date and Authorship of *Culhwch ac Olwen*: A Reassessment', *Cambrian Medieval Celtic Studies* 49 (Summer 2005): 21–44

Rojcewicz, Peter M., 'Between One Eye Blink and the Next: Fairies, UFOs, and Problems of Knowledge' in Peter Narváez (ed.), *The Good People: New Fairylore Essays* (Lexington: University Press of Kentucky, 1997), pp. 479–514

Roling, Bernd, 'Our White Ladies on the Graves: Historicisations of Nymphs in Early Modern Antiquarianism' in Karl A. E. Enenkel and Anita Traninger (eds.), *The Figure of the Nymph in Early Modern Culture* (Leiden: Brill, 2018), pp. 442–62

Rose, Herbert Jennings, '*Numen inest*: "Animism" in Greek and Roman Religion', *Harvard Theological Review* 28:4 (1935): 237–57

Ryan, W. F., 'The Witchcraft Hysteria in Early Modern Europe: Was Russia an Exception?', *Slavonic and East European Review* 76:1 (1998): 49–84

Salisbury, Joyce E., *Iberian Popular Religion 600 B.C. to 700 A.D.: Celts, Romans and Visigoths* (New York: Edwin Mellen Press, 1985)

Salve, Kristi, 'Forest Fairies in the Vepsian Folk Tradition' in Mare Kõiva and Kai Vassiljeva (eds.) *Folk Belief Today* (Tartu: Estonian Academy of Sciences, 1995), pp. 413–34

Sawyer, Rose A., *The Medieval Changeling: Health, Childcare, and the Family Unit* (Cambridge: D. S. Brewer, 2023)

Schacker, Jennifer, *Staging Fairyland: Folklore, Children's Entertainment, and Nineteenth-Century Pantomine* (Detroit, MN: Wayne State University Press, 2018)

Schefferus, Johannes, *Lapponia, id est, regionis Lapponum et gentis nova et verissima descriptio* (Frankfurt: Christian Wolff, 1673)

Schmiesing, Ann, *The Brothers Grimm* (New Haven, CT: Yale University Press, 2024)

Seaver, Kirsten A., '"Pygmies" of the Far North', *Journal of World History* 19:1 (2008): 63–87

Scholem, Gershom, *Kabbalah* (New York: Quadrangle, 1974)

Scot, Reginald, *The Discoverie of Witchcraft* (London: William Brome, 1584)

Scott, Walter, *Minstrelsy of the Scottish Border* (Edinburgh: Archibald Constable, 1802), 2 vols.

Scott, Walter, *Letters on Demonology and Witchcraft* (London: John Murray, 1830)

Sébillot, Paul, *Le folk-lore de France* (Paris: E. Guilmoto, 1904–7), 4 vols.

Seifert, Lewis C., *Fairy Tales, Sexuality, and Gender in France, 1690–1715* (Cambridge University Press, 1996)

Shippey, Tom A., 'Light-Elves, Dark-Elves, and Others: Tolkien's Elvish Problem', *Tolkien Studies* 1 (2004): 1–15

Shippey, Tom A., '*Alias oves habeo*: The Elves as a Category Problem' in Tom A. Shippey (ed.), *The Shadow-Walkers: Jacob Grimm's Mythology of the Monstrous* (Turnhout: Brepols, 2005), pp. 157–87

Silver, Carole G., 'On the Origin of Fairies: Victorians, Romantics and Folk Belief', *Browning Institute Studies* 14 (1986): 141–56

Silver, Carole G., *Strange and Secret Peoples: Fairies and Victorian Consciousness* (Oxford University Press, 1998)

Silverblatt, Irene M., *Moon, Sun and Witches: Gender Ideologies and Class in Inca and Colonial Peru* (Princeton University Press, 1987)

Simek, Rudolf, *Dämonen, Teufel, Hexenglaube: Böse Geister in europäischen Mittelalter* (Vienna: Böhlau, 2023)

Simina, Daniela, *Where Fairies Meet: Parallels Between Irish and Romanian Fairy Traditions* (Alresford: Pagan Portals, 2023)

Simpson, Jacqueline, 'On the Ambiguity of Elves [1]', *Folklore* 122:1 (2011): 76–83

Sims-Williams, Patrick, *Irish Influence on Medieval Welsh Literature* (Oxford University Press, 2010)

Skjebred, Ann Helene, 'Rites of Passage as Meeting Place: Christianity and Fairylore in Connection with the Unclean Woman and Unchristened Child' in Peter Narváez (ed.), *The Good People: New Fairylore Essays* (Lexington: University Press of Kentucky, 1997), pp. 215–23

Slimak, Ludovic (trans. Andrew Brown), *The Last Neanderthal: Understanding How Humans Die* (Cambridge: Polity, 2025)

Sloan, John, *Andrew Lang: Writer, Folklorist, Democratic Intellect* (Oxford University Press, 2023)

Smith, J. Z., 'Towards Interpreting Demonic Powers in Hellenistic and Roman Antiquity' in Wolfgang Haase (ed.), *Aufstieg und Niedergang der römischen Welt*, Band 16.1 (Berlin: De Gruyter, 1978), pp. 425–39

Smith, Paul, 'The Cottingley Fairies: The End of a Legend', in Peter Narváez (ed.), *The Good People: New Fairylore Essays* (Lexington: University Press of Kentucky, 1997), pp. 371–405

Smith, Peter Alderson, *W. B. Yeats and the Tribes of Danu: Three Views of Ireland's Fairies* (London: Colin Smythe, 1986)

Sneddon, Andrew, *Witchcraft and Magic in Ireland* (Basingstoke: Palgrave Macmillan, 2015)

Somfai, Anna, 'The Nature of Daemons: A Theological Application of the Concept of Geometrical Proportion in Calcidius' *Commentary* to Plato's *Timaeus* (40D–41A)', *Bulletin of the Institute of Classical Studies* 78 (2003): 129–42

Stanmore, Tabitha, *Love Spells and Lost Treasure: Service Magic in England from the Later Middle Ages to the Early Modern Era* (Cambridge University Press, 2023)

Strieber, Whitley, *Communion: A True Story* (New York: Beech Tree, 1987)

Sugg, Richard, *Fairies: A Dangerous History* (London: Reaktion, 2018)

Sugg, Richard, 'Fairy Magic and the Cottingley Photographs: Yorkshire' in Simon Young and Ceri Houlbrook (eds.), *Magical Folk: British and Irish Fairies 500 AD to the Present* (London: Gibson Square, 2018), pp. 54–64

Sutcliff, Rosemary, 'History and Time', in Fiona M. Collins and Judith Graham (eds.), *Historical Fiction for Children: Capturing the Past* (Routledge: Abingdon, 2012), pp. 109–17

Taagepera, Rein, *The Finno-Ugric Republics and the Russian State* (London: Hurst, 1999)

Thigpen, Paul, *Extraterrestrial Intelligence and the Catholic Faith: Are We Alone in the Universe with God and the Angels* (Gastonia, NC: TAN, 2022)

Thomas of Walsingham (ed. Henry Thomas Riley), *Thomae Walsingham, quondam monachi S. Albani, Historia Anglicana* (London: Longman, Green, Longman, Roberts, and Green, 1863), 2 vols.

Todd, Margo, 'Fairies, Egyptians, and Elders: Multiple Cosmologies in Post-Reformation Scotland' in Bridget Heal and Ole Peter Grell (eds.), *The Impact of the European Reformation: Princes, Clergy and People* (Aldershot: Ashgate, 2008), pp. 189–208

Toivo, Raisa Maria, *Faith and Magic in Early Modern Finland* (Basingstoke: Palgrave MacMillan, 2016)

Tolkien, J. R. R., 'On Fairy-Stories' in *Essays Presented to Charles Williams* (Oxford University Press, 1947), pp. 38–89

Tucker, Steven D., *The Hidden Folk: Are Poltergeists and Fairies Just the Same Thing?* (Bideford: CFZ Press, 2016)

Uljas, Sami, Landborg, Anne, and Müller, Matthias, 'Between the Superpowers: Some Remarks on the Role of Demons in Early Coptic Christianity', *Vigiliae Christianae* 75 (2021): 237–52

Unterman, Alan (ed.), *Dictionary of Jewish Lore and Legend* (London: Thames & Hudson, 1997)

Uttley, Alison (ed. Denis Judd), *The Private Diaries of Alison Uttley* (Barnsley: Pen and Sword, 2009)

Valk, Heiki, 'Christianisation in Estonia: A Process of Dual-Faith and Syncretism' in Martin Carver (ed.), *The Cross Goes North: Processes of Conversion in Northern Europe, AD 300–1300* (Woodbridge: Boydell & Brewer, 2002), pp. 571–9

Valk, Ülo, 'Angels in Estonian Folk Religion' in Ülo Valk (ed.), *Studies in Folklore and Popular Religion*, vol. II (University of Tartu, 1999), pp. 219–38

Valk, Ülo, 'The Guises of Estonian Water-Spirits in Relation to the Plot and Function of Legend' in Patricia Lysaght, Séamas Ó Cathain, and Daithi Ó hÓgain (eds.), *Islanders and Water Dwellers* (Dublin: Eaton, 1999), pp. 337–47

Valk, Ülo, 'The Devil and the Spirit World in Nineteenth-Century Estonia: From Christianization to Folklorization' in Michael Ostling (ed.), *Fairies, Demons, and Nature Spirits: 'Small Gods' at the Margins of Christendom* (Basingstoke: Palgrave Macmillan, 2018), pp. 213–32

Vallée, Jacques, *Passport to Magonia: From Folklore to Flying Saucers*, 2nd edn (Brisbane: Daily Grail, 2014)

Van der Horst, P. C., 'Fatum, Tria Fata; Parca, Tres Parcae', *Mnemosyne* 11 (1943): 217–27

Veenstra, Jan R., 'Paracelsian Spirits in Pope's *Rape of the Lock*', in Jan R. Veenstra and Karin Olsen (eds.), *Airy Nothings: Imagining the Otherworld of Faerie from the Middle Ages to the Age of Reason, Essays in Honour of Alasdair A. MacDonald* (Leiden: Brill, 2013), pp. 213–40

Veenstra, Jan R. and Olsen, Karin, 'Introduction' in Jan R. Veenstra and Karin Olsen (eds.), *Airy Nothings: Imagining the Otherworld of Faerie from the Middle Ages to the Age of Reason, Essays in Honour of Alasdair A. MacDonald* (Leiden: Brill, 2013), pp. vii–xvi

Vėlius, Norbertas, *Mitinės Lietuvių sakmių butybės* (Vilnius: Vaga, 1977)

Vėlius, Norbertas, *Chtoniškasis lietuvių mitologijos pasaulis* (Vilnius: Vaga, 1987)

Vėlius, Norbertas (trans. Birutė Kiškytė), *Lithuanian Mythological Tales* (Vilnius: Vaga, 2002)

Vídalín, Arngrímur, 'The Man Who Seemed Like a Troll: Racism in Old Norse Literature', in Rebecca Merkelbach and Gwendolyne Knight (eds.), *Margins, Monsters, Deviants: Alterities in Old Norse Literature and Culture* (Turnhout: Brepols, 2020), pp. 215–38

Vuković, Krešimir, *Wolves of Rome: The Lupercalia from Roman and Comparative Perspectives* (Berlin: De Gruyter, 2023)

Wade, James, *Fairies in Medieval Romance* (Basingstoke: Palgrave MacMillan, 2011)

Wahlen, Clinton, *Jesus and the Impurity of Spirits in the Synoptic Gospels* (Tübingen: Mohr Siebeck, 2004)

Walsham, Alexandra, *The Reformation of the Landscape: Religion, Identity, and Memory in Early Modern Britain and Ireland* (Oxford University Press, 2011)

Walter Map (ed. M. R. James, C. N. L. Brooke, and R. A. B. Mynors), *Walter Map:* De Nugis Curialium: *Courtiers' Trifles* (Oxford University Press, 1983)

Warburton, Andrew, *New England Fairies: A History of the Little People of the Hills and Forests* (Charleston, SC: The History Press, 2024)

Warner, Marina, *From the Beast to the Blonde: On Fairy Tales and Their Tellers* (London: Vintage, 1994)

Warner, Marina, *Once Upon a Time: A Short History of the Fairy Tale* (Oxford University Press, 2014)

Warner, Marina, *Fairy Tale: A Very Short Introduction* (Oxford University Press, 2018)

Waters, Thomas, *Cursed Britain: A History of Witchcraft and Black Magic in Modern Times* (New Haven, CT: Yale University Press, 2019)

Watkins, Carl, 'Fascination and Anxiety in Medieval Wonder Stories' in

Sophie Page (ed.), *The Unorthodox Imagination in Late Medieval Britain* (Manchester University Press, 2010), pp. 45–64

Watkins-Pitchford, D. J. ('BB'), *A Child Alone: The Memoirs of 'BB'* (London: Michael Joseph, 1978)

Watkins-Pitchford, D. J. ('BB'), *The Little Grey Men*, new edn (Oxford University Press, 2012)

Webster, John, *The Displaying of Supposed Witchcraft* (London: J. M., 1677)

Weeks, Andrew, 'Cosmic and Terrestrial Aliens in the German Renaissance', *Daphnis* 33 (2004): 255–66

Wells, Rosemary, 'The Making of an Icon: The Tooth Fairy in North American Folklore and Popular Culture' in Peter Narváez (ed.), *The Good People: New Fairylore Essays* (Lexington: University Press of Kentucky, 1997), pp. 426–53

White, Martin, *A Midsummer Night's Dream: A Guide to the Text and the Play in Performance* (Basingstoke: Palgrave Macmillan, 2008)

Wilby, Emma, *Cunning Folk and Familiar Spirits: Shamanistic Visionary Traditions in Early Modern British Witchcraft and Magic* (Eastbourne: Sussex Academic Press, 2005)

Wilby, Emma, 'Burchard's *strigae*, the Witches' Sabbath, and Shamanistic Cannibalism in Early Modern Europe', *Magic, Ritual & Witchcraft* 8:1 (2013): 18–49

Wilcox, Helen, 'Shaggie Thighs and Aery Formes: Satyres and Faeries in Ben Jonson's *Oberon*' in Jan R. Veenstra and Karin Olsen (eds.), *Airy Nothings: Imagining the Otherworld of Faerie from the Middle Ages to the Age of Reason, Essays in Honour of Alasdair A. MacDonald* (Leiden: Brill, 2013), pp. 195–212

Willard, T., 'Pimping for the Fairy Queen: Some Cozeners in Shakespeare's England' in A. Classen and C. Scarborough (eds.), *Crime and Punishment in the Middle Ages and Early Modern Age: Mental-Historical Investigations of Basic Human Problems and Social Responses* (Berlin: De Gruyter, 2012), pp. 491–508

Williams, Mark, *Ireland's Immortals: A History of the Gods of Irish Myth* (Princeton University Press, 2016)

Williams, Noel, 'The Semantics of the Word "Fairy": Making Meaning out of Thin Air' in P. Narváez (ed.), *The Good People: New Fairylore Essays* (Lexington: University Press of Kentucky, 1997), pp. 457–78

Wright, Thomas (ed.), *St. Brandan: A Medieval Legend of the Sea* (London: The Percy Society, 1844)

Wright, William A. (ed.), *The Metrical Chronicle of Robert of Gloucester* (London: HM Stationery Office, 1887), vol. I

Young, Francis, *English Catholics and the Supernatural, 1553–1829* (Farnham: Ashgate, 2013)

Young, Francis, *A History of Exorcism in Catholic Christianity* (Basingstoke: Palgrave Macmillan, 2016)

Young, Francis, *Magic as a Political Crime in Medieval and Early Modern England: A History of Sorcery and Treason* (London: I. B. Tauris, 2017)

Young, Francis, *A History of Anglican Exorcism: Deliverance and Demonology in Church Ritual* (London: I. B. Tauris, 2018)

Young, Francis, *Suffolk Fairylore* (Norwich: Lasse Press, 2018)

Young, Francis, *Magic in Merlin's Realm: A History of Occult Politics in Britain* (Cambridge University Press, 2022)

Young, Francis (ed.), *Pagans in the Early Modern Baltic: Sixteenth-Century Accounts of Baltic Paganism* (Leeds: Arc Humanities Press, 2022)

Young, Francis, *Twilight of the Godlings: The Shadowy Origins of Britain's Supernatural Beings* (Cambridge University Press, 2023)

Young, Francis, 'An Earthy History of the British Gnome', *Hellebore* 13 (Beltane 2025): 42–53

Young, Francis, *Silence of the Gods: The Untold History of Europe's Last Pagan Peoples* (Cambridge University Press, 2025)

Young, Francis and Kubiliūtė, Saulė, 'The Balts: *Laumės* and *Laimės*', in Simon Young and Davide Ermacora (eds.), *The Exeter Companion to Fairies, Nereids, Trolls and Other Social Supernatural Beings: European Traditions* (University of Exeter Press, 2024), pp. 233–42

Young, Simon, 'A History of the Fairy Investigation Society, 1927–1960', *Folklore* 124:2 (2013), 139–56

Young, Simon, 'Fairy Bread and Fairy Squalls: Atlantic Canada' in Simon Young and Ceri Houlbrook (eds.), *Magical Folk: British and Irish Fairies 500 AD to the Present* (London: Gibson Square, 2018), pp. 210–22

Young, Simon, 'When Did Fairies Get Wings?' in D. Caterine and J. W. Morehead (eds.), *The Paranormal and Popular Culture: A Postmodern Religious Landscape* (London: Routledge, 2019), pp. 253–74

Young, Simon, 'Fairy Ain't What It Used to Be: Traditional vs Contemporary Fairies' in J. Hunter (ed.), *Deep Weird: The Varieties of High Strangeness Experience* (n.p.: August Night Press, 2023), pp. 189–210

Young, Simon (ed.), *The Wollaton Gnomes: A Nottingham Fairy Mystery* (Siena: Pwca Books and Pamphlets, 2023)
Young, Simon, 'Elsie, Frances and the Beck: The Artist, the Mystic and the Cottingley Fairies' in Simon Young (ed.), *The Cottingley Fairy Photographs: New Approaches to Fairies, Fakes and Folklore* (Siena: Pwca Books and Pamphlets, 2024), pp. 50–73
Young, Simon and Ermacora, Davide, 'Introducing the Social Supernatural' in Simon Young and Davide Ermacora (eds.), *The Exeter Companion to Fairies, Nereids, Trolls and Other Social Supernatural Beings: European Traditions* (University of Exeter Press, 2024), pp. 1–17

Unpublished PhD theses

Forment, Bruno, '*La terra, il cielo e l'inferno*: The Representation and Reception of Greco-Roman Mythology in Opera Seria' (University of Ghent, 2006–7)
Hogan, Samuel Gillis, 'Communing with Nature: Fairies in English Ritual Magic and Occult Philosophy, 1400–1700' (University of Exeter, 2023)
Sawyer, Rose A., 'Child Substitution: A New Approach to the Changeling Motif in Medieval European Culture' (University of Leeds, 2018)

Online sources

Baines, Dan, 'The Derbyshire Mummified Fairy', danbaines.com/derbyshire-mummified-fairy
Fimi, Dmitra, 'Tolkien and the Fairies: Faith and Folklore' (paper delivered at Oxenmoot 2010), dimitrafimi.org/2023/12/06/tolkien-and-the-fairies-faith-and-folklore
Hart, David Bentley, 'God, Gods, and Fairies', *First Things*, 1 June 2013, firstthings.com/god-gods-and-fairies
Hickey-Hall, J., *Modern Fairy Sightings* podcast (2000), scarlettofthefae.com/category/the-modern-fairy-sightings-podcast
Prideaux, Ed, 'Glitchcraft: The Tale of Leilan and Peter Todd', *Ecstatic Integration*, 21 January 2025, ecstaticintegration.org/p/glitchcraft-the-tale-of-leilan-and
Saunders, Erwin (YouTube channel), youtube.com/@erwinsaunders/videos
The Schools Collection, duchas.ie/en/cbes/schools
Vickers, Salley, 'Why We Need Fairies: Our Perception of the World Has Lost All Wonder', *Unherd*, 21 June 2022, unherd.com/2022/06/why-we-need-fairies

Young, Francis, 'How Santa Came to Recruit His Elves', *Spectator*, 24 December 2024, spectator.co.uk/article/how-santa-came-to-recruit-his-elves

Young, Simon (ed.), *Fairy Census 2014–2017*, pp. 368–79, fairyist.com/wp-content/uploads/2014/10/The-Fairy-Census-2014-2017-1.pdf

Young, Simon (ed.), *Fairy Census 2: 2017–2023*, pp. 293–5, fairyist.com/wp-content/uploads/2023/12/Fairy-Census2FINAL.pdf

Index

Page numbers in bold type indicate an illustration.

aaskouandy, 194
Aberfoyle, Scotland, 174, 176
Aberystruth, Wales, 169, 170
Abigar (fairy), 192
Aboriginal Australians, 202, 203
Acadia, 193, 196
Adam, 58–60, 74, 81, 127, 214
Africa, 8, 185, 204
Agobard of Lyons, 252
Agricola, Georgius, 156
Agrippa, Cornelius, 175
Ahura Mazda (Persian deity), 42
aitvaras (Lithuanian spirit), 234
Albert the Great, 84
Albigensian Crusades, 110
alchemy, 128, 156
Alcinous, 155
Alcott, Louisa M., 199
Alexander the Great, 103
Alexandria, Egypt, 78
álfar, *see* elves
Algarotti, Francisco, 181
Allatius, Leo, 146, 151
Álvarez, Bartolomé, 190
älvkvarnar (elf-mills), 115
Ambrose of Milan, 265
ancestors, fairies as, 39, 45–8, 92, 190, 191
Andersen, Hans Christian, 230, 231
Anderson, Allan, 137
angelization, 66, 94
angelology, 56, 62, 63, 110
angels, 4, 5, 7, 18, 20, 25, 53, 55–6, 57, 63, 64–5, 94, 104, 112, 114, 125, 128, 129, 130, 157, 165, 166, 169, 181, 209, 220, 231, 255, 259, 260, 262, 268, 269
  apocryphal, 191–2
  evil, 56
  fallen, 55, 58–9, 60, 61–2, 65, 67, 68, 69, 75, 76, 79, 109–10, 128, 139, 157, 171, 176, 214
  'folk', 137
  guardian, 65, 149, 177, 191
  neutral, 69, 75, 80, 94–9, 107, 110, 115, 127, 170, 189, 270
Anglo-Saxon England, 82, 83, 92, 93, 115, 127
animals, fairy, 35, 37, 52, 60, 91, 135, 196, 246, 254, 264, *see also* therianthropy
animism, 10, 18, 25, 28–9, 30–3, 35, 36, 37, 39, 41–2, 45, 50, 51, 88, 101, 109, 139, 152
  neo-animism, 261–2, 265
Annwn (Welsh underworld), 106, 107, 119
Anthony of the Desert, 66, 78–9
anthropology, 4, 5, 9, 29, 30, 31, 32, 33, 35, 199, 200, 226, 255, 263
anthropomorphism, 28–9, 32, 36, 40, 70
anti-Catholicism, 143, 149, 163, 217
anti-Sadducism, 160–1, 261, 270
'Anti-Scot' (author), 169, 175
antipodes, 82, 202

INDEX

antiquarians, 26, 30, 132, 146, 149, 150, 151, 162, 182, 197, 210, 212–13
aōrai (Greek spirits), 151
aos sí (Irish spirits), 2, 11, 37, 52, 71–5, 83, 93, 125–6, 189
apes (orangutan), 91, 164, 173, 174, 226, 254, 264
apocrypha, 54, *see also* pseudepigrapha
Apuleius, 43
archaeology, 30, 35, 38, 39, 44, 47, 218, 235
archetypes, 2, 88, 253, 266
Árnason, Jón, 127
art, fairies in, 23, 26, 34, 153–4, 162, 177, 206, 208, 210, 226, 239
Arthur, king, 119, 124, 129, 137
Artificial Intelligence, 247, 265
Aquinas, Thomas, 110
Aristotelianism, 110
Asherah (Canaanite deity), 54, 70
Asia, 185, 192
atheism, 13, 160, 161, 262
Athena (Greek deity), 42
Atkins, William, 145
aua (Inuit spirit), 188
Aubrey, John, 26, 150, 167, 174, 197–8
Augustine of Hippo, 44, 64–5, 81–2, 89–90, 102, 109
Aurivillius, Carl, 164
Australasia, 9, 185, 201–3, 270
Australia, 32, 185, 201–2, 203, 204
Avesta, 42

Babylon, 54, 60
Bacchus (Roman deity), 39, 46
Bali, Indonesia, 39
Balkans, the, 102, 136, 146, 152, 247
Balkin (fairy king), 214
Ballyshannon, Ireland, 117
banshees, 198
Barra, isle of, 214
Barrett, Francis, 209
Barrie, J. M., 13, 22, 204, 206, 257

barrows, 48, 135
Baxter, Richard, 175
Beaumont, John, 168–9, 176
beauty, fairy, 21, 37, 44, 68, 71, 83, 84–5, 87, 89, 92, 107, 111, 114, 115, 151, 188–9
Beck, Richard, 260
Bedford, Arthur, 166
Bekker, Balthasar, 26, 166
Benwell, Northumbria, 44
Beothuk people, 200
Berkeley, USA, 255
berserkers, 36
bestiaries, 80
Bible, the, 18, 25, 54–6, 58, 60, 73–4, 81, 82, 88, 98, 108, 134–5, 145, 160, 164, 165, 166, 170, 175, 196, 198, 223, 224
Bigfoot, 254
birds, 73, 75, 94–5, 156
Birds, Isle of, 97, 189
Björnsson, Þorsteinn, 172
Black Death, the, 134
Blake, William, 177, 209
blast, fairy, 137, 200, 201, 252
Blefkenius, Dietmar, 187–8
Blount, Charles, 164
Bodmin, England, 159
bogeys, 8, 43–4, 111, 112
boggarts, 211
Böhme, Jakob, 176
bohpoli (Choctaw spirits), 196
bohyni (East Slavic spirits), 9, 37, 45
Boisman, Henrik, 145
Boney, Perry, 199
Bord, Janet, 243
Bordelon, Laurent, 164
Borri, Gioseppe, 180
Boulton, Richard, 168
Bourne, Henry, 182
Boyle, Robert, 159, 174, 176
Boyman, Jonet, 137
Bradford, William, 197

Bran, 74
Bray, Eliza, 213, 215
Brébeuf, Jean de, 194
Briggs, Katharine, 5, 11, 45, 114, 123, 225, 231–3, 234, 237, 259
Britain, Battle of, 235
Brittany, 89, 91, 104, 119, 196, 218
Britten, Emma Hardinge, 223
Bromyard, John, 111
Browne, Thomas, 174
brownies, 2, 13, 142, 147
Brucker, Jacob, 177
Buckingham, duke of, 169
Budapest, Hungary, 224
Bullein, William, 142
bunyip (Australian cryptid), 204
Burchard of Worms, 100–2, 103, 108–9, 129
Burnet, Gilbert, bishop of Salisbury, 160
Burton, Robert, 150, 164

Caenchomrac, 52
Caesarius of Heisterbach, 98–9
Cain, 81–2, 92
Calcidius, 43, 61
Calmet, Antoine Augustin, 171–2
Calvinism, 136, 170, 214
Cambry, Jacques, 212
Camden, William, 157
Campton, USA, 198
Canary Islands, 50, 119, 189
cannibalism, 44, 50
Cannock Chase, England, 145
Cardano, Girolamo, 175
Carmichael, Alexander, 214
Cascorach, 74
Cauchon, Pierre, 112
Cavendish, Margaret, 168
caves, 34, 36, 41, 210, 211, 212, 257
Celtiberians, 40
Celtic revival, 208, 215
Census, Fairy, 202, 243–6

centaurs, 39, 78–9, 144
changelings, 8, 21, 104, 121, 122–3, 135, 141, 143, 144, 170, 183, 201, 217, 247
chaniques (Mexican spirits), 189, 192
Chaucer, Geoffrey, 115, 120, 124–5, 165, 210, 270
Cherington, Anne, 145
Chesterton, G. K., 258–9, 260, 261
child-stealing, 89, 104, 116, 122–3, 152, 192
childhood, 3, 144, 203, 225, 226, 239, 244, 250, 266, 271
Children of Lir, the, 117, 125
Chios (Greece), 151
Chrétien de Troyes, 95
Christmas elves, 240
Christsonday (spirit), 137–8
chud (Komi spirits), 206
Church Fathers, 25, 53, 54, 64, 65, 75, 76, 102, 107, 108, 109, 261
Christianity, 6, 18–21, 25, 26, 27, 43, 45, 52, 53, 54, 56, 59, 61, 62, 63, 70–1, 73, 74, 75, 76, 77, 80, 81, 107–8, 109, 112, 123, 137, 145, 167, 170, 191, 205, 206, 214, 250, 257–60
early, 64–9
popular, 19, 20, 66, 69, 108, 125, 193, 220, 269
Christianization, 19–20, 25, 33, 36, 49, 53, 54, 63, 67, 71, 111, 112, 115, 125, 127, 146, 192, 217, 220
Cihuacóatl (Mexica deity), 192
Circe, 115
Civil War, English, 159–60
Cladh Hallan mummies, 47
classicizing, 26, 115, 119, 132, 133, 148–54, 155, 158, 164, 176, 179
Clavus, Claudius, 187
Cleary, Bridget, 217
Cleland, William, 142
Clement of Alexandria, 63, 65, 69
clergy, 20, 26, 109, 125, 141, 167–8, 172, 194, 217

INDEX

Clerk, Agnes, 123, 129
Clodd, Edward, 212
Clonmacnoise, Ireland, 52
clurichauns, 83
Collen, St, 106
colonialism, 9, 184, 201, 211
    settler-colonialism, 12, 185, 204, 270
commercialization, 90, 235, 240–3
consciousness, 3, 15, 29, 50, 169, 254, 255, 260, 264, 265, 269
conversion, 69–70, 71, 108, 193
Cook, James, 201
coraniaid, 84
Corbet, Richard, 141
Cornwall, 156, 159, 215, 218
corporeality, fairy, 15, 58, 65, 80, 112, 140, 173
cosmologies, 14, 18, 19, 20, 31, 53–6, 61, 62, 63, 66, 67, 76, 93, 95, 105, 167, 174, 185, 206, 224, 233, 257, 261, 268, 269
Cottingley fairies, 13, 27, 204, 206, 208, 220–6, 228, 234–5, 237, 239, 241, 249, 259
Counter-Reformation, 132, 145, 147, 158
Craufurd, Quentin, 235–6
credulity, revolution of, 134, 158, 163
Cree people, 193, 195
Croatia, 76, 146
Croker, Thomas Crofton, 212
Crombie, Robert Ogilvie, 248–9
crop circles, 253
cryptids, 204, 245, 254
cryptozoology, 254
Cú Chulainn, 73
Cyril of Alexandria, 65

daemons (*daimōnia*), 42–3, 61–2, 65–8, 97, 115, 150, 155, 175, 176–7, 209, 261
daevas (Persian spirits), 42
Dagworth, England, 121
Damick, Andrew Stephen, 260, 261

dancing, 8, 46–7, 76, 80, 89, 115, 116, 124, 131, 132, 140, 141, 142, 151, 153, 168, 169, 170
Daniel, Edmund, 170
Dante Alighieri, 55, 96, 118, 170, 171
Darwin, Charles, 80, 211, 227
D'Aulnoy, Marie-Catherine, 180
Deae Matres (Gaulish spirits), 100
deism, 168
degradation, 19, 112, 126, 146, 216
demonization, 26, 45, 50, 66, 73, 74, 75, 99, 100, 105, 106, 108–9, 111–12, 113–14, 117, 124, 130, 132, 138, 140, 142, 147, 148, 149, 158, 162, 173, 190, 206, 219, 248
demonology, 5, 21, 43, 50, 51, 56, 58, 60, 61, 62, 63, 64, 66–7, 69, 76, 99, 110, 134, 136, 138, 140, 144, 163, 164, 165, 172, 175, 180, 181, 251, 260
    'folk', 20
demons, 4, 5, 7, 11, 15, 18, 20, 44, 53, 55–6, 57, 59, 60, 61–4, 65, 66–7, 69, 70, 73, 76, 79, 96, 97, 101, 106, 108–9, 111, 112, 114, 128, 129, 131, 133, 134, 139, 140, 150, 157, 158, 165–6, 168, 169, 171, 173, 181, 191, 194, 245, 258, 260, 269
    helpful, 80, 95, 98–9, 107, 110
Denmark, 28, 98, 187
departure of the fairies, theme of, 107, 123–7, 141, 257, 266, 270–1
Derry, USA, 198–9
Descartes, René, 166
Devil, the, *see* Satan
Devon, England, 183, 215
diabolism, 134, 194
Diana (Roman deity), 103, 136, 253
Díaz, Bernal, 189
Dierpmis (Sámi deity), 28
diffusionism, 9
digitization, 247
Dionysus (Greek deity), 39, 47

disenchantment, 26, 262, 264
Disney, Walt, 236
Disney (corporation), 1, 203, 204, 240
divination, 13, 28, 49, 57, 136, 189
DMT (psychedelic), 255–7, 266
dogheaded men (*cynocephali*), 79
dolphins, 91, 264
domestic spirits, 1, 21, 39, 47–8, 121–2, 146, 147–8, 172, 188, 209, 247
Domrémy, France, 98, 112–14
Donegal, Ireland, 243
doubles, fairies as, 37–8, 156
Dowding, Hugh, 235
Doyle, Arthur Conan, 13–14, 27, 221, 222–6, 234–5, 243, 254, 270
Doyle, Richard, 222–3
dracs (French spirits), 91
dragons, 18, 91
drama, fairies in, 22, 26, 48, 143, 152, 154, 162, 177, 208, 240
Drayton, Michael, 230
dreams, 15, 73, 147, 163, 189, 194, 196, 262
Dreher, Rod, 260, 261
druids, 73, 210
Dryden, John, 169
dualism, demonological, 55, 62, 65, 66–7, 68, 76, 269
duendes (Hispanic spirits), 48, 103, 184, 188, 191, 192–3, 258
Dunlop, Bessie, 137
Dunvegan, Fairy Flag of, 235
dusii, 64, 150
duwendes (Filipino spirits), 192
dwarfs, 2, 48, 83, 87, 89, 90, 92, 125, 126, 128, 144, 188, 209, 210, 260

ears, pointed, 35
eco-protesters, 249
ecology, 27, 31, 32, 248, 262, 263
Edinburgh, Scotland, 137, 210, 248
Egypt, 55, 78
Einarsson, Guðmundur, 140

Einarsson, Oddur, bishop of Skálholt, 139
Elchyell (fairy queen), 128
elementals, 150, 155–8, 223, 227, 231, 249
elfshot, 50, 86, 167, 175, 195, 200
Elidyr, story of, 22, 83, 85–6, 87, 118, 173, 271
Elizabeth I, queen of England, 141, 142, 152
Elrond (character), 35
Elspeth (fairy queen), 137
elves, 2, 8, 21, 35, 37, 52, 71, 82, 83, 87, 91–4, 97–8, 104, 115–16, 118, 121, 122–3, 124, 127, 131–2, 138, 139–40, 144, 147, 149, 151, 153, 172–3, 216–17, 240, 241, 242, 248, 260, *see also* Christmas elves; machine elves
literary, 22, 229, 231, 259
Emancipation, Catholic (1829), 217
enchantment, 3, 21, 22, 26, 42, 49, 84, 85, 103, 107, 114, 128, 133, 189, 190, 229, 245, 248, 264, 267, 271, *see also* disenchantment; re-enchantment
England, 3, 9, 11, 82, 83, 87, 88, 90–3, 113, 122, 125, 127, 135, 136, 142, 144, 145, 156, 159, 161, 166, 174, 181, 182, 200, 202, 212, 216, 224, 234, 239
Enikel, Jansen, 96
Enlightenment, the, 5, 17, 26, 109, 144, 158, 160–2, 163, 165, 167, 168, 172, 173, 174, 175, 176–7, 178, 180, 182, 206, 208, 209, 250, 270
Ephialtes, 151
Erlkönig (fairy king), 209
Erszike (healer), 242–3
'Erwin Saunders', 226
Estonia, 1–2, 20, 35, 36, 88, 146, 147, 148, 214, 219–20
Étienne de Bourbon, 123
Ethiopia, 80
ethnography, 35, 131, 132, 146, 188, 202, 206, 218, 226

'eucatastrophe', 230
euhemerism, 25, 66, 72, 117, 173, 203, 210–11
euphemism, 4, 44
Eusebius, 66
Evans-Wentz, Walter, 29, 217–19, 243, 253, 255, 256
Evesham, England, 113
exorcism, 1, 42, 55, 61, 128, 145, 147–8, 167, 261
exotika (Greek spirits), 151
extinction, 16

Fair One of the Mountains, the, 68
fairies, definitions of, 3–9
Fairy Investigation Society (FIS), 27, 234–7, 243, 271
fairy tales, 13, 16, 21, 22, 23, 34, 37, 104, 118, 123, 134, 141, 178, 210, 211, 226, 230–2, 233, 236, 247, 255, 259
fairyland, *see* otherworlds, fairy
'fakelore', 241, 242
familiars, 37, 168, 135, 171, 209
fandoms, 230, 249
fantasy literature, 23, 93, 118, 228, 229–30, 239, 249
Farmer, Tessa, 226
'fatedness', 103
Fates, the, *see* Parcae (Roman deities)
Fátima, Portugal, 224
fauns, 15, 35, 39, 64–5, 66, 78–9, 80, 82, 84, 104, 109, 110, 118, 123, 132, 144, 149–53, 166, 181, 248
Faunus (Roman deity), 39, 64, 150
Fergus (hero), 84, 89
fief of hell, fairyland as, 121
Fielding, Fidelia, 200
Findhorn, Scotland, 248–9
Finland, 145, 205, 231
Finno-Ugric peoples, 1, 139, 205
First World War, 206, 224
Fison, Anna, 212
Flood, the, 57, 58, 81, 189

Flora (Roman deity), 197
flower fairies, 23, 202, 206, 227, 228, 234, 241
Folklore Commission, National (Ireland), 219
Folklore Society, the (UK), 237
'folkloresque', 215
follets (French spirits), 91, 122, 148, *see also* poltergeists
feu follets, 193
Fomorians, 82
food, fairy, 21, 107, 157, 159
forests, 8, 9, 21, 31–2, 35, 48, 50, 75, 88, 89, 112, 123, 128, 139, 147, 151, 187, 199, 205–6, 214, 242
Forman, Simon, 48
Forteana, 263
fossils, 8, 17
Fourth Lateran Council (1215), 110
Fowler, Edward, bishop of Gloucester, 159–60, 163
France, 88, 91, 98, 107, 117, 122, 132, 178, 179, 200
Francis of Assisi, 261
friars, 117, 123, 124, 125, 143, 190, 191, 261
functionalism, 17, 123, 247
funerals, fairy, 169, 209
fungi, 8, 257
fur trade, 193, 195
Fuseli, Henry, **120**, 177, 178, **179**

Galicia, Spain, 20, 40, 70, 121
Gardner, Edward, 221, 223–4, 227
Gardner, Gerald, 248, 249
Garner, Alan, 93
Gasca, Beatriz de la, 191
genii (Roman spirits), 39, 149, 150, 151, 168, 171, 209
gentiles (Iberian spirits), 140, 189, 191
Gervase of Tilbury, 90, 91, 99, 122
ghosts, 7, 13, 14, 18, 28, 33, 45, 50, 130, 148, 150, 161, 163, 164, 192, 196, 239, 245, 268

giants, 18, 57, 60, 76, 77, 81, 82, 83, 87, 109, 140, 144, 147, 189, 191, 276 n.20
Gibbs, Cecelia May, 202
glamour, fairy, 21, 107, 183, 189, 241, 245
Glanvill, Joseph, 161, 182
Glastonbury Tor, England, 106
gnomes, 2, 155–6, 171, 180, 181, 226, 231, 235, 242, 248, 255
  garden gnomes, 240
Gnosticism, 65, 69
goblins, 13, 48, 140, 163, 164, 166, 184, 211, 253, 255, 266
Goethe, Johann Wolfgang von, 209
gonks, 240
Gothicism, 209
Gowdie, Isobel, 9, 138
Granada, Spain, 140
granaries, 1, 2, 70
green (colour), 83, 116, 142, 157, 159, 220, 227
Greenland, 185, 186–8
Gregory Nazianzen, 65
Grendel, 82
Grey, George, 202
Greystoke, Lord, 83
Griffiths, David, 195
Griffiths, Frances, 220–2, 224, 226, 234, 257
Grimm, Jacob, 211, 212, 216, 219
Grimm, Wilhelm, 211, 212, 216, 219
grimoires, 128, 129, 162, 209
Guadalajara, Mexico, 192
Guinefort, St, 123
Guðmundsson, Einar, 172
Guðmundsson, Jón, 127
Gumnut Babies, 202
Gwyn ap Nudd (fairy king), 106–7, 119

Hacka (troll queen), 121
hags, 48, 49, 102, 111, 142, 144

Hallowe'en, 21, 146
hallucinogens, 246, 255
Ham (son of Noah), 81, 82
Harrisville, USA, 198
Hart, David Bentley, 259, 261
Hartmann, Hans, 219
healing, 46, 87, 112, 115, 123, 129, 137, 159, 242–3
heaven, 51, 53, 55, 56, 58, 75, 94–9, 138, 171, 184, 191, 214, 228, 229, 253
Heindel, Max, 227
Hekla, Mount (Iceland), 140, 214
hell, 14, 51, 53, 55, 57, 67, 96, 99, 106, 109, 119, 121, 139, 140, 144, 170–1, 184, 228
Hellenistic culture, 42, 43, 55, 56, 97, 115, 155, 176
Hendrick, Richard, 261
Henryson, Robert, 126
Hereford, England, 87
heresy, 65, 69, 95, 184
Herla, king, 84, 118
Herodotus, 82
heroes, 38, 57, 84, 89, 90, 195, 215, 232
Herrick, Robert, 142
Hesiod, 42
Hickey-Hall, Jo, 245, 261
hierarchy, 2, 5, 21, 31, 39, 42, 61, 68, 70, 93, 105, 107, 118–21, 259, 268
Hildur (elf queen), 121
hills, 8, 21, 42, 52, 74, 106, 107, 116, 136–9, 145, 150, 172, 176, 211, 219, 251, 257
Hitler, Adolf, 219
Hobbes, Thomas, 160, 163, 164
hobgoblins, 144, 166, 209
Hogg, James, 214
Hollingsworth, Arthur, 212, 213
Homer, 42, 84
homunculi, 156
Hooke, Robert, 159, 160
Hoole, Charles, 149–50
Hopkins, Matthew, 135

INDEX

horses, 17, 83, 84, 85, 90, 106, 137, 196, 198, 201, 225
Hotham, Durant, 176
Houma people, 196–7
household spirits, *see* domestic spirits
huacas (Incan spirits), 190
huldufólk (Icelandic spirits), 127, 140, *see also* elves
Hungary, 11, 37–8, 102, 121, 136, 156, 182, 242–3, 253, 255, 270
hunting, 31, 242
  hunter-gatherers, 33, 35
Hupel, August Wilhelm, 147
Huron people, 194–5
hybridity, 34, 38, 57, 58, 59–60, 80, 81, 91, 96, 114, 173
Hyde, Douglas, 219

iaras (Brazilian spirits), 192
Iberia, 48, 70, 140, 180, 185, 188, 191–3, 258, 270, *see also* Portugal; Spain
Iblis, 68–9
Iceland, 8, 21, 37, 52, 71, 92–4, 127, 139–40, 172, 173, 174, 187, 201, 214, 216–17, 241–2, 247
idolatry, 70, 145, 149, 177, 195
iele (Romanian spirit), 92
illness, 8, 87, 92, 159, 198, 242
immortality, fairy, 40, 43, 71, 103, 110, 128
immrama, 73, 94, 189
Incans, 190
incest, 47
incubi, 64, 78, 97, 102, 110, 111, 144
India, 185, 187, 190
Indigenous people, 16, 27, 184–8, 190–1, 192–5, 196, 197, 199, 200, 201, 202, 203–4, 225, 241, 258, 263
ingnersuit (Inuit spirits), 188
Inquisition, the, 180, 184, 190, 191
international fairies, *see* 'SWFs' (small winged fairies)
interpretatio Romana, 152

inugagulligait (Inuit spirits), 196
Inuit people, 29, 187, 188, 195, 196
invisibility, 4, 21, 31, 43, 58, 59, 90, 121–2, 127, 139, 140, 155, 157, 173, 205, 222, 231, 247
Iona, Scotland, 248
Ireland, 2, 4, 6, 8, 11, 12, 25, 27, 36, 38, 47, 49, 52, 53, 69–75, 76, 82, 83, 86, 88, 89, 91, 92, 95, 107, 117, 121, 122, 123, 125–6, 132, 135, 136, 140, 146, 157, 167–8, 173, 178, 198, 200, 201, 204, 207, 208, 212, 213, 215, 217, 218–19, 233, 235, 236, 240, 241, 261, 270
Iroquois people, 194
Isidore of Seville, 44, 66, 68, 84, 86, 119, 187
Islam, 8, 14, 20, 25, 52, 54, 68–9, 76, 185, 259
Iubdan (fairy king), 84, 85, 87, 118
Ívaldr (elf), 187

James VI and I, king of Scots / king of England, 136, 141, 144
Jeffries, Ann, 159–60
Jerome, 58, 60, 78–9, 82
Jerusalem, 54, 99
Jesuits, 143, 145, 147–8, 165, 166, 193–4, 195
Jews, fairies as, 143
Jinn (Islamic spirits), 8, 14, 20, 68–9, 76, 185, 259
Joan of Arc, 98, 112–14
John de Tregoz, 87
John of Salisbury, 102
Johnsdochter, Katherine, 138
Johnson, Marjorie Thelma, 236–7, 243, 246
Jones, David, 195
Jones, Edmund, 22, 26, 169–71, 235
Jones, Inigo, 153
Jonson, Ben, 151
Jordanes, 92

INDEX

Judaism, 25, 43, 52, 53, 54–60, 61, 63, 67, 76, 127, 161, 176–7
    Hellenistic, 54, 56, 61, 62, 63
Julius Caesar, 128
Juovlagázzi (Christmas men) (Sámi spirits), 28
Jupiter (Roman deity), 149
Justin Martyr, 65

Karaites, 53
Karksi, Estonia, 1
Keats, John, 209
Keightley, Thomas, 211–12
Kelly-Hopkinsville 'goblins', 253
kelpies (Scottish spirits), 90
Kennedy, John F., 198
Killeaden, Ireland, 234
Kimmeridge, England, 49
King, Fairy, 21, 84, 85, 87, 106–7, 115, 118–21, 126, 128, 138, 143, 148, 168, 190
kintji (Aboriginal Australian spirits), 202, 203
Kircher, Athanasius, 166
Kirk, Robert, 26, 140, 174–6, 180, 210
knockers (Cornish spirits), 156
Knox, John, 142
kobolds (Germanic spirits), 48, 210
Komi people, 130, 206, 242
Kokko, Yrjö, 231
Kunz, Dora van Gelder, 199

La Llorona (Latin American spirit), 189, 192–3
Labrador, Canada, 201
Laimės (Baltic spirits), 100
lakes, 8, 52, 80, 89, 91, 116, 198–9
Lamia (Greek spirit), 43–5, 50, 58, 89, 102, 104, 149
landvættir (Norse spirits), 40, 93
Lang, Andrew, 226–7
lares (Roman spirits), 39, 47, 150, 151
LARPing, 249, 260

Latin America, 26, 185, 188–93
Latvia, 36, 146
laumės (Baltic spirits), 9, 49–50, 83, 104, 111, 219, 234
Lavenham, England, 122
Le Jeune, Paul, 194
Lenihan, Eddie, 83, 243
leprechauns, 2, 82, 83, 85, 86, 88, 89–90, 118, 125, 126, 199, 202, 240
Lewis, C. S., 14, 27, 228–9, 232, 237, 258, 261, 268
Lewis, Meriwether, 195
LGBTQ+, 249
Lhuyd, Edward, 167
Lilith (Jewish spirit), 45, 58–60, 76, 77, 129
Linnaeus, Carl, 183
literature, 2, 11, 22–3, 26, 28, 40, 70, 71, 72–3, 74, 87, 105, 107, 114–18, 119, 125, 126, 129, 141, 148, 152, 157, 162, 165, 177, 179, 180, 189, 204, 206, 207, 209, 215, 216, 218, 227, 232, 242
    children's, 16, 202, 230, 241
    fantasy, 228–9, 230, 239
Lilly, William, 166
Lithuania, 9, 22, 36, 49, 104, 146, 147, 219, 234
ljúflingar (Icelandic spirits), 140
Llangynwyd Fawr, Wales, 170
Llyn y Fan Fach, Wales, 195
longaevi, 80–1, 228, 232
Lough Ree, Ireland, 52
Louis XIV, king of France, 178
Louisiana, 193, 196, 242
Louth, Ireland, 52
Lucifer, *see* Satan
luck, 19, 147, 201
Lupa (Loba) (fairy queen), 121
Lutheranism, 28, 131, 139, 145, 147, 177
lutins (francophone spirits), 88, 90–1, 193, 196, 201
lycanthropy, *see* werewolves

INDEX

maa-alused (Estonian spirits), 147
Mac Manus, Dermot, 83, 233–4, 243
Machen, Arthur, 211, 225, 259
machine elves, 254–7, 266
McKenna, Terence, 255–6, 266
MacRitchie, David, 211
Madagascar, 195
Maddarakka (Sámi deity), 28
magic, 7, 37, 38, 41, 47, 49, 57, 67, 68, 80, 84, 114, 124, 134, 146, 161, 171, 209, 228, 249, 252, 267
    ritual (fairy conjuring), 23, 26, 96, 105, 107, 111, 116, 127–30, 135, 136, 137, 156–8, 166, 168, 242–3
Magnússon, Ari, 140
Magonians, 252, 253
Maine, USA, 196, 197, 199
Malabron (fairy), 90
Malekin (fairy), 121–2, 182
Man, Andro, 137–8
Man, Isle of, 183, 218
Manannán mac Lir (Irish deity), 74–5, 112, 117–18, 126
Mandeville, John, 87
manitou (Native American spiritual concept), 194
Māori people, 202–3
Map, Walter, 84, 105, 118
Marblehead, USA, 198
Mari people, 139
Martianus Capella, 80–1, 228
Martin, Martin, 176
Martin of Braga, 70
Martínez, Miguel, 184
Marx, Karl, 234
Mary, Virgin, 28, 112, 191
Mary I, queen of England, 141–2
masques, 151, 152, 153, 162
Maximus of Turin, 70
May Day, 146, 197
maypoles, 197
mecan izhandaizhed (Vepsian spirits), 205

Medea, 115
medicalization, 166, 169
mekumwasuck (Passamaquoddy spirits), 199
Melusine (French spirit), 102
memeguayiwahk (Cree spirits), 193, 195, 203
memorates, 22
mental illness, 173
Merlin, 114, 119, 228
mermaids, 156, 166
Merrymount colony (Quincy, USA), 197
Mesopotamia, 10, 42, 55, 56, 60
mestizos, 191
Métis people, 195
Mexico, 189, 258
midwives, 21, 255
mikumweswak (Penobscot spirits), 199
Milton, John, 142, 181
miniaturization, 126–7
mining, 156, 171, 210
Minucius Felix, 65
Mississippi River, 185, 193
Mohegan people, 200
Moirai (Greek spirits), 100
Mompesson, John, 182
monolatry, 54
monotheism, 51, 52–3, 54–5, 56, 62, 63, 69, 70
    inclusive, 74, 76, 260, 269
monsters, 15, 78, 80–2, 89, 90–1, 92, 112, *see also* races, monstrous
Moomintrolls, 240
Moors, 140
morality, fairies' relationship with, 5, 18, 44, 53, 62, 67, 95, 109, 111, 157, 177, 206
More, Henry, 175
Morehouse, Lancelot, 150
Morgan Le Fay, 22, 115, 119
Mormo (Greek spirit), 43
Morton, Thomas, 197

334

Mother Earth, 19, 111
mouras encantadas (Portuguese/
 Brazilian spirits), 192–3
Muirchú moccu Machtheni, 73
Müller, Ulrich, 134
Multyfarnham, Ireland, 117
'mummified fairy' hoax, 226
Murray, Margaret, 247–8
Muscovy, 138–9
mystery plays, 122
mysticism, 14, 176–7, 218, 227, 248–9

Nairn, Scotland, 138
Näkk (Estonian spirit), 88
Napoleon Bonaparte, 209
Napoleonic Wars, 216
nationalism, 27, 157, 171, 215, 216, 217, 219
Native Americans, 35, 194, 195, 197, 198–9, 203, *see also* Beothuk people; Cree people; Houma people; Huron people; Mohegan people; Ojibwa people; Passamaquoddy people; Penobscot people
naturalia, 66, 80
Nazism, 205, 219
Neanderthals, 16
Neoplatonism, 43, 61, 65, 209
nereids (Greek spirits), 2, 6, 8, 88, 89, 102, 104, 151, 178, 181, 209
 queen of, 121
New Age spirituality, 241, 243, 250
New England, USA, 26, 185, 197–200
New France, 26, 193–4, 196
New Spain, 184, 191, 192, *see also* Latin America; Mexico
Newfoundland, Canada, 12, 26, 185, 186, 193, 196, 200–1, 203
Newman, John Henry, 231
Newton, Isaac, 159, 172
Nicholas V, pope, 187
Nicholas of Cusa, 155

nightmares, 115, 262
Nixen (Germanic spirits), 88
Noah, 81, 94
Norman Conquest, 86
Norn (language), 138
Norns (Germanic spirits), 48, 100
North America, 9, 29, 35, 185, 186–7, 193–201, 202, 203–4
Norway, 28, 31, 93, 212
Nova Scotia, Canada, 193
Nunavik, Canada, 195
nympholepsy, 41
nymphs (Greek spirits), 11, 15, 39, 40–2, 44, 45, 80, 88, 89, 100, 103, 144, 149–52, 155, 156, 166, 180, 181, 199, 209

O'Brien, Donchad, 118
O'Donnell, Hugh 'the Black', 117, 126
Oberon (fairy king), 128–9, 151, 157
Occitania, 91
occultism, 166, 168, 209, 227, 228
Oddson, Gísli, bishop of Skálholt, 140
Odin (Norse deity), 187
Ojibwa people, 29, 30
oky (Algonquian spirits), 194, 195
Olaus Magnus, 131–2, 153, 186, 187
Orford, wild man of, 82
Origen, 65–6, 95
Orkney, Scotland, 138, 187, 188, 214
Orpheus, 119
Orthodoxy, Eastern, 1, 138–9, 206, 260
ostension, 23, 116, 129, 150, 265
Ostoticapac, Mexico, 184
otherworlds, fairy, 5, 8, 10, 21, 25, 26, 27, 31, 38, 44, 46, 47, 52, 66, 72, 73, 83, 84, 85–6, 87, 88–9, 93, 94, 104, 106, 107, 115, 116, 117, 118–21, 122, 123, 125, 133, 135, 140, 149, 189, 208, 218, 228, 238, 261, 267, 270
Ovid, 39

paganism, 1, 19, 20, 25, 28, 29, 40, 43, 63–7, 70–3, 75, 77, 79, 87–8, 92, 102, 111, 112, 114, 115, 119, 132, 133, 146, 149, 170, 181, 182, 197–8, 216, 218, 219–20, 258, 269
  Catholicism as, 145
  contemporary, 27, 239, 247–51
Pan (Greek deity), 35, 36, 39, 42, 84, 248–9
Paracelsianism, 155–6, 157–8, 181
Paracelsus, 150, 155–6, 173, 175, 180
Parcae (Roman deities), 49, 100–5, 179, 209
Parham, England, 142
Paris, University of, 95
Parish, Mary, 143, 144, 162
Parsons, Robert, 143
Passamaquoddy people, 199
Patagonia, 189
paths, fairy, 201
Patrick, St, 69–70, 71–5
patupaiarehe (Māori spirits), 202, 203
Paul, St, 62–3, 108
Paul of Thebes, 78
Pell (Estonian spirit), 1–2
penates (Roman spirits), 39
Penobscot people, 199
penitentials, 100, 103–4, 132
perception, fairies as a mode of, 15, 16, 18, 30–1, 33, 256, 263, 265
Perks, Thomas, 166
Perrault, Charles, 141, 178, 204
Persians, 42, 56, 212
personhood, 29, 30, 33, 265
personification, 28–9, 30, 31, 32, 35, 40, 42, 62–3, 100, 111, 265, 266
Peter Pan, see Barrie, J. M.
Philip II, king of Spain, 190
Philip of Opus, 42
Philippines, the, 185, 192–3
Philo of Alexandria, 62
Piaget, Jean, 32
Pilgrim Fathers, 197

Pitt, Moses, 159–61, 174
pixies, 2, 13, 183, 213, 215, 226, 249
Plato, 42, 65
Platonism, 62, 155, 209, *see also* Neoplatonism
Plot, Robert, 167
Plotinus, 43
Plutarch, 43
Pluto (Roman deity), 115, 119, 120, 129
podcasts, 27, 245, 260, 261
Poland, 36, 50, 151
Pollok, Scotland, 169
poltergeists, 13, 80, 122, 145, 147–8, 150, 171–2, 182, 223, 245, 247, 266
polytheism, 33, 36, 39, 41–2, 65, 260
pooka (Irish spirit), 125, 233
Pope, Alexander, 178, 180–1
Portugal, 185, 188, 189, 191, 192, 224
Portunes (English spirits), 88, 90, 122
Portunus (Roman deity), 90
Poseidon (Greek deity), 89
Povelsen, Anders, 28, 31
Pratchett, Terry, 44
preachers, 20, 111, 117
prehistory, 8, 10, 17, 21, 24, 28, 30–1, 35, 40, 44, 45, 46, 47–8, 50, 51, 53, 86, 92, 115, 125, 135, 140, 167, 212, 248, 252
Presbyterians, 147
Procopius, 103
Proserpina (Roman deity), 115, 120, 129, 148
Protestantism, 14, 26, 133, 142, 143–4, 145, 146, 150, 158, 161, 165, 168, 214–15
Providence, USA, 198
Psellus, Michael, 67–8, 139, 151, 163
pseudepigrapha, 54, 55, 58, 60, 66
psychedelics, 27, 254–7
psychology, depth, 261, 263, 264
psychology, developmental, 29, 32
pucks (English spirits), 3, 13, 144, 178, **179**, 232

pukwudgies (New England spirits), 199, 204
purgatory, 97, 117, 144, 145, 150, 184, 196
Puritanism, 141, 197–8
pygmies, 79, 84–5, 86–7, 126, 156, 173–4, 186–8, 211
'pygmy theory', 248

Queen, Fairy, 21, 102–3, 115, 116, 118, 119–21, 124, 128, 137, 138, 143, 148, 149, 152, 163, 166, 168, 176, 199
Quebec, Canada, 193, 194, 195, 196
Qur'an, the, 14, 20, 68

races, monstrous, 25, 79, 81–2, 87–8, 91, 110, 155, 157, 173, 187, 189
Rádfalva, Hungary, 242
Ragueneau, Paul, 194
Ralph of Coggeshall, 121
Rambynas, Lithuania, 219
re-enchantment, 27, 250, 260, 261, 262
Reformation, 26, 106, 107, 125, 129–34, 136, 138, 142, 144, 145, 147, 148, 150, 157, 158
Regino of Prüm, 101, 136
Renaissance, the, 26, 132, 151, 161, 163
Reoch, Elspeth, 138
Rheen, Samuel, 152
Richard I, king of England, 121
rings, fairy, 8, 10, 17, 47, 50, 141, 167
Robert of Gloucester, 115
Robertson, David, 183
Robin Goodfellow (fairy), 142, 144, 150, **153**, 178, **179**
romances, medieval, 2, 22, 26, 90, 93, 114–18, 119–20, 128, 129, 148, 157, 165, 179, 189, 210, 228
Romania, 12, 92, 102, 224
Romans, 3, 25, 33, 39, 40, 43, 44, 47, 49, 61, 62, 63, 64, 70–1, 79, 80, 81, 86, 90, 100, 102–3, 108, 152, 153, **154**, 164, 197

Romanticism, 171, 181, 183, 208–9
Rosicrucians, 180, 227
Rouen, France, 112
rougarou (spirit of French North America), 195
Rowling, J. K., 129
Royal Society, the, 159–60, 162, 168
rusalkas (Slavic spirits), 45, 151
Russell, A. E., 218
Russia, 1, 38, 50, 103, 138–9, 206
Rye, Mother of (Baltic spirit), 111

sacrifice, 71, 72, 92, 94, 102, 198, 146, 177, 190, 206
Sadducees, 53, 161
sagas, 92, 186, 187, 200, 216
Saint-Paul-de-Varax, France, 78
Sámi people, 28–9, 35, 37, 152
Samson of Dol, 48, 89
Santa Claus, 35
Sápmi, 109
Sáráhkká (Sámi deity), 28
Satan, 5, 55, 61, 67, 68, 75, 94, 94, 97, 98, 99, 101, 108–11, 119, 121, 129, 134, 136, 138, 139, 144, 146, 160, 165–6, 190, 194, 214, 220, 258
satyrs, 15, 35, 39, 60, 64, 65, 66, 78, **79**, 80, 91, 132, 144, 149, 151, 153, 164, 166, 173, 174, 209, 214, 254, 264
sauna spirits, 148
Savery, Thomas, 159
Scandinavia, 8, 22, 25, 40, 83, 87, 100, 104, 107, 121, 127, 132, 138, 147, 183, 188, 240
'scarelore', 44, 112
scepticism, 13, 17, 68, 101, 114, 144, 151, 161–2, 163–5, 166, 168–9, 172, 176, 177, 180, 194, 234, 245, 255, 263
Schefferus, Johannes, 152
Scholasticism, 55, 109–10, 111
scientism, 250, 262, 263
Scot, Reginald, 144, 163, 165, 166, 169

Scotland, 14, 49, 135–8, 139, 142, 144–5, 146, 147, 172, 174, 210, 213, 218, 270, *see also* Orkney; Shetland; Western Isles
    Highlands of, 176, 213, 214–15, 248
    Lowland, 121, 122, 126
Scott, Walter, 210–11
seals, 214, 264
Seaton, Ethel, 232
Sebond, Raymond de, 175
second sight, 174–6, 195, 215
Second World War, 232, 235
Seneca, 152
sentimentality, 201, 207, 227, 237, 262
Seven Angels of Palermo, 191
Seven Years War, 193
sex, 44, 57, 58, 64, 101, 108, 109, 110, 124, 139, 157, 191, 236, 251
Shaftesbury, earl of, 163
Shakespeare, William, 152, 210, 232
    A Midsummer Night's Dream, 22, 121, 128, 177
    Macbeth, 48
shamanism, 25, 29, 31, 34–8, 41, 44, 45, 101, 195
shapeshifting, 90, 111, 170
Sherman, USA, 199
Shetland, UK, 138, 214
Shoney (Scottish spirit), 146
Sibylia (fairy), 157
Sikes, Wirt, 213
Silvanus (Roman deity), 39, 64
skogsrå (Scandinavian spirits), 9
Skraelings, 186–7
Skye, Isle of, 235
sleep paralysis, 10, 102, 151
Sleigh, Bernard, 235
Sloane, Hans, 168–9
'social supernatural', fairies as, 7–8, 9, 21, 31, 37, 40, 47, 49, 202
Socrates, 65, 150, 177
'sons of God' (Genesis 6), *see* Watchers

South Africa, 203, 204, 220
South America, *see* Latin America
Southey, Robert, 210
Soviet Union, 1, 205–6, 231, 234
Spain, 141, 165, 184, 185, 188–91, 192–3
Spenser, Edmund, 190
Spiritualism, 27, 199, 218, 222–4, 234–7, 253
SPR (Society for Psychical Research), 226
Sprat, Thomas, 162
squall, fairy, 201
Sri Lanka, 109
St Teath, England, 159
stage fairies, *see* drama, fairies in
Star Carr, England, 35
stature, diminutive, 37, 48, 83–4, 86–7, 89, 90, 91, 135, 153, 156, 186, 187, 188, 206, 210, 211, 255; *see also* dwarfs; miniaturization; pygmies
Stefánsdóttir, Erla, 241
Stefánsson, Sigurður, 140
Steiner, Rudolf, 227
Stoker, Bram, 221
Stothard, Thomas, 177–8
Stowmarket, England, 212
stray sod, 233
Strieber, Whitley, 252
Sturlusson, Snorri, 93, 94
Suárez, Francisco, 165
subterranean, fairies as, *see* underground, location of fairies as
Suffolk, England, 82, 121, 142, 212, 245–6, 249
Súñiga, Agustín de, 184
superstition, 17, 33, 40, 103, 112, 113, 133, 134, 142, 144, 145, 161, 164–5, 166, 168, 180, 181, 184, 185, 195, 210, 217, 233
Sweden, 28, 93, 115, 135, 152, 164, 183, 203, 240
Sweetman, Nicholas, bishop of Ferns, 167

'SWFs' (small winged fairies), 23, 203, 240–1
Syerston, England, 232
sylphs, 155, **178**, 180, 181
syncretism, 42, 71, 94, 98, 139, 192, 195
szépasszony (Hungarian spirits), 38, 224

Talmud, the, 45, 58
technology, 33, 160, 222, 227, 235, 242, 245, 247, 249, 252, 255, 257, 265, 266
Tecolote, Mexico, 192
Tedworth Drummer (poltergeist), 182
Tenochtitlan, Mexico, 189, 192
Tertullian, 65
theodicy, 53, 55
Theosophy, 27, 66, 199, 204, 218, 221, 223, 225–6, 227, 231, 241, 249, 250, 252, 253, 258, 259
therianthropy, 34–7, 45, 73, 84, 91, 96, 101, 131, 132, 139
theurgy, 191, 209
Thomas Cantilupe, bishop of Hereford, 87
Thomas of Cantimpré, 90
Thomas of Walsingham, 83
Thompson, Francis, 231
Thoms, William John, 211
Thorgilsson, Ari, 186
Thule people, 187
Tillotson, John, archbishop of Canterbury, 160
Tinker Bell, 1, 35, 204
Tírechán, 73
Titania (fairy queen), 121
Toland, John, 166
Tolkien, J. R. R., 14, 16, 22, 27, 33–4, 87, 93, 228–32, 237, 258, 259, 260, 261
tomte (Scandinavian spirit), 240
Tooth Fairy, the, 203
Torfason, Þormóður (Torfaeus), 172
tourism, 27, 240–2

trances, 15, 35, 37, 41, 44
Transcendentalism, 199
transgression, 34, 38, 44, 45, 67, 129, 250, 264
treasure, buried, 8, 135, 143, 152, 162–3, 192, 235
trees, fairy, 31, 98, 112–14, 170, 189, 192, 198, 233
Tregeagle, John, 159
Trenchard, John, 166
trolldómr, 83, 127, 135
trolls, 2, 8, 22, 83, 92, 94, 104, 121, 135, 138, 140, 152, 172, 199, 231, 240, 260
Trondheim, Norway, 187
trows, 138, 147
Tsienneto (fairy), 198–9
Tuath Luchra, 84, 87
Tuatha Dé Danaan, 72, 74, 75, 86, 117–18, 125, 173, 218
Tündér Ilona (fairy queen), 102, 121
Tunja, Colombia, 191
Tyson, Edward, 173

Udmurts, 139
UFOs, 27, 251–4, 264
Ukraine, 18, 45
unclean spirits (Jewish and early Christian concept), 43, 60, 61, 62
undemonization, 111
underground, location of fairies as, 41, 67, 82, 85, 86, 88, 118, 140, 147, 156, 175, 187, 188, 189, 192, 206
Uttley, Alison, 231

Vadsø, Norway, 28
Vallée, Jacques, 251–2
vampires, 43, 171, 221, 247
Vanir (Norse deities), 92
Vanstone, Henry, 227
Vazimba (Malagasy spirits), 195
Vedic religion, 39
Vélius, Norbertas, 22, 234

INDEX

Velnias (Baltic deity), 108
Venus (Roman deity), 149, 153, **154**
Vepsian people, 205–6
Vespucci, Amerigo, 189
Vézelay, France, 79
vilas (Slavic spirits), 2, 6, 8, 37, 46, 76, 83, 102–3, 152, 178
Villars, Nicolas-Pierre-Henri de Montfaucon de, 180, 181
Vinland, 186, 200
Visigoths, 40
vitalism, 155, 231
Volga-Ural region, 139
Voyage of St Brendan, 75, 94–7, 189
Vrouw Holle (fairy queen), 121

Waldron, George, 183
Wales, 12, 22, 106, 122, 136, 169, 171, 195, 213, 218
Wallace, Alfred Russel, 227
Walserands (Germanic spirits), 96
Walsh, John, 157
wanagemesmak (Penobscot spirits), 199
wands, 1, 141, 204
Warner, William, 142
Watchers (Jewish spirits), 57–8, 60, 67, 77, 102
water spirits, 40, 42, 80, 82, 88–91, 134, 155, 156, 192, 212, 214
Watkins-Pitchford, D. J., 231, 239
Webster, John, 58, 173, 211
weddings, fairy, 170
werewolves, 36, 90, 101, 195
Wesley, John, 168

Western Isles, Scotland, 146, 176, 187, 214
Wharton, Goodwin, 143, 162
Wicca, 247–8
wights, seely (Scottish spirits), 49, 136, 137
Wild Hunt, the, 253
William III, king of England, 159
William of Auvergne, 110
wings, 1, 3, 23, 153–4, 177–8, 204, **207**, 220, 225, 240, *see also* 'SWFs'
witchcraft, 49, 50, 83, 101, 132, 133–9, 142, 143, 157, 158, 159, 161, 163, 168, 174, 197, *see also* Wicca
Witchcraft Act, English (1604), 169
Witchcraft Act, Scottish (1563), 135–6
witches, 4, 7, 18, 37–8, 48–50, 101, 102, 133, 134, 136, 138, 143, 144, 162, 164, 166, 197, 248, 249
Wolfram von Eschenbach, 95
Wollaton gnomes, 242
Woolpit, England, 113
 Green Children of, 22, 82, 83
Wright, Elsie, 220–2, 225, 226, 234, 257
Wyrd Sisters (Scottish spirits), 100

Yahwism, 57, 70
Yeats, W. B., 13–14
yeti (Tibetan cryptid), 204
yowie (Australian cryptid), 204

Zeus (Greek deity), 42
zupay (Incan spirit), 190